D1599927

# TALENT IS NEVER ENOUGH

---

# BECOMING A PERSON OF INFLUENCE

THOMAS NELSON
*Since 1798*

NASHVILLE  DALLAS  MEXICO CITY  RIO DE JANEIRO

Published in Nashville, Tennessee, by Thomas Nelson. Thomas Nelson is a registered
trademark of Thomas Nelson, Inc.

Published in association with Yates & Yates, www.yates2.com.

Thomas Nelson, Inc., titles may be purchased in bulk for educational, business,
fund-raising, or sales promotional use. For information, please e-mail
SpecialMarkets@ThomasNelson.com.

Scripture quotations marked NIV are taken from the HOLY BIBLE: NEW
INTERNATIONAL VERSION®. © 1973, 1978, 1984 by International Bible
Society. Used by permission of Zondervan Publishing House. All rights reserved.

ISBN 978-1-4002-8099-5

**Library of Congress Cataloguing-in-Publication Data Available**

*Printed in the United States of America*
10 11 12 13 14 WC 6 5 4 3 2 1

# TALENT IS NEVER ENOUGH

Discover the Choices That Will
Take You Beyond Your Talent

## John C. Maxwell

*TALENT IS NEVER ENOUGH* IS DEDICATED TO JOHN PORTER MAXWELL, OUR THIRD GRANDCHILD.
HIS READY SMILE AND DESIRE TO BE WITH PAPA AND MIMI HAVE STOLEN OUR HEARTS.
WE PRAY THAT AS HE GROWS OLDER, HE WILL MAKE THE RIGHT CHOICES ENABLING HIM TO BE A TALENT-PLUS PERSON.

# CONTENTS

# ACKNOWLEDGMENTS

Thank you to
Charlie Wetzel, my writer
Stephanie Wetzel, who proofs and edits the manuscript
Linda Eggers, my assistant

# WHEN IS TALENT
# ALONE ENOUGH?

Talent is often overrated and frequently misunderstood. French poet and dramatist Edouard Pailleron pointed out, "Have success and there will always be fools to say that you have talent." When people achieve great things, others often explain their accomplishments by simply attributing everything to talent. But that is a false and misleading way of looking at success. If talent alone is enough, then why do you and I know highly talented people who are not highly successful?

Many American business leaders are obsessed with talent. Some think talent is the answer to every problem. Malcolm Gladwell, author of *The Tipping Point* and *Blink,* notes that many companies and consultants put finding people with talent ahead of everything else. He says, "This 'talent mind-set' is the new orthodoxy of American management." Certain companies hire dozens of MBAs from top universities, promote them quickly, reward them lavishly, and never accurately assess their performance. The prime example he gives is Enron. Its talent focus was legendary. For example, Lynda Clemmons, who started Enron's weather derivatives business, went from trader to associate to manager to director to head of her own business unit in only seven years! Gladwell asks, "How do you evaluate someone's performance in a system where no one is in a job long enough to allow such evaluation?"[1]

Talent is never enough. Peter Drucker, the father of modern management, said, "There seems to be little correlation between a man's effectiveness and his intelligence, his imagination, or his knowledge . . . Intelligence, imagination, and knowledge are essential resources, but only effectiveness converts them into results. By themselves, they only set limits to what can be contained." If talent were enough, then the

2 ～ TALENT IS NEVER ENOUGH

most effective and influential people would always be the most talented ones. But that is often not the case. Consider this:

- More than 50 percent of all CEOs of Fortune 500 companies had C or C- averages in college.
- Sixty-five percent of all U.S. senators came from the bottom half of their school classes.
- Seventy-five percent of U.S. presidents were in the Lower-Half Club in school.
- More than 50 percent of millionaire entrepreneurs never finished college![2]

Clearly talent isn't everything.

## THE HIGH-JUMP PRINCIPLE

This is not an anti-talent book. I believe in the importance of talent. How could I not? All successful leaders understand its importance. Legendary college football coach Lou Holtz once told me, "John, I've coached teams with good players and I've coached teams with bad players. I'm a better coach when I have good players!" The more talent that a sports, business, or service team possesses, the greater potential it has—and the better its leader can be.

Most leaders understand the dynamics of ownership, shared responsibility, division of labor, committee governance, and delegation. Often leaders accomplish great tasks by dividing a job into its parts and coordinating the whole effort. Remarkable feats, such as the building of the pyramids or the Great Wall of China, were accomplished in that fashion. However, there are some tasks that are not improved by adding more people. Brooks's Law states, "Adding people to a late software project makes it later." More isn't always better, and some things are best done by an individual.

A wonderful, simple illustration of the importance of talent can be seen in a sports event like the high jump. Winning the high jump requires one person who can jump seven feet, not seven people who can jump one foot. Such an example may seem obvious, yet don't we often believe that we can accomplish more by throwing more people at a task? That isn't always the right solution. In fact, there are many tasks that call for talent more than numbers. Like high jumping, they require the extraordinary talent of one person, not the mediocre talent of many.

## PUTTING TALENT INTO PERSPECTIVE

As I said, I don't mean to minimize the importance of talent. Talent is a God-given gift that should be celebrated. When we observe talented people . . .

### 1. We Should Marvel at Their Giftedness

Reading leadership books by Jack Welch, I am amazed by his deep wisdom mixed with common sense. It is no surprise that he was able to turn around GE and lift it to a dominant position in corporate America. He is a born leader.

Every time I have the opportunity, I go to Sarah Brightman's concerts. I find that her voice sets her apart from other vocal artists. I often close my eyes and just listen to her sing, marveling at the giftedness of this diva. Sarah Brightman is a born vocalist.

Professional football in Atlanta rose to a new level when Michael Vick came to town. His ability to run a football is guaranteed to thrill the crowd every game. He has lifted his team and the Falcons' fans with his extraordinary gifts. Michael Vick is a born athlete.

Talent can enable people to do extraordinary things, and we should acknowledge people's talent and marvel at their accomplishments.

## 2. We Should Recognize Their Contribution to Society

When we observe talented people, we should note their impact. Where would America be today if it had not been formed by talented leaders? I have been reading *Booknotes Life Stories: Notable Biographers on the People Who Shaped America* by Brian Lamb, the founding CEO of C-SPAN and host of C-SPAN's *Booknotes* program. The book has reminded me of the talent of America's Founding Fathers:

- THOMAS JEFFERSON, the nation's third president and primary writer of the Declaration of Independence, was a Renaissance man: He invented the first modern plow, was the president of the American Philosophical Society, sent Lewis and Clark on the country's first scientific expedition, redesigned Washington, D.C., so that the president in the White House would have to look up to see Congress on Capitol Hill, and offered his 6,500-volume personal library so that it could become the foundation of the U.S. Library of Congress.

- THOMAS PAINE produced the nation's first bestseller when he penned *Common Sense*. It sold half a million copies in a country of three million people.

- JAMES MADISON, the country's fourth president, was the primary thinker behind the U.S. Constitution. He was the MVP of the fifty-five men who created that world-changing document. He was a better thinker than Jefferson.

- HENRY CLAY, orator, statesman, and lawyer, was a mentor to Abraham Lincoln and prevented a move by the southern states to secede in 1850. Many historians believe that the decade-long delay gave the Union enough time to build its industrial base, thus leading to the preservation of the United States.

The course of history the world over has been changed by talented men and women who have maximized their skills.

## 3. We Should Separate What They Can Do from Who They *Are*

Fred Smith, author and former president of Fred Smith Associates, shared a bit of wisdom with me many years ago. He said, "The giftedness is usually greater than the person." By that he meant that the talent of some people is greater than other important personal attributes, such as character and commitment. As a result, they often fail to rise to the level of their talent. Talented people are always tempted to coast on their abilities. Or they want others to recognize their skills but overlook their deficiencies.

Haven't you known people who should have risen to the top but didn't? They had all the talent they should ever need, but they still didn't succeed. Philosopher Ralph Waldo Emerson must have known people like that, too, because he said, "Talent for talent's sake is a bauble and a show. Talent working with joy in the cause of universal truth lifts the possessor to a new power as a benefactor."

So is talent ever enough? Yes, but only in the very beginning. Novelist Charles Wilson says, "No matter the size of the bottle, the cream always rises to the top." Talent stands out. It gets you noticed. In the beginning, talent separates you from the rest of the pack. It gives you a head start on others. For that reason, natural talent is one of life's greatest gifts. But the advantage it gives lasts only a short time. Songwriter Irving Berlin understood this truth when he said, "The toughest thing about

> "The toughest thing about success is that you've got to keep on being a success. Talent is only a starting point in business. You've got to keep working that talent."
>
> —Irving Berlin

success is that you've got to keep on being a success. Talent is only a starting point in business. You've got to keep working that talent."

Too many talented people who start with an advantage over others lose that advantage because they rest on their talent instead of raising it. They assume that talent alone will keep them out front. They don't realize the truth: if they merely wing it, others will soon fly past them. Talent is more common than they think. Mega-best-selling author Stephen King asserts that "talent is cheaper than table salt. What separates the talented individual from the successful one is a lot of hard work." Clearly, more than just talent is needed for anyone who wants to achieve success.

## DO YOU HAVE WHAT IT TAKES?

So what does it take to succeed? Where does that leave you and me? Can anyone be successful? And where does talent fit in? Here's what I believe:

### 1. Everyone Has Talent

People have equal value, but not equal giftedness. Some people seem to be blessed with a multitude of talents. Most of us have fewer abilities. But know this: all of us have something that we can do well.

In their book *Now, Discover Your Strengths*, Marcus Buckingham and Donald O. Clifton state that every person is capable of doing something better than the next ten thousand people. And they support that assertion with solid research. They call this area the strength zone, and they encourage everyone to find it and make the most of it. It doesn't matter how aware you are of your abilities, how you feel about yourself, or whether you previously have achieved success. You have talent, and you can develop that talent.

## 2. Develop the Talent You Have, Not the One You Want

If I asked you who would be more successful, the person who relies on his talent alone or the person who realizes his talent and develops it, the answer would be obvious. Then I'll ask you this question: Why do most people spend the majority of their time focused on strengthening their weaknesses?

One thing I teach people at my conferences is to stop working on their weaknesses and start working on their strengths. (By this I mean abilities, not attitude or character issues, which *must* be addressed.) It has been my observation that people can increase their ability in an area by only 2 points on a scale of 1 to 10. For example, if your natural talent in an area is a 4, with hard work you may rise to a 6. In other words, you can go from a little below average to a little above average. But let's say you find a place where you are a 7; you have the potential to become a 9, maybe even a 10, if it's your greatest area of strength and you work exceptionally hard! That helps you advance from 1 in 10,000 talent to 1 in 100,000 talent—but only if you do the other things needed to maximize your talent.

## 3. Anyone Can Make Choices That Will Add Value to Talent

The question remains: What creates the effectiveness that Peter Drucker says is necessary for converting talent into results? It comes from the choices you make. *The key choices you make—apart from the natural talent you already have—will set you apart from others who have talent alone.* Orator, attorney, and political leader William Jennings Bryan said, "Destiny is not a matter of chance, it is a matter of choice; it is not a thing to be waited for, it is a thing to be achieved."

> The key choices you make—apart from the natural talent you already have—will set you apart from others who have talent alone.

I've discovered thirteen key choices that can be made to maximize any person's talent:

1. Belief lifts your talent.
2. Passion energizes your talent.
3. Initiative activates your talent.
4. Focus directs your talent.
5. Preparation positions your talent.
6. Practice sharpens your talent.
7. Perseverance sustains your talent.
8. Courage tests your talent.
9. Teachability expands your talent.
10. Character protects your talent.
11. Relationships influence your talent.
12. Responsibility strengthens your talent.
13. Teamwork multiplies your talent.

Make these choices, and you can become a talent-plus person. If you have talent, you stand alone. If you have talent *plus*, you stand out.

## YOU CAN DO IT!

I believe the ideas in this book can help you. *Talent Is Never Enough* was inspired by something that happened to me in 2004. Coach Jim Tressel asked me to speak to the Ohio State football team on the weekend that they played Michigan. It was more than just a speaking engagement for me—it was a dream come true! I grew up in Ohio, and I have been a lifelong Buckeye fan.

Coach Tressel had read my book *Today Matters*. Because his players were very young and he wanted to teach them to keep their focus on the 2004 football season, the team studied the book throughout the year. Coach Tressel wanted me to speak to the team on the last and most important game of their regular season schedule. It was an unforgettable experience. I spoke to the Buckeyes on Friday night, walked with them to the stadium on Saturday, and went into their locker room where I saw a countdown clock for the Michigan game that also said, "Today Matters."

Could it get any better? Yes! Coach Tressel turned to me while we were still in the locker room and said, "John, you and I will lead the team out on the football field."

In front of one-hundred thousand screaming fans, we ran onto the field. I'll never forget that moment. Could it get any better? Yes! I was on the sidelines with the team for the entire game. And it got even better than that! Ohio State won!

How does this relate to *Talent Is Never Enough*? Prior to my visit, Coach Tressel had sent me some information on Ohio State football to help me prepare. One item was "The Winner's Manuel," which contained an article titled "Things That Do Not Require Talent." It emphasized that characteristics such as punctuality, effort, patience, and unselfishness were important to the OSU football program. Not one of those things required any talent. Coach Tressel told me that he and his staff were trying to help their talented players realize that their talent alone was not enough.

I loved the article and thought that if I wrote a book on the subject, it could help a lot of people. You see, people who neglect to make the right choices to release and maximize their talent continually underperform. Their talent allows them to stand out, but their wrong choices make them sit down. Their friends, families, coaches, and bosses see their giftedness, but they wonder why they so often come up short of expectations. Their talent gives them opportunity, but their wrong choices shut the door. Talent is a given, but you must earn success.

In contrast, talent-plus people come as close as humanly possible to achieving their potential. They frequently overperform. People see their

giftedness and are amazed at how they continually rise above expectations. Their talent gives them opportunity, and their right choices open
the door for even greater success.

Life is a matter of choices, and every choice you make makes you.
What will you do for your career? Who will you marry? Where will you
live? How much education will you get? What will you do with today?
But one of the most important choices you will make is *who will you
become!* Life is not merely a matter of holding and playing a good hand
as you would hope to do in a card game. What you start with isn't up to
you. *Talent* is God-given. Life is playing the hand you have been dealt
well. That is determined by your choices.

## TALENT + RIGHT CHOICES = A TALENT-PLUS PERSON

The talent-plus people are the ones who maximize their talent, reach
their potential, and fulfill their destiny.

I was reading a book by Dr. Seuss to my grandchildren called *Oh,
The Places You'll Go!* In it, I found a wonderful truth. It said,

> You have brains in your head.
> You have feet in your shoes.
> You can steer yourself
> Any direction you choose.

I believe that with all my heart. My prayer is that *Talent Is Never Enough*
will help you to steer yourself in the right direction and make right
choices that will empower you to become a talent-plus person, build
upon the foundation of your abilities, and live your life to its
fullest potential.

# 1
## BELIEF LIFTS
## YOUR TALENT

The first and greatest obstacle to success for most people is their belief in themselves. Once people figure out where their sweet spot is (the area where they are most gifted), what often hinders them isn't lack of talent. It's lack of trust in themselves, which is a self-imposed limitation. Lack of belief can act as a ceiling on talent. However, when people believe in themselves, they unleash power in themselves and resources around them that almost immediately take them to a higher level. Your potential is a picture of what you can become. Belief helps you see the picture and reach for it.

## MORE THAN JUST GREAT TALENT

It has become an American sports legend. People call it the guarantee. At the time, it seemed like little more than an outrageous statement— bravado from a high-profile athlete whose team was the underdog before the big game. It occurred on January 9, 1969, just three days before the third world championship game of football, the first that was called the Super Bowl. And it was just eight simple words uttered by the Jets' quarterback, Joe Namath: "The Jets will win Sunday. I guarantee it."

That boastful statement may not seem remarkable today. Ever since the career of Muhammad Ali, bold statements by athletes have been commonplace. But people didn't hear those kinds of boasts from anyone playing in the upstart American Football League (AFL). The eight-year-old AFL was considered to be inferior, and in the previous two world championship football games, the AFL teams had been trounced. Most experts believed it would be many years before an AFL team could compete at the level of any NFL team. The NFL's Colts were favored to win this third championship game by 18 or 19 points.

Namath's guarantee might have seemed outrageous, but it was more than a hollow boast. It wasn't out of character for him either. Despite the fact that Namath was often quick to take the blame in interviews when the Jets lost, he always displayed a powerful self-confidence. He believed in himself, his team, and their ability to win the game. That ability to believe in himself was something that could be traced all the way back to his childhood.

## EARLY SIGNS

Joe Namath always possessed athletic talent. He came from a family of athletes. His first coaches were his family members. John, his father, spent a lot of time showing him how to throw, hit, and field a baseball and teaching him what to do in various game situations. His brothers contributed too. His brother Bobby started teaching him the position of quarterback when Joe was only six. And brother Frank drilled him and pounded him if he didn't perform well in their family practices.

Growing up, Joe was small and light for his age. Sometimes people underestimated him because of that. When he was in elementary school, a group of kids from an even tougher neighborhood than his own challenged his friend Linwood Alford to a game of two-on-two basketball. Linwood and Joe showed up to play, and Linwood recalled, "They were all laughing like: who's this little scrawny kid? How you gonna win with this guy?" Joe might have looked like an easy kid to beat, but he wasn't. "You knocked him down, he got right back up," observed Alford. "Joe wasn't no pretty boy."[1] Joe and Linwood beat the other kids and quickly earned their respect.

Joe had a certain fearlessness. He and Linwood used to go to a train trestle near their home, and they would hang from the trestle as the locomotive and its cars thundered overhead. But at first, that fearlessness didn't translate onto the athletic field. The key to unleashing the belief that lifted his talent occurred when Joe Namath was eight years old. He came home with his first team uniform for the Elks' Little League baseball team. Namath's biography recounts the exchange that occurred between young Joe and his father, John:

"That's real nice, son. Fits you good."

Joey was the smallest kid on that team. He was the youngest, too, probably by a year. "You know, Daddy, those other kids are so good," he said. "They're bigger than I am . . . I don't have a chance."

"Well, you take that uniform off right now," his father said. "Take it back to the manager and tell him that you can't make the team because the other boys are better than you are."

Joey looked at his father with those sad, dreamy eyes. "Oh, no, Daddy. I can't do that."

"If you can't make the team, what's the use of keeping the uniform?"

"But, Daddy," he said, "they're so good."

"You're good, too. You can field grounders. You can hit the ball. You know where to make the plays."

John gave the boy a choice: return the uniform or practice with the team. If, after the practice, he didn't feel that he was better than every other kid, he should quit.

Joey said he'd try.

As it happened, he turned out to be the best player on that Elks team.[2]

The belief that John Namath tried to instill in his son was not misplaced. The father used to sum up Joe's Little League career by telling about a particular game that represented his son's ability. John arrived late and asked about the score from someone who was at all of the games. There were no outs, the score was tied at 3, and all and the bases were loaded. "But don't worry," the man said. "They just put the little Namath kid in to pitch." Joe got three quick outs, including striking out the opposing team's best player, a boy who was two years older than Joe (and who later played football at Pitt). Then when Joe got up to bat, he hit the winning home run.[3]

## BUSINESS AS USUAL

That kind of confident performance became the norm for Namath. As a high school basketball player, he was fast, he could shoot, and unlike most of his opponents and teammates, he could dunk. As a football player, he led his Beaver Falls team to win the Western Pennsylvania Interscholastic Athletic League championship. Before one of the games when Joe had a sore ankle, the confident quarterback, who also punted for the team, assured his worried coach, "Don't worry, coach, we won't have to punt."[4]

Namath was heavily recruited out of high school, and some referred to him as the best quarterback in the country. He ended up at the University of Alabama, where he became a star and led the Crimson Tide to a national championship.

Entering the pros, Namath was again considered the best quarterback of his class. It's said that the NFL's New York Giants wanted him badly, but the AFL's New York Jets got him. Namath signed a contract in 1965 whose terms dwarfed anything previously seen in professional football—in any professional sport, for that matter.

For three years, Namath played his heart out, broke passing records, underwent knee surgeries, and led his team to losing seasons. But he never lost his belief in himself. He knew he could play and lead his team to victory. In the 1968 season, his fourth, he finally led his team to a winning season and a victory in the AFL championship. He didn't care that nobody gave the Jets a chance to win against the NFL team. He believed in himself and his ability to win. He also convinced his team. What most people didn't know was that Namath had watched hours of film on the Colts, as he did for every opponent. "The one-eyed monster—it never lies," Namath used to say, referring to the projector he kept in his apartment.[5] He showed his teammates what he saw. They could win that game. And that's exactly what they did. The Jets beat the Colts 16 to 7. Most people consider it to be the biggest upset in Super Bowl history.

What would have happened to Joe Namath if his father hadn't challenged him to believe in himself and his ability when he was only eight years old? Maybe he would have ended up like his brothers, talented athletes who dropped out of high school or college to work in the local mill or machine shop. Or maybe he would have ended up a pool hustler. It's hard to say. But one thing is certain: he wouldn't have ended up in the Pro Football Hall of Fame in Canton, Ohio. It takes more than talent to end up there; it also takes belief.

## BELIEFS WORTH BUYING INTO

I don't know what your talent is, but I do know this: it will not be lifted to its highest level unless you also have belief. Talent alone is never enough. If you want to become your best, you need to believe your best. You need to . . .

## 1. Believe in Your Potential

Your potential is a picture of what you can become. Inventor Thomas Edison remarked, "If we did all the things we are capable of doing, we would literally astonish ourselves."

Too often we see what is, not what could be. People looked at Joe Namath when he was young, and they saw a skinny, undersized kid. They looked at him when he was in high school, and they saw a kid who hung around with the wrong crowd and didn't do his homework. They looked at him when he was in the pros, and they saw a guy with bad knees. But he saw himself as a champion. If you could see yourself in terms of your true potential, you wouldn't recognize yourself.

When my daughter, Elizabeth, was in high school, she had a "glamour shot" taken of herself to give me as a gift. That was the rage at the time. A person would go into the photo studio and be made up to look like a movie star. When I first saw the picture, I thought, *That's not the way she looks every day, but that's Elizabeth. That's truly her.* Likewise, that's what it's like when you see and believe in your potential. If you were to see yourself as you could be, you would look better than you ever imagined. I just wish I could show you a picture of yourself with your potential intact.

Indian statesman Mohandas Gandhi said, "The difference between what we do and what we are capable of doing would suffice to solve most of the world's problems." Closer to home, it would also suffice to solve most of our *individual* problems. We must first believe in our potential if we are to do what we're capable of.

Too many people fall far short of their real potential. John Powell, author of *The Secret of Staying in Love*, estimates that the average person reaches only 10 percent of his potential, sees only 10 percent of the beauty that is all around him, hears only 10 percent of its music and poetry, smells only 10 percent of its fragrance, and tastes only 10 percent of the deliciousness of being alive. Most neither see nor seize their potential.

Executive coach Joel Garfinkle recounts a story by writer Mark Twain in which a man died and met Saint Peter at the pearly gates. Immediately realizing that Saint Peter was a wise and knowledgeable individual, the man inquired, "Saint Peter, I have been interested in military history for many years. Tell me who was the greatest general of all time?"

Saint Peter quickly responded, "Oh, that's a simple question. It's that man right over there."

"You must be mistaken," responded the man, now very perplexed. "I knew that man on earth and he was just a common laborer."

"That's right, my friend," assured Saint Peter. "He would have been the greatest general of all time, if he had been a general."[6]

Cartoonist Charles Schulz offered this comparison: "Life is a ten-speed bike. Most of us have gears we never use." What are we saving those gears for? It's not good to travel through life without breaking a sweat. So what's the problem? Most of the time it's self-imposed limitations. They limit us as much as real ones. Life is difficult enough as it is. We make it more difficult when we impose *additional* limitations on ourselves. Industrialist Charles Schwab observed, "When a man has put a limit on what he *will* do, he has put a limit on what he *can* do."

> "Life is a
> ten-speed bike.
> Most of us have
> gears
> we never use."
> —Charles Schulz

In *If It Ain't Broke . . . Break It!* Robert J. Kriegel and Louis Patler write,

> We don't have a clue as to what people's limits are. All the tests, stopwatches, and finish lines in the world can't measure human potential. When someone is pursuing their dream, they'll go far beyond what seems to be their limitations. The potential that exists within us is

limitless and largely untapped . . . When you think of limits, you create them.[7]

We often put too much emphasis on mere physical challenges and obstacles, and give too little credence to psychological and emotional ones. Sharon Wood, the first North American woman to climb Mount Everest, learned some things about that after making her successful climb. She said, "I discovered it wasn't a matter of physical strength, but a matter of psychological strength. The conquest lay within my own mind to penetrate those barriers of self-imposed limitations and get through to that good stuff—the stuff called potential, 90 percent of which we rarely use."

> "When a man has put a limit on what he *will* do, he has put a limit on what he *can* do."
>
> —Charles Schwab

In 2001, I was invited to Mobile, Alabama, to speak to six hundred NFL coaches and scouts at the Senior Bowl. That's the game played by two teams of college seniors who have been invited to participate because they are believed to have NFL potential. In the morning I taught from *The 17 Indisputable Laws of Teamwork*, which had just been published. And in the afternoon, I attended a workout session in which the players were tested for running speed, reaction time, jumping ability, and so forth.

One of the coaches in attendance, Dick Vermeil, chatted with me as I watched. At some point he said, "You know, we can measure many of their skills, but it's impossible to measure the heart. Only the player can determine that."

Your potential is really up to you. It doesn't matter what others might think. It doesn't matter where you came from. It doesn't even matter what you might have believed about yourself at a previous time in your life. It's about what lies within you and whether you can bring it out.

There's a story about a farm boy from Colorado who loved to hike and rock climb. One day while climbing in the mountains, he found an eagle's nest with an egg in it. He took the egg from the nest, and when he got home, he put it under a hen along with her other eggs.

Since he hatched among chicks, the eagle thought he was a chicken. He learned chicken behavior from his "mother" and scratched in the chicken yard along with his "siblings." He didn't know any better. And when he sometimes felt strange stirrings within him, he didn't know what to do with them, so he ignored them or suppressed them. After all, if he was a chicken, he should behave like a chicken.

Then one day an eagle flew over the farm, and the chicken-yard eagle looked up and saw him. In that moment, he realized he wanted to be like that eagle. He wanted to fly high. He wanted to go to the mountain peaks he saw in the distance. He spread his wings, which were much larger and stronger than those of his siblings. Suddenly he understood that he was like that eagle. Though he had never flown before, he possessed the instinct and the capabilities. He spread his wings once more, and he flew, unsteadily at first, but then with greater power and control. As he soared and climbed, he knew that he had finally discovered his true self.

Phillips Brooks, writer of the song "O Little Town of Bethlehem," remarked, "When you discover you've been leading only half a life, the other half is going to haunt you until you develop it." Not only is that true, but I'd also say this: Not reaching your potential is a real tragedy. To reach your potential, you must first believe in your potential, and determine to live way beyond average.

## 2. Believe in Yourself

It's one thing to believe that you possess remarkable potential. It's another thing to have enough faith in yourself that you think you can fulfill it. When it comes to believing in themselves, some people are agnostic! That's not only a shame; it also keeps them from becoming what they could be. Psychologist and philosopher William James emphasized that "there is but one cause of human failure. And that is man's lack of faith in his true self."

People who believe in themselves get better jobs and perform better in them than those who don't. Martin Seligman, professor of psychology at the University of Pennsylvania, did some research at a major life insurance company and found that the salespeople who expected to succeed sold 37 percent more insurance than those who didn't.[8] The impact of belief in self begins early. Some researchers assert that when it comes to academic achievement in school, there is a greater correlation between self-confidence and achievement than there is between IQ and achievement.

> When it comes to believing in themselves, some people are agnostic!

Attorney and marketing expert Kerry Randall observed, "Successful people believe in themselves, especially when others do not." That's no more evident than in sports. Coaches have told me that self-confidence within players is especially important in tight ball games. During crunch time, some players want the ball. Others want to hide. The ones who want the ball are the self-confident ones, like Namath, who held the ball down to the last second during a high school basketball game in which his team was one point behind. While his team's leading scorer kept shouting, "Give me the ball!" Namath was as cool as ever and sank the winning shot as the buzzer sounded.[9]

People with confidence live by a credo that is said to hang in the office of golfer Arnold Palmer. It reads,

> If you think you are beaten, you are.
> If you think you dare not, you don't.
> If you'd like to win, but think you can't
> It's almost certain you won't . . .

Life's battles don't always go
To the stronger or faster man,
But soon or late, the man who wins
Is the man who thinks he can.[10]

Only with belief in yourself will you be able to reach your potential.

## 3. Believe in Your Mission

What else is necessary to lift a person's talent? Believing in what you are doing. In fact, even if the odds are against your accomplishing what you desire, confidence will help you. William James asserted, "The one thing that will guarantee the successful conclusion of a doubtful undertaking is faith in the beginning that you can do it." How does this kind of belief help?

*Belief in your mission will empower you.* Having confidence in what you are doing gives you the power to achieve it. Architect Frank Lloyd Wright noted, "The thing always happens that you really believe in; and the belief in a thing makes it happen." Confident people can usually evaluate a task before undertaking it and know whether they can do it. In that belief is great power.

*Belief in your mission will encourage you.* A woman with a will to win will have her naysayers. A man on a mission will have his critics. What often allows such people to keep going in a negative environment? Belief in the mission.

Playwright Neil Simon advises, "Don't listen to those who say, 'It's not done that way.' Maybe it's not, but maybe you'll do it anyway. Don't listen to those who say, 'You're taking too big a chance.' Michelangelo would have painted the Sistine floor, and it would surely be rubbed out today." Simon should know. He has been awarded seventeen Tony Awards, five Drama Desk Awards, and two Pulitzer Prizes.

Obviously he believes in what he does.

*Belief in your mission will enlarge you.* The more you believe in your potential, yourself, and your mission, the more you will be able to accomplish. If you keep believing, you will someday find yourself doing what you once considered impossible.

Actor Christopher Reeve had that perspective, and it carried him far. He once told an audience,

> America has a tradition many nations probably envy: we frequently achieve the impossible. That's part of our national character. That's what got us from one coast to another. That's what got us the largest economy in the world. That's what got us to the moon. On the wall of my room when I was in rehab was a picture of the space shuttle blasting off, autographed by every astronaut now at NASA. On top of the picture says, "We found nothing is impossible." That should be our motto . . . It's something that we as a nation must do together. So many of our dreams at first seem impossible, then they seem improbable, and then, when we summon the will, they soon become inevitable. If we can conquer outer space, we should be able to conquer inner space, too. The frontier of the brain, the central nervous system, and all the afflictions of the body that destroy so many lives, and rob . . . so much potential.[11]

Do you believe in your mission? Are you confident that you can accomplish great tasks? Do you expect to achieve your goals? These are necessary ingredients to lift your talent from potential to fruition.

I need to say one more thing about mission. It needs to include people. Only a life lived for others is worthwhile. As you fulfill your mission, will others around you say . . .

> "My life is *better* as a result," or
> "My life is *worse* as a result"?

If you think it won't be the former, then the mission may not be worth doing.

One of my prized possessions is a simple crystal paperweight. It doesn't have an especially artistic design. It's not especially valuable monetarily. But it means a lot to me because of what is engraved in it and who gave it to me. It says,

> John—
> Pastor, Mentor, Friend
> "Thank you for believing in me."
> Love,
> Dan

It was a gift from Dan Reiland, who worked with me for twenty years as a staff member, as my second in command, and then as a senior vice president at one of my companies. Dan is someone I would go to battle with. He's like a kid brother to me. The mission we pursued together made *both* of us better. That's the kind of person you want working with you—and the kind of result.

## TALENT + *BELIEF* = A TALENT-PLUS PERSON
## PUTTING THE TALENT-PLUS FORMULA INTO ACTION

So how do you become a talent-plus person? You tap into a natural chain of actions that begins with belief and ends with positive action:

### Belief Determines Expectations

If you want your talent to be lifted to its highest level, then you don't begin by focusing on your talent. You begin by harnessing the power of your mind. Your beliefs control everything you do. Accomplishment is more than a matter of working harder or smarter. It's also a matter of believing positively. Someone called it the "sure enough" syndrome. If you expect to fail, sure enough, you will. If you expect to succeed, sure

> You will become
> on the outside
> what you believe
> on the inside.

enough, you will. You will become on the outside what you believe on the inside.

Personal breakthroughs begin with a change in your beliefs. Why? Because your beliefs determine your expectations, and your expectations determine your actions. A belief is a habit of mind in which confidence becomes a conviction that we embrace. In the long run, a belief is more than an idea that a person possesses. It is an idea that possesses a person. Benjamin Franklin said, "Blessed is he who expects nothing, for he shall never be disappointed." If you want to achieve something in life, you have to be willing to be disappointed. You need to expect to succeed. Does that mean you always will? No. You will fail. You will make mistakes. But if you expect to win, you maximize your talent, and you keep trying. Then like Joe Namath, you will eventually succeed.

Attorney Kerry Randall said, "Contrary to popular opinion, life does not get better by chance, life gets better by change. And this change always takes place inside; it is the change of thought that creates the better life." Improvement comes from change, but change requires confidence. For that reason, you need to make confidence in yourself a priority. You need to put believing in your potential, yourself, your mission, and your fellow human beings at the top of your list. President Franklin Delano Roosevelt asserted, "The only limit to our realization of tomorrow will be our doubts of today." Don't let your doubts cause your expector to expire.

Harvey McKay tells the story of a professor who stood before a class of thirty senior molecular biology students. Before he passed out the final exam, he stated, "I have been privileged to be your instructor this semester, and I know how hard you have worked to prepare for this test. I also know most of you are off to medical school or grad school next fall. I am well aware of how much pressure you are under to keep your GPAs up, and because I am confident that you know this material, I am prepared to offer an automatic B to anyone who opts to skip taking the final exam."

The relief was audible. A number of students jumped up from their desks, thanking their professor for the lifeline he had thrown them.

"Any other takers?" he asked. "This is your last opportunity."

One more student decided to go.

The instructor then handed out the final exam, which consisted of two sentences. "Congratulations," it read, "you have just received an A in this class. Keep believing in yourself."[12] It was a just reward for the students who had worked hard and believed in themselves.

## Expectations Determine Actions

Fred Smith Sr., one of my mentors and the author of *Leading with Integrity*, says that a linguist with Wycliffe Bible translators told him that in twenty of the world's most primitive languages, the word for *belief* is the same as the word for *do*. It is only as people become more "sophisticated" that they begin to separate the meaning of one word from the other. That insight is very telling because most people separate belief from action. So how can we bring these two things back together? Through our expectations.

We cannot live in a way that is inconsistent with our expectations for ourselves. It just doesn't happen. I once heard a story that I have not been able to confirm about an aviation pioneer

> We cannot live in a way that is inconsistent with our expectations for ourselves.

who built a plane the year before the Wright brothers made their historic flight in Kitty Hawk. The plane sat in this inventor's barn because he was afraid to fly it. Maybe it was because it had never been done before. Maybe it was because he expected it to fail—I don't know. It's said that after the news reached him about Orville and Wilbur Wright, the man flew his plane. Before then, he didn't believe in himself enough to take the risk.

There are two kinds of people in this world: those who want to get things done and those who don't want to make mistakes. The Wright brothers were of the first type. The would-be aviation pioneer was of the

> There are two kinds of people in this world: those who want to get things done and those who don't want to make mistakes.

second. If you're of the first type, then you already expect to believe in yourself and take risks. But what if you're of the second type? There's good news: you can grow.

A story in Robert Schuller's book *Tough Times Never Last, but Tough People Do!* is about Sir Edmund Hillary, who was the first person to reach the summit of Mount Everest along with Tibetan Tenzing Norgay. Prior to his success on Everest, Hillary had been part of another expedition, in which the team not only had failed to reach the summit but also had lost one of its members. At a reception for the expedition members in London, Hillary stood to address the audience. Behind the platform was a huge photograph of Everest. Hillary turned to face the image of the mountain and exclaimed, "Mount Everest, you have defeated us. But I will return. And I will defeat you. *Because you cannot get any bigger, and I can.*"[13]

I don't know what challenges you face. They may be getting bigger every day, or they may already be as big as they can get, like Mount Everest. But I do know this: the only way you can rise to meet the challenges effectively is to expect to. You don't overcome challenges by making them smaller. You overcome them by making yourself bigger!

## Actions Determine Results

Results come from actions. That may seem obvious in the physical realm. Sir Isaac Newton's third law of motion states that for every action, there is an equal and opposite reaction. However, in the human realm, many people don't make the connection. They simply hope for good results. Hope is not a strategy. If you want good results, you need to perform good actions. If you want to perform good actions, you must have positive expectations. To have positive expectations, you have to first believe. It all goes back to that. Radio personality Paul Harvey observed, "If you don't live it, you don't believe it." It all starts with belief.

A popular activity for tourists in Switzerland is mountain climbing—not the type of climbing that the world-class mountaineers do to scale the world's highest peaks. Maybe it would be more accurate to call it high-altitude hiking. Groups depart from a "base camp" early in the morning with the intention of making it to the top of the mountain by mid-afternoon.

I talked to a guide about his experiences with these groups, and he described an interesting phenomenon. He said that for most of these expeditions, the group stops at a halfway house where the climbers have lunch, catch their breath, and prepare themselves for the last leg of the rigorous climb. Invariably some members of the group opt for the warmth and comfort of the halfway house and decide not to climb to the

> "If you don't live it,
> you don't believe it."
>
> —Paul Harvey

top. As the rest of the group leaves, the ones who stay are happy and talkative. It's a party. But when the shadows begin to lengthen, many make their way over to the window that looks up the mountain. And the room gets quiet as they wait for the climbers to return. Why is that? They realize they've missed a special opportunity. Most of them will never be in that part of the world again. They won't ever have a chance to climb that mountain again. They missed it.

That's what it's like when people don't make the most of their talent, when they don't believe in themselves and their potential, when they don't act on their belief and try to make the most of every opportunity.

Don't allow that to happen to you! Live the life you were meant to. Try to see yourself as you could be, and then do everything in your power to believe that you can become that person. That is the first important step in becoming a talent-plus person.

# TALENT + *BELIEF*
# APPLICATION EXERCISES

At the end of each chapter of this book, you will find application exercises like the ones below to help you put into practice the ideas contained in the chapter. *Learning* an idea isn't enough to make a person grow; you must *put ideas into practice* to make the most of your talent and become a talent-plus person. I encourage you to create a growth journal and use it as you answer questions and record observations as you do assignments. It will help you to stay focused and chart your progress.

1.  Write a short description of yourself as you are today.

2.  What are your top five talents? If you have not explored them before, you may have to do some work to answer this question. If necessary, buy a book like *Now, Discover Your Strengths* by Marcus Buckingham and Donald O. Clifton and take the Strengths Finder quiz, or do the exercises in *What Color Is Your Parachute?* by Richard Nelson Bolles. In addition, think about your most significant and fulfilling accomplishments. And interview colleagues, family, and close friends to get their input concerning your talents. When you have completed your research, list those strengths.

3.  List the three activities you are most passionate about.

4.  Think about what opportunities may be presenting themselves to you. They may be related to where you live, where you work, who you know, or what's happening in your industry or area of interest. List as many opportunities as you can.

5. Take some time to consider what kind of picture emerges based on these talents, interests, and opportunities. How might they come together for someone other than you, someone with few obstacles or limitations—someone who was in the right place at the right time? Dream big—no idea is too outrageous. Brainstorm what someone in that situation might be able to do, what he or she could become. What would be this person's mission? Using a phrase or short description, write down these things.

6. What you just wrote is a description of who you could be. It is a picture of your potential. How does it compare with the description you wrote in Exercise 1? Believe in your potential, yourself, your mission, and your fellow human beings. How can you light the fire of your belief and increase your expectations to become that person? Give yourself an action plan to do it. Enlist the help of others if needed.

# 2

# PASSION ENERGIZES YOUR TALENT

W hat carries people to the top? What makes them take risks, go the extra mile, and do whatever it takes to achieve their goals? It isn't talent. It's passion. Passion is more important than a plan. Passion creates fire. It provides fuel. I have yet to meet a passionate person who lacked energy. As long as the passion is there, it doesn't matter if they fail. It doesn't matter how many times they fall down. It doesn't matter if others are against them or if people say they cannot succeed. They keep going and make the most of whatever talent they possess. They are talent-plus people and do not stop until they succeed.

## LOOKING FOR DIRECTION

What does a boy like Rueben Martinez do in a place like Miami, Arizona? Miami is a small mining town of two thousand people in the southeastern part of Arizona that has changed little since its founding in 1907. When Rueben was growing up in the 1940s and 1950s, most of the town's jobs came from the copper mining industry, as they still do. Rueben's parents, who were Mexican immigrants, worked in the mines.

There wasn't much to do in Miami. But Rueben had a curious mind, and he found his passion in books—not necessarily an easy task when your parents aren't big readers and your town is so small that it doesn't even have a public library.

"My mother always wanted me to put down my books and clean the yard," recalls Rueben. "So I would hide in the outhouse and read because no one would bother me there."[1]

The child was so desperate for reading material that he became very industrious. "Every morning at 6:45," he says, "the newspaper boy would deliver the newspaper and, when it hit my neighbor's side of the house, I would wake up, go out the back door, lean against my neighbor's house and read the newspaper every morning thoroughly. Then I'd fold that newspaper and put it back as neatly as I could."[2]

Eventually Rueben got caught. But his neighbor didn't mind and encouraged him to keep reading. Rueben was also inspired and assisted by two of his teachers. They continually encouraged his love of reading and loaned him books.

## NEW DIRECTION

When he was seventeen, Rueben moved to Los Angeles to find greater opportunities. The moment he saw the Pacific Ocean, he knew he'd never live in Arizona again. He took whatever jobs he could. He worked as a grocery clerk, crane operator, and factory worker, including at the Bethlehem Steel Mill in Maywood. But then one day he saw an ad for a barber college, and he was captivated by the idea of attending. "I saw those smocks they wore, so white," says Martinez. "It was the opposite of the dirt of the mining world. I wanted clean."[3]

In the 1970s, Rueben Martinez opened his own barbershop and became his own boss. He was making a better life for himself. But he never lost his passion for reading, a passion he wanted to pass on to others, especially young people in the Hispanic and Latino communities. According to a National Endowment for the Arts survey, the reading level among Hispanics is half that of non-Hispanic whites.[4] Martinez wanted to change that.

He started out by lending volumes from his two-hundred-book collection to people waiting for a haircut. The books ranged from Spanish-language masterpieces like *One Hundred Years of Solitude* by Gabriel Garcia Marquez and *Don Quixote* by Cervantes, to American books by Hemingway or Silverstein translated into Spanish, to a signed autobiography by actor Anthony Quinn. But often his patrons forgot to return the books, which frustrated Martinez and diminished his supply for other patrons. His solution? Start selling books. In 1993, Martinez offered books for sale for the first time. He started out with two titles. But it didn't take long for sales to increase, and he started carrying more titles. He became an advocate for literacy. He talked to parents about reading to their children. He talked to young people about diving into books. And he contacted high-profile authors, such as Isabel Allende, and invited them to his shop. Martinez recalls Allende's reaction when she showed up. "When she came into the barbershop bookstore, she said, 'Is this it?' And I said, 'This is it.' Because I only had two book shelves. I had art. I had a barber chair . . . And she said, 'I like it.' And we had a good time. But we also had one of the biggest audiences that ever came to see an author in the city of Santa Ana. We had quite a few people . . . about 3,000."[5]

A few years later, the barbershop with books became a bookstore with a symbolic barber chair. Martinez called his store Librería Martínez Books and Art Gallery. "We started out with two books," says Martinez, "then 10, then 25. Little by little, we've sold over 2 million books. That's what happens if you dare to dream."[6] The store now stocks seventeen thousand titles and has become one of the country's largest collections of Spanish-language books. Martinez opened a second store in 2001 and also a third store just for children. He tells parents, "Do you want your child to be ahead of the line or at the back of the line, moms and dads?

You have to support, endorse, and read to your kid . . . if you do that, your kid will be at the head of the line . . . and be someone special in this world. Reading does it."[7]

## MOMENTUM

Rueben Martinez's talent for promoting literacy has blossomed as he has allowed his passion to explode. He started hosting a weekly cable show on Univision. He cofounded the Latino Book Festival with actor Edward James Olmos. And he started speaking at schools and to other groups to promote literacy. He advises his audiences to read twenty minutes a day so that they consume one million words a year. One of his favorite sayings is that books can take a person all over the world—a library card will take you farther than a driver's license.

"I started reading at a very, very young age," says Martinez, "and I still do. I read a lot every day. I look forward to that. I love literature."[8]

People are starting to recognize Martinez's talent. In 2004, he won a MacArthur Foundation fellowship—often called a "genius grant"—for "fusing the roles of marketplace and community center to inspire appreciation of literature and preserve Latino literary heritage." He became the U.S. Small Business Administration's 2004 Minority Business Advocate of the Year. He received an honorary doctorate in humane letters from Whittier College in 2005 and was also named one of Inc.com's twenty-six most fascinating entrepreneurs. Carlos Azula of Random House points out that "Rueben isn't just selling books; he's selling reading."[9]

Martinez isn't stopping. In his midsixties, he has no intention of resting on his laurels. He is energized by what he does.

"I made more money cutting hair than selling books," notes Martinez, age sixty-four. "But the joy of my life is what I'm doing now."[10] Martinez wants to create a bilingual Borders-style chain of bookstores across the nation, hoping to establish twenty-five stores by 2012.

"If I had stayed with my factory jobs," observes Martinez, "I would have been living a comfortable retirement now. But I chose to go on my own as a barber. Now with the bookstores, I'm going to work for the rest of my life. My kids think I'm crazy."[11] No, he's not crazy. He's just filled with passion!

## YOUR PASSION CAN EMPOWER YOU

Passion can energize every aspect of a person's life—including his talent. Have you ever known a person with great passion who lacked the energy to act on what mattered to her? I doubt it. A passionate person with limited talent will outperform a passive person who possesses greater talent. Why? Because passionate people act with boundless enthusiasm, and they just keep on going! Talent plus passion energizes.

Authors Robert J. Kriegel and Louis Patler cite a study of 1,500 people over twenty years that shows how passion makes a significant difference in a person's career:

At the outset of the study, the group was divided into Group A, 83 percent of the sample, who were embarking on a career chosen for the prospects of making money now in order to do what they wanted later, and Group B, the other 17 percent of the sample, who had chosen their career path for the reverse reason, they were going to pursue what they wanted to do now and worry about the money later.

The data showed some startling revelations:

- At the end of the 20 years, 101 of the 1,500 had become millionaires.
- Of the millionaires, all but one—100 out of 101—were from Group B, the group that had chosen to pursue what they loved![12]

The old saying is true: "Find something you like to do so much that you'd gladly do it for nothing, and if you learn to do it well, someday people will be happy to pay you for it." When that's the case, then true are the words of a motto that Dr. Charles Mayo kept on his office wall: "There's no fun like work."

# THE POWER OF PASSION

There really is no substitute for passion when it comes to energizing your talent. Take a look at what passion can do for you:

## 1. Passion Is the First Step to Achievement

Loving what you do is the key that opens the door for achievement. When you don't like what you're doing, it really shows—no matter how hard you try to pretend it doesn't. You can become like the little boy named Eddie whose grandmother was an opera lover. She had season tickets, and when Eddie turned eight, she decided to take him to a performance of Wagner—in German—as his birthday present. The next day, at his mother's prompting, the child wrote the following in a thank-you note: "Dear Grandmother, Thank you for the birthday present. It is what I always wanted, but not very much. Love, Eddie."

It's difficult to achieve when you don't have the desire to do so. That's why passion is so important. There is a story about Socrates in which a proud and disdainful young man came to the philosopher and, with a smirk, said, "O great Socrates, I come to you for knowledge."

Seeing the shallow and vain young man for what he was, Socrates led the young man down to the sea into waist-deep water. Then he said, "Tell me again what you want."

"Knowledge," he responded with a smile.

Socrates grabbed the young man by his shoulders and pushed him down under the water, holding him there for thirty seconds. "Now, what do you want?"

"Wisdom, O great Socrates," the young man sputtered.

The philosopher pushed him under once again. When he let him up, he asked again, "What do you want?"

"Knowledge, O wise and . . . ," he managed to spit out before Socrates held him under again, this time even longer.

"What do you want?" the old man asked as he let him up again. The younger man coughed and gasped.

"Air!" he screamed. "I need air!"

"When you want knowledge as much as you just wanted air, then you will get knowledge," the old man stated as he returned to shore.

The only way you can achieve anything of significance is to really want it. Passion provides that.

## 2. Passion Increases Willpower

One of my roles as a motivational teacher is to try to help people reach their potential. For years, I tried to inspire passion in audiences by going about it the wrong way. I used to tell people about what made me passionate, what made me want to get out and do my best. But I could see that it wasn't having the effect I desired—people just didn't respond. I couldn't ignite others' passion by sharing my own.

I decided to change my focus. Instead of sharing my passion, I started helping others discover their passion. To do that, I ask these questions:

*What do you sing about?*
*What do you cry about?*
*What do you dream about?*

The first two questions speak to what touches you at a deep level today. The third answers what will bring you fulfillment tomorrow. The answers to these questions can often help people discover their true passion.

> The secret to willpower is what someone once called *wantpower*.

While everybody can possess passion, not everyone takes the time to discover it. And that's a shame. Passion is fuel for the will. Passion turns your have-to's into want-to's. What we accomplish in life is based less on what we want and more on how much we want it. The secret to willpower is what someone once called *wantpower*. People who want something enough usually find the willpower to achieve it.

You can't help people become winners unless they want to win. Champions become champions from within, not from without.

### 3. Passion Produces Energy

When you have passion, you become energized. You don't have to produce perseverance; it is naturally present in you. It helps you to enjoy the journey as much as reaching the destination. Without it, achievement becomes a long and difficult road.

For many years my wife, Margaret, has called me the Energizer Bunny because of the commercials where the battery-operated rabbit keeps going and going. I guess she does so with good reason. I do have a lot of energy. There are always things I hope to do, people I want to see, and goals I want to reach. The reason is passion! We often call people high energy or low energy based on how much they do, but I have come to the conclusion that it might be more appropriate to call them high or low *passion*.

During a Q-and-A session at a conference, an attendee once asked me, "What is the secret of your passion?" It took me only a moment to be able to articulate it:

1. I am gifted at what I do (strength zone).
2. What I do makes a difference (results).
3. When I do what I was made to do, I feel most alive (purpose).

I believe all passionate people feel that way. Aviation pioneer Charles Lindbergh observed, "It is the greatest shot of adrenaline to be doing what you've wanted to do so badly. You almost feel like you could fly without the plane."

Some people say that they feel burned out. The truth is that they probably never were on fire in the first place. Writer and editor Norman Cousins said, "Death isn't the greatest loss in life. The greatest loss is what dies inside of us while we live." Without passion, a part of us does becomes dead. And if we're not careful, we could end up like the person whose tombstone read, "Died at 30. Buried at 60." Don't allow that to happen to you. Be like Rueben Martinez who is still going strong beyond age sixty. People often describe him as acting half his age. What gives him such energy? His passion!

> "Death isn't the greatest loss in life. The greatest loss is what dies inside of us while we live."
>
> —Norman Cousins

## 4. Passion Is the Foundation for Excellence

Passion can transform someone from average to excellent. I can tell you that from experience. When I was in high school, I wasn't a great student. My priorities were basketball first, friends second, and studies a distant third. Why? Because playing basketball and spending time with friends were things I was passionate about. I studied, but only to please my parents. School held little appeal for me.

Everything changed when I went to college. For the first time I was studying subjects that mattered to me. They were interesting, and they would apply to my future career. My grades went up because my passion did. In high school I was sometimes on the principal's "list" (which was not a good thing), but in college I continually made the *dean's* list. Passion fired my desire to achieve with excellence.

Civil rights leader Martin Luther King Jr. asserted, "If a man hasn't discovered something that he will die for, he isn't fit to live." When you find purpose, you find passion. And when you find passion, it energizes your talent so that you can achieve excellence.

## 5. Passion Is the Key to Success

People are such that whenever anything fires their souls, impossibilities vanish. Perhaps that's why philosopher-poet Ralph Waldo Emerson wrote, "Every great and commanding movement in the annals of the world is the triumph of enthusiasm."

> "Every great and commanding movement in the annals of the world is the triumph of enthusiasm."
>
> —Ralph Waldo Emerson

I read about two hundred executives who were asked what makes people successful. The number one quality they cited was enthusiasm, not talent—80 percent of them recognized that there needed to be a fire within to achieve success.

The most talented people aren't always the ones who win. If they did, how could anyone explain the success of the 1980 U.S. Olympic hockey team, which was depicted in the movie *Miracle,* or the Hall of Fame careers of basketball's Larry Bird or football's Joe Montana? Of Montana, teammate Ronnie Lott said, "You can't measure the size of his heart with a tape measure or a stopwatch." It takes more than talent to create success. It takes passion.

## 6. Passion Makes a Person Contagious

Writer and promotional publicist Eleanor Doan remarked, "You cannot kindle a fire in any other heart until it is burning within your own." I believe that's true. One of my favorite subjects is communication. I have studied and taught it for years, and I always enjoy observing great communicators in action. I believe that people are instructed by reason, but they are inspired by passion.

Even a brief review of effective leaders and businesspeople through-out history illustrates that their passion "caught on" with others. One of my favorites is Winston Churchill. In the 1930s, Churchill was begin-ning to fade from view in British politics. But with the rise of Hitler came a rise in Churchill's passion. Long before others did, Churchill spoke out against the Nazis. He had a passion to protect freedom and democracy. And when Hitler declared war and sought to conquer Europe and crush England, Churchill's passion for resistance became infused in the people of Britain and eventually the United States. Without Churchill, the fate of the free world might have turned out to be quite different.

## TALENT + PASSION = A TALENT-PLUS PERSON
## PUTTING THE TALENT-PLUS FORMULA INTO ACTION

If you don't possess the energy that you desire, then you need to fire up your passion. Here is how I suggest you proceed:

### 1. Prioritize Your Life According to Your Passion

People who have passion but lack priorities are like individuals who find themselves in a lonely log cabin deep in the woods on a cold snowy night and then light a bunch of small candles and place them all around the room. They don't create enough light to help them see, nor do they produce enough heat to keep them warm. At best, they merely make the room seem a bit more cheerful. On the other hand, people who possess priorities but no passion are like those who stack wood in the fireplace of that same cold cabin but never light the fire. But people who have passion with priorities are like those who stack the wood, light the fire, and enjoy the light and heat that it produces.

In the early 1970s, I realized that my talent would be maximized and my potential realized only if I matched my passion with my priorities. I was spending too much of my time doing tasks for which I possessed nei-ther talent nor passion. I had to make a change—to align what I felt strongly about with what I was doing. It made a huge difference in my life. It didn't eliminate my troubles or remove my obstacles, but it empowered me to face them with greater energy and enthusiasm. For more than thirty years, I have worked to maintain that alignment of priorities and passion. And as I have, I've kept in mind this quote by journalist Tim Redmond, which I put in a prominent place for a year to keep me on track: "There are many things that will catch my eye, but there are only a few that catch my heart. It is those I consider to pursue."

> "There are many things that will catch my eye, but there are only a few that catch my heart. It is those I consider to pursue."
>
> —Tim Redmond

Prioritizing your life according to your passion can be risky. For most people, it requires a major realignment in their work and private lives. But you can't be a talent-plus person and play it safe. Advertising agency president Richard Edler stated this:

> Safe living generally makes for regrets later on. We are all given talents and dreams. Sometimes the two don't match. But more often than not, we compromise both before ever finding out. Later on, as successful as we might be, we find ourselves looking back longingly to that time when we should have chased our *true* dreams and our *true* talents for all they were worth. Don't let yourself be pressured into thinking that your dreams or your talents aren't prudent. They were never meant to be prudent. They were meant to bring joy and fulfillment into your life.[13]

If your priorities are not aligned with your passion, then begin thinking about making changes in your life. Will change be risky? Probably. But which would you rather live with? The pain of risk or the pain of regret?

## 2. Protect Your Passion

If you've ever built a fire, then you know this: the natural tendency of fire is to go out. If you want to keep a fire hot, then you need to feed it, and you need to protect it. Not everyone in your life will help you do that when it comes to your passion. In truth, there are two kinds of people: fire*lighters*, who will go out of their way to help you keep your fire hot, and fire*fighters*, who will throw cold water on the fire of passion that burns within you.

How can you tell the firelighters from the firefighters? Listen to what they say. Firefighters use phrases like these:

- "It's not in the budget."
- "That's not practical."
- "We tried that before and it didn't work."
- "We've never done that before."
- "Yeah, but . . ."
- "The boss won't go for it."
- "If it ain't broke, then don't fix it."
- "That's not the way we do things around here."
- "It'll never work."
- "But who will do all the extra work?"
- "You're not _____ [smart, talented, young, old, etc.] enough."
- "You're getting too big for your britches."
- "Who do you think you are?"

If you've heard one or more of these phrases coming from people you know, you may want to create some distance between yourself and them. These firefighters focus on what's wrong rather than what's right. They find the cloud that comes with every silver lining. They doubt. They resist change. They keep people from reaching their potential by trying to put out the fire of their passion. Stay away from them. Instead, spend more time with people who see you not just as you are but as you could be; people who encourage your dreams, ignite your passion. I try to schedule a lunch or two with firelighters like these every month. They really fire me up and energize me to do what I know is best for me.

### 3. Pursue Your Passion with Everything You've Got

Rudy Ruettiger, upon whose life the movie *Rudy* was based, observed, "If you really, really believe in your dream, you'll get there. But you have to have passion and total commitment to make it happen. When you have passion and commitment, you don't need a complex plan. Your plan is your life is your dream."

What do you want to accomplish in your lifetime? How do you want to focus your energy: on survival, success, or significance? We live in a time and place with too many opportunities for survival alone. And there's more to life than mere success. We need to dream big. We need to adopt the perspective of someone like playwright George Bernard Shaw, who wrote,

> I am convinced that my life belongs to the whole community; and as long as I live, it is my privilege to do for it whatever I can, for the harder I work the more I live. I rejoice in the life for its own sake. Life is no brief candle to me. It is a sort of splendid torch which I got hold of for a moment, and I want to make it burn as brightly as possible before turning it over to future generations.

Shaw had passion—for life and his work. Your passion has the potential to provide you energy far beyond the limitations of your talent. In the end, you will be remembered for your passion. It is what will energize your talent. It is what will empower you to make your mark.

# Talent + Passion
# Application Exercises

1. To get a better handle on what you are passionate about, answer these questions:
   What makes you sing?
   What makes you cry?
   What makes you dream?

2. Make a list of the people in your life who try to put out the fire of your passion. If you can simply stop spending time with some of them, then plan to distance yourself. For those with whom you *must* spend time, create a strategy for minimizing the damage they can do to you. If you're married and your spouse is on this list, then seek help from a professional to help you repair the damage and rebuild relational bridges.

3. Think about key firelighters in your life, both past and present. Make spending time with some current firelighters a priority in the coming weeks. Write a note to a firelighter from your past to thank him or her for inspiring you to succeed.

4. Spend some time identifying the top priorities in your life. Think broadly and include the areas of work, family, recreation, health, and so on. Try to write out the priorities in order of importance.

5. Compare what you have written about your passions and talent from Chapter 1 and the priority list you just completed. How do they

match up? What could you change to help align them? What price
will you likely pay if you neglect to make changes?

6. For whom can you be a firelighter? Where and when is your passion
   contagious? How can you add value to others by helping to light
   their fire?

# 3

## INITIATIVE ACTIVATES YOUR TALENT

I t's a cliché to say that every journey begins with the first step, yet it is still true. Talent-plus people don't wait for everything to be perfect to move forward. They don't wait for all the problems or obstacles to disappear. They don't wait until their fear subsides. They take initiative. They know a secret that good leaders understand: momentum is their friend. As soon as they take that first step and start moving forward, things become a little easier. If the momentum gets strong enough, many of the problems take care of themselves and talent can take over. But it starts only after you've taken those first steps.

## DISASTER

On January 17, 1994, at 4:30 in the morning, a 6.7 magnitude earthquake struck the Los Angeles area. The earthquake was considered moderate (in contrast, the San Francisco earthquake of 1906 was believed to be more than ten times as powerful), but it still did an incredible amount of damage. More than 50 people died and 9,000 were seriously injured.[1] More than 22,000 people were left homeless, and

7,000 buildings were judged uninhabitable with an additional 22,000 sustaining major damage. The quake closed 9 hospitals, ruined several freeways, and collapsed 9 bridges.

The disaster, called the Northridge earthquake, was centered beneath the San Fernando Valley and did $44 billion in damage. Some experts considered the people who lived in the area to be fortunate because the earthquake occurred so early in the morning and on a holiday—Martin Luther King Day. Yet it was still the most monetarily costly earthquake in the history of the United States.

## BREAKING GRIDLOCK

Los Angeles typically has the worst congestion and traffic delays of any large city in the nation. The effects of the Northridge earthquake made them worse. One of the most problematic areas was a section of Interstate 10 called the Santa Monica Freeway in the heart of Los Angeles—the most heavily used highway in the world. Every day it carries as many as 341,000 vehicles. Estimates were that it would cost California $1 million a day in lost wages, added fuel costs, and depressed business activity for every day it was closed.[2]

Environmental reviews and permitting requirements in California routinely take eighteen to twenty-four months. And construction on a project this size usually takes well over six months. At a cost of $1 million a day, that would mean the closure of the Santa Monica Freeway alone could create a negative impact costing Los Angeles more than $900 million!

Governor Pete Wilson knew that he needed to act to solve the problem. He initiated a plan to clear the way for quick reconstruction. Wilson recounts, "I issued an executive order suspending all statutes and regulations related to state contracting . . . My goal was to reopen I-10 within 6 months. Each contract included an incentive. If the work was late, we charged a fine, and if it was completed early, we paid a bonus."[3]

Demolition and removal work had begun a mere six hours after the earthquake. And on Monday, January 31, just two weeks after the earthquake, CalTrans, the state's agency responsible for freeway construction, invited five contractors to bid on the job of rebuilding the Santa Monica Freeway. Preliminary plans were made available to the contractors that night. But bids would be due Friday, February 4, at 10:00 a.m., just four days later! The contract would be awarded that night, and construction would commence on Saturday, February 5. And there were two other important pieces of information. First, the maximum amount of time allowed for construction was 140 days. Second, the financial stakes for finishing the project on time were high. If the winning contractor finished the project late, there would be a penalty of $200,000 per day. However, the contractor would receive $200,000 per day over the bid for each day it finished ahead of schedule.

## STEPPING FORWARD

One company that received the offer to bid was C. C. Myers, which had completed several CalTrans projects in the past. The company bid the project at $14.7 million with the promise to finish in 140 days.[4] However, the management team privately set the goal of completing it in 100 days. If all went well, the company could make an additional $8 million.

But of course, everything didn't go well. C. C. Myers planned to work its crews in twelve-hour shifts, twenty-four hours a day, seven days a week. The crews quickly became fatigued. The solution? The managers hired more workers. A job that size usually required 65 carpenters. They hired 228. Instead of 15 iron workers, they employed 134. They continually initiated steps to speed up the project, such as using an expensive fast-drying concrete rather than their usual material. And when the company was informed that the railroads would require three weeks to deliver the steel beams needed for the project, C. C. Myers chartered its own trains to get the supplies from Arkansas and Texas to Los Angeles.[5]

C. C. Myers's initiative paid off. The company didn't just beat the 140-day deadline or even its own internal goal of 100 days. The crews finished the job in a mere 66 days—74 days ahead of schedule. And in the process the organization earned bonuses totaling $14.5 million, nearly the amount of the original bid.

The C. C. Myers organization had expertise, experience, and a proven track record. But the leaders didn't rely on those things alone. Why? They knew that talent alone is never enough. They knew they needed talent plus! To complete the Santa Monica Freeway project, they needed to show initiative in the bidding process, in the leadership of their people, and in the management of the details. That initiative brought them great success. And the company continues to show initiative. In the wake of the Northridge earthquake, Myers began working with engineers at the University of Southern California on innovations to strengthen existing freeways against earthquake damage.

## Insights on Initiative

If you want to reach your potential, you have to show initiative, just as Governor Pete Wilson and the leaders at C. C. Myers did. Here's why:

### 1. Initiative Is the First Step to Anywhere You Want to Go

A tourist paused for a rest in a small town in the mountains. He sat down on a bench next to an old man in front of the town's only store. "Hi, friend," he said, "can you tell me something this town is noted for?"

"Well," answered the old man after a moment's hesitation, "you can start here and get to anywhere in the world you want."

That's true of nearly every location. Where you finish in life isn't determined so much by *where* you start as by *whether* you start. If you're willing to get started and keep initiating, there's no telling how far you might go.

That was the case for Les Brown. Les and his brother, Wes, were adopted when they were six weeks old, and they grew up in Liberty City, a poor section of Miami, Florida. As a child, Les was branded a slow learner and given little chance of success by many of his teachers. But with the encouragement of one of his high school teachers, who told him, "Someone else's opinion of you does not have to become your reality," Les managed to graduate from high school and later got a job as a radio DJ. With much hard work, he became a broadcast manager. He got involved in his community, became a community activist and leader, and eventually was elected to the state legislature for three terms. And then he turned his attention to public speaking, where he received the National Speakers Association's highest honor and was named one of the world's top five speakers according to Toastmasters in 1992. He has written books, hosts his own syndicated television show, owns a business, and commands $25,000 per appearance as a public speaker.

> Where you finish in life isn't determined so much by *where* you start as by *whether* you start.

When he started life, most people wouldn't have given him much of a chance to succeed. Few thought he had talent. But he just kept moving forward, and he has since moved far beyond his detractors. Successful people initiate—and they follow through.[6]

## 2. Initiative Closes the Door to Fear

Author Katherine Paterson said, "To fear is one thing. To let fear grab you by the tail and swing you around is another." We all have fears. The question is whether we are going to control them or allow them to control us.

In 1995, my friend Dan Reiland and his wife, Patti, went skydiving along with a group of friends (including my writer, Charlie Wetzel). They approached the event with a mixture of excitement and fear. At the skydiving center in Southern California, they received only a few minutes of training to prepare them for their tandem jumps. Dan said they were feeling pretty good about the whole thing until a guy walked into the room and made a pitch to sell them life insurance.

As the plane ascended to 11,000 feet, they became increasingly nervous. Then they opened the sliding door at the back of the plane, at which point the fear factor went through the roof. Wishing they had worn rubber pants, they approached the door, each of them harnessed to a jumpmaster, and then launched themselves out of the plane.

Within seconds, they were hurtling toward the earth at 120 miles an hour. And after a free fall of 6,000 feet, they pulled their rip cords. When the canopy opened, with a forceful jolt they went from 120 miles an hour to 25 miles an hour. Dan said, "It made my underwear find places it had never found before!"

I laugh whenever Dan tells the story, but I was really surprised to learn from Dan and Patti that as petrified as they were before they jumped, all their fear was gone the second they left the plane.

Author and pastor Norman Vincent Peale asserted, "Action is a great restorer and builder of confidence. Inaction is not only the result, but the cause, of fear. Perhaps the action you take will be successful; perhaps different action or adjustments will have to follow. But any action is better than no action at all." If you want to close the door on fear, get moving.

## 3. Initiative Opens the Door to Opportunity

Benjamin Franklin, one of our nation's Founding Fathers, advised, "To succeed, jump as quickly at opportunities as you do at conclusions." People who take initiative and work hard may succeed, or they may fail. But anyone who doesn't take initiative is almost guaranteed to fail. I'm willing to bet that you have . . .

a decision you should be making,
a problem you should be solving,
a possibility you should be examining,
a project you should be starting,
a goal you should be reaching,
an opportunity you should be seizing,
a dream you should be fulfilling.

No one can wait until everything is perfect to act and expect to be successful. It's better to be 80 percent sure and make things happen than it is to wait until you are 100 percent sure because by then, the opportunity will have already passed you by.

## 4. Initiative Eases Life's Difficulties

Psychiatrist M. Scott Peck famously stated, "Life is difficult." That's not most people's problem. Their response to life's difficulties is. Too many people wait around for their ship to come in. When they take that approach to life, they often find it to be hardship. The things that simply come to us are rarely the things we want. To have a chance at getting what we desire, we need to work for it.

> "Nothing is so fatiguing as the hanging on of an uncompleted task."
>
> —William James

Philosopher and author William James said, "Nothing is so fatiguing as the hanging on of an uncompleted task." The longer we let things slide, the harder they become. The hardest work is often the accumulation of many easy things that should have been done yesterday, last week, or last month. The only way to get rid of a difficult task is to do it. That takes initiative.

## 5. Initiative Is Often the Difference Between Success and Failure

A man who was employed by a duke and duchess in Europe was called in to speak to his employer.

"James," said the duchess, "how long have you been with us?"

"About thirty years, Your Grace," he replied.

"As I recall, you were employed to look after the dog."

"Yes, Your Grace," James replied.

"James, that dog died twenty-seven years ago."

"Yes, Your Grace," said James. "What would you like me to do now?"

Like James, too many people are waiting for someone else to tell them what to do next. Nearly all people have good thoughts, ideas, and intentions, but many of them never translate those into action. Doing so requires initiative.

Most people recognize that initiative is beneficial, yet they still frequently underestimate its true value. Perhaps the best illustration of the power of initiative is a story about the patenting of the telephone. In the 1870s, two men worked extensively on modifying and improving tele-graphy, which was the current technology. Both had ideas for transmitting sounds by wire, and both explored the transmission of the human voice electrically. What is remarkable is that both men— Alexander Graham Bell and Elisha Gray—filed their ideas at the patent office on the same day, February 14, 1876. Bell was the fifth person on record that day who filed for a patent. Gray, on the other hand, sent his attorney, and the man arrived more than an hour after Bell, applying for a caveat, a kind of declaration of intention to file for a patent. Those minutes cost Gray a fortune. Bell's claim was upheld in court, even though Gray complained that he had come up with the idea first.

Talent without initiative never reaches its potential. It's like a caterpillar that won't get into its cocoon. It will never transform, forever relegated to crawling on the ground, even though it had the potential to fly.

# PEOPLE WHO LACK INITIATIVE

When it comes to initiative, there are really only four kinds of people:

1.  People who do the right thing without being told
2.  People who do the right thing when told
3.  People who do the right thing when told more than once
4.  People who never do the right thing, no matter what

Anyone who wants to become a talent-plus person needs to become the first kind of person. Why doesn't everyone do that? I think there are several reasons.

## 1. People Who Lack Initiative Fail to See the Consequences of Inaction

King Solomon of ancient Israel is said to have been the wisest person who ever lived. Every time I read Proverbs, which he is believed to have authored, I learn something. In recent years, I've enjoyed reading his words in a paraphrase called *The Message*:

> You lazy fool, look at an ant.
> > Watch it closely; let it teach you a thing or two.
> Nobody has to tell it what to do.
> > All summer it stores up food;
> > at harvest it stockpiles provisions.
> So how long are you going to laze around doing nothing?
> > How long before you get out of bed?
> A nap here, a nap there, a day off here, a day off there,
> > sit back, take it easy—do you know what comes next?
> Just this: You can look forward to a dirt-poor life,
> > poverty your permanent houseguest![7]

British civil servant and economist Sir Josiah Stamp remarked, "It is easy to dodge our responsibilities, but we cannot dodge the consequences of dodging our responsibilities." That is true. Whatever we do—or neglect to do—will catch up with us in the end. Those who never initiate often end up like the subject of English playwright James Albery's verse,

> He slept beneath the moon;
> He basked beneath the sun.
> He lived a life of going-to-do;
> And died with nothing done.[8]

Don't let that happen to you.

## 2. People Who Lack Initiative Want Someone Else to Motivate Them

There's a silly story of a man in a small town who was known as a great fisherman. Every morning he went out on a lake in his small boat, and in a short time, he returned with his boat loaded with fish.

One day a stranger showed up in town and asked if he could accompany the man the next time he went out. The fisherman said, "Sure, you can come. Meet me at the dock at five a.m."

The next morning the two men went far out into the lake and made their way to a remote cove. As they traveled, the stranger noticed that the fisherman didn't have any poles or other equipment—just a rusty tackle box and a scoop net.

After the fisherman shut off the motor, he opened the tackle box and pulled out a stick of dynamite. He struck a match, lit it, and then tossed it into the water. After a deafening explosion, he grabbed his net and started scooping up fish.

With a hard look, the stranger reached into his pocket and pulled out a badge with the words *game warden* on it. "You're under arrest," he said evenly.

His words didn't faze the fisherman. He simply reached into the tackle box again, lit another stick of dynamite, and held it while the fuse burned down. He then handed it to the game warden and said, "So, are you going to just sit there, or are you going to fish?"

Successful people don't need a lighted fuse to motivate them. Their motivation comes from within. If we wait for others to motivate us, what happens when a coach, a boss, or other inspirational person doesn't show up? We need a better plan than that.

Tom Golisano, founder of Paychex, Inc., offered this considered opinion: "I believe you don't motivate people. What you do is hire motivated people, then make sure you don't demotivate them." If you want to get ahead, you need to light your own fire.

## 3. People Who Lack Initiative Look for the Perfect Time to Act

Timing is important—no doubt about that. The Law of Timing in my book The 21 Irrefutable Laws of Leadership states, "When to lead is as important as what to do and where to go." But it's also true that all worthwhile endeavors in life require risk. I love this Chinese proverb: "He who deliberates fully before taking a step will spend his entire life on one leg." For many people, the tragedy isn't that life ends too soon; it's that they wait too long to begin it.

> "He who deliberates fully before taking a step will spend his entire life on one leg."
>
> —Chinese proverb

## 4. People Who Lack Initiative Like Tomorrow Better Than Today

One of the reasons noninitiators have such a difficult time getting started is that they focus their attention on tomorrow instead of today. Jazz musician Jimmy Lyons remarked, "Tomorrow is the only day in the year that appeals to a lazy man." But that attitude gets us into trouble because the only time over which we have any control is the present.

Edgar Guest wrote a poem that captures the fate of those who have this problem. It is appropriately titled "To-morrow":

> He was going to be all that a mortal should be
> To-morrow.
> No one should be kinder or braver than he
> To-morrow.
> A friend who was troubled and weary he knew,
> Who'd be glad of a lift and who needed it, too;
> On him he would call and see what he could do
> To-morrow.
> Each morning he stacked up the letters he'd write
> To-morrow.
> And thought of the folks he would fill with delight
> To-morrow.
> It was too bad, indeed, he was busy to-day,
> And hadn't a minute to stop on his way;
> More time he would have to give others, he'd say
> To-morrow.
> The greatest of workers this man would have been
> To-morrow.
> The world would have known him, had he ever seen
> To-morrow.
> But the fact is he died and he faded from view,
> And all that he left here when living was through
> Was a mountain of things he intended to do
> To-morrow.[9]

The idea of tomorrow can be very seductive, but the promise that it holds is often false. I heard about a customer who went into a furniture store in Santa Fe, New Mexico, and saw an old, faded sign on the wall that said, "Tomorrow we will give away everything in the store." For a moment, the customer got excited. Then he realized the sign would say the same thing tomorrow—putting off the giveaway another day and then another day. That particular *tomorrow* would never come.

Spanish priest and writer Baltasar Gracian said, "The wise man does at once what the fool does finally." Anything worth doing is worth doing immediately. Remember that for people who never start, their difficulties never stop.

## TALENT + *INITIATIVE* = A TALENT-PLUS PERSON PUTTING THE TALENT-PLUS FORMULA INTO ACTION

To be honest, all of us are plagued by procrastination in some area of our lives. If something is unpleasant, uninteresting, or complex, we tend to put it off. Even some things we *like* doing can cause us difficulty. Johann Wolfgang von Goethe observed, "To put your ideas into action is the most difficult thing in the world." Yet to reach our potential and become talent-plus people, we must show initiative. Here are some suggestions to help you as you strive to become a talent-plus person in this area:

### 1. Accept Responsibility for Your Life

Greek philosopher Socrates said, "To move the world we must first move ourselves." Show me those who neglect to take responsibility for their own lives, and I'll show you people who also lack initiative. Responsibility and initiative are inseparable.

Everyone experiences setbacks. We all face obstacles. From time to time, we all feel that the deck is stacked against us. We need to show initiative anyway. Dick Butler asserted, "Life isn't fair. It isn't going to be fair. Stop sniveling and whining and go out and make it happen for

> "To move the world
> we must first move
> ourselves."
>
> —Socrates

you. In business I see too many people who expect the financial tooth fairy to come at night and remove that ugly dead tooth from under the pillow and substitute profitability just in the nick of time at the end of the fiscal year." There's a saying that great souls have wills but feeble ones have only wishes. We cannot wish our way to success. We need to take responsibility and act.

## 2. Examine Your Reasons for Not Initiating

Chinese philosopher Mencius made this point: "If your deeds are unsuccessful, seek the reason in yourself. When your own person is correct, the whole world will turn to you." If you lack initiative, the only way you will be able to change is to first identify the specific problem. Think about the reasons people lack initiative already outlined in this chapter. Are you in denial about the consequences of not taking initiative and responsibility for yourself? Are you waiting for others to motivate you instead of working to motivate yourself? Are you waiting for everything to be perfect before you act? Are you fantasizing about tomorrow instead of focusing on what you can do today? Or is there some other issue that is preventing you from taking action?

What's important is that you separate legitimate reasons from excuses. An excuse puts the blame on someone or something outside you. Excuses are like exit signs on the road of progress. They take us off track. Know this: it's easier to move from failure to success than from excuses to success. Eliminate excuses. Once you've done that, you can turn your attention to the reasons—and how to overcome them.

## 3. Focus on the Benefits of Completing a Task

It is extremely difficult to be successful if you are forever putting things off. Procrastination is the fertilizer that makes difficulties grow. When you take too long to make up your mind about an opportunity that presents itself, you will miss out on seizing it. In the previous chapter, I wrote about the importance of aligning your priorities with your passion. To become effective and make progress in your area of talent or responsibility, you can't spend your valuable time on unimportant or unnecessary tasks. So I'm going to make an assumption that if you do procrastinate about a task, it is a necessary one. (If it's not, don't put it off; eliminate it.) To get yourself over the hump, focus on what you'll get out of it if you get it done. Will completing the task bring a financial benefit? Will it clear the way for something else you would *like* to do? Does it represent a milestone in your development or the completion of something bigger? At the very least, does it help to clear the decks for you emotionally? If you seek a positive reason, you are likely to find one.

Once you find that idea, start moving forward and act decisively. U.S. admiral William Halsey observed, "All problems become smaller if you don't dodge them, but confront them. Touch a thistle timidly, and it pricks you; grasp it boldly, and its spines crumble."

## 4. Share Your Goal with a Friend Who Will Help You

No one achieves success alone. As the Law of Significance states in my book *The 17 Indisputable Laws of Teamwork*, "One is too small a number to achieve greatness." Lindbergh didn't fly solo across the Atlantic without help, Einstein didn't develop the theory of relativity in a vacuum, and Columbus didn't discover the New World on his own. They all had help.

My primary partner in life has been my wife, Margaret. She has been a part of every significant goal that I have achieved. She is the first to know when I identify a goal, and she is both the first and the last to support me along the way. And of course, many others have helped me and encouraged me along the way, particularly my parents and my brother, Larry.

In recent years, a key person in supporting me has been John Hull, the president and CEO of EQUIP. When I set the goal of EQUIP to train one million leaders around the globe, the task seemed formidable.

As much as I was dedicated to that vision, I had moments when I wondered if it were really possible. John not only was encouraging, but he took ownership of the vision and launched the plan to accomplish it. As you read this book, we have surpassed the goal of training one million leaders and are now working on training another million. One of the reasons I love and admire John is his initiative.

There is no way to put a value on the assistance that others can give you in achieving your dreams. Share your goals and dreams with people who care about you and will encourage and assist you in accomplishing them. It means taking a risk because you will have to be vulnerable in sharing your hopes and ambitions. But the risk is worth taking.

## 5. Break Large Tasks Down into Smaller Ones

Once you remove some of the internal barriers that may be stopping you from taking initiative and you enlist the help of others, you're ready to get practical. Many times large tasks overwhelm people, and that's a problem because overwhelmed people seldom initiate.

Here's how I suggest you proceed in breaking an intimidating goal into more manageable parts:

*Divide it by categories*. Most large objectives are complex and can be broken into steps for functions. The smaller pieces often require the effort of people with particular talents. Begin by figuring out what skill sets will be required to accomplish the smaller tasks.

*Prioritize it by importance*. When we don't take initiative and prioritize what we must do according to its importance, the tasks begin to arrange themselves according to their urgency. When the urgent starts driving you instead of the important, you lose any kind of initiative edge, and instead of activating your talent, it robs you of the best opportunities to use it.

*Order it by sequence*. Dividing the task according to its categories helps you to understand *how* you will need to accomplish it. Prioritizing by importance helps you to understand *why* you need to do each part of it. Ordering by sequence helps you to know *when* each part needs to be done. The important thing here is to create a timetable, give yourself deadlines, and stick to them. The biggest lie we tell ourselves when it comes to action is, "I'll do it later."

**Assign it by abilities**. When you divide the large task into smaller ones by category, you begin to understand what kinds of people you'll need to get the job done. At this stage, you very specifically answer the *who* question. As a leader, I can tell you that the most important step in accomplishing something big is determining who will be on the team. Assign tasks to winners and give them authority and responsibility, and the job will get done. Fail to give a specific person ownership of the task or give it to an average person, and you may find yourself in trouble.

**Accomplish it by teamwork**. Even if you break a task down, strategically plan, and recruit great people, you still need one more element to succeed. Everyone has to be able to work together. Teamwork is the glue that can bring it all together.

## 6. Allocate Specific Times to Tasks You Might Procrastinate

Dawson Trotman, author and founder of The Navigators, observed, "The greatest time wasted is the time getting started." Haven't you found that to be true? The hardest part of writing a letter is penning the first line. The hardest part of making a tough phone call is picking up the receiver and dialing the number. The most difficult part of practicing the piano is sitting down at the keyboard.

> "The greatest time wasted is the time getting started."
>
> —Dawson Trotman

It's the start that often stops people. So how do you overcome that difficulty? Try scheduling a specific time for something you don't like doing. For example, if dealing with difficult people is a regular part of your job, but you tend to avoid doing it, then schedule a set time for it. Maybe the best time would be between two and three o'clock every day. Treat it like an appointment, and when three o'clock rolls around, stop until tomorrow.

## 7. Remember, Preparation Includes Doing

One of the questions I often hear concerns writing. Young leaders frequently ask me how I got started, and I tell them about my first book, *Think on These Things*. It's a small book comprised of many three-page chapters, but it took me nearly a year to write it. I remember many nights when I spent hours scribbling on a legal pad only to have a few sentences to show for my effort.

"I want to sell a lot of books and influence a lot of people like you do," these young leaders will declare.

"That's great," I'll answer. "What have you written?"

"Well, nothing yet" is typically the response.

"Okay," I say. "What are you working on?" I ask the question hoping to give some encouragement.

"Well, I'm not actually writing yet, but I have a lot of ideas," they'll say, explaining that they hope they'll have more time next month or next year or after they get out of school. When I hear an answer like that, I know that it will never happen. Writers write. Composers compose. Leaders lead. You must take action in order to become who you desire to be. Novelist Louis L'Amour, who wrote more than 100 books and sold more than 230 million copies, advised, "Start writing, no matter about what. The water does not flow until the faucet is turned on."

> "The water does not flow until the faucet is turned on."
>
> —Louis L'Amour

Desire isn't enough. Good intentions aren't enough. Talent isn't enough. Success requires initiative. Michael E. Angier, founder of SuccessNet, stated, "Ideas are worthless. Intentions have no power. Plans are nothing . . . unless they are followed with action. Do it now!"

# TALENT + *INITIATIVE*
# APPLICATION EXERCISES

1. Spend some time creating a list of all the reasons why you do not display greater initiative. Be thorough and list everything you can think of. Once the list is complete, go through and mark each entry with either an *E* for excuse or an *R* for reason.

   Now, create three new lists from your original list. The first is to be called "No More Excuses." On it, rewrite each excuse as a statement of responsibility. For example, if one of your excuses stated, "I don't have enough money," rewrite it to say, "I will no longer blame not having enough money." Post this list where you can see it every day.

   The second list comes from the remaining reasons on your original list and will be called "Facts of Life." Anything you have no control over and cannot change—such as the actions of others, your age, or the economy—is to go on this list. These are things you must simply accept.

   Whatever remains from your list of reasons goes on the third list called "My Responsibility." Since these things are your responsibility, you must solve them. Put them on your to-do list and get to work.

2. What causes you to procrastinate?
   - Are you in denial about the consequences of not taking initiative and responsibility for yourself?
   - Are you waiting for others to motivate you instead of working to motivate yourself?

- Are y ou waiting for everything to be perfect before you act?
- Are you fantasizing about tomorrow instead of focusing on what you can do today?
- Are you trying to go it alone?

Identify a specific action you can take to overcome your procrastination, designate a specific time on your calendar to take it, and if needed, enlist someone to help you follow through.

3. Think about something you strongly desire to do but are currently afraid of. As Dan Reiland did when he jumped out of the plane, what step can you take to put yourself into action mode, thus taking your focus off your fear?

4. What are you currently neglecting that is preventing your talent from becoming activated? Is it a decision you should be making? A problem you should be solving? A possibility you should be examining? A project you should be starting? A goal you should be reaching? An opportunity you should be seizing? A dream you should be fulfilling? Figure out what it is and determine to tackle it using the steps outlined in the chapter:

- Divide it by categories.
- Prioritize it by importance.
- Order it by sequence.
- Assign it by abilities.
- Accomplish it by teamwork.

# 4
## FOCUS DIRECTS
## YOUR TALENT

Watch small children playing, and what do you see? They move quickly from one toy to another and from activity to activity. They expend tremendous amounts of energy but get little done. That's to be expected. They are exploring their world and learning by doing.

Focus does not come naturally to us, yet it is essential for anyone who wants to make the most of his talent. Having talent without focus is like being an octopus on roller skates. You can be sure that there will be plenty of movement, but you won't know in what direction it will be. Talent with focus directs you and has the potential to take you far.

In 2004, I traveled to Buenos Aires, Argentina, to do leadership training for a group of about seven thousand people. Whenever I travel to a part of the world that is new to me, I do some research to find out what's unique about the area. I always want to visit special places or engage in experiences that aren't available anywhere else in the world.

I learned that Argentina has the greatest dove hunting in the world. There is a place about seventy-five to one hundred miles north of Buenos Aires where there are literally millions upon millions of doves, and anybody who hunts loves to go there for the experience.

## A-HUNTING WE WILL GO

Although I have been hunting before, I'm not really a hunter. Some people are passionate about it, and they enjoy hunting game of all kinds. I go mostly because I love a new experience. So when I went to Argentina, I talked one of my team members, Ray Moats, into going with me. We planned to fly up and go hunting together.

When the guide picked us up from the airport, he took one look at me and said, "You're not a hunter, are you?" I confessed that I wasn't. "That's what I thought. The first thing we'll have to do is get rid of that red jacket you're wearing. Even doves will see that. We'll get you some camouflage."

The guide got Ray and me all set up, and there we were, in a beautiful valley. And sure enough, flocks of doves flew over our heads along the valley. In an hour's time, at least fifty thousand doves flew over us. There were moments when the sky was black with them. So for an hour I shot . . . and shot . . . and shot. It was one of those situations where there are so many that you say to yourself, *How can I miss?* And you just start shooting everywhere.

But do you know how many doves I hit in that hour? None! I was surrounded by empty shotgun shells, and I didn't have a single dove to show for it.

## INTERVENTION

After an hour of watching my technique and seeing me come up empty-handed, my guide finally couldn't take it anymore. At that rate, we were on track to break a record—for the fewest doves ever shot on a hunt. So he tried to help me.

"Your problem is, you are trying to shoot *all* of the doves," he said. "You don't try to shoot all the doves. You don't even worry about the doves that get away. Trust me," he continued, "in another twenty-five to thirty seconds another whole flock of doves will come. So don't worry about the doves; they'll keep coming all day. Quit worrying about what you lost. Focus on getting *one*."

While the guide was saying all this, Ray was right there beside me soaking it in. Why? Because he wasn't a hunter either, and he was doing as poorly as I was.

## MEET SOME REAL HUNTERS

A couple of hours later, our guide decided it was time for us to take a break, and we went back to camp for lunch. There we met some good ol' boys from Arkansas who were real hunters. You could tell by taking one look at them. They were wearing camouflage—and not something they had just bought for the trip. Their clothes, like their shotguns, were well broken in. And these boys were talking very seriously about their hunting experience.

Ray and I sat down across from the Arkansans, and one of them looked at us and said to Ray, "Say, son, how many did you shoot this morning?"

"Three," Ray answered kind of sheepishly.

"Three, huh? Well, you shouldn't feel bad," he said. "Three hundred's not bad at all. Really, that's pretty good. We got about four hundred fifty, but three hundred's not bad, especially if it's your first time down here."

"No, you don't understand," Ray said. "We got three. Not three hundred. You know, *three!*" Ray counted on his fingers. "One. Two. Three."

For a moment, the boys from Arkansas just stared at us. "Son, son," one finally said, "you don't even have to *aim* to get three. You just shoot in the air and you're gonna get three. Heck, you can't get just three *on purpose*. You can only get three *by accident*."

> If you want
> to be successful,
> you must focus
> on what you
> *can* do, not on
> what you can't.

After lunch, we did a little better, but not much. It's true that Ray and I are not good hunters, so that was definitely a problem. In an area where there is little talent, you can't expect much success. However, our hunting trip is a great example of a situation where there are so many opportunities that you miss all of them. In hunting as in anything else, what we should have

done was focus on the few that we could hit and forget about any opportunities we missed. If you want to be successful, you must focus on what you *can* do, not on what you can't.

## THE POWER OF FOCUS

Focus can bring tremendous power. Without it, you will often feel drained and unable to accomplish much. With it, you will find that your talents and abilities gain direction and intentionality. And those qualities pay off by producing results.

Here are some facts you need to know about focus:

### 1. Focus Does Not Come Naturally to Most People

We live in a culture with almost infinite choices and opportunities, and because of that, most people find themselves pulled in dozens of directions. What's worse is that people often find themselves expending much of their time and energy on things they don't really care about. Don Marquis, author of *Archy and Mehitabel*, put it this way: "Ours is a world where people don't know what they want and are willing to go through hell to get it."

The solution to such a predicament is focus. Poet William Matthews wrote, "One well-cultivated talent, deepened and enlarged, is worth 100 shallow faculties. The first law of success in this day, when so many things are clamoring for attention, is concentration—to bend all the energies to one point, and to go directly to that point, looking neither to the right nor to the left."

I try to maintain my focus in the moment by heeding the advice of the martyred missionary Jim Elliott, who said, "Wherever you are, be all there." But I also look at the bigger picture. As a leader, I am always asking myself, *Am I helping others make progress?* I am vigilant about how I spend my time, with whom I am spending it, how it fits into the bigger picture, and whether it produces results. And my assistant, Linda Eggers, also keeps me on track by overseeing my calendar. She is a tremendous asset for helping me maintain my priorities. If I feel that I'm not moving forward and helping others throughout the day, then I know that I'm off track in some way. Linda helps me monitor that.

## 2. Focus Increases Your Energy

If you desire to achieve something, you first need to know what your target is. That's true even when it comes to personal development. If you lack focus, you will be all over the place. Attempting everything, like attempting nothing, will suck the life out of you. It will sap you of energy and new opportunities. And whatever momentum you have going for you will be diminished.

In contrast, focus gives you energy. Polar explorer Admiral Richard E. Byrd asserted, "Few men during their lifetime come anywhere near exhausting the resources dwelling within them. There are deep wells of strength that are never used." One of the reasons that those wells often go untapped is lack of focus. Something wonderful happens when we narrow our focus and set goals. That is where the real magic starts. The mind doesn't reach toward achievement until it has clear objectives.

After American astronauts successfully landed on the moon, Albert Siepert, deputy director of the Kennedy Space Center, attributed their success, at least in part, to NASA's focus. For a decade, the organization

> Attempting everything,
> like attempting nothing,
> will suck the life out of you.

put nearly all of its time and energy into reaching the moon. Siepert observed, "The reason NASA has succeeded is because NASA had a clear-cut goal and expressed its goal. By doing this, we drew the best of men to our goal and the support of every phase of government to reach our goal."

## 3. Focus Lifts You

Scholar and educator David Star Jordan said, "The world stands aside to let anyone pass who knows where he or she is going." In a sea of mediocrity, just knowing what you want to do and then making an effort to pursue it distinguishes you from almost everybody else.

The plain-spoken American writer Henry David Thoreau asked, "Did you ever hear of a man who had striven all his life faithfully and singly toward an object, and in no measure obtained it? If a man constantly aspires, is he not elevated?" Focus always has an impact. Just by striving to become better than you are, you become elevated—even if you don't accomplish what you desire, and even if others *don't* step aside for you. You can't shoot for the stars and remain unaffected by the effort.

## 4. Focus Expands Your Life

A few years ago, I wrote a book called *Thinking for a Change* in which I described the various thinking skills that can help a person become more successful. Included was a chapter on focused thinking, the ability to remove distractions and mental clutter so that a person can concentrate with clarity. In it I explained how I often bring together a team of people to help me brainstorm when working on a project. Because we focus our attention on the subject at hand, we are able to expand ideas in a way that we wouldn't be able to do otherwise.

Mike Kendrick asserts, "What you focus on expands." That may seem ironic, but it's true. Have you noticed that if you consider buying a particular kind of car, you begin seeing them everywhere? Narrowing your view widens your perspective. On the other hand, if you actually try to expand your view, instead of taking more in, it simply wears you out. If you want to expand your capacity, then focus.

## 5. Focus Must Be Intentionally Sustained

People do not naturally remain focused. Just as light naturally loses its focus and gets diffused, so does a person's attention. It takes a lot of effort, but the payoff is significant. Hall of Fame baseball player Hank Aaron says, "I think what separates a superstar from the average ballplayer is that he concentrates just a little bit longer." Aaron demonstrated that he was able to sustain his concentration. He holds the major-league baseball record for the most home runs hit in a career.

> "I think what separates a superstar from the average ballplayer is that he concentrates just a little bit longer."
> —Hank Aaron

In his book *Laughter, Joy, and Healing*, Donald E. Demaray wrote about a young journalist who was receiving tough criticism from his father because he didn't seem to be making much progress in his career. Undaunted, the young man wrote back to his father explaining that he had a plan for success upon which he was focused. His intentions were as follows:

- At 30, he would be a great newspaper reporter.
- At 40, he would be a great editor.
- At 50, he would be a great story writer.
- At 60, he would be a great fiction writer.

- At 70, he would be a great grandfather.
- At 80, he would be a great admirer of beautiful women.
- At 90, he would be a great loss to the community.

Demaray said that the father got a good laugh from the letter and was gratified when he began to see that his son's career was progressing along those lines.[1]

Several years ago, I memorized a definition of success to help me in my career: "Success is the progressive realization of a predetermined worthwhile goal." What I learned most from that definition is that success is not an event; it is a process. And anytime you engage in a process that takes time, focus is essential. Only people capable of remaining focused can expect to direct their talent and achieve a level of success.

## TALENT + *FOCUS* = A TALENT-PLUS PERSON
## PUTTING THE TALENT-PLUS FORMULA INTO ACTION

If you desire to become a talent-plus person, you need to make focus your friend. Here's how:

### 1. Be Intentional—Make Every Action Count

A family who had moved to a new neighborhood got a late start one morning, and as a result their six-year-old missed her bus to school. Though it would make him late for work, the father agreed to take her to school if she could give him directions.

They left their neighborhood, and the young girl began directing her father to take one turn after another. Following twenty minutes of circuitous driving, they arrived at the school, which turned out to be only eight blocks away. Steaming, the father asked the kindergartener why she had him drive all over the place when the school was so close to home.

"We went the way the bus goes," she said. "That's the only way I know."

If you want to maximize your talent and become a talent-plus person, you need to make every action count. You must determine where you want to go and

> "You've removed most of the roadblocks to success when you know the difference between motion and direction."
>
> —Bill Copeland

how to get there. You cannot be like Alice in Lewis Carroll's *Through the Looking Glass*, who asks for directions in this way during her encounter with the Cheshire Cat:

> "Would you tell me please, which way ought I to go from here?" she asks.
>
> "That depends a good deal on where you want to get," the cat replies with a grin.
>
> "I don't care much where," she answers.
>
> "Then it doesn't matter which way you go," the cat responds.

People who are undecided about what they want to do or where they want to go cannot tap into their strength of will—or their talent. As a result, they will merely drift along.

Private investigator and author Bill Copeland advises, "You've removed most of the roadblocks to success when you know the difference between motion and direction." Have you asked yourself what you really want to do? And have you determined that you will pursue it against the odds, despite the obstacles, and regardless of the circumstances? Being intentional is about focusing on doing the right things, moment by moment, day to day, and then following through with them in a consistent way. As President John F. Kennedy asserted, "Efforts and courage are not enough without purpose and direction."

## 2. Challenge Your Excuses

A sign on the desk of an officer who works at the Pentagon reads, "The secrecy of my job does not permit me to know what I'm doing." It's a clever joke, but it's not funny when it's actually true. People who don't know what they're doing soon become frustrated.

We all have reasons for not doing what we ought to do. We don't have enough time. We don't have enough resources. We don't have enough help. We have problems. We have shortcomings. We have distractions. Should we let these things get us off track? No!

## 3. Don't Let Yesterday Hijack Your Attention

Humorist and entertainer Will Rogers shared this thought: "Don't let yesterday take up too much of today." I've never known a person focusing on yesterday who had a better tomorrow. Too many people *yearn* for the past and get stuck in it. Instead, they should *learn* from the past and let go of it.

Alvin Dark, who was once the manager of the Kansas City Athletics, used to say, "There's no such thing as taking a pitcher out. There's only bringing another pitcher in." That runs contrary to what you hear during most baseball broadcasts, but here's the point. When you say you're going to take a pitcher out, you're probably focused on the mistakes he made—the players he walked, the hits he allowed. That doesn't help you win the game. In contrast, when you say you're putting a pitcher in, you are focusing on what that new pitcher is going to do now to try to help you beat the other team. That can make a big difference in your team's attitude—and in the players' ability to succeed.

> "Don't let yesterday take up too much of today."
>
> —Will Rogers

Editor and publisher Elbert Hubbard wrote,

A retentive memory may be a good thing, but the ability to forget is the true token of greatness. Successful people forget. They know the past is irrevocable. They're running a race. They can't afford to look behind. Their eye is on the finish line. Magnanimous people forget. They're too big to let little things disturb them. They forget easily. If anyone does them wrong, they consider the source and keep cool. It's only the small people who cherish revenge. Be a good forgetter. Business dictates it, and success demands it.

If you desire to make the most of your talent and achieve success, then you need to make what you're doing now your focus. Striving for achievements is a lot like driving a car. It's a good idea to check your rearview mirror occasionally, but not to give it your complete attention. If you do, you will eventually be incapable of moving forward at all.

## 4. Focus on the Present

Just as you should keep your focus off yesterday, you shouldn't have it on tomorrow. If you're always thinking about tomorrow, then you'll never get anything done today. Your focus needs to remain in the one area where you have some control—today. What's ironic is that if you focus on today, you get a better tomorrow.

I try to do certain things every day to help me in this area. I read daily to grow in my personal life. I listen to others daily to broaden my perspective. I spend time thinking daily to apply what I am learning. And I try to write daily so that I can remember what I've learned. I also try to share those lessons with others. (Today's lessons become tomorrow's books.) Every day I read aloud to myself the daily dozen list from my book *Today Matters* to help me focus and have the right mind-set.

You should do something similar. You can't change yesterday. You can't count on tomorrow. But you can choose what you do today. Giving it your focus will pay dividends.

## 5. Stay Focused on Results

Anytime you concentrate on the difficulty of the work at hand instead of its results or rewards, you're likely to become discouraged. Dwell on the difficulties too long and you'll start to develop self-pity instead of self-discipline, and your attention will become scattered instead of focused. As a result, you will accomplish less and less. By focusing on results, you will find it easier to stay positive and encouraged.

Another thing that can distract you from results is interaction with difficult people. You will come in contact with a lot of people who can impact your efforts as you work on achieving your dreams—some in a negative way. Here are five types of people you are likely to encounter:

- *Refreshers*—they inspire your dreams and energize your talents.

- *Refiners*—they sharpen your ideas and clarify your vision.

- *Reflectors*—they mirror your energy, neither adding nor subtracting from it.

- *Reducers*—they try to reduce your vision and efforts to their comfort level.

- *Rejecters*—they deny your talent, hinder your efforts, and impede your vision.

If you remain focused on results, you will stay grounded. The praise of others is less likely to go to your head, and the negative impact of people such as the reducers and rejecters will be minimized.

## 6. Develop and Follow Your Priorities

There's an old saying that if you chase two rabbits, both will escape. Unfortunately that is what many people seem to do. They don't focus their attention, and as a result, they become ineffective. Perhaps the reason is that people in our culture have too many choices—nearly unlimited options. Management expert Peter Drucker recognized this phenomenon. He said, "Concentration is the key to economic results. No other principle of effectiveness is violated as constantly today as the basic principle of concentration . . . Our motto seems to be, 'Let's do a little bit of everything."

If you want to develop your talent, you need to focus. If you're going to focus, you need to work on knowing what your true priorities are and then following them. This is something I have learned to do over time. I love options. I like to have the freedom to pursue the best course of action at any given moment. When I was in my twenties, I spent a lot of time doing things that had little return. In my thirties, I did better, but I still wasn't as focused as I should have been. It wasn't until I reached forty that I started to become highly selective about where I spent my time and energy. Today, as I approach sixty, I filter just about everything I do through my top priority: *Am I adding value to people?* For me, it all comes down to that.

## 7. Focus on Your Strengths, Not Your Weaknesses

There's a story about a couple who bought a new piece of property upon which they intended to establish a farm. It was good land, and they could hardly wait to move there and get started. As they made plans for the move one night, they began to argue about what to do first. The wife wanted to build the house first. After all, once they moved, the new property would be their home. The husband, who had grown up working on a farm, wanted to build the barn first to house their animals. They went back and forth for a while until the man finally said, "Look, we have to build the barn first—because the barn will build the house, and the garage, the silo, the kids' swing set, and everything else!" When you focus on your priorities and put first things first, everything else is more likely to fall into place.

Anthony Campolo, professor emeritus of sociology at Eastern University in Pennsylvania, says,

What you commit yourself to will change what you are and make you into a completely different person. Let me repeat that. Not the past but the future conditions you, because what you commit yourself to become determines what you are—more than anything that ever happened to you yesterday or the day before. Therefore, I ask you a very simple question: What are your commitments? Where are you going? What are you going to be? You show me somebody who hasn't decided, and I'll show you somebody who has no identity, no personality, no direction.

Focusing on weaknesses instead of strengths is like having a handful of coins—a few made of pure gold and the rest of tarnished copper—and setting aside the gold coins to spend all your time cleaning and shining the copper ones in the hopes of making them look more valuable. No matter how long you spend on them, they will never be worth what the gold ones are. Go with your greatest assets; don't waste your time.

## 8. Delay Rewards Until the Job Is Done

One of the tricks I've used with myself for years is to reward myself when I've done something that I ought to do. My father taught me that when I was a kid—pay now and play later. I think too often people want the rewards before the results, and for that reason they don't stay as focused as they could.

One secret of a life well lived is making every action count—being intentional. That kind of focus helps people live without regrets because it directs and makes the most of their talent and their opportunities. If you know that you have talent, and you are energetic and active, but you don't see concrete results, then lack of focus is likely your problem. It takes talent plus focus to reach your potential and become the person you desire to be.

# TALENT + *FOCUS*
# APPLICATION EXERCISES

1. In what area has lack of focus tapped your energy in the past? Is this a recurring problem? If so, try to determine why.

2. Give an example of a time when your ability to focus well helped you to achieve excellent results. What helped you to maintain your focus? What can you learn from that experience?

3. Where have you been putting your focus? Do you spend a great part of your time thinking about what happened in the past? Are you placing much hope in the future, when you hope to get a raise, establish a relationship, take a vacation, or enjoy retirement? Or are you concentrating on the here and now? Try to break down your thinking time according to percentages and write them here (making sure they total 100 percent):

   _____ Past
   _____ Present
   _____ Future

I believe it is healthy to spend 90 percent of your time focused on the present. Considering the past 5 percent of the time is useful if you learn from your successes and mistakes. Contemplating the future 5 percent of the time is useful to make sure your current activities are pointed in the right direction. Anything more may be detrimental to your productivity. You will have to begin making adjustments to refocus yourself on the present.

4. At the end of Chapter 1, I asked you to identify your strengths. Do you typically focus on developing and maximizing them? Or do you gravitate to shoring up your weaknesses? What can you do to place an even greater emphasis on your strengths? What can you give up that is undermining your focus? What untapped strength or talent do you suspect that you possess but have neglected? What concrete step can you take to start utilizing it?

5. Since the present is the only time over which you have any control, how can you "up the ante" and make your activities even more focused? Your goal should be to make every action count toward the results you desire.

6. Think about something you would like to have. It can be anything—a book or CD, a set of golf clubs, a vacation, or even a new car. Instead of just buying it, consider making it a reward that you will allow yourself to have once you have earned it by producing some kind of desired result. Make sure that the effort matches the reward. (If you're not sure about whether they match, ask a friend or your spouse.)

# 5

# Preparation Positions Your Talent

What happens when you don't prepare? Things you hoped *won't* happen do happen—and they occur with greater frequency than the things you hoped *would* happen. The reason is simple: being unprepared puts you out of position. Ask negotiators what happens at the bargaining table when they are out of position. Ask athletes what happens when they are out of position. They lose. Preparation positions people correctly, and it is often the separation between winning and losing. Talent-plus people who prepare well live by this motto: "All's well that begins well."

## Great Challenges

What was the greatest adventure humankind faced in the twentieth century? Exploring the polar ice caps? Conquering the world's highest mountains? Sending ships into space and landing people on the moon? Good cases could be made for each adventure.

How about in the nineteenth century? It was undoubtedly the exploration of the interior of Africa, Australia, and the Americas. Much global exploration had occurred from 1492 to 1800. Bold adventurers had explored the globe and been able to map and define all the conti- nents in broad strokes, having accurately mapped their shorelines. But what lay within the boundaries of some of those continents remained a mystery.

In North America, the leaders of the newly formed United States were anxious to know details about the interior of their continent. Much of the territory between the Atlantic Ocean and the Mississippi River (south of St. Louis) had been explored, but in 1801 when Thomas Jefferson became president of the United States, two-thirds of the nation's 5.3 million occupants lived within fifty miles of the coast, and few had traveled west of the Appalachian Mountains. The land west of the Mississippi River was unknown and still up for grabs. The fate of the nation would be determined by who controlled that land— the United States, France, England, Spain, or the native populations who inhabited it.

No American leader was more interested in knowing about North America than was Thomas Jefferson. Historian Stephen E. Ambrose asserts that Jefferson's interest in exploration began in the 1750s. Ambrose writes, "In the decade following the winning of independ- ence, there were four American plans to explore the West. Jefferson was the instigator of three of them."[1] In the 1790s, as a member of the American Philosophical Society, Jefferson tried to launch an exploratory expedition. He knew the key to its success would be selecting the right leader. He chose a trained scientist from France named André Michaux and directed him to find the shortest route between the United States and the Pacific Ocean, presumably up the Missouri River and somehow connected to the Columbia River in the West. In 1793, Michaux made it as far as Kentucky before Jefferson recalled the mission after discovering that the scientist was a secret agent of the French government given the mission to incite people to attack Spanish possessions in the West.

# THE RIGHT PERSON FOR THE JOB

Jefferson's best opportunity to launch the expedition of the American West wouldn't come until he became president of the United States. The key still would be the leader of the expedition. It would require an extremely talented person. And Jefferson thought he knew who that would be: Meriwether Lewis.

Ironically, back in 1792, when Jefferson and the American Philosophical Society were preparing the ill-fated expedition that would be headed by Michaux, one of the people who asked to be selected to lead it was Lewis. Like Jefferson, Lewis was born in Albemarle County, Virginia, but at that time Lewis was only eighteen years old. It was true that Lewis had lived on the frontier in Georgia for three or four years where he had learned many frontier skills. As a boy of eight, he was known to go out hunting in the middle of the night on his own. Lewis's cousin, Peachy Gilmer, described the young Lewis as "always remarkable for persevereance [sic], which in the early period of his life seemed nothing more than obstinacy in pursuing the trifles that employ that age; a martial temper; great steadiness of purpose, self-possession, and undaunted courage."[2] Lewis also already had experience as a leader. Because of his father's early death, Lewis had taken charge of a two-thousand-acre plantation when he was still a teenager. But back then he didn't have the wherewithal to lead an expedition. He was talented but green.

Years later, Jefferson explained why he selected Lewis instead of a credentialed scientist. He said it was impossible to find a person possessing "a compleat science in botany, natural history, mineralogy & astronomy" who could add to it "the firmness of constitution & character, prudent, habits adapted to the woods, & a familiarity with the Indian manners & character, requisite for this undertaking. *All the latter qualifications Capt. Lewis has.*"[3]

Lewis further honed those character qualities and frontier skills during six years in the army where he rose from the rank of private to captain. He served much of his time on the frontier as far west as Ohio and Michigan. At one point as a regimental paymaster, he traveled extensively, learned to understand much about the Native Americans in that part of the country, and refined his leadership skills.

What Lewis most lacked was formal education. His other responsibilities kept him from studying as much as he would have liked. Why would that matter? The expedition to the West that Jefferson envisioned would be more than just the search for an all-water route to the Pacific Ocean. It was also to be a scientific and diplomatic mission. The president wanted to know the quality of the land for farming and for the support of future settlers. He wanted reliable information on previously unknown plants, animals, and fossils from the regions, and he expected many specimens to be collected, catalogued, and brought back east.

Jefferson directed the party to create accurate maps of previously unexplored regions. He wanted to know about the geography and weather. He desired facts concerning the culture and habits of the native populations. He also intended the party to initiate friendly relations with those populations and convince them of the value of trading with the United States. It was to be so much more than a mere trailblazing adventure.

## EARLY PREPARATION

The way Jefferson decided to deal with Lewis's raw but still largely undeveloped talent was characteristic of the president's leadership and genius. As Jefferson prepared to assume his role as president, he invited Lewis to become his personal secretary, telling him it "would make you know & be known to characters of influence in the affairs of our country, and give you the advantage of their wisdom."[4] Lewis's time at the White House did that and much more. The young man was treated as a member of Jefferson's family, and he was, in fact, the only resident of the White House along with Jefferson, a widower, besides the servants.

Lewis's first task was to help Jefferson as he reduced the size of the nation's army. He frequently gathered information for the president, and he also copied and drafted documents. He was a frequent messenger to Congress. He functioned as the president's aide-de-camp. They spent long hours working together, Lewis read extensively from Jefferson's library, and the young captain always dined with Jefferson as he entertained the great thinkers, scientists, and leaders of the day. Lewis biographer Richard Dillon states that his experience in the White House functioned as "an ideal finishing school for Lewis."[5]

But Jefferson wasn't finished getting Lewis ready. In the summer of 1802, Jefferson procured and read a copy of *Voyages from Montreal, on the River St. Lawrence, Through the Continent of North America, to the Frozen and Pacific Ocean*, an account of Scotsman Alexander Mackenzie's exploration across Canada. It spurred Jefferson's desire to launch an American expedition. And it prompted him to become highly intentional in Lewis's preparation. Jefferson helped Lewis study geography, botany, celestial observation with a sextant, and more. Ambrose says, "In short, between the time Mackenzie's book arrived at Monticello [August 1802] and December 1802, Jefferson gave Lewis a college undergraduate's introduction to the liberal arts, North American geography, botany, mineralogy, astronomy, and ethnology."[6] Their preparations for the expedition had formally begun.

## Becoming More Intentional

Two kinds of preparations were going on in the months prior to Lewis's departure. The first was Lewis's gathering and preparing the supplies and equipment for the trip. The second was Lewis's preparation of himself. It's hard for us in the age of Internet communication, worldwide overnight delivery services, and corner convenience stores to imagine how complex the logistical and physical preparations were. Today if you go on vacation and discover that you forgot to pack a book, you simply buy one. If you get sick, you visit a drugstore. If your clothes get lost or ruined, you buy new ones. If you forget your glasses, you can ask someone at home to overnight them to you. It may cost you more than you would like to spend, but in a pinch you can always charge it. These problems are solvable.

In the age before motorized transportation or rapid communication, mistakes of preparation could be devastating. In addition, the logistical preparations of Lewis were massive. He had to secure *tons* of supplies from an amazing variety of manufacturers and purveyors, everything from rifles and ammunition to delicate scientific equipment to paper and ink to medical supplies to food to gifts for the Native Americans they would encounter. He had to have a keel boat built for travel up the Mississippi and Missouri Rivers (which he designed himself). He had to select the members of the expedition.

As daunting as those tasks were, they paled in comparison to the importance of the preparation of the man. If Lewis was not ready for the task, then the entire expedition—no matter how well planned and equipped—would be a failure. Lewis spent months with some of the top experts in America continuing to learn scientific skills and to prepare himself for his mission. Here is a list of the most notable ones along with how they helped Lewis:

- ALBERT GALLATIN, map collector—knowledge of the geography of western North America

- ANDREW ELLICOTT, astronomer and mathematician—skill in celestial observation using the sextant, chronometer, and other instruments

- ROBERT PATTERSON—additional assistance with celestial observation and with the purchase of the chronometer for the journey

- DR. BENJAMIN RUSH, physician—medical matters, the selection and purchase of medicines, and the creation of questions to be asked of the native populations

- DR. BENJAMIN SMITH BARTON, botany professor—skill in preserving specimens and properly labeling them, and knowledge of botanical terminology (later experts judge Lewis's knowledge to have been remarkable for an amateur)

- DR. CASPAR WISTAR, anatomy professor and expert on fossils—fossil discovery and collection[7]

All the preparation paid off. Ambrose describes the result:

Two years of study under Thomas Jefferson, followed by his crash course in Philadelphia, had made Lewis into exactly what Jefferson had hoped for in an explorer—a botanist with a good sense of what was known and what was unknown, a working vocabulary for description of flora and fauna, a mapmaker who could use celestial instruments properly, a scientist with keen powers of observation, all combined in a woodsman and an officer who could lead a party to the Pacific.[8]

The final pieces in the preparation process were the selections of a fellow officer and the men who would become members of the "corps of discovery." That was no small task. Lewis knew who the officer should be: William Clark, a captain under whom Lewis had served while in the army and with whom he had developed a remarkable friendship. Assembling the twenty-nine men who would make the trip took more time since, as Clark and Lewis agreed, "a judicious choice of our party is of the greatest importance to the success of this vast enterprise."[9] As Lewis traveled west from Philadelphia toward St. Louis, he continued collecting supplies, searching for suitable men, and making financial arrangements. It was during this phase that he got word from Jefferson that Jefferson had transacted the Louisiana Purchase.

## FINALLY GETTING OUT!

On May 22, 1804, Lewis and Clark set off up the Missouri River from their winter camp just north of St. Louis where they had completed the last of their preparations. Counting from the time Lewis began working for the president in April of 1801, the preparations had taken a little more than three years for a trip that they hoped could be completed in eighteen to twenty-four months. Actually the trip took longer than that. The explorers made it to the Pacific and back to St. Louis in two and a half years, and to Washington four months later.

The expedition was an amazing success. The corps of discovery made their way across the continent. They skirted or passed through modern-day Missouri, Kansas, Iowa, Nebraska, South Dakota, North Dakota, Montana, Idaho, Washington, and Oregon. They were the first non-indigenous people to see and cross the Rocky Mountains. James P. Ronda, the H. G. Barnard Professor of Western American History at the University of Tulsa, points out that they strengthened the claims of the United States in the West. They established peaceful contact with many groups of Native Americans. They set the pattern for scientific exploration in the U.S. They discovered 122 animal species or subspecies and 178 new plant species. And Ronda says, "The journals, maps, plant and animal specimens, and notes on Native American societies amounted to a Western encyclopedia."[10] Ambrose goes even farther: "Since 1803 and the return of the expedition in 1806, every American everywhere has benefited from Jefferson's purchase of Louisiana and his setting in motion the Lewis and Clark Expedition."[11]

> Spectacular achievement comes from unspectacular preparation.

What's sad is that as prepared as Lewis was for his expedition and as well as he performed, he was not prepared for life after its completion. Jefferson made Lewis governor of Louisiana, a task for which he was *not* prepared, and he did not succeed in that post. As much as he tried to work on his extensive journals, he never completed their preparation for publication. Others had to work on them after his death. Lewis began to drink heavily. And when he was ill, he began taking medicine laced with opium or morphine, a practice he continued, though he vowed to stop. On October 11, 1809, in a bout of despair, Lewis shot himself and died a few hours later.

## WHY PEOPLE FAIL TO PREPARE

The life of Meriwether Lewis shows a truth about preparation: spectacular achievement comes from unspectacular preparation. Talent, much like the eighteen-year-old Lewis, wants to jump into action, but preparation positions talent to be effective. Talent plus preparation often leads to success. Talent minus preparation often leads to disaster.

In hindsight, it's easy to recognize the value of preparation. So why do so many people fail to prepare?

### They Fail to See the Value of Preparation Before Action

Authors Don Beveridge Jr. and Jeffrey P. Davidson believe that lack of preparation is the primary reason for business failure today. "Poorly educated, poorly prepared, and poorly trained people fail because they do not have the skills or expertise to perform," they say. "Inadequate financing, the number-one reason businesses fail, can also be traced to lack of preparation."[12]

> Talent may be a given, but success you must earn.

In the introduction to this book I wrote about how talent early in life or in the beginning of a career makes a person stand out—but only for a short time. Why? Talent may be a given, but success you must earn. Proverbs 18:16 states, "A man's gift makes room for him."[13] In other words, your talent will give you an opportunity. But you must remember that the room it makes is only temporary.

Preparation is a major key to achieving any kind of success. It alone can position your talent to achieve its potential. Military people know this. General Douglas MacArthur said, "Preparedness is the key to success and victory." He also stated it more bluntly: "The more you sweat in peace, the less you bleed in war." The actions of Meriwether Lewis demonstrated that he had a similar attitude. Despite all the dangers and deprivations, the brutal weather and hostile Native Americans, Lewis lost only one member of his party, Sergeant Charles Floyd, probably from peritonitis cause by a ruptured appendix. No preparation on Lewis's part could have saved him from that. In fact, in 1804, Floyd probably would have died under the care of a trained physician.

## They Fail to Appreciate the Value of Discipline

It's been said that discipline is doing what you really *don't want* to do so that you can do what you really *do want* to do. Meriwether Lewis's most evident weakness was a tendency to be a bit rash and take offense. In fact, one of Jefferson's serious concerns was that Lewis might alienate the Native Americans and either start a war or get himself and his party killed. Lewis came close several times, including a tense standoff with the Teton Sioux. The explorers were one wrong move away from being wiped out and becoming little more than an obscure footnote in American history. What saved the day? Ambrose says Lewis's rashness was compensated by his tremendous self-discipline. With guns loaded and aimed and dozens of arrows pointed in their direction, Lewis waited out the situation. Eventually a Sioux chief managed to get the angry braves to stand down and defuse the conflict. Lewis understood the value of discipline.

A frustrating thing about preparation is that it usually takes much more time than the actual event one prepares for. Musicians may practice many hours preparing to perform a three-minute piece. Stage actors practice for weeks to prepare for a performance that lasts two hours. I know that when I create a leadership lesson that may take me less than an hour to deliver, it usually takes me eight to ten hours to write it. Discipline is required to keep preparing long hours for something that will be over quickly.

Alexander Hamilton, a Founding Father of the United States and its first secretary of the treasury, said, "Men give me credit for genius; but all the genius I have lies in this: When I have a subject on hand I study it profoundly." Hamilton was a disciplined and highly productive man. He understood that no matter your circumstances, resources, or natural talent, certain things were always within your control—your ability to work harder and smarter than anybody else. That bears remembering as you prepare yourself for the challenges that lay ahead of you.

## PREPARATION PRINCIPLES

Automaker Henry Ford observed, "Before everything else, getting ready is the secret of success." Ford understood the power of preparation and all the things it can do for someone:

### 1. Preparation Allows You to Tap into Your Talent

While I was working on this book, I was scheduled to make a trip to Latin America to teach leadership and meet national leaders in Guatemala, El Salvador, Honduras, Panama, Venezuela, Bolivia, and Peru. I would be gone more than ten days, so before I left, I spent an entire day making sure I had the materials I would need to keep working on the book. I reviewed the chapter outlines, gave some thinking time to the subject of the first couple of chapters, and pulled quotes and other materials from my files to take with me. And of course, I packed several new legal pads!

I also wrote the book's introduction. A group of excellent leaders and thinkers would be accompanying me on the trip, and I wanted their comments on the direction I was taking the book. I had copies made of that introduction so that I could hand them out to my fellow travelers, and I asked everyone to give me feedback and ideas. (I'm a strong believer in teamwork when related to talent too. I'll write more about that in Chapter 13.) And since we spent a lot of hours flying on a plane, during much of that time I pulled out the materials I had packed and did some writing.

As the trip concluded and we were flying back home, one of my travel mates, David McLendon, said to me, "I've learned a valuable lesson on this trip. You came prepared to maximize your time because you knew what you wanted to accomplish. While the rest of us read and talked, you got a lot of work done. You outlined two chapters. You even engaged all of us in the writing of your book!"

What he observed was possible because I had prepared. "You know, David," I replied, "I've found that every minute spent in preparation saves ten in execution." And that had been the case here. Because I spent a day preparing, I was able to work for ten days on that trip. It's not difficult; it just takes planning. The questions I ask myself before a trip like this are really very simple:

- *What work is to be done?*

- *How is it to be done?*

- *When is it to be done?*

- *Where is it to be done?*

- *How fast can it be done?*

- *What do I need to get it done?*

Answering these questions prepares me for what lies ahead. And when I am prepared, my talent is positioned for maximum effect.

## 2. Preparation Is a Process, Not an Event

We live in a quick-fix society. We think in terms of events and instant solutions. But preparation doesn't work that way. Why? Because it's about you. Anything having to do with people is process-oriented. The Law of Process in *The 21 Irrefutable Laws of Leadership* states, "Leadership develops daily, not in a day." The same can be said of maximizing your talent.

Legendary UCLA basketball coach John Wooden says that the best way to improve your team is to improve yourself. He learned that lesson from his father, Joshua Wooden, who used to tell young John, "Don't try to be better than somebody else, but never cease trying to be the best you can be." That's good advice whether you're playing basketball, parenting, or conducting business.

In 1983, I began teaching and recording monthly leadership lessons. Today, more than two decades later, I am still teaching them, and I have produced more than three hundred different leadership lessons. How was I able to do it? By continually feeding my mind and adding to my pool of resources. Every day, I read and file quotes, stories, and idea starters. Every month, I draw upon those filed resources. Every year, I use some of those lessons to write new books. My productivity comes more from my preparation than anything

> The best way to improve your team is to improve yourself.

else. That positions whatever talent I have so that I can use it to my maximum potential. It is an ongoing process. And if the daily learning and preparation ever stop, so will my productivity.

## 3. Preparation Precedes Opportunity

There's an old saying: "You can claim to be surprised once; after that, you're unprepared." If you want to take advantage of opportunities to use your talent, then you *must* be prepared when the opportunities arise. Once the opportunity presents itself, it's too late to get ready.

If you study the lives of dynamic men and women, you will find that preparation for opportunity is a common theme. President Abraham Lincoln said, "I will prepare and some day my chance will come." Prime Minister Benjamin Disraeli of England remarked, "The secret of success in life is for a man to be ready for his time when it comes." Oprah Winfrey asserted, "Luck is a matter of preparation meeting opportunity." And President John F. Kennedy observed, "The time to repair the roof is when the sun is shining." All of these people had talent, prepared themselves, and then made the most of their opportunities when they arose. Many people believe that their greatest barrier to opportunity is having one, but the reality is that their greatest barrier is being ready when one arrives.

> You can claim
> to be surprised once;
> after that,
> you're unprepared.

## 4. Preparation for Tomorrow Begins with the Right Use of Today

Recently, a few friends and I were privileged to have dinner with former New York City mayor Rudy Giuliani and his wife, Judith, in Orlando after a speaking engagement. I found the mayor to be a very warm and personable man who was an easy conversationalist. During our conversation, I of course asked him about his experience during 9-11. He talked about his impressions from that day and how the event impacted him as a leader. He said that leaders need to be ready for anything. They need to study, acquire skills, and plan for every kind of situation.

"Your success will be determined by your ability to prepare," he said. He went on to explain that when a situation like that on September 11 occurs—for which there was no plan in place—leaders must take action and rely on whatever preparation had taken place. In his case, it was the emergency drills they had followed. Both helped during the crisis.

Preparation doesn't begin with what you do. It begins with what you believe. If you believe that your success tomorrow depends on what you do today, then you will

> If you are *preparing* today, chances are, you will not be *repairing* tomorrow.

treat today differently. What you receive tomorrow depends on what you believe today. If you are *preparing* today, chances are, you will not be *repairing* tomorrow.

## 5. Preparation Requires Continually Good Perspective

When I was a kid, my first love was basketball. From the time I was ten until I graduated from high school, I was shooting hoops at every free moment. One thing that I still enjoy about basketball is how quickly one player can change the tempo and momentum of a game. That's true not only of the stars and starters but also of the players who come off the bench. That's why the "sixth man," the player of starting caliber who is often the first substitute in the game, is so important. Former Boston Celtics coach Tom Heinsohn observed, "The sixth man has to be so stable a player that he can instantly pick up the tempo or reverse it. He has to be able to go in and have an immediate impact. The sixth man has to have the unique ability to be in a ball game while he is sitting on the bench." What makes the sixth man capable of that? Perspective. He has to have both a coach's mind-set as he watches the game from the bench and a player's ability once he steps into it. If he does, then he is prepared to impact the game.

Howard Coonley, the executive after whom the American National Standards Institute named its award honoring service to the national economy, stated, "The executive of the future will be rated by his ability to anticipate his problems rather than to meet them as they come."

Perspective not only helps people prepare, but it can also *motivate* them to prepare. I love the quote from Abraham Lincoln, who said, "If I had eight hours to chop down a tree, I'd spend six sharpening my ax." Lincoln had split rails with an ax as a young man, so he knew the value of a sharp ax. Perspective always prompted him to prepare—whether he was getting ready to cut wood, study law on his own to pass the bar, or lead the country.

### 6. Good Preparation Leads to Action

What value has preparation if it never leads to action? Very little. As William Danforth, former chancellor of Washington University in St. Louis, noted, "No plan is worth the paper it is printed on unless it starts you going."

People who enjoy preparation sometimes find themselves caught in the trap of overpreparing, and they sometimes do so to the point that they fail to act. Kathleen Eisenhardt, professor of management science and engineering at Stanford University, studied the decision-making process at twelve technology companies. She found that the fast deciders, who took two to four months to make major decisions, were much more effective than their slower counterparts who wanted to get all the facts of their situation and create consensus. The slower group took up to eighteen months to plan and decide, and by the time they did find resolution, the decision they made was often irrelevant.

> "No plan is worth the paper it is printed on unless it starts you going."
> —William Danforth

Preparation does not mean mastery of the facts. It does not mean knowing all the answers. It does not necessarily mean achieving consensus. (Former British prime minister Margaret Thatcher remarked that "consensus is the negation of leadership.") It means putting yourself in a better position to succeed.[14]

# TALENT + *PREPARATION* = A TALENT-PLUS PERSON
## PUTTING THE TALENT-PLUS FORMULA INTO ACTION

Sports have always been an area in which you can see the value of preparation. It doesn't matter what sport—good athletes talk about it all of the time. Tennis champion Arthur Ashe explained, "One important key to success is self-confidence. An important key to self-confidence is preparation." Quarterback Joe Namath said simply, "What I do is prepare myself until I know I can do what I have to do."

Friend and fellow golfer Rick Bizet once told me that his golf coach taught him that the only thing that relieves pressure is preparation. If you want to see that preparation in action, observe any professional golfer's pre-shot routine. I particularly appreciate the routine of professional golfer Tom Kite.

> The only thing that relieves pressure is preparation.

It contains three main steps: assessment, alignment, and attitude. In fact, I use it as a guideline, not only when playing golf, but also in other situations when I need to prepare myself. I believe you can do the same.

## 1. Assessment—Am I Evaluating Correctly?

Good preparation always begins with assessment. If you don't accurately evaluate where you need to go and what it will take to get there, then you're likely to get into trouble. In golf, good players typically ask themselves these questions to assist in the assessment process:

- *Where do I need to go?* The process begins with finding the right target. That target must be appropriate to your talent. You don't want to be like the Miss America contestant that Jay Leno quoted as saying, "My goal is to bring peace to the entire world—and to get my own apartment."

- *How far is my goal?* Next, a person needs to assess the distance. I enjoy telling my fellow golfers that I have a great short game—but unfortunately only off the tee! It may sound obvious, but you've got to know the distance to your goal to have a shot at making it there.

- *What are the conditions?* Good golfers always take the wind into account. The conditions make all the difference in the world. One of my personal highlights related to golf was the opportunity to play at St. Andrews in Scotland. And I shot really well that day—a 79. How did I do it? There was no wind! My caddie told me, "It's a whole different game with the wind."

- *What will it take to get there?* The final step in the assessment process is knowing what club to use. Gary Player says that bad club selection is the number one error of amateurs. They hit the ball short. It's important to know your skills and limitations when making your assessment.

How would I translate these questions for non-golfing situations? I'd say that you need to know *what* exactly you should be doing, what it will *cost* you in time, effort, and resources to get there, what *obstacles* you are likely to face, and what your *personal limitations* are. If you know these things, you will be well on your way to preparing yourself to achieve your goals.

## 2. Alignment—Am I Lined Up Correctly?

A good golfer can perform the assessment process flawlessly and still miss his or her target horribly. How? By lining up poorly. Psychologist James Dobson said, "What is the use of climbing the ladder of success only to find that it's leaning against the wrong building?"

When I first started playing golf, I tried to teach myself the game. I held the club with a baseball grip and lined up in a baseball stance, and more often than not, if I hit the ball any distance, I sent it into the woods. To improve my game, I had to change the way I played golf. I had to relearn the game, and that meant getting help.

If you want to take your game to the next level—personally, professionally, relationally, or recreationally—you need to find someone who is better than you to help you with the preparation process. Be open and honest with that person, and he or she will be able to evaluate your "alignment" and help you get on course.

## 3. Attitude—Am I Visualizing Correctly?

The final step after assessment and alignment is attitude. In golf, after you select a target and line it up, it's really a mental game. You're not just training your body—you're training your mind. But that's true for any endeavor. You have to believe in yourself and what you're doing. You have to be able to see yourself doing it with your mind's eye. If you can't imagine it, you probably will not be able to achieve it.

Preparation is one of the most obvious choices you must make in order to maximize your talent and become a talent-plus person. Sometimes the preparation process is long and slow. It may require formal education. It may necessitate your finding wise mentors. It may mean getting out of your comfort zone. Or it could mean simply fine-tuning a skill you've nearly mastered. But whatever it requires, remember that you must be ready when your time comes. People don't get a second chance to seize a once-in-a-lifetime opportunity.

# Talent + Preparation
## Application Exercises

1. What process are you currently using to assess where you should be going and what you should be doing? How has it been working?

2. Find a mentor to help you check your current "alignment." Here are some questions you can ask him or her to help you get started:

   - Am I looking at the right "target"?
   - Am I seeing the potential problems?
   - Is where I'm headed going to put me in the best place for my next step?
   - What strengths do you see in me?
   - What is the potential downside of where I'm headed?
   - What is the potential upside?
   - What is my most urgent need?

3. Trainer and consultant Dru Scott Becker says that one of the best ways that people can prepare is to make use of the "Grab 15" principle. Whether you want to improve your garden, learn a new language, or get ready to start a new business, find fifteen minutes a day and work at it. She says fifteen-minute blocks add up fast, keep your head continually in the game, and often lead to even more concentrated time working on your goals. But even if you don't go beyond the fifteen-minute blocks, stick with it six days a week for a year, and you'll devote seventy-eight hours to your goal.

   Where and when can you grab fifteen minutes every day? Identify a goal and lay out a plan to achieve it—fifteen minutes at a time.

---

# 6

# PRACTICE SHARPENS
# YOUR TALENT

It is a fact: you play at the level at which you practice. Consistently good practice leads to consistently good play. It sharpens your talent. Successful people understand this. They value practice and develop the discipline to do it. If you want to sum up what lifts most successful individuals above the crowd, you could do it with four little words: *a little bit more*. Successful people pay their dues and do all that is expected of them—plus a little bit more.

## LOOKING FOR SUCCESS

In London, England, a young man sought to find his way in life. Only fifteen years old in 1827, young Charles possessed intelligence, ambition, and—he hoped—talent enough within himself to make his dreams for success a reality.

The boy grew up in a lower-middle-class family that had always struggled financially. His parents tended to spend a little more money than his father earned. And they had many mouths to feed, since the couple had eight children. As a result, they were continually borrowing money, putting off creditors, and moving from one place to another. In 1824, when his father was sent to debtors' prison, twelve-year-old Charles was put to work gluing labels on bottles in a factory. He hated it.

Charles had gone to school for several years before his time in the factory, and when the family's financial situation became less dire, he attended school again. He was a good student, but at age fifteen, with the family facing more hard times, he knew his school days were over. He was sent off to work, this time as a law clerk. At first he was glad to be doing tasks much different from those of his previous experience. In the factory, he had been among poor, illiterate boys doing dirty and tedious work. But it didn't take long for his work in the law office to become tedious to him. After a year and a half apprenticing there, he switched legal firms, but it was not much better. After a few months, he resigned.

Unlike his parents, with whom he still lived, Charles had managed to save some money while working, so he decided to take his time figuring out what kind of work he wanted to do. He spent long hours in the reading room at the British Museum. A profession that interested him was journalism. Not only did it appeal to his love of literature, but it would require no further formal education or any kind of apprenticeship. His uncle was a reporter, and his father wrote occasional pieces as well. How could he achieve his goal? Through hard work and lots of practice. With the benefit of books from the museum and some coaching from his uncle, John Henry Barrow, Charles began teaching himself the Gurney system of shorthand writing. Because of his diligence, it didn't take him long. Having "tamed the savage stenographic mystery," he became a freelance court stenographer at age eighteen.[1]

## FROM OBSCURITY TO EXCELLENCE

His choice surprised his family, and they did not believe he would be successful. "None of us guessed at it," his father said, "and when we heard that he had become a reporter . . . my brother-in-law Barrow . . . and other relations anticipated a failure."[2] But he didn't fail. He was so good that his uncle soon hired him as a staff member of the *Mirror of Parliament* and later gave him managerial duties. By the time he was twenty-one, he was considered to be "the most rapid, the most accurate, and the most trustworthy reporter then engaged on the London press."[3]

Charles felt good about his professional progress and he was earning money, but he desired more. He desired greater income and greater fulfillment. He decided to start doing another kind of writing—more creative works. He wanted to be more than just a reporter; he wanted to become an author. He began by writing "sketches" of people and places, drawing upon his experiences traveling throughout Britain as a reporter and upon his observations while taking long daily walks throughout London. When the first sketch, "A Dinner at Poplar Walk," was complete, Charles hoped to get it published, dropping it into "a dark letter box, in a dark office, up a dark court in Fleet Street . . . with fear and trembling."[4] He was ecstatic when in December of 1833, his piece appeared in the *Monthly Magazine*. He was paid nothing for his effort, nor was his name included with his work. But that didn't matter. He was developing his talent by practicing his craft. He was on his way to becoming a professional author.

## PRACTICING HIS CRAFT

He wrote more sketches in his "spare" time. With the creation of each new piece, he sharpened his talent. For a year and a half, he wrote for no payment, receiving only recognition from editors and readers as his pieces were published. His work was gaining such attention that his employer, the *Evening Chronicle*, requested that he create sketches regularly for the magazine. He agreed to do it at no charge, but also suggested that he would welcome some extra money in addition to his regular pay. His employer raised his salary from five to seven guineas a week.

The first half dozen sketches he had written were published unsigned. Later, he used the pen name "Boz." Over the next three years, he published sixty sketches in various magazines. Much to his surprise and delight, he was approached in 1836 by a young publisher who wanted to collect his writings into a volume along with ten prints from a well-known illustrator. It would be called *Sketches by Boz*. It was such a success that it went through four printings in its first year. It also earned him enough respect and recognition to be hired for another writing job: a collection of stories to be offered in monthly installments with illustrations. His years of practicing his craft by writing sketches were finally about to pay off. He knew he wanted to call this new work *The Pickwick Papers*, and he decided he would use his real name: Charles Dickens.

## From Excellence to Fame

When we hear the name Charles Dickens today, most people think of long, old-fashioned novels that are required reading in English literature classes. But in his day, Charles Dickens's works were as popular as today's biggest hit television shows or movies. And there was no author in the entire world more popular than Dickens.

Jane Smiley, a Pulitzer Prize–winning novelist and biographer of Dickens, suggests that Dickens was "the first true celebrity of the popular arts—that is, a man whose work made him rich and widely famous, as close to a household name as any movie star is today" and the "first person to become a 'name brand.'"[5]

Dickens is also considered by many to be the most talented author in England's history—after Shakespeare. But before his fame, many people didn't recognize his talent. Dickens biographer Fred Kaplan writes, "When he left his legal clerkship to attempt to be a reporter, his family thought he had aimed too high. When, in the next two years, he went from legal to parliamentary reporting, they expected a failure. Understandably, they were unprepared for the explosive release of energy and talent that transformed him in a three-year period into an internationally celebrated writer."[6] How did he transform that talent? He practiced his craft by writing those sketches. Kaplan says, "The sketches were a testing ground for an apprentice author whose talent enabled him to progress precociously."[7]

The idea for Dickens to write his first novel in installments was a good one. He went on to write all of them in that fashion. Most were published in monthly installments called monthly numbers. People bought and read each installment similar to the way we now tune in to our favorite television series. People who missed the novel as a series could buy a complete bound version once the series was finished—just as we can now purchase a complete season of a TV series on DVD.

*The Pickwick Papers* was Dickens's first novel written in this fashion. The first monthly number sold fewer than 500 copies in April of 1836. However, Dickens kept fine-tuning the story and characters, and by the fourth "number," sales were up to 4,000. That may not seem like much, but consider this. The novel as an art form was only 100 years old, and most novels sold an average of only 300 to 400 copies. And with each episode, Dickens's sales continued growing. As the last few numbers came out, each sold a remarkable 40,000 copies. Dickens's first novel was more successful than any other novel in history to that point. At age twenty-five, he achieved success as an author that was unmatched until the next century. Over the next twenty years, more than 1.6 million copies of *Pickwick* sold in one form or another.[8]

Jane Smiley believes that Dickens's first three major works— *Sketches by Boz, The Pickwick Papers,* and *Oliver Twist*—were examples of his practicing his craft to sharpen his talent. She writes,

> Every novelist seeks . . . to extend his range of expression . . . In his twenties, [Dickens] was not unlike other youthful authors. Even

though he was a genius, he had artistic ambitions that he was not yet technically equipped to fulfill, and he used his first three books to write his way toward fulfilling them.[9]

During his thirty-five-year career, Dickens wrote more than a dozen full-length novels (some of which are considered masterpieces), several travel books, and numerous Christmas stories. And all those years, he also edited various monthly magazines and traveled extensively giving readings of his work. He was probably the most popular author in Britain's history. But as talented as he was, he didn't start out at the top. Even a genius needs practice to sharpen his talent and reach his potential.

## The Power of Practice

There's a myth about highly talented people—it's that they are simply born that way. But the truth is that no people reach their potential unless they are willing to practice their way there. Recently I was traveling with Tom Mullins, a former football coach who wrote *The Leadership Game*, which contains successful leadership principles he gleaned from interviewing eight college national champion football coaches. As I talked about the idea of practice with him, he nearly leaped out of his seat. When Tom talks about anything related to leadership, it's like he's back in the locker room talking to his team at halftime when they're losing. I mean he gets excited!

> Preparation positions talent and practice sharpens it.

"Let me tell you, John," he said, "all the national champion coaches told me the key to going from good to great came in two areas: the preparation of the team and the practice of the players. They were forever upgrading their preparation and sharpening their practices."

That made sense to me because preparation positions talent and practice sharpens it.

Before we go any further, there are three things you need to know about practice:

## 1. Practice Enables Development

How do we grow and develop? Through practice. People refine old skills and acquire new ones through practice. That is where the tension between where we are and where we ought to be propels us forward.

Former pro basketball player and U.S. senator Bill Bradley says that he attended a summer basketball camp when he was fifteen years old. There former college and pro basketball star "Easy" Ed Macauley told him, "Just remember that if you're not working at your game to the utmost of your ability, there will be someone out there somewhere with equal ability who will be working to the utmost of his ability. And one day you'll play each other, and he'll have the advantage."

If you desire to improve and develop, then you must practice. It allows you to break your own records and outstrip what you did yesterday. Done correctly, practice keeps making you better than you were yesterday. If you don't practice, you shortchange your potential.

## 2. Practice Leads to Discovery

In one of Charles Schulz's *Peanuts* strips, Charlie Brown laments to his friend Linus, "Life is just too much for me. I've been confused from the day I was born. I think the whole trouble is that we're thrown into life too fast. We're not really prepared."

"What did you want," Linus responds, "a chance to warm up first?"

> "A good leader understands that anything that has been done in a particular way for a given amount of time is being done wrong. Every single performance can be improved."
>
> —Harvey Mackay

We may not get a chance to warm up before entering childhood, but we *can* warm up by practicing the many activities we pursue once life has begun. And it is often during these "warm-ups" that we learn valuable things about ourselves. If you commit yourself to practice, here are a few things you are likely to learn:

**Practice both shows and builds commitment.** The true test of commitment is action. If you say, for example, that you are committed to becoming a great dancer but you never practice, that's not commitment. That's not dance. That's just talk. But when you follow through and practice, you show your commitment. And every time you follow through, your commitment becomes stronger.

**Your performance can always be improved.** Consultant and author Harvey Mackay says, "A good leader understands that anything that has been done in a particular way for a given amount of time is being done wrong. Every single performance can be improved." Since there is always a better way, your job is to find it.

**The "sharpening" process is better in the right environment.** You can't discover your abilities and improve your skills in an environment where you are not allowed to make mistakes. Improvement always requires some degree of failure. You must seek a practice area where experimentation and exploration are allowed.

**You must be willing to start with small things.** Human relations expert Dale Carnegie advised, "Don't be afraid to give your best to what seemingly are small jobs. Every time you conquer one it makes you that much stronger. If you do little things well, the big ones tend to take care of themselves." As you first start to practice, the gains you make may be small. But they will grow. They compound like interest. Swimming coach Daniel F. Chambliss says

> "Don't be afraid to give your best to what seemingly are small jobs. Every time you conquer one it makes you that much stronger."
>
> —Dale Carnegie

that great athletes pay attention to small details and practice them consistently. He observes, "Swimming is swimming, we can say—in practice, or in meets, it's all the same. If you swim sloppily for 364 days a year, nothing great is going to happen on the day of that big meet, no matter how excited you get."

*Very small differences, consistently practiced, will produce results.* A curious thing happens when you practice. At first the gains are small, as I said. Then they begin to grow. But there comes a time, if you persevere, when the gains become small again. However, at this season these small gains make big differences. In the Olympics, for example, the difference between the gold medalist and the athletes who finish without a medal is often just hundredths of a second.

*There is a price to pay to reach the next level.* One of the things you often learn in practice is what it will cost to reach a goal or go to the next level. As you get ready to practice, I recommend that you abide by the Taxicab Principle, which is something I learned traveling overseas: Before you get into the cab, find out how much the ride is

> "One half of knowing what you want is knowing what you must give up before you get it."
>
> —Sidney Howard

going to cost. If you don't, you may end up paying much more than the ride is worth! As you practice, keep in mind the words of screenwriter Sidney Howard, who remarked, "One half of knowing what you want is knowing what you must give up before you get it."

Many people regard practice as an essentially negative experience. It doesn't have to be that way. The best way to make practice exciting is to think of it in terms of discovery and development.

## 3. Practice Demands Discipline

One reason some people see practice as a grind is that it requires discipline. Even activities with intense physical demands also require lots of mental discipline. Bill McCartney, former national championship head football coach of the Colorado Buffaloes, used to tell me, "Mental preparation to physical preparation is four to one."

Developing discipline always begins with a struggle. There is no easy way to become a disciplined person. It has nothing to do with talent or ability. It is a matter not of conditions, but of choice. But once the choice is made and practice becomes a habit, two things become obvious. The first is a separation between the person who practices and the one who doesn't. Cyclist Lance Armstrong emphasizes that "success comes from training harder and digging deeper than others." He would know, having won a record seven Tour de France championships. The second thing that emerges is a winning spirit. The harder you work, the harder it becomes to surrender.

Greek philosopher Aristotle observed, "Excellence is an art won by training and habituation. We do not act rightly because we have virtue or excellence, but we rather have those because we have acted rightly. We are what we repeatedly do. Excellence, then, is not an act, but a habit." That habit is developed during practice.

# THE FIVE PILLARS OF PRACTICE

I talked to a lot of leaders and coaches about practice while I was working on this chapter. And each one of them had a little different take on how to approach practice effectively. Warren Bottke is a PGA master professional who has helped thousands of amateurs and professionals improve their golf game. As Warren and I talked, we settled on five elements upon which great practice rests.

## Pillar #1: An Excellent Teacher or Coach

One of my core beliefs is that everything rises and falls on leadership. I teach that truth to businesspeople all the time, but it also applies in other areas of life, including practice. People who perform at their peak practice effectively, and they practice effectively under the leadership of a great teacher.

Howard Hendricks, professor and chairman of the Center for Christian Leadership in Dallas, says, "Teaching is causing people to learn." How do good coaches do that? In part, they inspire. But good teachers do more than that. They tailor their instruction to their students. A good teacher or coach, like all good leaders, knows the strengths and weaknesses of each person. He knows whether a person is a right-brain creative/intuitive type or a left-brain analytical type. He knows whether a person learns visually, verbally, or kinesthetically. And he can tell when someone needs a pat on the back or a kick in the pants.

When Dickens started in his career, his uncle coached him as a reporter. With practice, he became the best in England. As he began writing creative pieces, a few key editors gave him feedback and, more important in his case, encouraged him to keep doing that kind of writing. Because his talent was so great, Dickens quickly outpaced the ability of those who would coach him. But throughout his life, he remained connected with other professional writers from whom he could receive advice and feedback, people such as Thomas Carlyle, Wilkie Collins, William Makepeace Thackeray, Edward Bulwer-Lytton, and John Forster.

## Pillar #2: Your Best Effort

Industrialist and philanthropist Andrew Carnegie declared, "There is no use whatever trying to help people who do not help themselves. You cannot push anyone up a ladder unless he is willing to climb himself." People don't improve and reach their potential without putting forth great effort. That's why composer and orchestra leader Duke Ellington used to make a simple but demanding request of the musicians who played for him. "Just give me your best," he asked. Ellington worked hard and expected the same from others, knowing that hard work would not kill anybody (although it does seem to scare some people half to death).

Joe Theismann, who currently works as an announcer for ESPN, quarterbacked the Washington Redskins to two Super Bowl appearances in 1983 and 1984. The team won the first time and lost the second time. Today he wears his Super Bowl winner's ring and his "loser's" ring as reminders of the importance of effort. Why? Because his two experiences couldn't have been more different. During their championship season, Theismann was thrilled to be in the Super Bowl and gave his very best to win. But not the next year. About the next year, Theismann explained, "I was griping about the weather, my shoes, practice times, everything." He clearly wasn't giving his best effort. "The difference in those two rings," said Theismann, "lies in applying oneself and not accepting anything but the best."[10]

> "There is no use whatever trying to help people who do not help themselves. You cannot push anyone up a ladder unless he is willing to climb himself."
>
> —Andrew Carnegie

## Pillar #3: A Clear Purpose

PGA Golfer Warren Bottke says that when he works with a new client, the first thing he does is to establish the purpose of practice. That usually means identifying a specific goal for each practice session. But the overarching purpose of practice is always improvement leading to excellence.

Pepperdine University sociology professor Jon Johnston makes a distinction between excellence and mere success:

Success bases our worth on a comparison with others. Excellence gauges our value by measuring us against our own potential. Success grants its rewards to the few but is the dream of the multitudes.

Excellence is available to all living beings but is accepted by the . . . few. Success focuses its attention on the external—becoming the tastemaker for the insatiable appetites of the . . . consumer. Excellence beams its spotlight on the internal spirit . . . Excellence cultivates principles and consistency.[11]

As you practice, make excellence your target, and give your best to achieve it. Willow Creek founder Bill Hybels says, "Most people feel best about themselves when they have given their very best." If excellence is your goal and you arrive at it, you will be satisfied even though you never achieve success.

## Pillar #4: The Greatest Potential

Have you ever noticed that two people on the same team with the same coach can practice with equal focus, effort, and purpose and have very different results? It's a fact that equal practice does not mean equal progress. I learned this fact when I was nine. By then I had been taking piano lessons for a couple of years. As I played, I thought to myself, *I'm pretty good at this*. But then one day I played at a piano recital, and it turned out to be a reality check. Elaine, a girl who had been taking piano lessons for only six months, played a more difficult piece than mine. How could she be so much better than I was so quickly? The answer is simple: her potential was much greater than mine. It didn't matter how much focused effort I put into practicing the piano. I was never going to go as far as Elaine could. Music wasn't one of my best gifts. I enjoyed playing, but I wasn't going to achieve excellence in it.

A few years ago after I spoke on leadership for Chick-fil-A, someone asked me during a Q&A session how to develop future leaders. I

> "Most people feel best about themselves when they have given their very best."
>
> —Bill Hybels

believe that when I quickly answered, "Find potential leaders," people thought I was being flippant. But my point was that it's much easier to train people in the area of their greatest potential. When I evaluate people's potential, I ask two questions: (1) Can they? and (2) Will they? The answers to these questions reveal something about their ability and their attitude. If both are right, the potential for excellence is high.

When Charles Dickens began thinking about writing fiction, he was already the best reporter in England. He could have remained where he was and been at the top of his profession. But something inside him must have known that as good as he was, he was not in the area of his most remarkable strength. So he took the risk of shifting his focus in search of his greatest potential.

You need to do the same. And once you figure out where your greatest potential lies, then start to practice there. If you don't, not only will you fail to increase your ability, but you'll eventually lose some of the ability you started with. You see, having potential works exactly opposite from the way a savings account does. When you put your money in a savings account, as time goes by, your money compounds and grows. The longer you leave it untouched, the more it *increases*. But when it comes to potential, the longer you leave it untouched, the more it *decreases*. If you don't tap into your talent, it wastes away.

One way that you can get the best from yourself is to set high standards for your greatest potential. Dianne Snedaker, cofounder and general partner of Wingspring, advises,

> If you are interested in success, it's easy to set your standards in terms of other people's accomplishments and then let other people measure you by those standards. But the standards you set for yourself are always more important. They should be higher than the standards anyone else would set for you, because in the end you have to live with

yourself, and judge yourself, and feel good about yourself. And the best way to do that is to live up to your highest potential. So set your standards high and keep them high, even if you think no one else is looking. Somebody out there will always notice, even if it's just you.

You can tell that you're not making the most of your potential when the standards set for you by others are higher than the ones you set for yourself. Anytime you require less of yourself than your boss, spouse, coach, or other involved person does, your potential will go untapped.

## Pillar #5: The Right Resources

Even if you do many things right, including finding a good coach or mentor, focusing in your area of greatest potential, giving your best, and doing so with purpose, you can still fall short without the right resources. During World War II, General George Patton was one of the most talented and accomplished commanders for the Allied forces. He was innovative, focused, and fearless. He was a good strategist and tactician. And he possessed the tanks and men to strike boldly against the Nazis to help bring an end to the war. But one thing he often lacked: gasoline. Without fuel, his tanks were useless.

Resources are nothing more than tools you need to accomplish your purpose. Every human endeavor requires resources of some kind. To practice well, you need to be properly equipped.

## TALENT + PRACTICE = A TALENT-PLUS PERSON
## PUTTING THE TALENT-PLUS FORMULA INTO ACTION

There is one more secret to successful practice that will help you to sharpen your talent, and I believe it elevates top achievers above everyone else. Dickens displayed it. So did Joe Namath, Rueben Martinez, Meriwether Lewis, and the other highly talented people whose stories I recount in this book. It's summed up by the phrase "a little extra." Here's what I believe it takes for someone to become a talent-plus person in the area of practice:

## 1. A Little Extra Effort

Historian Charles Kendall Adams, who was president of Cornell University and later the University of Wisconsin, observed, "No one ever attains very eminent success by simply doing what is required of him; it is the amount of excellence of what is over and above the required that determines greatness." All accomplishments begin with the willingness to try—and then some. The difference between the ordinary and the extraordinary is the *extra!*

> "No one ever attains very eminent success by simply doing what is required of him; it is the amount of excellence of what is over and above the required that determines greatness."
>
> —Charles Kendall Adams

A little extra effort always gives a person an edge. Art Williams, the founder of Primerica Financial Services, once told me, "You beat fifty percent of the people in America by working hard; you beat forty percent by being a person of honesty and integrity and standing for something; and the last ten percent is a dogfight in the free enterprise system." If you want to win that dogfight, then do a little extra.

## 2. A Little Extra Time

Successful people practice harder and practice longer than unsuccessful people do. Success expert Peter Lowe, who has gleaned success secrets from hundreds of people who are at the top of their profession, says, "The most common trait I have found in all successful people is that they have conquered the temptation to give up."

Giving a little extra time requires more than just perseverance. It requires patience. The Law of Process in my book *The 21 Irrefutable*

*Laws of Leadership* says, "Leadership develops daily, not in a day." That can be said of any talent we try to cultivate and improve.

As you work to give a little extra time to your efforts, it is wise to maintain a longer view of the process of improvement. Such a perspective really helps. Gutzon Borglum, the sculptor who created the memorial to the American presidents at Mount Rushmore, was asked if he considered his work to be perfect. It's

> "The most common trait I have found in all successful people is that they have conquered the temptation to give up."
>
> —Peter Lowe

said he replied, "Not today. The nose of Washington is an inch too long. It's better that way, though. It will erode to be exactly right in 10,000 years." Now that's patience!

## 3. A Little Extra Help

Anybody who succeeds at anything does so with the help of others. Alex Haley, the author of *Roots,* used to keep a reminder of that in his office. It said, "If you see a turtle on top of a fence post, you know he had help getting there."

I know that in my professional pursuits, I've always needed help. And I've been fortunate that others were willing to give it to me. Early in my career in the 1970s, I contacted the top ten leaders in my field and offered them $100 to meet with me for thirty minutes so that I could ask them questions. Many granted my request, and (fortunately for my thin wallet at the time) most declined to accept the $100. And today, I still make it a point to meet with excellent leaders from whom I desire to learn.

When I think about the ways that people have helped me in all aspects of my life, I am humbled and grateful. Some have given me advice. Others have presented me with opportunities. And a few, like my wife, Margaret, have lavished unconditional love on me. I know I am a very fortunate man.

## 4. A Little Extra Change

A letter was returned to the post office. Handwritten on the envelope were the words, "He's dead." Through an oversight, the letter was inadvertently sent again to the same address. It was again returned to the post office with another handwritten message: "He's still dead!"

> "We cannot become what we need to be by remaining what we are."
> —Max DePree

Let's face it. Most people are resistant to change. They desire improvement, but they resist changing their everyday routine. That's a problem because, as leadership expert Max DePree says, "We cannot become what we need to be by remaining what we are." To sharpen your talent through practice, you need to do more than just be *open* to change. You need to *pursue* change—and you need to do it a little bit more than other achievers. Here's what to look for and how to focus your energy to get the kinds of changes that will change you for the better:

- Don't change just enough to *get away* from your problems—change enough to *solve* them.

- Don't change your *circumstances* to improve your life—change *yourself* to improve your circumstances.

- Don't do *the same old things* expecting to get different results—get different results by doing *something new.*

- Don't wait to *see the light* to change—start changing as soon as you *feel the heat.*

- Don't see change as something *hurtful* that *must* be done—see it as something *helpful* that *can* be done.

- Don't avoid paying the *immediate* price of change—if you do, you will pay the *ultimate* price of never improving.

Poet and philosopher Johann von Schiller wrote, "He who has done his best for his own time has lived for all times." You can do your best only if you are continually seeking to embrace positive change.

When you have worked hard in practice to sharpen your talent and you begin to see results, please don't think that it's time to stop practicing. You never arrive at your potential—you can only continue to strive toward it. And that means continual practice.

Charles Swindoll's friend William Johnson, who owns the Ritz-Carlton hotels, was pleased when the organization won the Malcolm Baldridge National Quality Award. When Swindoll congratulated him, Johnson quickly gave others the credit for the achievement. But he also said that it made him and others in the organization work even harder to earn the respect that came with the award. Johnson summed up his attitude: "Quality is a race with no finish line." If you don't strive for excellence, then you are soon settling for acceptable. The next step is mediocrity, and nobody pays for mediocre! If you want to reach your potential and remain a talent-plus person, you have to keep practicing with excellence.

> "He who has done his best for his own time has lived for all times."
> —Johann von Schiller

# TALENT + PRACTICE
# APPLICATION EXERCISES

1. If you want to practice well, then you need to make sure you are incorporating the Five Pillars of Practice into your routine. Think about each one:

   - *An excellent teacher or coach.* Have you sought out someone who can help you learn your craft, sharpen your skills, or practice well? If you already have a coach, is he or she the best person to help you during this season? Do you need to find a specialist to help you improve in a specific area? You can't maximize your potential on your own.

   - *Your best effort.* Are you practicing in a way that allows you to give your best effort? Are you practicing at the right time? Are you in the best place? Are you giving yourself incentives to give your best? Do what you must to give your best.

   - *A clear purpose.* Every time you practice, do you know what you are trying to accomplish? Do you have the larger goal in mind as well as the specific improvement you are trying to make?

   - *The greatest potential.* Are you focused on developing your greatest talent? Are you staying in your strength zone? Your greatest progress and your greatest contributions will come from your areas of greatest talent.

   - *The right resources.* Do you have everything you need to practice well? What could you invest in that would facilitate your going to the next level?

2. Where are you on the practice continuum? Are you just starting out and facing a big learning curve? Are you at the phase of rapid progress? Have you already made the greatest gains of this season of your practice life and are now working on fine-tuning? Knowing where you are helps you tailor your practice routine to get the most out of it.

3. How disciplined are you when it comes to practice? Track yourself. Use a practice journal to record your practice sessions for thirty days. Write down not only when you practice and for what duration, but also make notes of what you worked on and how it went. At the end of that period, review your progress.

4. Elmer G. Letterman asserted, "The average human being in any line of work could double his productive capacity overnight if he began right now to do all the things he knows he should do, and to stop doing all the things he knows he should not do." How can you apply this piece of wisdom to your practice routine? What currently wastes your time? What task do you perform as a matter of habit that could be replaced by something that would sharpen your talent? "Audit" yourself and reinvent your practice routine.

5. Talent-plus people are always striving to do a little bit more. Upon which of the four areas outlined in the chapter do you currently need to focus more: effort, time, help, or change? What will you do to create that little extra that can take you from ordinary to *extra*ordinary?

# 7

# PERSEVERANCE SUSTAINS YOUR TALENT

Perseverance is not an issue of talent. It is not an issue of time. It is about finishing. Talent provides hope for accomplishment, but perseverance guarantees it. Playwright Noel Coward commented, "Thousands of people have talent. I might as well congratulate you for having eyes in your head. The one and only thing that counts is: Do you have staying power?"

## DARING TO DREAM

In July 2000, Vonetta Flowers landed in Sacramento, California, ready to compete in the U.S. Olympic trials for a place on the American team that would travel to Sydney, Australia, for the summer games. She had been training for it her whole life.

Vonetta had dreamed about being in the Olympics since she was a small child. She ran everywhere as a kid, and at age nine, when she had a chance to try out with an inner-city track club called the Alabama Striders in Birmingham, she gladly seized it. When the coach later looked over the list of times children ran in the 50-yard dash and saw that V. Jeffrey had the fastest time of all the kids in Jonesboro Elementary School, he assumed the time had come from one of the older boys. He was shocked to find out that it belonged to Vonetta—a third grade girl! Vonetta quickly became a star among the club's runners.

An excellent athlete, Vonetta lettered in track, volleyball, and basketball in high school and was named MVP of her track team three seasons. In college she focused exclusively on track, competing in the 200- and 400-meter sprints, long jump, triple jump, heptathlon, and relays. She was named all-American seven times.

At age twenty-six, Vonetta was competing as an elite athlete, and she was on course to make the Sydney team. She had tried out for the 1996 team at age twenty-two, competing in the 100-meter dash and long jump, but she hadn't made it. That had been tough for her. But she had dreamed of competing in the Olympics since she was nine, so she decided to put in four more years of grueling training, delayed starting a family, and gave it one more try. "In the years after college, while I worked as an assistant track coach," writes Flowers, "I continued my own training. I devoted countless hours to lifting weights, eating right, and staying mentally tough. I knew that my time as an athlete was coming to an end, and I'd hoped that the 2000 Olympic trials would prove to be my year to finally find out what it's like to be an Olympian."[1] But despite all her hopes, all her efforts, all her talent, Vonetta's best effort at the 2000 trials wasn't good enough. She did not finish with a good enough jump to make the team. Seventeen years of training had ended in failure. Her Olympic dream was over.

## GIVE UP OR GO ON?

But a funny thing happened while she was in Sacramento. Her husband, Johnny, saw a flyer posted in a hallway. It read,

Continue Your Olympic Dream
by Trying Out for the Bobsled Team

Ideal candidates should be able to perform the following:

30 meters
60 meters
100 meters
Five Consecutive Hops

Vertical Jump
Shot Put Toss

Please call Bonny at [number] or come to
Davidson High School track on [date] for tryouts.

Johnny was very excited about it, but Vonetta wasn't. She knew nothing about bobsleds, she had never lived anywhere that it snowed, and she was still crestfallen about failing in the summer games trials.

Vonetta was at a crossroads. Her talent had seemed almost limitless, yet it hadn't carried her to her dream. Now here was another opportunity. But it wasn't in *her* sport. It wasn't even in her Olympics—the summer games. And even if she succeeded in passing the "audition," it would mean starting over again in a new sport on unfamiliar ground—ice. It would require a degree of perseverance beyond what she had already displayed.

Reluctantly Vonetta agreed to attend the tryouts. She discovered that her experience as a sprinter and triple jumper and her training with weights had prepared her well to become a bobsled brakewoman (the person who pushes the bobsled and rides with the driver). It took her two years of learning, training, and competing—along with the ability to survive the soap opera of drivers changing brakewomen multiple times—but she finally fulfilled her dream of making it to the Olympics, not as a track athlete in the summer games, but as a bobsledder in the winter Olympics. And in 2002, her perseverance paid off beyond her wildest dreams. Much to everyone's surprise, Vonetta and her driver, Jill Bakken, won the gold medal! And with that, Vonetta went into the record books as the first African-American to win a gold medal in a winter Olympics.

## PRINCIPLES OF PERSEVERANCE

No matter how talented people are, there is no success without perseverance. World War I flying ace Eddie Rickenbacker said, "I can give you a six-word formula for success: Think things through—then follow through." Many people like to think things through; few follow through.

If you desire to become a talent-plus person, you need to understand some things about perseverance:

### 1. Perseverance Means Succeeding Because You Are Determined to, Not Destined To

Green Bay Packers coach Vince Lombardi said, "The difference between a successful person and others is not lack of strength, not a lack of knowledge, but rather a lack of determination." The greatest achievers don't sit back and wait for success because they think they deserve it. They keep moving forward and persevering because they are determined to achieve it.

> "We will either find a way or make one."
>
> —Hannibal

You can see this determination in successful people in every walk of life and in every age. Hannibal, the Carthaginian general who fought the Romans during the Second Punic War, asserted, "We will either find a way or make one." He lived out that attitude of perseverance when he led an unexpected campaign that took him over the Alps to defeat the Romans.

Talented people who succeed show similar determination. Joseph Lanier, one-time chairman and CEO of West Point-Pepperell, Inc., stated, "We are determined to win the battle. We will fight them until hell freezes over, and then, if we have to, we'll fight them on the ice." That kind of determination serves people well whether they are running an organization or pursuing a profession.

Actor Tom Hanks has been in some incredible movies of seemingly every type: comedy, suspense, action, romantic comedy, fantasy, and mystery. From *Sleepless in Seattle*, *Forrest Gump*, and *Toy Story* to *Apollo 13*, *Saving Private Ryan*, and *Philadelphia*, his movies have received popular and critical acclaim. He has been called a modern-day Jimmy Stewart. As of early 2006, the movies he's appeared in have made more than $3 billion at the box office.[2] He has also expanded his efforts into writing, directing, and producing. What actor wouldn't want a career like his?

Looking back, one might be tempted to assume that he was so talented that he was destined to succeed. Yet it didn't appear that way early on. When he started in his career, he couldn't seem to get any steady work. He tried to act in commercials but couldn't break in. He auditioned repeatedly for television shows but was constantly rejected. Finally in 1980, he landed a steady job on a sitcom called *Bosom Buddies*. It lasted two years and paid Hanks only $5,000 per episode. But it also earned him the opportunity to guest star on other TV shows. That exposure eventually led to his first big break, a starring role in the movie *Splash*.

What made the difference for Hanks? Perseverance! He never let rejection dissuade him from persevering in his career. He kept going—when he couldn't get a part, when he couldn't land a regular job, when the parts he was offered were mediocre. Ten years into his career, Hanks is reported to have said, "I've made over twenty movies and five of them are good." Today he has made nearly fifty movies, many of them first-rate. He has won two Academy Awards. And he earns $25 million per film now![3] His success has nothing to do with destiny—it has to do with determination.

## 2. Perseverance Recognizes Life Is Not a Long Race, but Many Short Ones in Succession

Have you heard the saying, "Life is a marathon"? Whoever first said it was almost certainly trying to encourage people to keep trying when things get tough and to have a patient yet tenacious approach to life. But I think whoever said it didn't quite get it right. Life isn't one very long race. It's actually a long series of shorter races, one after another. Each task has its own challenges. Each day is its own event. True, you have to get out of bed the next day and race again, but it's never exactly the same race as before. To be successful, you just need to keep plugging away. Talk show host Rush Limbaugh observed, "In life or in football, touchdowns rarely take place in seventy-yard increments. Usually it's three yards and a cloud of dust."

I've read that explorer Christopher Columbus faced incredible difficulties while sailing west in search of a passage to Asia. He and his crews encountered storms, experienced hunger and deprivation, and dealt with extreme discouragement. The crews of the three ships were near mutiny. But Columbus persevered. The account of the journey written by Columbus said the same thing, day after day: "Today we sailed on." And his perseverance paid off. He didn't discover a fast route to the spice-rich Indies; instead he found new continents. But as he sailed, his focus was clear—making it through the day. Winning each short race. And that's key. Management consultant Laddie F. Hutar affirmed that "success consists of a series of little daily victories."

> "Success consists of a series of little daily victories."
>
> —Laddie F. Hutar

## 3. Perseverance Is Needed to Release Most of Life's Rewards

At a sales convention, the corporate sales manager got up in front of all two thousand of his firm's salespeople and asked, "Did the Wright brothers ever quit?"

"No!" the sales force shouted.

"Did Charles Lindbergh ever quit?" he asked.

"No!" the salespeople shouted again.

"Did Lance Armstrong ever quit?"

"No!"

He bellowed for a fourth time, "Did Thorndike McKester ever quit?" There was a confused silence for a long moment.

Then a salesperson stood up and asked, "Who in the world is Thorndike McKester? Nobody's ever heard of him."

The sales manager snapped back, "Of course you never heard of him—because he quit!"[4]

How many highly successful people do you know who gave up? How many do you know who have been richly rewarded for quitting? I don't know any, and I bet you don't either. It's said that Walt Disney's request for a loan was rejected by 301 banks before he finally got a yes. The loan he received allowed him to build Disneyland, the first and most famous theme park in history.

Inventor Thomas Edison asserted, "Many of life's failures are people who did not realize how close they were to success when they gave up." It's the last step in the race that counts the most. That is where the winner is determined. That is where the rewards come. If you run every step of the race well *except* the last one and you stop before the finish line, then the end result will be the same as if you never ran a step.

> "Many of life's failures are people who did not realize how close they were to success when they gave up."
>
> —Thomas Edison

## 4. Perseverance Draws Sweetness Out of Adversity

The trials and pressures of life—and how we face them—often define us. Confronted by adversity, many people give up while others rise up. How do those who succeed do it? They persevere. They find the benefit to them personally that comes from any trial. And they recognize that the best thing about adversity is coming out on the other side of it. There is a sweetness to overcoming your troubles and finding something good in the process, however small it may be.

I came across a poem by Howard Goodman called "I Don't Regret a Mile" that expresses this idea well. It says, in part:

> I've dreamed many a dream that's never come true,
> I've seen them vanish at dawn,
> But enough of my dreams have come true
> To make me keep dreaming on
>
> I've prayed many a prayer that seemed no answer would come,
> Though I'd waited so patient and long;
> But enough answers have come to my prayers
> To make me keep praying on
>
> I've sown many a seed that's fallen by the wayside,
> For the birds to feed upon
> But I've held enough golden sheaves in my hands
> To make me keep sowing on
>
> I've trusted many a friend that's failed me
> And left me to weep alone
> But enough of my friends have been true-blue
> To make me keep trusting on
>
> I've drained the cup of disappointment and pain,
> And gone many a day without song
> But I've sipped enough nectar from the roses of life
> To make me want to live on[5]

Giving up when adversity threatens can make a person bitter. Persevering through adversity makes one better.

## 5. Perseverance Has a Compounding Effect on Life

Author Napoleon Hill says, "Every successful person finds that great success lies just beyond the point when they're convinced their idea is not going to work." How do you get beyond that point? How do you go beyond what you believe is your limit? How do you achieve *lasting* success? Do the right thing, day after day. There are no shortcuts to anything worthwhile.

Every day that you do the right things—work hard, treat others with respect, learn, and grow—you invest in yourself. To do these things every day takes relentless perseverance, but if you do them, your success compounds over time. Weight-loss expert and author Judy Wardell Halliday supported this idea: "Dreams become reality when we keep our commitment to them."

## 6. Perseverance Means Stopping Not Because You're Tired but Because the Task Is Done

Former diplomat and recipient of the Presidential Medal of Freedom Robert Strauss commented, "Success is a little like wrestling a gorilla. You don't quit when you're tired—you quit when the gorilla is tired." If you think about it, perseverance doesn't really come into play until you *are* tired. When you're fresh, excited, and energetic, you approach a task with vigor. Work is fun. Only when you become tired do you need perseverance.

> "Success is a little like wrestling a gorilla. You don't quit when you're tired—you quit when the gorilla is tired."
>
> —Robert Strauss

To successful people, fatigue and discouragement are not signs to quit. They perceive them as signals to draw on their reserves, rely on their character, and keep going. One problem of many people is that they underestimate what it will take to succeed. Enlightenment political philosopher Montesquieu declared, "In most things success depends on knowing how long it takes to succeed." When we haven't counted the cost of success, we approach challenges with mere interest; what is really required is total commitment. And that makes all the difference.

**7. Perseverance Doesn't Demand More Than We Have but All That We Have**

Author Frank Tyger observed, "In every triumph there is a lot of try." But perseverance means more than trying. It means more than working hard. Perseverance is an investment. It is a willingness to bind oneself emotionally, intellectually, physically, and spiritually to an idea or task until it has been completed. Perseverance demands a lot, but here's the good news: everything you give is an investment in yourself.

# THE FIVE ENEMIES OF PERSEVERANCE

French scientist Louis Pasteur said, "Let me tell you the secret that has led me to my goal. My strength lives solely in my tenacity." Perseverance begins with the right attitude—an attitude of tenacity. But the desire to persevere alone isn't enough to keep most people going when they are tired or discouraged. Perseverance is a trait that can be cultivated. And the initial step to developing it is to eliminate its five greatest enemies:

## 1. A Lifestyle of Giving Up

A little boy had been promised an ice-cream cone if he was good while accompanying his grandfather on some errands. The longer they were gone, the more difficult the boy was finding it to be good. "How much longer will it be?" the boy asked.

"Not too long," replied the grandfather. "We've got just one more stop before we get ice cream."

"I don't know if I can make it, Grandpa," the little boy responded. "I can be good. I just can't be good enough long enough."

When we were kids and we didn't follow through a task, people often gave us a break. That's to be expected. Children tend to jump from one activity to another and to bounce from idea to idea. Adults can't do that and expect to be successful. Scientist L. G.

Elliott advised, "Vacillating people seldom succeed. They seldom win the solid respect of their fellows. Successful men and women are very careful in reaching decisions and very persistent and determined in action thereafter."

If you desire to be successful and to maximize your talent, you need to be consistent and persistent. Talent without perseverance never comes to full fruition. Opportunities without persistence will be lost. There is a direct correlation between perseverance and potential. If you have a habit of giving up, you need to overcome it to be successful.

## 2. A Wrong Belief That Life Should Be Easy

Debra K. Johnson tells about an incident with her seven-year-old daughter who wanted to take violin lessons. When they went to a music store together to rent an instrument, Debra began lecturing her about the expense of lessons and the commitment that would be required of her if she got her the violin. "There will be times you'll feel like giving up," Debra said, "but I want you to hang in there and keep on trying."

Her daughter nodded and, in her most serious voice, responded, "It will be just like marriage, right, Mom?" Having the right expectations going into anything is half the battle. John C. Norcross, a clinical psychologist and professor at the University of Scranton, has studied people and their goals, and he has found a characteristic that distinguishes those who reach their goals from those who don't: expectations. Both types of people experience the same amount of failure during the first month they strive for their goals. But members of the successful group don't expect to succeed right away, and they view their failures as a reason to recommit and a reminder to refocus on their goals with more determination. Norcross says, "Those who are unsuccessful say a relapse is evidence that they can't do it."[6]

## 3. A Wrong Belief That Success Is a Destination

The NBA's Pat Riley has won many championships as a basketball coach. In his book *The Winner Within*, he writes, "Complacency is the last hurdle any winner, any team must overcome before attaining potential greatness. Complacency is the success disease: it takes root when you're feeling good about who you are and what you've achieved." It's ironic, but past success can be the fiercest enemy to future success.

In February 2006, I was invited to join some friends who were going to the Super Bowl on a private plane. I sat next to Lester Woerner, the owner of the plane and a very successful entrepreneur and businessman. He started investing in real estate when he was a teenager, helped build one of the finest turf grass companies in the country in his twenties and thirties, and now in his forties is the chairman of Woerner Holdings with investments in agriculture, real estate, and financial securities. Within minutes we were engaged in conversation, and one of the questions I asked him was how he maintained success after having achieved it.

Lester described a day when he came to the realization that he had "made it," and he started to wonder what was next for him. "I started to change," Lester explained. "I went from thinking *why not* about every opportunity that approached me to thinking *but why* when an opportunity arose. I lost the hunger."

When Lester stopped seizing opportunities, the opportunities began drying up. And he hit a plateau.

"How did you break out of it?" I asked.

"The first thing was to recognize that I was on a plateau; the second was to close the door on yesterday's success," he answered. "Once I did that, I was able to take steps to change, to begin going after opportunities again."

I told Lester that I found that people tend to celebrate and then to relax when they see success as a destination.

"It's good to celebrate and even take a rest," Lester responded, "but not for long. We must close the door on yesterday's success."

If you think you have arrived, then you're in trouble. As soon as you think you no longer need to work to make progress, you'll begin to lose ground.

## 4. A Lack of Resiliency

Harvard professor of psychiatry George E. Vaillant, in his book *Aging Well*, identifies resiliency as a significant characteristic of people who navigate the many transitions of life from birth to old age. He writes, "Resilience reflects individuals who metaphorically resemble a twig with a fresh, green living core. When twisted out of shape, such a twig bends, but it does not break; instead it springs back and continues growing."[7]

> "You can't get much done in life if you only work on the days you feel good."
>
> —Jerry West

That's an excellent description of how we must be if we desire to persevere through adversity and make the most of the talent we have. We must not become dry, brittle, and inflexible. And we must endeavor to bounce back, no matter how we may feel. We would be wise to remember the words of former NBA player, coach, and executive Jerry West: "You can't get much done in life if you only work on the days you feel good."

## 5. A Lack of Vision

Everything that is created is actually created twice. First it is created mentally; then it is created physically. Where does that mental creation come from? The answer is vision.

People who display perseverance keep a larger vision in mind as they toil away at their craft or profession. They see in their mind's eye what they want to create or to do, and they keep working toward it as they labor. For example, years ago I read an account of an amateur golfer who played a round with Sam Snead, member of the World Golf Hall of Fame, recipient of the PGA Tour Lifetime Achievement Award, and three-time captain of the U.S. Ryder Cup team. On the first hole, Snead shot a seven—three over par, an unusually poor score for a golfer of his caliber. As the pair exited the green, Snead didn't seem to be bothered by his triple bogey. When his amateur companion asked Snead about it, he responded, "That's why we play eighteen holes." Snead's vision of the big picture helped him to maintain perspective, remain resilient, and persevere. By the end of the round, Snead finished four strokes under par.

## TALENT + PERSEVERANCE = A TALENT-PLUS PERSON PUTTING THE TALENT-PLUS FORMULA INTO ACTION

Clearing away the five enemies of perseverance is a preliminary step to becoming a talent-plus person in the area of perseverance. Right thinking always precedes right action. If you want to be able to sustain your talent, then take the following steps:

### Purpose: Find One

Rich De Voss, owner of the NBA's Orlando Magic, remarked, "Persistence is stubbornness with a purpose." It is very difficult for people to develop perseverance when they lack a sense of purpose. Conversely, when one has a passionate sense of purpose, energy rises, obstacles become incidental, and perseverance wins out.

> "Persistence is stubbornness with a purpose."
>
> —Rich De Voss

Perhaps you've seen *America's Most Wanted*, the television program that re-creates the crime stories and encourages viewers to help authorities locate and capture the criminals who are wanted for these often violent crimes. The program's host is John Walsh. Many people think he is an actor or journalist—a television professional hired to host the show. But he isn't, and his story is quite remarkable.

Walsh owned his own company, and along with three partners, he built deluxe hotels. But one day his six-year-old son, Adam, disappeared. The child had been abducted, but because there was no evidence of a crime, the authorities were slow to help Walsh and his wife find their only child. They searched for sixteen days. Tragically, by the time he was found, it was too late. He was dead.

Walsh's life was thrown into chaos. He lost thirty pounds. His house went into foreclosure. And he lost his business—he just couldn't bring himself to return to his work. He had lost all hope. Then one day Dr. Ronald Wright, the county coroner, looked at Walsh and asked, "You're thinking about suicide, aren't you?"

"What do I have to live for?" Walsh replied. "I have nothing. My only child has been murdered. I can't even talk to my wife. I have no job, my house is in foreclosure, my whole life is over."

"No, it isn't," Wright responded. "You are articulate. You mounted the greatest campaign for a missing child in the history of Florida. Go out and try to change things."

Walsh says that it was the best advice he'd gotten from anyone. It gave him purpose. And that sense of purpose did more than give him a reason not to kill himself. It energized him to serve and help others. In 1988, he began hosting *America's Most Wanted*, which he continues to do as I write this. The show has been responsible for the capture of hundreds of fugitives, including fourteen who were on the FBI's Ten Most Wanted lists.

If you want to maximize your talent as a talent-plus person, you need to find your purpose. That is the only way you will be able to persevere, as John Walsh did, even when facing the most difficult circumstances.

## Excuses: Eliminate Them

One of the most striking things that separates people who sustain their success from those who are only briefly or never successful is their strong sense of responsibility for their own actions. It is easier to move from failure to success than it is from excuses to success.

According to Bruce Nash, author of a series of "Hall of Shame" books on sports figures, one notorious person for making excuses was Rafael

> It is easier to move from failure to success than it is from excuses to success.

Septien, former placekicker for the NFL's Dallas Cowboys. Nash writes, "We're all guilty of using excuses. When we do, we place ourselves in the company of great sports heroes. Take Rafael Septien, for example. Rafael Septien has no peers—when it comes to making up lamebrained excuses for missed field goals." Among the excuses, perhaps tongue-in-cheek, that Septien offered:

- "I was too busy reading my stats on the scoreboard."

- "The grass was too tall." (Texas Stadium doesn't even have grass; its surface is artificial turf.)

- "The 30-second clock distracted me."

- "My helmet was too tight and it was squeezing my brain. I couldn't think."

- "No wonder [I missed]. You placed the ball upside down" (said to his holder).[8]

If you want to maximize and sustain your talent, don't allow yourself to offer excuses when you don't perform at the best of your ability. Instead, take complete responsibility for yourself and your actions. And keep in mind the words of George Washington Carver, who said, "Ninety-nine percent of failures come from people who have the habit of making excuses."

## Stamina: Develop Some

Former world heavyweight champion boxer Muhammad Ali, called "The Greatest," asserted, "Champions aren't made in the gyms. Champions are made from something they have deep inside them—a desire, a dream, a vision. They have to have last-minute stamina, they have to be a little faster, they have to have the skill, and the will. But the will must be stronger than the skill." All people who achieve and maintain success possess stamina. Truly, stamina is a key to perseverance, and perseverance is a key to becoming a talent-plus person.

In February 2006, I accompanied a group of leaders from two organizations, EQUIP and Lidere, on a trip to Central and South America. We traveled together by private plane. Our mission was to launch a leadership training initiative in seven countries.

The first leg of our journey was to Honduras. We were scheduled to train a group of leaders there at a conference, and part of our plan was to have leadership books available for anyone who might want to buy them. Abraham Diaz, who works with Marcos Witt at Lidere, took charge of working out the details of getting the books through customs in Guatemala and then on to Honduras, which we needed to happen in one day in order for them to make it to the conference on time the next day. Little did we know that getting those books to the conference was going to be an exercise in perseverance. Here, in Abraham's own words, is what happened after he landed in Guatemala:

> Before I left Atlanta, where we were to meet with the rest of the group, I spent two days in Houston receiving all the instructions I needed. The books were coming down in another plane, and the plan was to keep the books in the plane so that when we arrived we wouldn't have to go through the process of importing all the material. But the company in Guatemala that we hired to bring the books in didn't follow instructions. They said that they had turned all the books over to Customs officials. It took two and a half hours to find this out. Now they didn't have any control of those boxes, and I had to go directly to Customs to see where they were located.
>
> 2:30 p.m.—I went to Customs' main office to find the boxes. But they couldn't search for them. They needed me to go back to the company

which brought in the books and get the documents they received when they turned over the boxes. I went back to get them, but was told I would have to wait for the person in charge of this matter.

3:00 p.m.—The person in charge arrived. He informed me that I needed to pay a fee at another location so that he could release these documents. I went to the other location and made the payment.

3:30 p.m.—I went back to the handling company and received the papers which included the airway bill number and invoice that Customs required.

4:00 p.m.—I arrived back at Customs and they started searching for the hundreds of boxes. As they reviewed their information, they realized the number of boxes that arrived was one less than the number reported in the documents, so they said they could not release them to me. To get them, I needed to provide a letter, stamped and approved by another Customs official, stating that I relinquished my right to the missing box.

4:30 p.m.—I walked to this office. I saw a man there who appeared to be important. When I started to explain my problem, he invited me into his office. It turned out he was the administrative director of Customs for all of Guatemala. He started typing the letter I needed himself. Then he got all of the signatures and stamps I needed to get the boxes out. I finally felt like I might succeed.

5:15 p.m.—I went back to the warehouse where international shipments are held. They kept me waiting for forty-five minutes while they processed other orders.

6:00 p.m.—The warehouse official said that in order for them to release the boxes, I had to make two different payments for storage and other charges. I went to the other location to make the payment, but I had only U.S. dollars with me, which they wouldn't take. So I jumped into a cab and went to a nearby bank to exchange money.

6:30 p.m.—I returned to make the payment and waited in line for more than twenty minutes before I could pay the fees.

7:00 p.m.—I returned to the warehouse and waited for the person who would take the receipts showing I made the proper payments. After waiting forty-five minutes, he finally arrived. He looked over the papers. He couldn't believe I had been able to do all the procedures in a few hours. He made some phone calls and looked over the papers again.

8:00 p.m.—He finally gave the okay and called the people who would operate the machinery to move the boxes to the front of the warehouse.

9:00 p.m.—I found out the workers who move the boxes in the warehouse were not the same people who would move them to the plane, so I started searching for someone who could perform this service. I waited for nearly an hour for the person in charge to show up so that I could find out how much it was going to cost and whether he had workers to do it.

10:00 p.m.—After coming to an agreement, workers started loading boxes and moving them to where the plane was. I then realized that the FBO [fixed base of operations] at this airport had no place to store the boxes overnight, so I worked it out for the people who moved them to stay with the boxes until 5:00 a.m. the next morning.

11:00 p.m.—The captain of our plane called me to let me know that his aircraft could not take all the boxes we had because of the weight. As the boxes arrived from the warehouse, I began contacting other pilots with small planes near ours to find one who was willing to take the remaining boxes to Honduras. I finally found one who was willing to do it.

The next morning, we departed and flew to Honduras—where we had to start a similar process all over again!

A lot of leaders in Honduras were very grateful for the perseverance of Abraham Diaz. Because of him, they were able to get the books they needed.

Earlier in this chapter I stated that life is not one long race but a series of many short ones in succession. Abraham Diaz's experience is a perfect illustration of this truth. On that day in Guatemala, he ran race after race for eight and a half hours—and the official who finally gave the okay to him was amazed that he had been able to do it. The next day he ran another race. And the day after that.

Abraham is a talented leader. He demonstrates the number one characteristic of good leaders: the ability to make things happen. That takes perseverance. That's true no matter what your talent is or what skills you possess. Without perseverance, a talented person is little more than a flash in the pan.

# TALENT + PERSEVERANCE APPLICATION EXERCISES

1. Purpose gives passion, and passion feeds perseverance. What is your purpose? If you haven't defined it and written it out, do so now.

2. How often do you think you make excuses when you fail to accomplish something you set out to do? Is it 20 percent of the time? Perhaps 60 percent of the time? Define it as a percentage. Now do this: ask three people who know you well (and who see you at your worst) to define how often you make excuses.

   If the figure they give you averages more than 10 percent, then you need to work on this area. First, ask those people to hold you accountable for not making excuses. Second, train yourself to ask, *What can I learn from this?* rather than, *What went wrong?*

3. What is your attitude toward life's challenges? Do you expect obstacles and failures? What do you do if you don't succeed right away? Do you give up and try something else, or do you keep working at it?

   Stamina comes from expecting life to be difficult, from developing the habit of overcoming adversity, and from taking one more step when you think you have nothing left. What recent obstacle, failure, or setback that stopped you can you revisit and attack again with renewed energy? Take it on again. And when you feel like quitting again, push yourself to take one more step. *Then* reevaluate it and see if you need to take *one more step* again.

4. How can you personally apply the concept of life as a series of short races? Where will this idea most benefit you? How will it change your approach to a task, responsibility, or opportunity?

5. What are you willing to give to realize your potential and maximize your talent as a talent-plus person? Give it some think time and create two lists: things you are willing to give up to go to the next level, and things you are unwilling to compromise.

# 8

# COURAGE TESTS
# YOUR TALENT

People think of courage as a quality required only in times of extreme danger or stress, such as during war or disaster. But it is much larger than that—and more ordinary than we think. Courage is an everyday virtue. Professor, writer, and apologist C. S. Lewis wrote, "Courage is not simply one of the virtues, but the form of every virtue at its testing point." You can do nothing worthwhile without courage. The person who exhibits courage is often able to live without regrets.

## BRITISH BULLDOG

When I think about people whose talent was elevated—and tested—by their courage, one individual who immediately comes to mind is Winston Churchill. As a young man, Churchill anticipated greatness for himself. While he was in school at Harrow at age sixteen, Churchill's response to a classmate's queries about his future were bold. "I can see vast changes coming over a now peaceful world," said the teenage Churchill, "great upheavals, terrible struggles, wars such as one cannot imagine; and I tell you London will be in danger, London will be attacked and I shall be very prominent in the defence [*sic*] of London . . . In the high position I shall occupy, it will fall to me to save the Capital, to save the Empire."[1] The vision Churchill had of his role was remarkably on target.

After Europe fell to the Nazis, Great Britain stood alone against them for two years with Churchill as their leader. He defied Hitler and continually rallied the people of the nation while they suffered under repeated German bombings and faced the threat of a possible German invasion. In the 1930s prior to war, Britain's strategy had been to appease Hitler. All during that time, Churchill vocally expressed his opposition to such actions. In 1940, when Prime Minister Neville Chamberlain was forced from office, Britain looked for a strong leader to replace him. The natural successor to Chamberlain would have been Lord Halifax, the foreign secretary. But Halifax knew that he didn't possess the qualities needed to lead Britain in war, and he declined the potential appointment. That's when Churchill, then age sixty-six, was called to step into the gap.[2]

Why would Churchill be chosen as prime minister? He had been out of favor for many years. Why would anyone believe Churchill had the courage to lead the nation in what appeared to be a cause for which many believed there was little hope? The answer is that his courage had been tested time and time again, and it had proven his talent.

## A Desire to Distinguish Himself

Growing up, Churchill was a merely average student. He was clumsy and accident prone. As a teenager in boarding school at Harrow, he didn't really begin to shine until he prepared for a career in the army. He excelled at history, was an excellent rider, and won the school's fencing championship. After Harrow, he completed his military officer's training at Sandhurst, and in 1895, at twenty years old, he was commissioned into the 4th Hussars, a cavalry unit that was destined for India.

His long-term goal was to enter politics, as his father had. But first he wanted to make a name for himself in the military. While waiting to ship out to India, he was eager for action, and he managed to join with Spanish forces, which were in combat in Cuba, as an observer to test his mettle. He later wrote, "I thought it might be as well to have a private rehearsal, a secluded trial trip in order to make sure that the ordeal was not unsuited to my temperament."[3] He proved himself courageous under fire and was even recommended for the Cross of the Order of Military Merit.

Once stationed in quiet Madras, India, he quickly grew bored, and once again, he sought action. He managed to get attached as a correspondent to the Malakand Field Force on the northwest frontier of India more than two thousand miles from Madras, but soon he ended up joining the commanding general's staff. "I mean to play this game out and if I lose, it is obvious that I could never have won any other," he wrote to his family. "I am more ambitious for a reputation for personal courage than anything else in the world."[4]

## A HISTORY OF COURAGE

He didn't have to wait long to begin proving himself. He saw battle twice. The first time the unit was attacked, Churchill was under fire for thirteen hours. He was clearheaded in battle and even assisted another officer in carrying a wounded soldier to safety. He later wrote, "Bullets are not worth considering . . . I do not believe the gods would create so potent a being as myself for so prosaic an ending."[5] He described his second experience as the hardest fighting on the northwest frontier for forty years. During the five-hour battle, the unit suffered fifty wounded and seventeen killed, including the regimental commander.

When things quieted down, Churchill again looked for action. His mother's influence helped him get into the 21st Lancers in Cairo. With them, he participated in what's been called the last great cavalry charge in the history of the British Army. His unit was on reconnaissance that day near Khartoum and spotted 150 enemy spearmen. The British charged them, only to find that they had ridden into a trap. They ended up in fierce hand-to-hand combat. Within two minutes, 119 of the British army's horses were wounded, 21 of their force were killed, and 50 more were wounded. Churchill fought valiantly, and his unit was victorious

In 1899, Churchill was ready to start his political career. He resigned from the army and ran for a seat in Parliament. He lost. Later that year, when war broke out in South Africa, Churchill went there to cover it as a correspondent for the *Morning Post*. Two weeks later, as he traveled with troops on an armored train, rebels attacked and derailed it. Churchill calmly took charge and rallied the troops. He helped to clear the rails, allowing the locomotive and tender to escape with the wounded. Then he went back to try to help the troops commander, only to be captured. He was taken to a temporary prison in Pretoria.

But Churchill refused to give in to defeat. After a month of captivity, he made a daring escape from the prison. He climbed over the prison wall and hopped a freight train. The Boer rebels posted a reward for his capture—dead or alive—but Churchill managed to make it to Durban. When he arrived there, he found that he had become a national hero and an international celebrity. After a six-month stint in the South African Light Horse, an irregular cavalry regiment, he returned to England where he once again ran for Parliament. This time he won. He was twenty-six years old.

Churchill's grandson, Winston S. Churchill, wrote,

When one considers the number of occasions on which he hazarded his life, even after he resigned his commission and entered Parliament at the age of 26 in 1900, walking out of the wreck of a crashed airplane in the earliest days of aviation, serving in the trenches of Flanders where he commanded the 6th Battalion of the Royal Scots Fusiliers in the line in 1917, and again when he was knocked down by a New York taxi in 1930 one cannot help but reflect that his preservation through all these hazards was nothing short of miraculous.[6]

So when Winston Churchill was chosen to be prime minister in 1940, people who knew him understood what the country was getting. His courage, toughness, and talent had been well tested. His entire life had prepared him for what he would face during those five war years. And his performance didn't disappoint.

## WHY DOES TALENT NEED COURAGE?

The stakes were high for Churchill as he carried out his duties as prime minister. He was doing more than just defending London and the empire, though those responsibilities were obviously monumental. Freedom and democracy were hanging in the balance. But his first tests didn't come when the stakes were so high. They came early. If he hadn't possessed the courage to step up when he was young and untested, he never would have discovered the depth of his talent, nor would he have been ready when he had to perform on the world stage.

> "A great deal of talent is lost to the world for want of a little courage."
>
> —Sydney Smith

English writer and clergyman Sydney Smith asserted, "A great deal of talent is lost to the world for want of a little courage." To develop and discover our talent, we need courage. The English word *courage* comes from the French word *coeur*, which means "heart." And we need to recognize that if we display courage, our hearts will be tested continually. Here's what I mean:

### Our Courage Will Be Tested . . .
### As We Seek a Truth That We Know May Be Painful

Before he joined the army, Winston Churchill had a desire to create a reputation for bravery, but he didn't know whether he had the talent for it. To make that discovery, he went to Cuba. His goal was to test his courage in a relatively controlled and somewhat safer environment than he thought he would face in India, what he called "a private rehearsal."

> "The truth that makes men free is for the most part the truth which men prefer not to hear."
>
> —Herbert Agar

He understood that a person doesn't know what he's really made of until tested. If we fear the test, then we will never get a chance to develop the talent.

Most of us will never be asked to face flying bullets in a physical battle. Often our tests are much more private and involve an internal battle, and many people find that painful. Pulitzer Prize–winning columnist Herbert Agar said, "The truth that makes men free is for the most part the truth which men prefer not to hear."

In order to grow, we need to face truths about ourselves, and that is often a difficult process. It usually looks something like this:

- *The issue.* Often it is something we do not want to hear about.
- *The temptation.* We want to ignore it, rationalize it, spin it, or package it.
- *The decision.* To grow, we must face the truth and make personal changes.
- *The challenge.* Change is not easy; our decision to change will be tested daily.
- *The response.* Others will be slow to acknowledge it; they will wait to see if our behavior changes.
- *The respect.* Respect is always gained on difficult ground, and it comes from others only when our behavior and words match.

Winston Churchill said, "Courage is what it takes to stand up and speak; courage is also what it takes to sit down and listen." It takes a brave person to listen to unpleasant truths. I have to admit that this has been a challenging area for me. I find it much easier to cast vision, motivate people, and lead the charge than to sit, listen to others speak truth, humble myself, and respond appropriately, but I'm continuing to work on it.

## Our Courage Will Be Tested . . . When Change Is Needed but Inactivity Is More Comfortable

Being inactive and never leaving what is familiar may mean that you are comfortable, but having the willingness to continually let go of the familiar means that you are courageous. American historian James Harvey Robinson asserted, "Greatness, in the last analysis, is largely due to bravery—courage in escaping from old ideas and old standards and respectable ways of doing things."

Our situation doesn't make us; we make our situation. Our circumstances don't have to define us; we can redefine our circumstances by our actions. At any given time, we must be willing to give up all we have in order to become all we can be. If we do that, if we are willing to leave our comfort zone and bravely keep striving, we can reach heights we thought were beyond us. We can go farther than others who possess greater talent than we do. Italian actress Sophia Loren observed, "Getting ahead in a difficult profession requires avid faith in yourself. That is why some people with mediocre talent, but with the inner drive, go much farther than people with vastly superior talent."

> "Getting ahead in a difficult profession requires avid faith in yourself. That is why some people with mediocre talent, but with the inner drive, go much farther than people with vastly superior talent."
>
> —Sophia Loren

## Our Courage Will Be Tested . . . When Our Convictions, Once Expressed, Are Challenged

Anytime you are willing to stand up for something, someone else will be willing to take a shot at you. People who express their convictions and attempt to live them out will experience conflict from others with opposing views. Ralph Waldo Emerson wrote, "Whatever you do, you need courage. Whatever course you decide upon, there is always someone to tell you you are wrong. There are always difficulties arising which tempt you to believe that your critics are right. To map out a course of action and follow it to an end, requires some of the same courage which a soldier needs. Peace has its victories, but it takes brave men to win them." So should we simply keep a low profile, swallow our convictions, and keep the peace? Of course not! The opposite of courage isn't cowardice; it is conformity. It's not enough just to believe in something. We need to live for something. Howard Hendricks said, "A belief is something you will argue about. A conviction is something you will die for." You cannot really live unless there are things in your life for which you are willing to die.

## Our Courage Will Be Tested . . . When Learning and Growing Will Display Our Weakness

Learning and growing always require action, and action takes courage—especially in the weak areas of our lives. That is where fear most often comes into play. It's easy to be brave in an area of strength; it's much more difficult in an area of weakness. That is why we need courage most. General Omar Bradley remarked, "Bravery is the capacity to perform properly even when scared half to death."

When I am striving to learn and grow in an area of weakness and I am afraid of failing or looking foolish, I encourage myself with these quotations:

- "Courage is fear holding on a minute longer."
  —George S. Patton

- "The difference between a hero and a coward is one step sideways."—Gene Hackman
- "Courage is fear that has said its prayers."—Karl Barth
- "Courage is doing what you're afraid to do. There can be no courage unless you're scared."—Eddie Rickenbacker
- "Courage is being scared to death but saddling up anyway." —John Wayne

We often mistakenly believe that learning is passive, that we learn by reading a book or listening to a lecture. But to learn, we must take action. As Coach Don Shula and management expert Ken Blanchard state, "Learning is defined as a change in behavior. You haven't learned a thing until you can take action and use it." And that is where fear often comes into play. The learning process can be summarized in the following five steps:

1. Observe.
2. Act.
3. Evaluate.
4. Readjust.
5. Go back to step 2.

Every time you prepare to take action, fear will to some degree come into play. It is at those times that you must rely on courage.

David Ben-Gurion, the first prime minister of Israel, observed, "Courage is a special kind of knowledge; the knowledge of how to fear what ought to be feared, and how not to fear what ought not to be feared. From this knowledge comes an inner

> "Learning is defined as a change in behavior. You haven't learned a thing until you can take action and use it."
>
> —Don Shula and Ken Blanchard

strength that subconsciously inspires us to push on in the face of great difficulty. What can seem impossible is often possible, with courage." Courage is a releasing force for learning and growth.

## Our Courage Will Be Tested . . . When We Take the High Road Even as Others Treat Us Badly

In 2004 I wrote a book called *Winning with People: Discover the People Principles That Work for You Every Time*. In it is the High Road Principle, which says, "We go to a higher level when we treat others better than they treat us." When it comes to dealing with others, there are really only three routes we can take:

*The low road*—where we treat others worse than they treat us

*The middle road*—where we treat others the same as they treat us

*The high road*—where we treat others better than they treat us[7]

The low road damages relationships and alienates others from us. The middle road may not drive people away, but it doesn't attract them either. But the high road creates positive relationships with others and attracts people to us—even in the midst of conflict.

Taking the high road requires two things. The first is courage. It certainly isn't one's immediate inclination to turn the other cheek and treat people well while they treat you badly. How does one find the courage to do that? By relying on the second thing, about which clergyman Dr. James B. Mooneyhan writes:

> There is a great cancer working at the integrity of our society. It gets in the way of our efficiency and hampers our success. It robs us of the promotions we seek and the prestige we desire. The great tragedy is that none of us are immune to it automatically. Each of us must work to overcome it.

This malignancy is the lack of the ability to forgive. When someone wrongs us we make mental notes to remember what was done or we think of ways to "get back at them." Someone gets the promotion we wanted so badly and resentment toward that person begins to build. Our spouse makes a mistake or does something offensive to us and we see what we can do to get even or at least make sure they never forget the hurt they have caused us.

When we keep score of wrongs committed against us, we reveal a lack of maturity. Theodore Roosevelt once said, "The most important single ingredient in the formula of success is knowing how to get along with people." Those who do not forgive are persons who have not yet learned this truth and they are usually unsuccessful people.

If you wish to improve this area of your life, here are some things that should help. First, practice forgiving . . . Secondly, think good thoughts of those persons . . . It is difficult to have hostile feelings toward one in whom you see good. Finally, let people know through your actions that you are one who can forgive and forget. This will gain respect for you.

Remember this: Committing an injury puts you below your enemy; taking revenge only makes you even with him, but forgiving him sets you above.

No one makes the most of his talent in isolation. Becoming your best will require the participation of other people. When you take the high road with others, you make yourself the kind of person others want to work with—and you put yourself in the best position to help others at the same time.

## Our Courage Will Be Tested . . . When Being "Out Front" Makes Us an Easy Target

Many people admire leaders and innovators. Organizations give them honors; historians write books about them; sculptors chisel their images on the face of mountains. However, while many people lift leaders up, others want to knock them down. C. V. White describes this tension well:

> The man who makes a success of an important venture never waits for the crowd. He strikes out for himself. It takes nerve, it takes a lot of grit; but the man that succeeds has both. Anyone can fail. The public admires the man who has enough confidence in himself to take the chance. These chances are the main things after all. The man who tries to succeed must expect to be criticized. Nothing important was ever done but the greater number consulted previously doubted the possibility. Success is the accomplishment of that which people think can't be done.

If you are a leader or even an innovative thinker, you will often be ahead of the crowd, and that will at times make you an easy target. That requires courage.

For many years, I hosted an event in Atlanta called Exchange. It was a weekend leadership experience for executives. I usually did some leadership teaching, brought in some high-profile leaders to answer questions, and arranged a unique leadership experience. One year we took the group to the King Center so that they could be impacted by the life and legacy of a great leader, Martin Luther King Jr. We then took them over to Ebenezer Baptist Church. And as a surprise we had arranged for King's widow, Coretta Scott King, and daughter Bernice to be there so that everyone could meet them.

One question asked of Mrs. King was what it was like being with Dr. King during the civil rights movement, and she talked about the loneliness of being a pioneer and taking new territory. She said that her husband was often misunderstood, and she pointed out how much courage it took to stand alone.

We will almost certainly never have to face the hatred and violence that Martin Luther King Jr. did, but that doesn't mean that we don't need courage to lead. Often leaders are misunderstood, their motives are misconstrued, and their actions are criticized. That, too, can be a test— one that makes us stronger and sharpens our talent if only we have the courage to endure it.

## Our Courage Will Be Tested . . . Whenever We Face Obstacles to Our Progress

Advice columnist Ann Landers wrote, "If I were asked to give what I consider the single most useful bit of advice for all humanity, it would be this: Expect trouble as an inevitable part of life and when it comes, hold your head high, look it squarely in the eye and say, 'I will be bigger than you. You cannot defeat me."

Adversity is always the partner of progress. Anytime we want to move forward, obstacles, difficulties, problems, and predicaments are going to get in the way. We should expect nothing less. And we should even welcome such things. Novelist H. G. Wells asked, "What on earth would a man do with himself if something didn't stand in his way?" Why would he make such a comment? Because he recognized that adversity is our friend, even though it doesn't feel that

> Adversity is always the partner of progress. Anytime we want to move forward, obstacles, difficulties, problems, and predicaments are going to get in the way.

way. Every obstacle we overcome teaches us about ourselves, about our strengths and weaknesses. Every obstacle shapes us. When we succeed in the midst of difficulty, we become stronger, wiser, and more confident. The greatest people in history are those who faced the most difficult challenges with courage and rose to the occasion. That was certainly true of Winston Churchill.

Pat Williams, in his book *American Scandal*, writes about Churchill's last months. He says in 1964, former president and World War II general Dwight D. Eisenhower went to visit the former prime minister.

Eisenhower sat by the bold-spirited leader's bed for a long period of time, neither speaking. After about ten minutes, Churchill slowly raised his hand and painstakingly made the "V" for victory sign, which he had so often flashed to the British public during the war. Eisenhower, fighting back tears, pulled his chair back, stood up, saluted him, and left the room. To his aide out in the hallway, Eisenhower said, "I just said good-bye to Winston, but you never say farewell to courage."[8]

## TALENT + COURAGE = A TALENT-PLUS PERSON
## PUTTING THE TALENT-PLUS FORMULA INTO ACTION

It's tempting to learn about the life of someone like Churchill or Eisenhower and believe that certain people are born with courage and are destined for greatness while others must sit on the sidelines and simply admire them. But I don't think that is true. I believe that anyone can develop courage. If you desire to become a more courageous person, then do the following:

### 1. Look for Courage Inside, Not Outside, Yourself

During the Great Depression, Thomas Edison delivered his last public message. In it he said, "My message to you is: Be courageous! I have lived a long time. I have seen history repeat itself again and again. I have seen many depressions in business. Always America has come out stronger and more prosperous. Be as brave as your fathers before you. Have faith! Go forward!" Edison knew that when we experience fear, we must be willing to move forward. That is an individual decision. Courage starts internally before it is displayed externally. We must first win the battle within ourselves.

I love the story about the shortest letter to the editor written to England's newspaper the *Daily Mail*. When the editor invited readers to send in their answers to the question, "What's wrong with the world?" writer G. K. Chesterton is reputed to have sent the following:

Dear Sir,
I am.
Yours sincerely,
G. K. Chesterton

The old saying goes, "If we could kick the person responsible for most of our troubles, we wouldn't be able to sit down for a week." Courage, like all other character qualities, comes from within. It begins as a decision we make and grows as we make the choice to follow through. So the first step toward becoming a talent-plus person in the area of courage is to decide to be courageous.

## 2. Grow in Courage by Doing the Right Thing Instead of the Expedient Thing

Florence Nightingale observed, "Courage is . . . the universal virtue of all those who choose to do the right thing over the expedient thing. It is the common currency of all those who do what they are supposed to do in a time of conflict, crisis, and confusion." The acquisition of courage can often be an internal battle. We often desire to do what is most expedient. The problem is that what is easy and expedient is frequently not what is right. Thus the battle. But psychotherapist and author Sheldon Kopp stated, "All the significant battles are waged within self."

As you strive to do what you know to be right, you must know yourself and make sure you are acting in integrity with your core values. There's a saying that inside every individual there are six people. They are . . .

Who You Are Reputed to Be
Who You Are Expected to Be
Who You Were
Who You Wish to Be
Who You Think You Are
Who You Really Are

You must strive to be true to who you really are. If you do and you do the right thing, then you will increase in courage.

## 3. Take Small Steps of Courage to Prepare You for Greater Ones

Most of us want to grow quickly and be done with it. The reality is that genuine growth is slow, and to be successful, we should start with small things and do them every day. St. Francis de Sales advised, "Have patience with all things, but chiefly have patience with yourself. Do not lose courage in considering your own imperfections, but instantly start remedying them—every day begin the task anew."

People's lives change when they change something they do every day. That's how they change the "who they wish to be" into "who they really are." What kinds of things can you do every day? You can have the courage to be positive as you get up in the morning to face the day. You can have the courage to be gracious in defeat. You can have the courage to apologize when you hurt someone or make a mistake. You can have the courage to try something new—any small thing. Each time you display bravery of any kind, you make an investment in your courage. Do that long enough, and you will begin to live a *lifestyle* of courage. And when the bigger risks come, they will seem much smaller to you because you will have become much larger.

> People's lives change when they change something they do every day.

## 4. Recognize That a Leadership Position Won't Give You Courage, but Courage Can Make You a Leader

In my years of teaching leadership, I have found many people who believed that if only they could receive a title or be given a position, that would make them a leader. But life doesn't work that way. Former British prime minister Margaret Thatcher remarked, "Being a leader is a lot like being a lady. If you have to tell people you are one, you aren't." The position doesn't make the leader; the leader makes the position.

In similar fashion, people should not expect the acquisition of a leadership position to give them courage. However, anytime people continually display courage, they will likely become leaders because others will look up to them, emulate them, and follow

> Leadership is "the expression of courage that compels people to do the right thing."
>
> —Jim Mellado

them. Jim Mellado, president of the Willow Creek Association, described leadership as "the expression of courage that compels people to do the right thing."

## 5. Watch Your Horizons Expand with Each Courageous Act

The life you live will expand or shrink in proportion to the measure of courage you display. Those who are willing to take risks, explore their limits, face their shortcomings, and sometimes experience defeat will go farther than people who timidly follow the safe and predictable path. Founder of *Success* magazine, Orison Swett Marden, stated it this way:

> The moment you resolve to take hold of life with all your might and make the most of yourself at any cost, to sacrifice all lesser ambitions to your one great aim, to cut loose from everything that interferes with this aim, to stand alone, firm in your purpose, whatever happens, you set in motion the divine inner forces the Creator has implanted in you for your own development. Live up to your resolve, work at what the Creator meant you to work for the perfecting of His plan, and you will be invincible. No power on earth can hold you back from success.

If you want to become a talent-plus person, you must show courage. There is no other way to reach your potential.

When I began my leadership career, I was very ineffective as a leader. I believed I had talent. I had been able to influence and lead others at every phase of my school career. But when I got out into the real world, I fell far short of my expectations. My talent was being tested, and I was falling short. My problem was that I wanted to please everybody. Making people happy was the most important thing to me. The bottom line was that I lacked the courage to make right but unpopular decisions. How did I turn things around? By making small decisions that were difficult. With each one, I gained more confidence and more courage, and I began to change. The process took me four years.

At the end of that time, I felt I had learned many valuable lessons, and I wrote the following to help me cement what I had learned:

### Courageous Leadership Simply Means I've Developed:

1. Convictions that are stronger than my fears.
2. Vision that is clearer than my doubts.
3. Spiritual sensitivity that is louder than popular opinion.
4. Self-esteem that is deeper than self-protection.
5. Appreciation for discipline that is greater than my desire for leisure.
6. Dissatisfaction that is more forceful than the status quo.
7. Poise that is more unshakeable than panic.
8. Risk taking that is stronger than safety seeking.
9. Right actions that are more robust than rationalization.
10. A desire to see potential reached more than to see people appeased.

You don't have to be great to become a person of courage. You just need to want to reach your potential and to be willing to trade what seems good in the moment for what's best for your potential. That's something you can do regardless of your level of natural talent.

# TALENT + COURAGE
## APPLICATION EXERCISES

1. How often do you fail? The frequency is a sure indication of your inclination to take risks. Successful people understand that failure is a natural part of the process of making progress. For seven days, make it a point to record every failure in a journal or planner. At the end of the week, evaluate your willingness to take risks.

2. Talk to your spouse or a trusted friend and ask where you most need to change and grow. Promise this individual that if he or she will confide in you, you will hold your peace and not defend yourself or make excuses for a week. Then keep your promise and use those seven days to reflect on the person's assessment of you. Remember, it takes courage to seek a truth that may be painful to you.

3. Which do you value more highly, pleasure or progress? One of the ways to assess the honesty of your answers is to examine your goals. Do your goals involve comfort or accomplishment? If pleasure and comfort are higher on your priority list, you may not be taking enough chances to maximize your talent and reach your potential.

4. Plan to develop your courage by doing something uncomfortable or scary once or twice a week for two months. Put them on your calendar and to-do list. These actions can be small. You don't have to skydive or bungee jump, although you can do those kinds of things if you are inclined to. The more actions requiring courage that you take, the braver you will become. Your goal is to develop a lifestyle of courage.

5. When others treat you poorly, how do you respond? Do you respond in kind, giving tit for tat? It's often not easy to take the high road. However, if you can, you will find that your life has less conflict, you will experience less stress, and others will be attracted to you. Begin by forgiving others for past hurts. Make a list of any grudges you are currently holding or ill feelings you are carrying toward others. Then work through them on your own. If you need to go to anyone on the list to forgive him, do so. Then make it a point to treat others better than they treat you, not only for their sake, but also for your own.

# 9
# TEACHABILITY EXPANDS YOUR TALENT

If you are a highly talented person, you may have a tough time with teachability. Why? Because talented people often think they know it all. And that makes it difficult for them to continually expand their talent. Teachability is not so much about competence and mental capacity as it is about *attitude*. It is the desire to listen, learn, and apply. It is the hunger to discover and grow. It is the willingness to learn, unlearn, and relearn. I love the way Hall of Fame basketball coach John Wooden states it: "It's what you learn after you know it all that counts."

When I teach and mentor leaders, I remind them that if they stop learning, they stop leading. But if they remain teachable and keep learning, they will be able to keep making an impact as leaders. Whatever your talent happens to be—whether it's leadership, craftsmanship, entrepreneurship, or something else—you will expand it if you keep expecting and striving to learn. Talented individuals with teachable attitudes become talent-plus people.

## More Than Enough Talent

Who is the most talented person who ever lived? There's really no way for us to make that determination. How would you even pick your criteria? What talent would you value? Intelligence? Creativity? Athletic prowess? Musical ability? Business acumen? Artistic mastery? Charisma? People skills? Professional influence? You could perhaps make a strong argument for any of these criteria. But what if you used *all* of these characteristics to judge who was most talented? If you did, Leonardo da Vinci would certainly be a strong candidate.

Leonardo has been called *Homo Universalis*, a "universal man," for his incredible ability to master diverse disciplines. The term *Renaissance man* was coined for him because he embodied the rebirth movement and displayed so many talents. He was admired by his peers, by his protégés, and by the artists, scientists, and historians who have studied his life. Giorgio Vasari, author of the classic work *The Lives of the Artists*, captured the common opinion of da Vinci when he wrote:

> The greatest gifts often rain down upon human bodies through celestial influences as a natural process, and sometimes in a supernatural fashion a single body is lavishly supplied with such beauty, grace, and ability that wherever the individual turns, each of his actions is so divine that he leaves behind all other men and clearly makes himself known as a genius endowed by God (which he is) rather than created by human artifice. Men saw this in Leonardo da Vinci, who displayed great physical beauty (which has never been sufficiently praised), a more than infinite grace in every action, and an ability so fit and so vast that wherever his mind turned to difficult tasks, he resolved them completely with ease. His great personal strength was joined to dexterity, and his spirit and courage were always regal and magnanimous. And the fame of his name spread so widely that not only was he held in high esteem in his own times, but his fame increased even more after his death.[1]

If Leonardo had only sculpted, he would have been famous as a sculptor. If he had only painted, he still would have been revered as a master. If he had only studied anatomy, hydraulics, and optics, he would have been viewed as a groundbreaking scientist. If he had only engineered fortifications, designed buildings, and manufactured heavy weapons—for which he was employed much of his professional life—he would have been held in high regard. He was a good athlete, a fine musician, and an excellent singer. He assisted the Italian mathematician Luca Pacioli in creating the *Divina Proportione*. He seemed able to do anything.

## HUNGER TO LEARN

What set Leonardo apart? Was it a simple case, as Vasari says, of all talents coming together in a single person? I believe it was more than that. Da Vinci's talent was extraordinary—but so was his teachability. And the evidence for it can be found in his notebooks. They are a physical record of a mind that never stopped discovering and never ceased learning.

Many artists create notebooks to record their ideas and to make practice sketches. For example, Picasso produced 178 sketchbooks during his life, often using them to explore themes and make compositional studies before creating a painting. But Leonardo's notebooks go far beyond an artist's sketches. They display a highly teachable mind at work, and they show the breadth of his learning and the depth of his thinking.

Microsoft founder Bill Gates purchased one of those notebooks in 1994. The notebook is called the Codex Leicester and was created by da Vinci between 1506 and 1510. Its seventy-two pages contain sketches and text on water, light, and several other subjects. Sometimes his writings were motivated by his desire to discover more about art, such as his observations about how light is reflected off paint. Other times, like the great scientists who lived before and after him, he made acute observations and rendered scientific explanations. For example, da Vinci noted that sometimes when viewing the crescent moon in the twilight sky, the entire circular outline of the moon was faintly visible. He deduced that sunlight reflected from the earth's oceans to create the effect, which was confirmed more than a hundred years later.[2]

Gates says, "I've been fascinated by da Vinci's work since I was 10. Leonardo was one of the most amazing people who ever lived. He was a genius in more fields than any scientist of any age, and he was an astonishing painter and sculptor. His notebooks were hundreds of years ahead of their time. They anticipated submarines, helicopters and other modern inventions.

"His scientific 'notebooks' are awe inspiring," continues Gates, "not simply as repositories of his remarkable ideas but as records of a great mind at work. In the pages of the Codex Leicester, he frames important questions, tests concepts, confronts challenges, and strives for answers."[3]

In one notebook, da Vinci wrote, "Iron rusts from disuse; stagnant water loses its purity and in cold weather becomes frozen; even so does inaction sap the vigor of the mind."[4] That distaste for inaction drove his intellectual curiosity his entire life. Leonardo da Vinci's love for learning never stopped. He was learning and writing his discoveries in his notebooks until the very end of his life. And it is the main reason we remember him.

## TEACHABILITY TRUTHS

The good news is that we don't have to have the talent of a Leonardo da Vinci to be teachable. We just need to have the right attitude about learning. To do that, consider the following truths about teaching:

## 1. Nothing Is Interesting If You Are Not Interested

Management guru Philip B. Crosby writes in his book *Quality Is Free*:

> There is a theory of human behavior that says people subconsciously retard their own intellectual growth. They come to rely on clichés and habits. Once they reach the age of their own personal comfort with the world, they stop learning and their mind runs on idle for the rest of their days. They may progress organizationally, they may be ambitious and eager, and they may even work night and day. But they learn no more.[5]

It's a shame when people allow themselves to get in a rut and never climb out. They often miss the best that life has to offer. In contrast, teachable people are fully engaged in life. They get excited about things. They are interested in discovery, discussion, application, and growth. There is a definite relationship between passion and potential.

German philosopher Goethe advised, "Never let a day pass without looking at some perfect work of art, hearing some great piece of music and reading, in part, some great book." The more engaged you are, the more interesting life will be. The more interested you are in exploring and learning, the greater your potential for growth.

> "Never let a day pass without looking at some perfect work of art, hearing some great piece of music and reading, in part, some great book."
>
> —Goethe

## 2. Successful People View Learning Differently from Those Who Are Unsuccessful

After more than thirty-five years of teaching and training people, I've come to realize that successful people think differently from unsuccessful ones. That doesn't mean that unsuccessful people are unable to think the way successful people do. (In fact, I believe that just about anyone can retrain himself to think differently. That's why I wrote *Thinking for a Change*—to help people learn the thinking skills capable of making them more successful.) Those successful thinking patterns pertain to learning as well.

> "A winner knows how much he still has to learn, even when he is considered an expert by others. A loser wants to be considered an expert by others, before he has learned enough to know how little he knows."
>
> —Sydney J. Harris

Teachable people are always open to new ideas and are willing to learn from anyone who has something to offer. American journalist Sydney J. Harris wrote, "A winner knows how much he still has to learn, even when he is considered an expert by others. A loser wants to be considered an expert by others, before he has learned enough to know how little he knows." It's all a matter of attitude.

It's truly remarkable how much a person has to learn before he realizes how little he knows. Back in 1992, I wrote a book called *Developing the Leader Within You*. At the time, I thought, *I've had some success at leadership. I'll write this book, and it will be my contribution to others on this important subject.* I then put *everything* I knew about leadership in that book. But that book was only the beginning. Writing it made me want to learn more about leadership, and my drive to learn went to another level. I searched out more books, lectures, people, and experiences to help me learn. Today, I've written a total of *eight* books on leadership. Am I finished with that topic? No. There are still things to learn—and to teach. My leadership world is expanding, and so am I. The world is vast, and we are so limited. There is much for us to learn—as long as we remain teachable.

## 3. Learning Is Meant to Be a Lifelong Pursuit

It's said that the Roman scholar Cato started to study Greek when he was more than eighty years old. When asked why he was tackling such a difficult task at his age, he replied, "It is the earliest age I have left." Unlike Cato, too many people regard learning as an event instead of a process. Someone told me that only one-third of all adults read an entire book after their last graduation. Why would that be? Because they view education as a period of life, not a way of life!

Learning is an activity that is not restricted by age. It doesn't matter if you're past eighty, like Cato, or haven't yet entered your teens. Author Julio Melara was only eleven years old when he began to acquire major life lessons that he has been able to carry with him into adulthood and to teach others. Here are some of the things he's learned, taken from his book *It Only Takes Everything You've Got!: Lessons for a Life of Success*:

Here is a list of all the jobs you will not find on my resume but lessons that have lasted a lifetime:

- Started cutting grass for profit at age 11

  *Lesson learned*: It is important to give things a clean, professional look.

- Stock clerk at a local food store

  *Lesson learned*: Making sure that if I am going to sell something, the merchandise needs to be in stock.

- Dishwasher at local restaurant

  *Lesson learned*: Somebody always has to do the job no one else wants to do. Also, most people have a lot of food on their plates. (They do not finish what they start.)

- A janitor at an office building

  *Lesson learned*: The importance of cleanliness as it related to image.

- Fry and prep cook at a steak house

  *Lesson learned:* The importance of preparation and the impact of the right presentation.

- Construction helping hand (lug wood and supplies from one place to another)

  *Lesson learned:* I do not want to do this for the rest of my life.

- Sold newspaper subscription for daily paper

  *Lesson learned:* The job of rejection—had to knock on at least 30 doors before I ever sold one subscription.

- Shipping clerk at a plumbing supply house

  *Lesson learned:* Delivering your project or service on time is just as important as selling it.

- Breakfast cook at a 24-hour restaurant stop

  *Lesson learned:* How to do 15 things at once. Also learned about the weird things people like to eat on their eggs.

- Cleaned cars at detailing shop

  *Lesson learned:* The importance of details (washing vs. detailing). You can pay $15 just to wash the outside of the car or $150 to clean the car inside and out and cover all the details. Details are a pain, but details are valuable.

- Shoe salesman at a retail store

  *Lesson learned:* To sell customers what they want and like. Also, learned to compliment people and be sincere.

- Busboy at a local diner

  *Lesson learned:* People enjoy being served with a smile and they love a clean table.

Every stage of life presents lessons to be learned. We can choose to be teachable and continue to learn them, or we can be closed-minded and stop growing. The decision is ours.

## 4. Talented People Can Be the Toughest to Teach

The other day I was having lunch with my friend Sam Chand, and we were talking about talent and teachability. Sam mentioned that he had a lot of musical talent. "I can play any type of keyboard, accordion, drums, guitar, saxophone, fiddle," he said. "I can basically play anything. If I hear a tune once, I can play it."

That sounds like a wonderful gift. But Sam said that when he decided to raise his saxophone playing to a new level by taking jazz lessons, he quickly became frustrated. Because he had played by ear and music had always come so easily to him, he didn't possess the patience and perseverance he needed to succeed. Eventually he gave up.

> One of the paradoxes of life is that the things that initially *make* you successful are rarely the things that *keep* you successful.

One of the paradoxes of life is that the things that initially *make* you successful are rarely the things that *keep* you successful. You have to remain open to new ideas and be willing to learn new skills. J. Konrad Hole advises,

If you cannot be teachable, having talent won't help you.
If you cannot be flexible, having a goal won't help you.
If you cannot be grateful, having abundance won't help you.
If you cannot be mentorable, having a future won't help you.
If you cannot be durable, having a plan won't help you.
If you cannot be reachable, having success won't help you.[6]

This may sound strange, but don't let your talent get in the way of your success. Remain teachable.

## 5. Pride Is the Number One Hindrance to Teachability

Author, trainer, and speaker Dave Anderson believes that the number one cause of management failure is pride. He writes,

> There are many reasons managers fail. For some, the organization outgrows them. Others don't change with the times. . . A few make poor character choices. They look good for a while but eventually discover they can't get out of their own way. Increasingly more keep the wrong people too long because they don't want to admit they made a mistake or have high turnover become a negative reflection on them. Some failures had brilliant past track records but start using their success as a license to build a fence around what they had rather than continue to risk and stretch to build it to even higher levels. But all these causes for management failure have their root in one common cause: pride. In simplest terms, pride is devastating . . . the pride that inflates your sense of self-worth and distorts your perspective of reality.

While envy is the deadly sin that comes from feelings of *inferiority*, the deadly sin of pride comes from feelings of *superiority*. It creates an arrogance of success, an inflated sense of self-worth accompanied by a distorted perspective of reality. Such an attitude leads to a loss of desire to learn and an unwillingness to change. It makes a person unteachable.

# THE PROBLEMS WITH PRIDE

Pride is such a huge barrier to success and the development of talent that we need to examine it in greater detail. Here are just a few of the negative effects of pride as they relate to teachability:

## Pride Closes Our Minds to New Ideas

I've yet to meet a conceited, arrogant, or prideful person who possessed a teachable spirit. How about you? The writer of Proverbs observed,

"Do you see a man who is wise in his own eyes? There is more hope for a fool than for him."[7] Teachability in its most fundamental form is a willingness to open our minds to new ideas. Pride prevents that.

## Pride Closes Our Minds to Feedback

Stephen Covey comments, "It takes humility to seek feedback. It takes wisdom to understand it, analyze it, and appropriately act on it." I've already confessed to you that I have not always been a good listener. But I've learned over the years that I cannot do anything of real value alone. Achievement requires teamwork, and none of us is as smart as all of us. Having learned that lesson, I am continually asking members of my team to give me input on my ideas. I find this most valuable before team members or I take action, but I also solicit feedback throughout the process. The communication process looks something like this:

TEAM
FEEDBACK

IDEA

TEAM
INPUT

CORRECTION

TEAM
FEEDBACK

ACTION

The process begins with an idea, which becomes improved through the interaction of the team. But what also happens is that because of the input and feedback I receive, my next idea improves. As long as I am willing to listen to and embrace feedback, it not only improves whatever task we're working on; it also improves me!

## Pride Prevents Us from Admitting Mistakes

The commanding admiral ordered a group of navy pilots on maneuvers to maintain radio silence. But one young pilot mistakenly turned on his radio and was heard to mutter, "Man, am I fouled up!"

> "The most important thing in life is not to capitalize on our gains. Any fool can do that. The really important thing is to profit from our losses. That requires intelligence; and makes the difference between a man of sense and a fool."
>
> —William Bolitho

When the admiral heard it, he grabbed the microphone from the radio operator and barked into it, "Will the pilot who broke radio silence identify himself immediately!"

After a long pause, a voice on the radio was heard to say, "I may be fouled up, but I'm not *that* fouled up!"

Fear may keep some people from admitting mistakes, but pride is just as often the cause. The problem is that one of the best ways we grow is by admitting mistakes and learning from them. Writer William Bolitho observed, "The most important thing in life is not to capitalize on our gains. Any fool can do that. The really important thing is to profit from our losses. That requires intelligence; and makes the difference between a man of sense and a fool."

## Pride Keeps Us from Making Needed Changes

Anytime we do a job and think we did it well, we become reluctant to make changes to our work. We become dedicated to the status quo instead of progress. Why? Because we have an emotional investment in it. For example, anytime in the past when I've taken a leadership position in which I inherited a staff, I had little reluctance to make changes for the good of the organization. If someone wasn't doing the job and would not or could not grow and improve, I would replace him or her. However, if someone I selected was falling short, I was much slower to make the needed change. Pride caused me to defend what sometimes should not have been defended. When it comes to changing others, we want to do it immediately. But changing ourselves? Not so fast! That's a problem.

# HOW TO OVERCOME A PRIDE PROBLEM

If pride is an obstacle to your growth, then you need to take some deliberate and strategic steps to overcome it. That may not be easy. Founding Father Benjamin Franklin observed, "There is perhaps not one of our natural passions so hard to subdue as pride. Beat it down, stifle it, mortify it as much as one pleases, it is still alive. Even if I could conceive that I had completely overcome it, I should probably be proud of my humility." To start the process, here is what I suggest:

## 1. Recognize and Admit Your Pride

The first and most difficult step in overcoming pride is recognizing that it's a problem since those who are bound by it are often unaware of it. To defeat pride, we need to embrace humility, and few desire that. Writer and apologist C. S. Lewis remarked, "If anyone would like to acquire humility, I can, I think, tell him the first step. The first step is to realize that one is proud. And a biggish step, too. At least, nothing whatever can be done before it. If you think you are not conceited, you are very conceited indeed."

To try to maintain perspective, I have carried a poem by Saxon White Kessinger with me. And when I'm starting to think that I'm really important, I pull it out and read it. The poem is called "Indispensable Man."

Sometime when you're feeling important;
  Sometime when your ego's in bloom
Sometime when you take it for granted
  You're the best qualified in the room,

Sometime when you feel that your going
  Would leave an unfillable hole,
Just follow these simple instructions
  And see how they humble your soul;
Take a bucket and fill it with water,
  Put your hand in it up to the wrist,
Pull it out and the hole that's remaining
  Is a measure of how you'll be missed.

You can splash all you wish when you enter,
  You may stir up the water galore,
But stop and you'll find that in no time
  It looks quite the same as before.

The moral of this quaint example
  Is do just the best that you can,
Be proud of yourself but remember,
  There's no indispensable man.

People have a natural tendency to believe—or to hope—that they are indispensable, that the world will stop and take notice if anything happens to them. But I have to tell you, as someone who has presided over many funerals, life goes on. When someone dies, the family and friends closest to him grieve. But the rest of the people who attend the reception after the funeral are more worried about the potato salad than the dearly departed. So Kessinger's advice is really good: do your best but remember that no one is indispensable.

## 2. Express Gratitude Often

Once when I was chatting with Zig Ziglar, he told me that he thought the least expressed of all virtues is gratitude. I think that is true. I also think that it is the most appreciated expression by recipients. I think Oprah Winfrey's suggestion for cultivating gratitude is excellent. She says,

> Keep a grateful journal. Every night, list five things that happened this day that you are grateful for. What it will begin to do is change your perspective of your day and your life. If you can learn to focus on what you have, you will always see that the universe is abundant; you will have more. If you concentrate on what you don't have, you will never have enough.

Therein lies the problem of people filled with selfish pride. They are not grateful because they never think they get as much as they deserve. Expressing gratitude continually helps to break this kind of pride.

## 3. Laugh at Yourself

I love the Chinese proverb that says, "Blessed are they that laugh at themselves, for they shall never cease to be entertained." People who have the problem of pride rarely laugh at themselves. But engaging in humor at your own expense shows that pride isn't a problem, and it is a way of breaking a pride problem.

> "Blessed are they that laugh at themselves, for they shall never cease to be entertained."
>
> —Chinese proverb

There's a story about a judge named Robert S. Gawthorp who had a distinguished career on the bench beginning in 1977 at age forty-four. But he refused to take himself too seriously and maintained his sense of humor. Gawthorp commented, "Just because people stand up when you walk into court and you wear a black dress to work and sit on an elevated chair . . . you have to remind yourself you're just another person who happens to be a lawyer elected to serve as a judge." To remind himself of this, he used to keep a small framed statement near his private courtroom door—a gift from relatives—that said, "To us, you'll always be just the same old jackass."[8]

## TALENT + *TEACHABILITY* = A TALENT-PLUS PERSON PUTTING THE TALENT-PLUS FORMULA INTO ACTION

If you want to expand your talent, you must become teachable. That is the pathway to growth. Futurist and author John Naisbitt believes that "the most important skill to acquire is learning how to learn." Here is what I suggest as you pursue teachability and become a talent-plus person:

### 1. Learn to Listen

The first step in teachability is learning to listen. American writer and philosopher Henry David Thoreau wrote, "It takes two to speak the truth—one to speak and one to hear." Being a good listener helps us to know people better, to learn what they have learned, and to show them that we value them as individuals.

Abraham Lincoln was one of the most teachable presidents. When he began his career, he was not a great leader. But he grew into his presidency. He was always an avid listener, and as president, he opened the doors of the White House to anyone who wanted to express an opinion to him. He called these frequent sessions his "public opinion baths." He also asked nearly everyone he met to send him ideas and opinions. As a result, he received hundreds of letters every month—many more than other presidents had received in the past. From this practice, he learned much. And even if he didn't embrace the arguments, he learned more about how the letter writers thought, and he used that knowledge to help him craft his policies and persuade others to adopt them.

As you go through each day, remember that you can't learn if you're always talking. As the old saying goes, "There's a reason you have one mouth but two ears." Listen to others, remain humble, and you will begin to learn things every day that can help you to expand your talent.

## 2. Understand the Learning Process

Sometimes things are painfully obvious and need little explanation. For example, read the following humorous warnings and pieces of advice collected from the military:

- "Aim towards enemy."—Instruction printed on U.S. rocket launcher
- "When the pin is pulled, Mr. Grenade is not our friend." —U.S. Army
- "If the enemy is in range, so are you."—Infantry Journal
- "It is generally inadvisable to eject directly over the area you just bombed."—U.S. Air Force Manual
- "If your attack is going too well, you're probably walking into an ambush."—Infantry Journal
- "Never tell the platoon sergeant you have nothing to do." —Unknown army recruit
- "Don't draw fire; it irritates the people around you."—Your buddies
- "If you see a bomb technician running, try to keep up with him."—U.S. Ammo Troop[9]

When things aren't so obvious, it is helpful to understand the learning process in order to learn and grow. Here is how it typically works:

STEP 1: Act.
STEP 2: Look for your mistakes and evaluate.
STEP 3: Search for a way to do it better.
STEP 4: Go back to step 1.

> The greatest enemy
> of learning is knowing.

Remember, the greatest enemy of learning is knowing, and the goal of all learning is action, not knowledge. If what you are doing does not in some way contribute to what you or others are doing in life, then question its value and be prepared to make changes.

### 3. Look for and Plan Teachable Moments

I recently read a book called *The Laws of Lifetime Growth* that presents an excellent perspective on this idea. The second law states, "Always make your learning greater than your experience." Authors Dan Sullivan and Catherine Nomura go on to explain,

> Continual learning is essential for lifetime growth. You can have a great deal of experience and be no smarter for all the things you've done, seen, and heard. Experience alone is no guarantee of lifetime growth. But if you regularly transform your experience into new lessons, you will make each day of your life a source of growth. The smartest people are those who can transform even the smallest events or situations into breakthroughs in thinking and action. Look at all of life as a school and every experience as a lesson, and your learning will always be greater than your experience.[10]

The authors are describing a lifestyle of teachability. If you look for opportunities to learn in every situation, you will become a talent-plus person and expand your talent to its potential. But you can also take another step beyond that and actively seek out and plan teachable moments. You can do that by reading books, visiting places that will inspire you, attending events that will prompt you to pursue change, listening to lessons, and spending time with people who will stretch you and expose you to new experiences.

I've had the privilege to spend time with many remarkable people, and the natural reward has been the opportunity to learn. In my personal relationships, I've also gravitated toward people from whom I can learn. My closest friends are people who challenge my thinking—and often change it. They lift me up in many ways. And I've found that I often live out something

> "Make your friends your teachers and mingle the pleasures of conversation with the advantages of instruction."
>
> —Baltasar Gracian

stated by Spanish philosopher and writer Baltasar Gracian: "Make your friends your teachers and mingle the pleasures of conversation with the advantages of instruction." You can do the same. Cultivate friendships with people who challenge and add value to you, and try to do the same for them. It will change your life.

## 4. Make Your Teachable Moments Count

Years ago I saw a *Peanuts* cartoon by Charles Schulz that showed Charlie Brown at the beach building a magnificent sand castle. With it completed, he stood back to admire his work, at which point he and his work were engulfed by a downpour that leveled his beautiful castle. In the last frame, he says, "There must be a lesson here, but I don't know what it is."

Unfortunately that's the way many people feel after a potentially valuable experience. Even people who are strategic about seeking teachable moments can miss the whole point of the experience. I say this because for thirty years I've been a speaker at conferences and workshops—events that are designed to help people learn. But I've found that many people walk away from an event and do very little with what they heard after closing their notebooks. It would be like a jewelry designer going to a gem merchant to buy fine gems, placing them carefully into a case, and then putting that case on the shelf to collect dust. What's the value of acquiring the gems if they're never going to be used?

We tend to focus on learning events instead of the learning process. Because of this, I try to help people take action steps that will help them implement what they learn. I suggest that in their notes, they use a code to mark things that jump out at them:

**T** indicates you need to spend some time thinking on that point.

**C** indicates something you need to change.

☺ A smiley face means you are doing that thing particularly well.

**A** indicates something you need to apply.

**S** means you need to share that information with someone else.

After the conference I recommend that they create to-do lists based on what they marked, then schedule time to follow through.

### 5. Ask Yourself, Am I Really Teachable?

Someone sent me a list of statements that are reported to have come from actual employee performance evaluations. They display the lack of teachability at its most humorous:

- Since my last report, this employee has reached rock bottom and has started to dig.
- Works well when under constant supervision and when cornered like a rat.
- When she opens her mouth, it seems that it is only to change feet.
- He would be out of his depth in a parking lot puddle.
- This young lady had delusions of adequacy.

- He sets low personal standards and consistently fails to achieve them.

- This employee should go far, and the sooner he starts, the better.

- He doesn't have ulcers, but he is a carrier.

- He's been working with glue too much.

- He brings a lot of joy whenever he leaves the room.

- If you see two people talking and one looks bored, he's the other one.

- Gates are down, the lights are flashing, but the train isn't coming.

- If you give him a penny for his thoughts, he'd give you change.

- Takes him two hours to watch 60 Minutes.

- The wheel is turning but the hamster is dead.

- Some drink from the fountain of knowledge; he only gargled.[11]

I've said it before, but it bears repeating: all the good advice in the world won't help if you don't have a teachable spirit.

To know whether you are *really* open to new ideas and new ways of doing things, answer the following questions:

1. Am I open to other people's ideas?

2. Do I listen more than I talk?

3. Am I open to changing my opinion based on new information?

4. Do I readily admit when I am wrong?

5. Do I observe before acting on a situation?

6. Do I ask questions?

7. Am I willing to ask a question that will expose my ignorance?

8. Am I open to doing things in a way I haven't done before?

9. Am I willing to ask for directions?

10. Do I act defensive when criticized, or do I listen openly for the truth?

If you answered no to one or more of these questions, then you have room to grow in the area of teachability. You need to soften your attitude and learn humility, and remember the words of John Wooden: "Everything we know we learned from someone else!"

> "Everything we know we learned from someone else!"
>
> —John Wooden

Thomas Edison was the guest of the governor of North Carolina when the politician complimented him on his creative genius

"I am not a great inventor," countered Edison.

"But you have over a thousand patents to your credit," the governor stated.

"Yes, but about the only invention I can really claim as absolutely original is the phonograph," Edison replied.

"I'm afraid I don't understand what you mean," the governor remarked.

"Well," explained Edison, "I guess I'm an awfully good sponge. I absorb ideas from every course I can, and put them to practical use. Then I improve them until they become of some value. The ideas which I use are mostly the ideas of other people who don't develop them themselves."

What a remarkable description of someone who used teachability to expand his talent! That is what a talent-plus person does. That is what all of us should strive to do.

# TALENT + *TEACHABILITY* APPLICATION EXERCISES

1. How would you describe your attitude toward teachability? To get a realistic view, name all the things within the last twelve months that you initiated and followed through with in order to learn. (If your list is short, your attitude is probably not as good as you think.)

2. On a scale from 1 to 10 (with 10 the highest), how talented do you think you are in general? How talented in your area of greatest expertise? If you rate yourself above a 7 in either area, you may be prone to resist learning because of either pride or a belief that you already know "enough." These attitudes can be a major hindrance to your teachability. To combat them, employ gratitude and laughter to help you change. For a month, keep a gratitude journal similar to the one Oprah Winfrey describes. Or make it a point to find something funny in mistakes you made in the last fourteen days and tell others about it in a humorous way. (If they look shocked or don't laugh, it probably means you take yourself too seriously and you need to do this kind of thing often until you get different responses.)

3. For the next week, practice active listening. Make it a point to ask others for their advice and to withhold advice you would usually give. At the end of each day, write down something you learned by being attentive to others.

4. Seek out, plan, and schedule teachable moments for the next year. Select one conference to attend, one inspiring location to visit, a minimum of six books to read, another six lessons or books to listen to, and

at least two important people to meet. Don't forget to create an action plan to apply what you've learned after each of these events.

5.  Take the advice of Ian Harvey, CEO of London-based BTG, who asks people in his inner circle to tell him:

> *Two things he should stop doing*
> *Two things he should keep doing*
> *Two things he should start doing*

# 10
# CHARACTER PROTECTS YOUR TALENT

Many people with talent make it into the limelight, but the ones who have neglected to develop strong character rarely stay there long. Absence of strong character eventually topples talent. Why? Because people cannot climb beyond the limitations of their character. Talented people are sometimes tempted to take shortcuts. Character prevents that. Talented people may feel superior and expect special privileges. Character helps them to know better. Talented people are praised for what others see them build. Character builds what's inside them. Talented people have the potential to be difference makers. Character makes a difference in them. Talented people are often a gift to the world. Character protects that gift.

When it comes to talent, everything is not always as it seems to the casual observer. Sometimes what appears to be a huge success isn't. And in time, the truth comes out. That was the case for Dr. Hwang Woo Suk.

## STRONG ON THE SURFACE

In 2004, *Time* published its annual list of "People Who Mattered" in a special issue of the magazine. Among those cited was Hwang Woo Suk. The brief article accompanying his picture stated,

A veterinarian by training, Hwang began to research cloning for a practical purpose: he wanted to create a better cow. But his work didn't stop in the barnyard. Hwang and his team at Seoul National University became the first to clone human embryos capable of yielding viable stem cells that might one day cure countless diseases. While such research raises troubling ethical questions, Hwang has already proved that human cloning is no longer science fiction, but a fact of life.[1]

The recognition by *Time* was just the latest in many honors and much adulation Hwang had received. His was an incredible success story. He grew up in a poor mountain town in South Korea. The son of a widow, he had worked his way through school, earning money by laboring on a farm. After receiving his bachelor's degree, he was advised to become a medical doctor. But he had another vision. He wanted to create a genetically superior cow for his nation. He earned his doctorate in veterinary medicine, and then after a couple of years practicing as a veterinarian, he entered the field of scientific research.

His talent was incredible—his drive remarkable. Both carried him all the way to a professorship at Seoul National University. It was there that he first gained attention in the scientific community. In 1999 he announced that he had succeeded in cloning a dairy cow. He became a national celebrity in South Korea. But he made a much greater impression in early 2004 when he announced that he had succeeded in creating human embryonic stem cells through cloning. Up to that time most experts around the world believed that cloning any kind of primate would be impossible because of the complexity of the genetic structure. Hwang followed his announcement to the media with an article in a prestigious scientific journal.

In 2005, Hwang announced additional breakthroughs and published them as well. He also announced that he had successfully cloned a dog—an Afghan hound that he named Snuppy. Hwang became an international celebrity among scientists and a national hero in Korea where he was a favorite of the nation's president. He was regarded as one of the top experts on stem cells in the world. He already held the prestigious POSCO (Pohang Iron and Steel Company) Chair as a professor at Seoul National University. To that were added an appointment to lead the World Stem Cell Hub, the title "Supreme Scientist" by Korea's Ministry of Science and Technology, and the creation of a postage stamp in his honor, depicting a man in a wheelchair getting up and walking as a result of his research. And he was receiving the equivalent of millions of dollars in financial support for his work. His talent and hard work had paid off, and he was at the pinnacle of his career and one of the most respected scientists in the world.

# QUESTIONS

But later that year a shadow was cast over Hwang's work. An American scientist with whom he had published his stem cell research suddenly announced that he would no longer collaborate with Hwang. The other scientist said his reason was a concern about the way eggs had been collected from donors during Hwang's work. Soon afterward, another colleague of Hwang, Roh Sung-il, admitted that he had collected eggs from their junior researchers and had paid some donors, both ethical violations. Of great concern was the possibility that donors had been coerced. Hwang claimed that he hadn't been aware of Roh's actions until after the fact and that he later hadn't identified the researchers as egg donors to protect their privacy.

Despite these ethical concerns, support for Hwang remained high. In South Korea, people who criticized him were often deemed unpatriotic. There were large public rallies to support the scientist. And Korea's president, Roh Moo-hyun, had always supported Hwang. He stated, "It is not possible nor desirable to prohibit research, just because there are concerns that it may lead to a direction that is deemed unethical," and "Politicians have a responsibility to manage bioethical controversies, not to get in the way of this outstanding research and progress."[2] What mattered most to the people was that there had been a scientific breakthrough.

However, while most of his countrymen cheered, a group of young Korean scientists grew skeptical of his claims. And a Korean investigative television show, similar to 60 Minutes in the United States, criticized Hwang's research methods and questioned his work. In response, Hwang offered to resign from all of his official posts, but also defended himself. "I was blinded by work and my drive for achievement," he stated.[3] Even as late as December 2005, Hwang insisted that he had merely acted to protect the identity of the egg donors.[4] A month later, the truth came out.

# THE REAL STORY

Things began to unravel when a journal that had published one of Hwang's articles issued a retraction and Seoul National University created a panel to investigate Hwang's work. On January 10, 2006, the panel announced an amazing conclusion: Hwang had fabricated all of his stem cell research.[5] Then other reports surfaced, saying Hwang had forced one female researcher to donate her own eggs after she accidentally knocked over petri dishes containing eggs from other donors.[6] Questions followed about how he had spent $2.6 million of the nearly $40 million in funding he had received.[7] On May 12, 2006, Hwang was indicted on embezzlement and bioethics law violations.

Had Hwang told the truth about anything? Was there any evidence that the scientist really did have talent? Or were all of his claims lies? No, as it turns out, he did tell the truth about one breakthrough—Snuppy the Afghan hound. Hwang and his team truly *had* been the first in the world to clone a dog. But the rest simply wasn't true.

What happened to Hwang Woo Suk? Had his talent let him down? No, he had enough talent. What failed him was his character. Because it was weak, it neglected to protect his talent. And now his talent—no matter how great—is irrelevant. His career is over.

## THE COMPONENTS OF CHARACTER

People are like icebergs. There's much more to them than meets the eye. When you look at an iceberg, only about 15 percent is visible—that's talent. The rest—their character—is below the surface, hidden. It's what they think and never share with others. It's what they do when no one is watching them. It's how they react to terrible traffic and other everyday aggravations. It's how they handle failure—and success. The greater their

> People are like icebergs. There's much more to them than meets the eye.

talent is, the greater their need is for strong character "below the surface" to sustain them. If they are too "top heavy" with talent, then they are likely to get into trouble, as Dr. Hwang did.

Tim Elmore, who worked for me many years and is the founder and president of Growing Leaders, is the first person I heard compare character to an iceberg. When he speaks to college students, he often tells some little-known details about the infamous sinking of the *Titanic*:

The huge and unsinkable ship received five iceberg warnings that fateful night of April 14, 1912, just before it went down. When the sixth message came in during the wee hours of the next morning, "Look out for icebergs," the operator wired back, "Shut up! I'm busy." Those were his last words over the wire before it all happened. Exactly thirty minutes later, the great vessel—the one whose captain said even God couldn't sink this ship—was sinking . . . They underestimated the power of the iceberg and overestimated their own strength. What an accurate description of so many people today.

No one can expect to succeed without strong character below the surface to protect his talent and sustain him during difficult times. Character holds us steady, no matter how rough the storm becomes. Or to put it another way, as David McLendon did when we spent time together recently, "Character is the pedestal that determines how much weight a person can sustain. If your character is the size of a tooth pick, you can only sustain a postage stamp. If your character is as thick as a column, you can sustain a roof."

So what exactly comprises character? Ask a dozen people and you'll get a dozen answers. I believe it boils down to four elements: (1) self-discipline, (2) core values, (3) a sense of identity, and (4) integrity. Let's consider each of them:

## 1. Self-Discipline

At the most basic level, self-discipline is the ability to do what is right even when you don't feel like doing it. Outstanding leaders and achievers throughout history understood this. Greek philosopher Plato asserted, "The first and best victory is to conquer self."

> Self-discipline is the ability to do what is right even when you don't feel like doing it.

The greatest victories are internal ones. Oswald Sanders, the author of the book on leadership that launched my personal journey as a leader, *Spiritual Leadership*, wrote that the future is with the disciplined. He said that without self-discipline, a leader's other gifts—however great—will never realize their maximum potential. That's true not only of leaders but also of anyone who wants to reach his or her potential. Talent alone is never enough. A person must have talent plus character. The battle for self-discipline is won within. The notable mountain climber Sir Edmund Hillary observed, "It's not the mountains we conquer, but ourselves."

One of the joys of my life is playing golf. I only wish my talent matched my passion! I have had the privilege of playing the East Lake course in Atlanta, home course of golf legend Bobby Jones, considered by some to be the greatest golfer who ever played the game. The club house is filled with pictures of him playing and with many of his championship trophies. Yet many people don't know that Jones's most significant victory was over himself.

Jones began playing golf at age five and won his first tournament at age six. By age twelve he was winning tournaments against adults. But Jones had a temper. His nickname was "Club Thrower." An older gentleman called Grandpa Bart, who had retired from golf but worked in the pro shop, recognized Jones's talent *and* his character issues. After Jones made it to the third round of the U.S. Amateur Championship, the older man advised, "Bobby, you are good enough to win that tournament, but you'll never win until you can control that temper of yours. You miss a shot— you get upset—and then you lose." Jones did master his temper and won his first U.S. Open when he was twenty-one. Grandpa Bart used to say, "Bobby was fourteen when he mastered the game of golf, but he was twenty-one when he mastered himself."

> "What we do on some great occasion will probably depend on what we already are; and what we are will be the result of previous years of self-discipline."
>
> —Henry Parry Liddon

English theologian and orator Henry Parry Liddon observed, "What we do on some great occasion will probably depend on what we already are; and what we are will be the result of previous years of self-discipline." The first step to strong character is conquering self.

## 2. Core Values

Our core values are the principles we live by every day. They define what we believe and how we live. Ideally we should write out our core values so that they become a clear beacon we can always use to guide us.

One person I most admire is John Wooden, the Hall of Fame former coach of UCLA's basketball team. When he graduated from grade school at twelve years old, his father gave him a seven-point creed. From that time, Wooden has carried a written copy of that creed with him every day. Here is what it says:

1. Be true to yourself.

2. Help others.

3. Make each day your masterpiece.

4. Drink deeply from good books, especially the Bible.

5. Make friendship a fine art.

6. Build a shelter against a rainy day.

7. Pray for guidance and give thanks for your blessings every day.

I had read about the creed, and when I got to meet Coach Wooden, I asked him about it. Sitting in a restaurant at breakfast, he pulled a copy out of his pocket and showed it to me. Of course, since he has it memorized, he doesn't need to carry a copy with him, but it has been his lifelong practice. Most important, he has always carried it in his heart and sought to live it out every day.

> "The man who has no inner life is the slave of his surroundings."
>
> —Henri Frederic Amiel

Swiss philosopher Henri Frederic Amiel stated, "The man who has no inner life is the slave of his surroundings." Core values give order and structure to an individual's inner life, and when that inner life is in order, a person can navigate almost anything the world throws at him.

## 3. A Sense of Identity

When it comes to character, each of us must answer the critical question, "Who am I?" That answer often provides the motivation to practice self-discipline. It is fundamental for the identification of core values. And it helps to establish emotional security. Our sense of security—or lack of it—often drives what we do.

American novelist Nathaniel Hawthorne recognized this truth: "No man can for any considerable time wear one face to himself and another to the multitude without finally getting bewildered as to which is the true one." How do you identify yourself? Where does your personal value come from? What is your motivation as it relates to money and power?

If you live with a chip on your shoulder, believe deep down you have no intrinsic value, or see yourself as a victim, you will have a distorted view of yourself

> People are set up to fail if they envision what they want to do before they figure out what kind of person they should be.

and your surroundings. That, in turn, will impact your character. No matter how hard you try, you cannot consistently behave in a way that is inconsistent with how you see yourself. Thus, a strong and accurate sense of identity is essential. To paraphrase author Ruth Barton, people are set up to fail if they envision what they want to do before they figure out what kind of person they should be.

## 4. Integrity

The final component in strong character is integrity, which is an alignment of values, thoughts, feelings, and actions. People who possess the consistency that comes with strong integrity can be very compelling. In his book *American Scandal*, Pat Williams tells the story of Mahatma Gandhi's trip to England to speak before Parliament. The British government had opposed Indian independence, and Gandhi, one of its most vocal proponents, had often been threatened, arrested, and jailed as a result. Gandhi spoke eloquently and passionately for nearly two hours, after which the packed hall gave him a standing ovation.

Afterward, a reporter asked Gandhi's assistant, Mahadev Desai, how the Indian statesman had been able to deliver such a speech without any notes.

"You don't understand Gandhi," Desai responded. "You see, what he thinks is what he feels. What he feels is what he says. What he says is what he does. What Gandhi feels, what he thinks, what he says, and what he does are all the same. He does not need notes."

When values, thoughts, feelings, and actions are in alignment, a person becomes focused and his character is strengthened. Visually it could be represented by this:

However, when these components aren't aligned, it creates confusion and internal conflict, which looks more like this:

Developing talent without developing character is a dead end. It won't take people where they want to go. The lives of people who are long on talent but short on character always get out of balance.

A joint study conducted by Korn/Ferry International and the UCLA Graduate School of Management asked 1,300 senior executives to identify the top trait needed to enhance a business executive's effectiveness. Coming in first was integrity. In second place was concern for results, with responsibility third. What's true for the boardroom is also true in the classroom, living room, soup kitchen, or gym. If you want your talent to take you far, you need to protect that talent with integrity.

## CHARACTER COMMUNICATES

The choice to develop strong character may not be the most important one to make the *most* of your talent. But it is certainly the most important to make sure you don't make the *least* of your talent. You can't really underestimate its impact. Entrepreneur Roger Babson, who founded Babson College and Webber International University, asserted, "A character standard is far more important than even a gold standard. The success of all economic systems is still dependent upon both righteous leaders and righteous people. In the last analysis, our national future depends upon our national character—that is, whether it is spiritually or materially minded."

As I hope I've already made clear, character creates a foundation upon which the structure of your talent and your life can build. If there are cracks in that foundation, you cannot build much. That's why you must first develop within before you can achieve much without. But once you build strong character, it does more than provide a platform for your personal success and the maximization of your talent. It also impacts others and allows you to build with them. It does that through what it communicates to people:

### 1. Character Communicates Consistency

Cultural anthropologist Margaret Mead stated, "What people say, what people do, and what people say they do are entirely different things." That is true of people who live without character, without integrity. Such people communicate confusion to others. They can say anything they like, but their actions determine the message we receive. It was philosopher-poet Ralph Waldo Emerson who said, "What you do thunders so loudly in my ears I cannot hear what you say."

Amazingly there are people who actually promote this inconsistency. Designer Ralph Lauren was quoted as saying, "The crux of a person's identity . . . resides in the trappings, not in the person himself . . . One needn't be well read, so long as one surrounds himself with books. One needn't play the piano, so long as one has a piano. In short, one can be whoever one wants to be. Or—more accurately—one can seem to be whoever one wants to be."[8] While one may be able to make an *impression* with "trappings," the real person always comes through in the end. Impressions are like shadows—they disappear when a strong enough light is shone on them. Character is the genuine article—and the more you shine light on it, the more of its details you can see. Character shows that who you are and who you appear to be are one and the same, and that, according to Greek philosopher Socrates, is the first key to greatness.

> Character shows that who you are and who you appear to be are one and the same, and that is the first key to greatness.

## 2. Character Communicates Choices

Earlier in this chapter, I mentioned that Bobby Jones needed to overcome a terrible temper to succeed at golf. Not only did Jones do that, but he actually became a model of sportsmanship and character. Both could be seen in his play. During the final play-off of a U.S. Open tournament, Jones's ball ended up in the rough just off the fairway. As he set up to play his shot, he accidentally caused his ball to move. He immediately turned to the marshals and announced the foul. The marshals discussed the situation among themselves. They hadn't seen the ball move. Neither did anyone in the gallery. They left it up to Jones whether to take the penalty stroke, which he did.

Later, when a marshal commended Jones on his high level of integrity, Jones replied, "Do you commend a bank robber for not robbing a bank? No, you don't. This is how the game of golf should be played at all times." Jones lost the match that day—by one stroke. But he didn't lose his integrity. His character was so well-known that the United States Golf Association's sportsmanship award came to be named the Bob Jones Award.[9]

It's an interesting paradox. Our character creates our choices, yet our choices create our character. Author and speaker Margaret Jensen observed, "Character is the sum total of all our everyday choices. Our character today is a result of our choices yesterday. Our charac-ter tomorrow will be a result of our choices today. To change your character, change your choices. Day by day, what you think, what you choose, and what you do is who you become." Once you get a handle on the character of a person, you can understand his choices and even pre-dict what they will be.

> "Character is the sum total of all our everyday choices."
>
> —Margaret Jensen

## 3. Character Communicates Influence

Today, many people try to demand respect. They believe that influ-ence should be granted to them simply because they have position, wealth, or recognition. However, respect and influence must be earned over time, and they are built and sustained by character. First and fore-most, influence is based on character. U.S. Army General J. Lawton Collins asserted, "No matter how brilliant a man may be, he will never engender confidence in his subordinates and associates if he lacks simple honesty and moral courage."

I've taught leadership for three decades, and I've written many books on it. During that time, I've tried to help people develop skills that will benefit them as leaders. However, all the skills in the world won't assist someone whose character is hopelessly flawed. Experienced leaders understand this. Author Stephen Covey writes,

> If I try to use human influence strategies and tactics of how to get other people to do what I want, to work better, to be more motivated to like me and each other while my character is fundamentally flawed, marked by duplicity or insincerity then, in the long run, I cannot be successful. My duplicity will breed distrust, and everything I do—even using so-called good human relations techniques will be perceived as manipulative.

It simply makes no difference how good the rhetoric is or even how good the intentions are; if there is little or no trust, there is no foundation for permanent success.[10]

Character cannot be inherited. It cannot be bought. It is impossible to weigh, and it cannot be physically touched. It can be built, but only slowly. And without it, one cannot lead others.

## 4. Character Communicates Longevity

If you want to know how long it will take to get to the top, consult a calendar. If you want to know how long it can take to fall to the bottom, try a stopwatch. Character determines which will happen. Dreams become shattered, possibilities are lost, organizations crumble, and people are hurt when a person doesn't have character protecting his talent. Character provides the opportunity for longevity in any career, any relationship, and any worthwhile goal.

Author and pastor J. R. Miller wrote, "The only thing that walks back from the tomb with the mourners and refuses to be buried is the character of a man. This is true. What a man is, survives him. It can never be buried." If you want your talent to last, and you want to sleep well at night, depend upon good character. Asked about the secret of a long and happy life, Coach John Wooden remarked on his ninetieth birthday, "There is no pillow as soft as a clear conscience." Character protects your talent, and it also guards you from regret.

## TALENT + CHARACTER = A TALENT-PLUS PERSON
## PUTTING THE TALENT-PLUS FORMULA INTO ACTION

Never forget that talent is a gift—either you have it or you don't—but character is a choice. If you want it, you must develop it. Here's how to become a talent-plus person in the area of character:

### 1. Don't Give Up or Give In to Adversity

It takes character to weather life's storms. At the same time, adversity develops character. Author and activist Helen Keller, who could not hear or see, remarked, "Character cannot be developed in ease and quiet. Only through experience of trial and suffering can the soul be strengthened, vision cleared, ambition inspired, and success achieved."

Anyone who does what he must only when he is in the mood or when it is convenient isn't going to develop his talent or become successful. The core foundation of character is doing what you don't want to do to get what you want. It is paying a higher price than you wanted to for something worthwhile. It is standing up for your principles when you know someone is going to try to knock you down. Every time you face adversity and come through it with your core values affirmed and your integrity intact, your character becomes stronger.

In his first novel, *One Day in the Life of Ivan Denisovich*, Russian dissident author Alexander Solzhenitsyn wrote about Ivan Denisovich Shukhov, a political prisoner in a Siberian labor camp. In one part of the novel, Shukhov is forced to build a wall in weather that is twenty degrees below zero. As it gets dark and even colder, the foreman gives the order to hurry the job by throwing leftover mortar over the wall, instead of using it, so that they can be finished for the day. "But Shukhov wasn't made that way," wrote Solzhenitsyn, telling how the man resists the order, determined to finish the job right. "Eight years in a camp couldn't change his nature. He worried about anything he could make use of, about every scrap of work he could do—nothing must be wasted without good reason."

The foreman yells at him and then hurries away. "But Shukhov— and if the guards had put the dogs on him it would have made no difference—ran to the back and looked about," writes the author. "Not bad. Then he ran and gave the wall a good look over, to the left, to the right. His eye as accurate as a carpenter's level. Straight and even." Only *then* does Shukhov stop working.[11]

German philosopher-poet Johann Wolfgang von Goethe observed, "Talent can be cultivated in tranquility; character only in the rushing stream of life." The irony is that if you have never experienced the resistance of the rushing stream, then whatever talent you have cultivated in tranquility may not survive. If you want your talent to take you far, then don't quit under duress. Don't give up in the midst of a storm. Don't bail out in the middle of conflict. Wait until the trouble is behind you before assessing whether it's time to change course or stop. Do that, and you may have additional opportunities to develop your talent.

## 2. Do the Right Thing

Doing the right thing doesn't come naturally to any of us. As America's first president, George Washington, said, "Few men have virtue enough to withstand the highest bidder." Yet that is what we must do to develop the kind of character that will sustain us.

It's not easy to do the right thing when the wrong thing is expedient. Molière commented, "Men are alike in their promises. It is only in their deeds that they differ. The difference in their deeds is simple: People of character do what is right regardless of the situation." It's not easy to do the right thing when it will cost you. It's not easy to do the right thing when no one but you will know. But it's in those moments that a person's character becomes strong. Civil rights leader Martin Luther King Jr. asserted this:

> *Cowardice asks the question:* Is it safe?
> *Consensus asks the question:* Is it popular?
> *Character asks:* Is it right?

That is the bottom line. Are you going to do what's right?

One way that I've tried to control my natural bent to do wrong is to ask myself some questions (adapted from questions written by business ethicist Dr. Laura Nash):[12]

1. Am I hiding something?

2. Am I hurting anyone?

3. How does it look from the other person's point of view?

4. Have I discussed this face-to-face?

5. What would I tell my child to do?

If you do the right thing—and keep doing it—even if it doesn't help you move ahead with your talent in the short term, it will protect you and serve you well in the long term. Character builds—

> "Men are alike in their promises. It is only in their deeds that they differ."
>
> —Molière

and it builds you. Or as Dr. Dale Bronner, a board member of my non-profit organization EQUIP, puts it, "Honesty is not something you do; honesty is who you are."

## 3. Take Control of Your Life

I have observed that the people with the weakest character tend to place the blame on their circumstances. They often claim that poor

upbringing, financial difficulties, the unkindness of others, or other circumstances have made them victims. It's true that in life we must face
many things outside our control. But know this: while your circumstances
*are* beyond your control, your character *is not*. Your character is always
your choice.

People can no sooner blame their character on their circumstances
than they can blame their looks on a mirror. Developing character is
your personal responsibility. It
cannot be given to you; you must
earn it. Commit yourself to its
development because it will protect your talent. Every time you
make a character-based decision,
you take another step toward becoming a talent-plus person. The
process begins with deciding to make good character your goal and to
stop making excuses. French writer François La Rochefoucauld asserted,
"Almost all our faults are more pardonable than the methods we think
up to hide them." The process continues with the determination to
manage that decision every day.

> While your circumstances
> *are* beyond your control,
> your character *is not*.

You have God-given talent; develop it. You have opportunity before
you; pursue it. You have a future that is bright; look forward to it. But
above all else, you have the potential to become a person of character;
follow through with it. Character, more than anything else, will make
you a talent-plus person. It will protect everything in your life that you
hold dear.

# TALENT + CHARACTER
# APPLICATION EXERCISES

1. Have you ever taken time to identify and write down your core values? If you haven't, you need to. There is no substitute for taking what may be some vague, general notions and making them specific and tangible by putting them in writing. Taking the time to do it can change your life.

2. Most people think of integrity as being the same thing as honesty. However, if you think of integrity as *consistency*—where your values, thoughts, feelings, and actions all line up—would you still consider yourself to have high integrity? If you completed the previous exercise, you've already written your core values. How do your thoughts match up to those values? Think about the various intellectual, moral, political, or religious issues that are important to you. How about your feelings? Are they consistent with your values and thinking? What about your actions? If you need help judging your consistency, enlist the assistance of people close to you and ask them to weigh in. And if you discover inconsistencies, try to discover where the breakdowns lie.

3. How would you rate yourself on a scale of 1 to 10 when it comes to self-discipline (with 10 being perfect)? Is yours what you would consider to be an acceptable score? How can you improve in this area? Identify specific goals that will help you. Remember that self-discipline is a lifestyle to be achieved. The more disciplined you are in one area, the more it helps you become disciplined in others. Each victory makes you stronger.

4. Jot down the times in your life when you faced great adversity. Try to remember at least ten. Put them in chronological order. Now next to each, note your response: paralysis, escape, avoidance, endurance, perseverance, or victory. What pattern do you see? If your responses don't tend to become stronger over time and lean more toward perseverance and victory, then this is probably a problem area for you. How will you learn to better handle adversity? Through teamwork? Better health and fitness? Stronger relationships? Professional counseling? Explore the options.

5. Write down the incidents, circumstances, choices, and habits that have helped to create your character until now. Try to list everything you can think of. How many of the things on the list are beyond your control, and how many are the result of actions you took or choices you made? If many of the things you list are due to circumstances and other things beyond your control, then you need to take greater control of your life. Start by making a choice every day that will strengthen your character. (Note: these kinds of choices usually involve doing things you would rather not do.)

# 11

## RELATIONSHIPS INFLUENCE YOUR TALENT

In his book *My Personal Best*, John Wooden writes, "There is a choice you have to make in everything you do, so keep in mind that in the end, the choice you make makes you." Nowhere is this more evident than in your relationships. Nothing will influence your talent as much as the important relationships in your life. Surround yourself with people who add value to you and encourage you, and your talent will go in a positive direction. Spend time with people who constantly drain you, pull you in the wrong direction, or try to knock you down, and it will be almost impossible for your talent to take flight. People can trace the successes and failures in their lives to their most significant relationships.

## MUSIC LEGEND

In 2005, Margaret and I went to see the movie *Walk the Line*. I have to admit, I didn't know very much about Johnny Cash before I saw the movie, but I was fascinated by his relationship with June Carter. And that got me reading about them.

During his career, Johnny Cash recorded more than 1,500 songs, had 14 number one hit songs, was awarded 11 Grammys, and sold 50 million albums.[1] He was inducted into the Rock and Roll Hall of Fame, the Songwriters Hall of Fame, and the Country Music Hall of Fame. He was a huge star. In 1959, he made a quarter of a million dollars by playing concerts.[2] In 1961, he performed at 290 concerts attended by nearly a million people.[3] He was a major influence on performers such as Elvis and Bob Dylan. And he was as much of a mess as the movie depicted him to be.

## LEGENDARY MESS

Cash took his first pill—an amphetamine tablet called Benzedrine—in 1957. He was instantly hooked.

"It increased my energy, it sharpened my wit, it banished my shyness, it improved my timing, it turned me on like electricity flowing through a light bulb," Cash recalled. For the next ten years, Cash was addicted to pills. "Every pill I took was an attempt to regain the wonderful, natural feeling of euphoria I experienced the first time. Not a single one of them, not even one among many thousands that slowly tore me away from my family and my God and myself, ever worked. It was never as great as the first time, no matter how hard I tried to make it so."[4] And Cash tried hard to make it so.

The damage that it did him was all that the movie *Walk the Line* showed and even more. At one point, Cash decided that he couldn't stand to live with it anymore. In his autobiography, Cash explained what happened:

> I just went on and on. I was taking amphetamines by the handful, literally, and barbiturates by the handful too, not to sleep but just to stop the shaking from the amphetamines. I was canceling shows and

recording dates, and when I did manage to show up, I couldn't sing because my throat was too dried out from the pills. My weight was down to 155 pounds on a six-foot, one-and-a-half-inch frame. I was in and out of jails, hospitals, car wrecks. I was a walking vision of death, and that's exactly how I felt. I was scraping the filthy bottom of the barrel of life.[5]

Having lost all hope, Cash traveled to Tennessee to Nickajack Cave, a series of deep caves he had visited before, where spelunkers and explorers had sometimes lost their way and died failing to find a way out. Cash intended to share their fate. He parked his Jeep, went in, and crawled for hours—until the batteries in his flashlight gave out. Then he lay down in the dark to die.

Cash said in the dark he experienced an encounter with God, and he realized his life was not his own to throw away. With newfound hope, he decided to start crawling in the dark. Miraculously he found his way out. And when he emerged blinking in the sunlight, he was dumbfounded and confused to find his mother and June Carter waiting for him. "I knew there was something wrong. I had to come and find you," his mother told him.[6] She had traveled all the way from California.

## RECOVERY

During the next few weeks and months, June Carter and her mother cared for him, shielded him from negative influences, and nursed him back to health, similar to the way it was depicted in the movie. In the past June had tried to help Cash, encouraging him to give up the drugs, and often getting rid of them. Now Cash readily accepted her help. A few months later, they were married. For the next thirty-five years, they were inseparable. And in the 1980s when Cash got addicted to painkillers due to a stomach problem, she helped him recover again. The battle was so hard-fought that when Cash later underwent heart bypass surgery, he refused any painkillers.

*Walk the Line* depicted June Carter as a positive influence on Johnny Cash, but even as good a job as it did, it couldn't capture her true character. Perhaps the best description came from Rosanne Cash, Johnny's daughter from his first marriage. At June's funeral, Rosanne said:

> In her eyes, there were two kinds of people in the world: those she knew and loved, and those she didn't know and loved. She looked for the best in everyone; it was a way of life for her. If you pointed out that a particular person was perhaps not totally deserving of her love, and might in fact be somewhat of a lout, she would say, "Well, honey, we just have to lift him up." She was forever lifting people up. It took me a long time to understand that what she did when she lifted you up was to mirror the very best parts of you back to yourself. She was like a spiritual detective: she saw into all your dark corners and deep recesses, saw your potential and your possible future, and the gifts you didn't even know you possessed, and she "lifted them up" for you to see. She did it for all of us, daily, continuously. But her great mission and passion were lifting up my dad. If being a wife were a corporation, June would have been the CEO. It was her most treasured role. She began every day by saying, "What can I do for *you*, John?" Her love filled up every room he was in, lightened every path he walked, and her devotion created a sacred, exhilarating place for them to live out their married life. My daddy has lost his dearest companion, his musical counterpart, his soul mate and best friend.[7]

The bottom line is that June Carter made Johnny Cash a better man. He reached his potential as an artist and as a human being in large part because of her influence. Cash put her impact on him in perspective a few years before they died:

The publicity in the 1960s was that June saved my life, and I some-times still hear it said that she's the reason I'm alive today. That may be true, but knowing what I do about addiction and survival, I'm fully aware that the only human being who can save you is yourself. What June did for me was post signs along the way, lift me up when I was weak, encourage me when I was discouraged, and love me when I felt alone and unlovable. She's the greatest woman I have ever known.[8]

## THE IMPACT OF RELATIONSHIPS

I think many people mistakenly minimize the impact that other people can have on their lives. My parents understood the influence of relation-ships. Today as I look back on my formative years, I see how intentional they were about who we spent time with and who we selected as our friends. My parents made our house the place to be in the neighborhood. We had a pool table, a Ping-Pong table, and a chemistry set in our basement. We had a shuffleboard court, a basketball court, and a Wiffle ball diamond in our yard. Everybody wanted to come to our house. And that was the strategy. My parents wanted to be able to

> Almost all our sorrows can be traced to relationships with the wrong people and our joys to relationships with the right people.

know the kids we played with. Typical of the times (it was the 1950s and 1960s), my mom didn't work outside the home, so she was always there to keep an eye on us.

Mom was always on the periphery of our play, fixing us lunch or a cold drink, putting Band-Aids on cuts, and observing the interaction and behavior of each person. Every now and then, she would ask my brother, Larry, my sister, Trish, or me about a particular friend. As chil-dren, we had no idea of the importance of associating with good kids rather than bad ones, but our parents did. They made sure the influences on our lives were positive.

Years later when I was an adult and I spent several hours a week counseling people, I learned through daily observation what my parents knew. Almost all our sorrows can be traced to relationships with the wrong people and our joys to relationships with the right people.

# The Direction Relationships Take Us

The relationships in our lives really do make or break us. They either lift us up or take us down. They add, or they subtract. They help to give us energy, or they take it away. Here's what I mean:

## Some Relationships Take from Us

There are a couple of good ways to tell whether a relationship is positive or negative. The first is to note whether a person makes you feel better or worse about yourself. The second relates to how much energy the relationship requires. Let's face it, some relationships feel as if they could suck the life out of you. In his book *High Maintenance Relationships*, Les Parrott identifies the types of people who are likely to hurt us and take energy from us. Here are some of them:

*Critics* constantly complain or give unwanted advice.

*Martyrs* are forever the victim and wracked with self-pity.

*Wet blankets* are pessimistic and habitually negative.

*Steamrollers* are blindly insensitive to others.

*Gossips* spread rumors and leak secrets.

*Control freaks* are unable to let go and let things be.

*Backstabbers* are irrepressively two-faced.

*Green-eyed monsters* seethe with envy.

*Volcanoes* build steam and are always ready to erupt.

*Sponges* are always in need but never give anything back.

*Competitors* always keep track of tit for tat.

Les also offers a straightforward quiz that can help you tell whether someone in your life is a negative person who takes energy from you. Answer yes or no to each of the following questions:

_____ Do you feel especially anxious when a particular person has called and left a message for you to return the call?

_____ Have you recently been dealing with a relationship that drains you of enthusiasm and energy?

_____ Do you sometimes dread having to see or talk to a particular person at work or in a social situation?

_____ Do you have a relationship in which you give more than you get in return?

_____ Do you find yourself second-guessing your own performance as a result of an interaction with this person?

_____ Do you become more self-critical in the presence of this person?

_____ Is your creativity blocked, or is your clarity of mind hampered somewhat, by the lingering discomfort of having to deal with a difficult person?

_____ Do you try to calm yourself after being with this person by eating more, biting your nails, or engaging in some other unhealthy habit?

_____ Do you ever have imaginary conversations with this person or mental arguments in which you defend yourself or try to explain your side of a conflict?

_____ Have you become more susceptible to colds, stomach problems, or muscle tension since having to deal with this difficult person?

_____ Do you feel resentful that this person seems to treat other people better than she or he treats you?

_____ Do you find yourself wondering why this person singles you out for criticism but rarely acknowledges things you do well?

_____ Have you thought about quitting your job as a result of having to interact with this difficult person?

_____ Have you noticed that you are more irritable or impatient with people you care about because of leftover frustrations from your interaction with this difficult person?

_____ Are you feeling discouraged that this person has continued to drain you of energy despite your efforts to improve the relationship?

Les says that if you answered yes to ten or more of the questions, then you are certainly in a high-maintenance relationship.[9]

I don't mean to imply that only negative relationships require you to put energy into them. All relationships require you to give *some* energy. Relationships don't cultivate and sustain themselves. The question is, how much energy do they require? And do they give anything in return? For example, some of the positive relationships that require a tremendous amount of energy in my life include:

- My *family*—every family has ups and down, but that's okay; that's what it means to be in a family.

- My *inner circle of friends*—these people get everything I've got, and they give their all, too; that's what friendship is all about.

- My *team*—leadership begins with a serving attitude; I always try to give more than I receive.

- *Those less fortunate than I am*—every year I travel to developing countries to train leaders and add value to people through EQUIP, my nonprofit organization.

If a relationship requires you to expend energy some of the time, that's normal. If a relationship saps your energy all the time, then that relationship has a negative effect on you. You may be able to see its effects in many areas of your life. It dilutes your talent because it robs you of energy that you could be using toward your best gifts and skills. It distracts you from your purpose. And it detracts from your best efforts. In the long run, a negative relationship cannot influence your talent in a positive direction.

## Some Relationships Add to Us

Some relationships clearly make us better. They energize, inspire, and validate us. They lift us up and give us joy. We should consider the people in these relationships friends and value them highly. Helen Keller remarked, "My friends have made the story of my life. In a thousand ways they have turned my limitations into beautiful privileges, and enabled me to walk serene and happy in the shadow cast by my deprivation."

In my book *The Treasure of a Friend*, I reflect on the nature of friendship. Who else but a friend is there . . .

to believe in your dreams,
to share your joys,
to dry your tears,
to give you hope,
to comfort your hurts,
to listen,
to laugh with you,
to show you a better way,

to tell you the truth,

to encourage you.

Who else can do that for you?

That's what friends are for.

Not long ago, I sat down and listed the types of people who add value to my life and give me energy. Here is what I wrote:

1. *My family*—the best moments with my family are *my* best moments.

2. *Creative people*—they unleash creativity within me like no others.

3. *Successful people*—I love to hear their stories.

4. *Encouraging people*—encouragement is like oxygen to my soul.

5. *Fun people*—laughter always lifts my spirit.

6. *Good thinkers*—conversations with them are my favorite things.

7. *My team*—they always add value to me.

8. *Learners*—interested people are interesting people.

Positive relationships take us to a higher level. They encourage us and bring out the best in us. They make us better than we otherwise would be without them. They are some of life's greatest gifts!

## Some Relationships Are Pivotal to Our Lives

Throughout a lifetime, people are in contact with thousands of people in varying levels of relationships. Most have a very limited impact on us. But a few relationships have such a tremendous impact that they change the course of our lives. They are pivotal to who we are and what we do.

Relationships commonly go through four stages:

1. *Surface relationships.* These require no commitment from either person. Examples include the clerk who helps you at the post office, acquaintances at church or the gym, and your favorite waiter at the neighborhood restaurant. You recognize these people and they recognize you. You may even know their names, but you don't know much beyond what you can observe from a distance.

2. *Structured relationships.* The next level is a little more involved than surface relationships. Structured relationships occur around routine encounters, usually at a particular place at a particular time. They often develop around a common interest or activity. The people you know from school or work, the parents at your kid's activities, and people who share your hobbies fall into this category.

3. *Secure relationships.* When a surface or structured relationship grows, trust develops, and the people involved begin to want to spend time together, it starts to develop into a genuine personal relationship. This is the level where you develop friendships.

4. *Solid relationships.* When people in a secure relationship build on their friendship and develop complete trust and absolute confidentiality, it can go to the solid relationship level. These relationships are long term and are characterized by a mutual desire to give and serve one another. Your desire should be to cultivate the most important relationships in your life: your spouse, your best friends, and your inner circle.

As the level of relationship increases, so does the influence of people on one another. And each time people try to take the relationship higher, it creates a period of testing. During that time, the relationship can go one way or another, positive or negative. If the dynamic becomes lose-lose or win-lose, the relationship is negative. Positive relationships are *always* overall win-win.

Every now and then, a relationship goes beyond *solid* to become *significant*, a relationship that is pivotal to your life. I don't think anyone can try to create one of these relationships. I call them simply God's gift to me. I don't deserve them—but I do need them. People with whom I have enjoyed this kind of relationship give beyond reason and lift me up to a level I *could not* achieve without them.

Tom Phillippe is one such friend. Tom and I have been friends for more than thirty years. We have traveled the world together, yet we also enjoy just sitting at home talking with no other agenda. Not long ago a group of Tom's friends got together with him to celebrate his seventieth birthday. Each of us had the chance to tell the others how Tom has affected our lives. I wrote what I wanted to say and read it to the group:

> Tom has loved me unconditionally. Victor Hugo said, "The supreme happiness of life is being loved in spite of yourself." Tom has also loved me continually. In 1980, he encouraged me to join the Wesleyan denomination. In 1981, he began assisting me in starting leadership conferences. He gave me an opportunity to enter the business world. He managed my personal development organization when time would not allow me to do it. He financially kept my nonprofit organization alive in its beginning days. Today it trains millions of leaders internationally. One of God's gifts to me was Tom's friendship.

I then closed with a poem called "Your Name Is Written . . . at the Top of My List."[10] Tom has changed my life forever. He has been a lifter in so many areas of my life. If you ever encounter someone who has that impact on you, fight to preserve that relationship, show your gratitude often, and give whatever you can in return.

# FIVE SIGNS OF A SOLID RELATIONSHIP

Relationships at the secure level validate us and help us to become more comfortable with who we are and to discover our gifts and talents. Solid relationships add value to us so that our talent is actually enhanced. Our solid friends tell us the truth in a supportive way. They keep us grounded. If we start to get off course, they help keep us on track. They encourage us when we're down and inspire us to go higher. A few solid relationships can make all the difference in where a talented person ends up in life.

As you engage in relationships, try to find people with whom you can build solid relationships that are mutually beneficial. Here are the signs that a relationship is headed toward that level:

## 1. Mutual Enjoyment

In solid relationships, people spend time together just for the enjoyment of being together. What they do is not of significance. For example, my wife, Margaret, and I often run errands together. What's enjoyable about dropping off the dry cleaning, buying groceries, or picking up items at a neighborhood shop? Nothing—except spending time with her.

I think when many of us were kids, we intuitively understood the value of spending time with someone special. Do you remember how it felt to sit on the lap of your mother or father when you were small? Or how excited you got when a favorite uncle or a grandparent came to visit? Or how it felt when you first started dating? Unfortunately the busyness and pressures of life often cause us to forget what a joy this can be. I've always valued time with Margaret. Now that she and I are grandparents, time with people I love means even more to me. Try not to let the stresses of life make you lose track of that.

## 2. Respect

When you value someone on the front end of a relationship, you earn respect on the back end. And that's foundational to all solid relationships.

> Respect
> is almost always
> built on
> difficult ground.

When do people respect you? When you don't let obstacles or circumstances become more important to you than the relationship. When the pressure is on and you still treat them with patience and respect. When the relationship is struggling and you are willing to work hard to protect and preserve it. That's when you have proven worthy of others' respect. Respect is almost always built on difficult ground.

Proverbs, the book of wisdom, teaches about the strength of relationships:

- Friends are scarce (18:24).
- Friends will not jump ship when the going gets rough (17:17).
- Friends will be available for counsel (27:9).
- Friends will speak the truth to you (27:6).
- Friends will sharpen you (27:17).
- Friends will be sensitive to your feelings (26:18–19).
- Friends will stick with you (16:28; 18:24).

People who respect each other and build a solid relationship enjoy all of these benefits of friendship.

## 3. Shared Experiences

Going through a significant experience with another person creates a mutual bond. The experience can be positive or negative. Families come together and enjoy reminiscing about vacations they took years before (often the more disastrous, the more fondly remembered!). Colleagues build relationships as they work together on high-pressure projects. Soldiers talk about the bond that occurs as they train together and how it only increases if they go to war together. We all need others to lean on and to celebrate with. Shared experiences give us those opportunities.

I still remember vividly my father taking me out of school when I was ten years old so that I could accompany him on a business trip. At the time, he was a district superintendent in our denomination, which meant that he was a pastor and leader to many pastors of local churches in our region. Dad and I packed for the trip and traveled from town to town by car. As we rode along, we talked. As he met with the various pastors, I watched him encouraging them. It not only created a special bond between us, but it modeled the kind of work with people that I would one day be doing myself. It was an experience I will treasure until the day I die.

> "The glory of friendship is
> not in the outstretched hand,
> nor the kindly smile,
> nor the joy of companionship;
> it is in the spiritual inspiration
> that comes to one when he
> discovers that someone else
> believes in him and
> is willing to trust him."
>
> —Ralph Waldo Emerson

## 4. Trust

Ralph Waldo Emerson wrote, "The glory of friendship is not in the outstretched hand, nor the kindly smile, nor the joy of companionship; it is in the spiritual inspiration that comes to one when he discovers that someone else believes in him and is willing to trust him." Trust is both a joy of relationships and a necessary component. In my book *Winning with People*, I described the Bedrock Principle, which says, "Trust is the foundation of any relationship." Nothing is more important in relationships. If you don't have trust, you don't have much of a relationship.

## 5. Reciprocity

All relationships experience ebb and flow. Sometimes one person is the primary giver. Sometimes the other person is. But relationships that continue to be one-sided will not remain solid. When they continue to be out of balance, they become unstable and often unhealthy. If you want the relationship to continue, you will need to make changes. Here's how it works:

- When you are getting the better of the relationship, changes must be made.
- When the other person is getting the better part, changes must be made.
- When you're both getting an equally good deal, continue as before.

> Relationships that continue to be one-sided will not remain solid.

Friendships are like bank accounts. You cannot continue to draw on them without making deposits. If either of you becomes overdrawn and it stays that way, then the relationship won't last.

Solid relationships must be beneficial to both parties. Each person has to put the other first, and both have to benefit. Hall of Fame football coach Vince Lombardi described this when he was asked what made a winning team. He observed,

> There are a lot of coaches with good ball clubs who know the fundamentals and have plenty of discipline but still don't win the game. Then you come to the third ingredient: if you're going to play together as a team, you've got to care for one another. You've got to *love* each other. Each player has to be thinking about the next guy and saying to himself, "If I don't block that man, Paul is going to get his legs broken. I have to do my job in order that he can do his." The difference between mediocrity and greatness is the feeling these guys have for each other.

Solid relationships are always win-win. If both people aren't winning, then the relationship isn't solid, and it won't last.

## TALENT + *RELATIONSHIPS* = A TALENT-PLUS PERSON
## PUTTING THE TALENT-PLUS FORMULA INTO ACTION

If you desire to become a talent-plus person in the area of relationships—a person whose relationships influence him or her in a positive direction—then here is what I suggest you do:

### 1. Identify the Most Important People in Your Life

Who are the significant people in your life, the people you spend the most time with, the people whose opinions mean the most to you? These people are your greatest influencers. You need to identify who they are before you can assess how they are influencing your talent.

### 2. Assess Whether They Are Influencing You in the Right Direction

Once you have identified the people who are influencing you, you would be wise to discern *how* they are influencing you. The easiest way to do that is to ask the following questions about each person:

**What does he think of me?** People tend to become what the most important person in their lives believes they can be. Think about small children. If their parents tell them they are losers, stupid, or worthless, they believe they are. If their parents tell them they are smart, attractive, and valuable, they believe they are. We embrace the opinions of people we respect.

Ralph Waldo Emerson asserted, "Every man is entitled to be valued by his best moments." If you want to be influenced in a positive direction, you need to spend time with people who think positively about you. They need to believe in you.

**What does he think of my future?** Novelist Mark Twain advised, "Keep away from people who try to belittle your ambitions. Do the most important people in your life envision a positive future for you? Do they see great things ahead of you?

Margaret, my wife, has given me many wonderful gifts during the course of our relationship. One that I cherish is the ministry log book she gave me the year before we were married, knowing that a pastoral career was ahead of me. In it, I could record my activities such as sermon topics, weddings, and funerals. It is a record of my life leading local churches. But I value it most for something she wrote in it in 1968. It said simply,

> John,
> You're going to accomplish great things.
> Love,
> Margaret

Her few words weren't poetic or profound, but they communicated her confidence in me and her belief in my future. And she has demonstrated that belief in me every day of our marriage.

*How does he or she behave toward me in difficult times?* There's an old saying: "In prosperity our friends know us. In adversity we know our friends." Haven't you found that to be true? When times are tough and you're having difficulties, a friend who is influencing you in the right direction is . . .

| Slow to | but | Quick to |
| --- | --- | --- |
| Suspect | | Trust |
| Condemn | | Justify |
| Offend | | Defend |
| Expose | | Shield |
| Reprimand | | Forbear |
| Belittle | | Appreciate |
| Demand | | Give |
| Provoke | | Help |
| Resent | | Forgive |

When you get knocked down, good friends don't kick you while you're down or say, "I told you so." They pick you up and help you keep going.

*What does he bring out of me?* British prime minister Benjamin Disraeli observed, "The greatest good you can do for another is not just to share your riches but to reveal to him his own." That is really the essence of positive relationships that influence people to rise up and reach their potential. They see the best in you and encourage you to strive for it, as June Carter did for Johnny Cash.

Author William Allen Ward remarked, "A true friend knows your weaknesses but shows you

> "In prosperity our friends know us. In adversity we know our friends."

your strengths; feels your fears but fortifies your faith; sees your anxieties but frees your spirit; recognizes your disabilities but emphasizes your possibilities." That's what positive relationships should do.

## 3. If Your Friends Aren't Friends, Then Make New Friends

A friend sent me a hilarious story that he said was called "Bob's Last Letter." Here's what it said:

Dear Friends:

It is important for men to remember that as women grow older it becomes harder for them to maintain the same quality of housekeeping as they did when they were younger. When men notice this, they should try not to yell.

Let me relate how I handle the situation.

When I got laid off from my consulting job and took "early retirement" in April, it became necessary for Nancy to get a full-time job, both for extra income and for health benefits that we need. It was shortly after she started working that I noticed that she was beginning to show her age.

I usually get home from fishing or hunting about the same time she gets home from work. Although she knows how hungry I am, she almost always says that she has to rest for half an hour or so before she starts supper. I try not to yell, instead I tell her to take her time and just wake me when she finally does get supper on the table. She used to do the dishes as soon as we finished eating. It is now not unusual for them to sit on the table for several hours after supper.

I do what I can by reminding her several times each evening that they aren't cleaning themselves. I know she appreciates this, as it does seem to help her get them done before she goes to bed.

Now that she is older she seems to get tired so much more quickly. Our washer and dryer are in the basement. Sometimes she says she just can't make another trip down those steps. I don't make a big issue of this. As long as she finishes up the laundry the next evening I am willing to overlook it.

Not only that, but unless I need something ironed to wear to the Monday lodge meeting or to Wednesday's or Saturday's poker club or to Tuesday's or Thursday's bowling or something like that, I will tell her to wait until the next evening to do the ironing. This gives her a little more time to do some of those odds and ends things like shampooing the dog, vacuuming or dusting.

Also, if I have had a really good day fishing, this allows her to gut and scale the fish at a more leisurely pace.

Nancy is starting to complain a little occasionally. For example, she will say that it is difficult for her to find time to pay the monthly bills during her lunch hour. In spite of her complaining, I continue to try to offer encouragement. I tell her to stretch it out over two or even three days. That way she won't have to rush so much. I also remind her that missing lunch completely now and then wouldn't hurt her any, if you know what I mean.

When doing simple jobs she seems to think she needs more rest periods.

She had to take a break when she was only half finished mowing the yard. I try not to embarrass her when she needs these little extra rest breaks. I tell her to fix herself a nice, big, cold glass of freshly squeezed lemonade and just sit for a while. I tell her that as long as she is making one for herself, she may as well make one for me and take her break by the hammock so she can talk with me until I fall asleep.

I know that I probably look like a saint in the way I support Nancy on a daily basis. I'm not saying that the ability to show this much consideration is easy. Many men will find it difficult. Some will find it impossible. No one knows better than I do how frustrating women can become as they get older. However, guys, even if you just yell at your wife a little less often because of this article, I will consider that writing it was worthwhile.

Signed, Bob

P.S. Bob's funeral was on Saturday, January 25th.
P.P.S. Nancy was acquitted Monday, January 27th[11]

If the people close to you are dragging you down, then it may be time to make some changes. Speaker Joe Larson remarked, "My friends didn't believe that I could become a successful speaker. So I did something about it. I went out and found me some new friends!"

When you really think about it, the things that matter most in life are the relationships we develop. Remember:

You may build a beautiful house, but eventually it will crumble.
You may develop a fine career, but one day it will be over.
You may save a great sum of money, but you can't take it with you.
You may be in superb health today, but in time it will decline.
You may take pride in your accomplishments, but someone will
　surpass you.

Discouraged? Don't be, for the one thing that really matters, lasts forever—your friendships.

Life is too long to spend it with people who pull you in the wrong direction. And it's too short not to invest in others. Your relationships will define you. And they will influence your talent—one way or the other. Choose wisely.

# Talent + Relationships
# Application Exercises

1. Make a list of the important people in your life. Next to each person's name, write a plus sign if the person adds value to you and a minus sign if that individual primarily takes from you. Use the questions in the chapter as criteria:

   • What does he think of me?
   • What does he think of my future?
   • How does he behave toward me in difficult times?
   • What does he bring out of me?

   For people on the list who are subtractors, you will need to develop a strategy to deal with them.

   If you work with some of the negative people, you will have to try to find a way to distance yourself. If that isn't possible, consider changing jobs.

   If the negative people are friends or acquaintances, it's time to find new ones. Separate yourself from the people who are having a negative influence on your life, and start looking for friends who will lift you up.

   If the negative people are family members, you may have to limit the amount of time you spend with them and counteract their impact by spending more time with positive people. (It's said that it takes at least five positive remarks to counteract the effects of one negative one.)

   If one of the negative people is your spouse, seek professional help. It is highly unlikely that you will be able to turn around the relationship without assistance.

2. Pick the relationship that matters most to you, and evaluate it. Write two columns: "What I Give" and "What I Get." Under each column, write all the benefits you receive from your relationship and all the benefits the other person receives.

   If the relationship is healthy, the two columns should balance each other. That doesn't necessarily mean they will have the same number of entries. Not all benefits are equal in value. Take that into account. But if the two columns are out of balance, you will need to make adjustments to preserve the relationship.

   If you are the primary giver, then first ask yourself *why*. Second, make plans to step back and give less. Sometimes the other person has just been waiting to step up and contribute more. If the other person is the primary giver, consider how you can add more value to the relationship and take action.

3. Write a thank-you note to a pivotal person in your life, expressing your gratitude and explaining what the person has done for you and what it has meant.

# 12

## RESPONSIBILITY STRENGTHENS YOUR TALENT

Nothing adds "muscle" to talent like responsibility. It lifts talent to a new level and increases its stamina. However, as I consider the thirteen choices that help to create a talent-plus person, I realize that responsibility is often the last choice people desire to make. The result is "flabby" talent that fails to perform and never realizes its potential. How sad for the person who fails to take responsibility. How sad for others. Author and editor Michael Korda said, "Success on any major scale requires you to accept responsibility . . . In the final analysis, the one quality that all successful people have . . . is the ability to take on responsibility." If you desire success, make responsibility your choice.

### EXTREME TALENT

One day when I was flipping through television channels, I came across a program on PBS about rock climbers. What amazed me were their Spiderman-like qualities. The program focused on Dan Osman, a man in his midthirties who scrambled up a rock face in record time without the benefit of safety ropes. At one point in his climb, he literally jumped in order to reach a handhold and was momentarily airborne. If he had missed the hold he was reaching for, the fall would have killed him.

Intrigued, I did some research. I discovered that this particular climb was in California at a place called Lover's Leap. The route he took is called Bear's Reach. Evidently specific routes are named and rated by the first climber to successfully navigate them. Bear's Reach is considered a 5.7 in difficulty on the Yosemite Decimal System. I didn't know what that meant, so I looked it up. Any climb that begins with a 5 involves "climbing involving technical moves and protective hardware in case of a fall" or "thin, exposed climbing, requiring skill (the holds are not obvious to a novice—this is where weird moves such as laybacks, underclings, and evangelical hammerlocks come into play) . . . where serious injury or death is very likely if you take an unprotected fall."[1]

In other words, it was very difficult. One rock climbing guide estimated that the average time it would take to climb the 400-foot-tall cliff face of Bear's Reach was three hours.[2] That would typically be done using safety ropes. On camera, Osman did what's called a free solo climb—with no help and no ropes—just him against the rock face. He accomplished the feat in 4 minutes, 25 seconds! (Go to the Internet, type in his name on a search engine, and you will find a video of him in action.)

## Developing His Skills

Osman started rock climbing when he was twelve years old. The son of a police officer father and a champion barrel racer mother, he is the descendant of samurai warriors. As a kid, he studied kung fu and aikido, a Japanese martial art that places high value on balance, control, and economy of motion. It took Osman eight years to become an expert climber, slow in his opinion, but he developed into a world-class climber and an expert rope rigger.

After more than a decade of climbing, Osman began experimenting with free falling. That's where a person jumps bungee-fashion from a high place, such as a bridge or cliff, but instead of being connected to a springy bungee cord, he is connected to a climber's rope. The rope has some stretch, but the fall is much more dramatic. It requires expert rigging and iron nerves. Osman began setting and breaking records for free falls. He became a legend among climbers and BASE jumpers (people who parachute from fixed objects). His fame grew, and soon creators of TV commercials and print ads started calling him.

## UNLIMITED TALENT—LIMITED RESPONSIBILITY

But there was another side to Dan Osman. He had a difficult time functioning in the real world. His friends joked about Dano time—showing up to appointments hours late or sometimes not at all. His mother's childhood nickname for him was "Danny I Forgot." He continually received tickets for speeding and driving with a suspended license or unregistered vehicle—which he neglected to pay. He regularly depended on others to rescue him. Andrew Todhunter, who was so intrigued with Osman that he spent time with him over the course of three years and wrote a book about the experience, writes about Osman's arrest for unpaid traffic violations. As Osman was being led away, he asked the writer to call friends, a retired couple who had "adopted" him. They were used to bailing him out. The woman, a retired executive, remarked, "I do worry a lot for him . . . What scares me is his jumping. He continues to want to jump farther and farther. I told him, 'You're not getting any younger, Dan. You're going to have to think about your future a little more.'" Her concern was not for just him. Osman had a twelve-year-old daughter named Emma. He also had a live-in fiancée with a daughter.

Todhunter was amazed that Osman had such intense attention to detail and a strong sense of responsibility when climbing but so little for the rest of life. And he asked Osman about his responsibility to his daughter.

"If I fell while soloing I'd go against everything I represent, which is not pushing it, which is having the route 'in hand.' By dying I would let everybody down—my family, my friends," said Osman. "I'd be robbing her if I fell. She knows her dad's rad. Other dads don't do this. She's afraid, but she's proud of what I'm doing. It's like my father: I worry about him, getting shot, but then I hear what a good cop he is. And there's a plaque on the wall: Officer of the Year."[3]

## RECORD BREAKER

On November 23, 1998, Dan Osman attempted his longest free fall— 1,000 feet. He had originally intended to set the new record on October 26. He had prepared his rigging at Yosemite's Leaning Tower and did some intermediate-distance jumps all the way up to 900 feet. Then he got a call from Emma. She was crying; she was worried about him. He dropped everything and went to see her. Two days later he was back at Yosemite and ready to resume his jumps, but he was arrested for the kinds of things he never took responsibility for: parking tickets and a suspended license. He spent fourteen days in jail.

His friend filmmaker Eric Perlman, who had offered his house against Osman's bail, talked to him after he got out of jail. Perlman recalls, "I told him, 'You've gone far enough, pushed it probably farther than it should be pushed. Nobody's going to touch this one [record] for a long time. Take the rig down, show the judge you're serious, that you're playing by the rules here.' And he agreed absolutely. He said, 'You know, you're right. It's what I should do. And my guardian angels need a break anyway. They've been working overtime for me.'"[4]

But when Osman went back with a friend on November 22 to take down his rigging and pack up all his equipment, he couldn't resist the urge to go for another record. First, he jumped at 925 feet. The next day, he talked his friend into jumping. Then Osman hastily rerigged everything for his own longer jump. By then it was late in the day, the sun was going down, and he couldn't see well. He jumped anyway. When the sound of the rope going taut didn't sound right, his friend knew something had gone wrong. He went to the base of the cliff where he found Osman dead.[5] His rope had snapped.

## CHANGE IN PERSPECTIVE

While Todhunter was researching his book and spending time with Osman, he at first admired the climber and made allowances for his frequent displays of irresponsibility. He compared Osman's behavior to "Picasso's philandering" and "Faulkner's drunkenness," saying that great artists and athletic geniuses had an "inability or refusal to live within ordinary parameters."[6] But as Todhunter witnessed one reckless act after another, his point of view changed. He writes, "There are those professionals and volunteers who consciously and repetitively risk their lives in public service—and not infrequently lose them—for a worthy cause. Many of them, like Osman, have families to support. Watching the bridge jumping, I am struck for the first time by its profound pointlessness, by the immeasurable *gratuity* of the risk."[7]

Dan Osman's talent was off the charts. Few people in the world can do what he did. His physical gifts, like those of Michael Jordan, Tiger Woods, or Lance Armstrong, were phenomenal. But his lack of responsibility limited his life, and it eventually killed him. What a tragedy.

## THE STRENGTH OF RESPONSIBILITY

We live in a culture that overvalues talent and undervalues responsibility. If you doubt that, then examine the way we treat our athletes. When

We live in a culture that overvalues talent and undervalues responsibility.

athletes are in high school and college, their reckless or irresponsible acts are often overlooked in proportion to the talent they display on the court or playing field. What a disservice to them. Responsibility actually strengthens talent and increases the opportunity for long-term success. Here is how it helps:

## 1. Responsibility Provides the Foundation of Success

Sociology professor Tony Campolo points out the importance of having a strong sense of responsibility, especially in a culture like ours that values freedom. Of the American system, he writes,

> While I think it lays down the principles that make for the best political system ever devised, the Constitution has one basic flaw. It clearly delineates the Bill of Rights, but it nowhere states a Bill of Responsibilities . . . Government that ensures people of their rights but fails to clearly spell out their responsibilities, fails to call them to be the kind of people God wants them to be.[8]

I agree wholeheartedly with Campolo's call for responsibility. In fact, for years I've taught leaders that as they move up the ladder and take on greater responsibility, their rights actually *decrease*. Leadership requires sacrifice. And while taking on responsibility is also a sacrifice, it is one that brings tremendous rewards.

Recently I had the opportunity to spend time on the aircraft carrier USS *Enterprise*. I received a tour of the ship and listened to many officers explain the various tasks and functions of the 5,500 people aboard the ship. What struck me was that the officers' messages had a common theme. They talked about the importance of their area to the overall mission of the ship and how the responsibility for those functions was shouldered by a bunch of nineteen-year-old sailors. The officers made these statements with pride.

One officer told me about leading a former gang member under his command. The young man had been given the choice of jail or the navy. The troubled youth became an effective part of the team and was then the leader of his squad. His proudest moments in the military, this officer said, came from helping troubled kids to succeed.

What turned kids into productive citizens and troublemakers into leaders? Responsibility! When they entered the service, they became immersed in a culture of responsibility. That culture demanded that they act accordingly, that they become responsible and productive. When people respond to a call for responsibility by giving their best, good things happen.

The young men and women I met had made the choice to embrace responsibility, and it was creating success for them in the military. It will continue to provide a foundation for their success in the coming years, no matter what they do.

## 2. Responsibility, Handled Correctly, Leads to More Responsibility

Years ago the editor of the *Bellefontaine (Ohio) Examiner*, Gene Marine, sent a new sports reporter to cover a big game. The reporter returned to the paper with no report.

"Where's the story?" asked Marine.

"No report," replied the reporter.

"What?" growled Marine. "And why not?"

"No game."

"No game? What happened?" quizzed the editor.

"The stadium collapsed."

"Then where's the report on the collapse of the stadium?" demanded Marine.

"That wasn't my assignment, sir."

People who handle their responsibilities well get the opportunity to handle additional responsibilities. Those who don't, don't.

### 3. Responsibility Maximizes Ability and Opportunity

During the major-league baseball players' strike of 1994, many trading card manufacturers found themselves in a tough spot. Pinnacle Brands, however, was determined not to lay off any of its employees. Yet the company had to make some changes to be able to pay everyone until business picked up again. So what did management do? Placed the responsibility on the workers for finding ways to replace the $40 million in lost revenue. CEO Jerry Meyer told his employees, "I'm not going to save your jobs. You're going to save your jobs. You know what you can change and what you can do differently."

The people did not let themselves down. A custodian reported that the company spent $50,000 on sodas for conference rooms, an expense that was cut. A finance department worker found a way to streamline trademark searches that saved the company $100,000. A PR manager signed a deal to distribute pins at the Olympics, generating $20 million. In the end, Pinnacle was the only one of the top trading card manufacturers that didn't lay off workers during the baseball strike.[9]

Responsibility has value, not just in hard times, but at all times. It increases our abilities and gives us opportunities. One reason it does is that it causes us to take action, to make things happen. On the job, we need to take responsibility, not just for what we're assigned, but for the contribution we make. For example, if you're in business, at the end of every day you should ask yourself, *Did I make a profit for my employer today?* If the answer is no, then you may be in trouble. Take responsibility for being a contributor. Every worker needs to be an asset to the company, not an expense.

Author Richard L. Evans remarked, "It is priceless to find a person who will take responsibility, who will finish and follow through to the final detail—to know when someone has accepted an assignment that it will be effectively, conscientiously completed." When leaders find responsible people, they reward them with opportunities and resources that help them to become more effective.

## 4. Responsibility, Over Time, Builds a Solid Reputation

Responsible people enjoy an increasingly better reputation. And that is one of the greatest assets of sustained responsibility. Others discover what they can expect from you, and they know they can depend on you. You're solid.

In contrast, the longer you know a person who lacks responsibility, the *less* you trust him. It is not surprising to me that the better Andrew Todhunter got to know Dan Osman, the more reservations he had about him and what he was doing. A person may try to compartmentalize his life—taking responsibility in one area and shirking it in another—but in the long run it doesn't work. Irresponsibility, left unchecked, inevitably grows and spreads into other areas of a person's life.

A general from American history whose reputation continued to grow was Dwight D. Eisenhower. In fact, his reputation became so strong that it got him elected president. Though he was only an average president, he was an excellent general. One reason was his willingness to take responsibility for his decisions.

During World War II, Eisenhower was responsible for planning the D-Day invasion of Normandy, France. Giving the okay for the assault was a painful decision, one he knew that would lead to the deaths of many servicemen. Yet he also knew that if it was successful, it would be a pivotal point in the war against the Nazis.

Pat Williams, in his book *American Scandal*, writes that in the hours prior to the assault, Eisenhower handwrote a press release that would be used in the event of the invasion's failure. It read,

Our landings have failed . . . and I have withdrawn the troops. My decision to attack at this time and this place was based upon the best information available. The troops, the air, and the Navy did all that bravery and devotion to duty could do. If any blame or fault attaches to the attempt, it is mine alone.[10]

Eisenhower had determined that he would take responsibility for whatever happened. That mind-set earned the admiration of his fellow officers, his soldiers, and citizens alike.

If you want others to trust you, to give you greater opportunities and resources to develop and strengthen your talent, and to partner with you, then embrace responsibility and practice it faithfully in every area of your life.

## TALENT + RESPONSIBILITY = A TALENT-PLUS PERSON
## PUTTING THE TALENT-PLUS FORMULA INTO ACTION

There's no way for me to know your personal history in regard to responsibility. Maybe assuming responsibility has been a problem for you. Or you may have a strong sense of responsibility, and you never drop the ball. Either way, please review the following steps to help you become a talent-plus person when it comes to responsibility:

### 1. Start Wherever You Are

Greek philosopher Aristotle observed, "We become what we are as persons by the decisions that we ourselves make." Each time you make a responsible decision, you become a more responsible person. Even if your track record hasn't been good up to now, you can change. Successful people take personal responsibility for their actions and their attitudes. They show response-ability—the ability to choose a correct response, no matter what situation they face. Responsibility is always a choice, and only you can make it.

If being responsible has not been one of your strengths, then start small. You can't start from anyplace other than where you are. I think you'll find that when it comes to responsibility, the best helping hand you will ever find is at the end of your arm.

## 2. Choose Your Friends Wisely

Since I've devoted an entire chapter to relationships and how they influence talent, I don't need to say very much here. Heed the advice of trainer and consultant Kevin Eikenberry, who says, "Look carefully at the closest associations in your life, for that is the direction you are heading." If you have started your journey on the road to responsibility, just make sure that you have the right traveling companions. You will find it difficult or impossible to be responsible when you spend most of your time with irresponsible people.

## 3. Stop Blaming Others

The sales manager of a dog food company asked his sales team how they liked the company's new advertising program.

"Great!" they replied. "The best in the business."

"What do you think of the product?" he asked.

"Fantastic," they replied.

"How about the sales force?" he asked.

They were the sales force, so of course they responded positively, saying they were the best.

"Okay then," the manager asked, "so if we have the best brand, the best packaging, the best advertising program, and the best sales force, why are we in seventeenth place in our industry?"

> "My philosophy is that not only are you responsible for your life, but doing the best at this moment puts you in the best place for the next moment."
>
> —Oprah Winfrey

After an awkward silence, one of the salesmen stated, "It's those darned dogs—they just won't eat the stuff!"

If you want to be successful and to maximize your talent as a talent-plus person, you need to stop blaming others, take a good look in the mirror, and take responsibility for your own life. Television host Oprah Winfrey says, "My philosophy is that not only are you responsible for your life, but doing the best at this moment puts you in the best place for the next moment."

Ron French of the Gannett News Service writes that failing to take responsibility has become pervasive in America:

> Ducking responsibility has become an American pastime. We all have learned to play the blame game, where the seven deadly sins are acceptable syndromes, and criminals are victims. From life-long smokers suing tobacco companies, to students rationalizing cheating, we've become a nation of whiners and cry babies. "It's part of the American character nowadays," says Charles Sykes, A Nation of Victims. "We've gone from a society of people who were self-reliant to a people who inherently refuse to accept responsibility."

People who think others are responsible for their situation assign the blame to various individuals, institutions, or entities. Some fault society or "the times." Some point at the system or "the man." (Criminals serving time in prison are notorious for blaming others and declaring their innocence.) Others rail against the previous generation as the cause of their problems. But do you know why? Cartoonist Doug Larson observed, "The reason people blame things on previous generations is that there's only one other choice."

> "Do what you can with what you have, where you are."
>
> —Theodore Roosevelt

Some of the best advice you could follow on this subject came from President Theodore Roosevelt: "Do what you can with what you have, where you are." That's all any of us can do. Don't make excuses. Don't look for others to blame. Just focus on the present and do your best. And if you make a mistake or fail, find whatever fault you can inside yourself and try to do better the next time around.

## 4. Learn Responsibility's Major Lessons

There are four core lessons we need to learn if we want to display the kind of responsibility that makes us talent-plus people. The lessons are simple and obvious. They are also very difficult to master:

*Recognize that gaining success means practicing self-discipline.* The first victory we must win is over ourselves. We must learn to control ourselves. You can use any incentive you want to do this: the desire to follow moral or ethical values, rewards for delayed gratification, even the threat of public exposure. Business executive John Weston commented, "I've always tried to live with the following simple rule: Don't do what you wouldn't feel comfortable reading about in the newspaper the next day." Every time you stop yourself from doing what you shouldn't or start yourself doing what you should, you are strengthening your self-discipline and increasing your capacity for responsibility.

*What you start, finish.* There are two kinds of people in the world: those who do and those who might. Responsible people follow through. If they make a commitment, they see it through. They finish. And that is how others evaluate them. Are they dependable or not? Can I rely on them? Writer Ben Ames Williams observed, "Life is the acceptance of responsibilities or their evasion; it is a business of meeting obligations or avoiding them. To every man the choice is continually being offered, and by the manner of his choosing you may fairly measure him."

*Know when others are depending on you.* Talent does not succeed on its own. (I'll discuss that in detail in the next chapter.) If you desire to be successful, you will need others. Sometimes you will have to depend on them. And there will be times they need to depend on you. In my book *The 17 Indisputable Laws of Teamwork*, I write about the Law of Countability, which says, "Teammates must be able to count on each other when it counts."

The first step in making yourself the kind of person others can depend on is being dependable. The second is taking the focus off yourself and becoming aware that others are depending on you. Having the *intention* to be responsible isn't enough. Your *actions* need to come through.

**Don't expect others to step in for you.** The following challenge was issued to the 1992 graduating class of the University of South Carolina by Alexander M. Saunders Jr., chief judge of the South Carolina Court of Appeals:

> As responsibility is passed to your hands, it will not do, as you live the rest of your life, to assume that someone else will bear the major burdens, that someone else will demonstrate the key convictions, that someone else will run for office, that someone else will take care of the poor, that someone else will visit the sick, protect civil rights, enforce the law, preserve culture, transmit value, maintain civilization, and defend freedom.
>
> You must never forget that what you do not value will not be valued, that what you do not remember will not be remembered, that what you do not change will not be changed, that what you do not do will not be done. You can, if you will, craft a society whose leaders, business and political, are less obsessed with the need for money. It is not really a question of what to do but simply the will to do it.

Many people sit back and wait for someone else to step up and take responsibility. Sometimes that is because of weak character—laziness, lack of resolve, and so on. But more often it comes from poor judgment or low self-esteem. People believe that someone else is more qualified or better situated to stand up and make a difference. But the truth is that most of the people who make a difference do so not because they are the best for the job but because they decided to try.

## 5. Make Tough Decisions and Stand by Them

When he was mayor of New York City, Rudy Giuliani kept a sign on his desk that stated, "I'm responsible." In his book *Leadership*, he writes,

> Throughout my career, I've maintained that accountability—the idea that the people who work for me are answerable to those we work for—is the cornerstone, and this starts with me . . . Nothing builds confidence in a leader more than the willingness to take responsibility for what happens during his watch. One might add that nothing builds a stronger case for holding employees to a high standard than a boss who holds himself to an even higher one. This is true in any organization, but it's particularly true in government.[11]

That mind-set served him well during the crisis of 9-11 in 2001. He had to make many tough decisions very quickly. And whether they were right or wrong, he stood by them. His tough-minded responsibility coupled with strong leadership served the people well during that difficult time.

> "You cannot escape the responsibility of tomorrow by evading it today."
>
> —Abraham Lincoln

President Abraham Lincoln said, "You cannot escape the responsibility of tomorrow by evading it today." Easy decisions may make us look good, but making tough ones—and taking ownership of them—makes us better.

## 6. Live Beyond Yourself

There is one more aspect of responsibility that I want to share with you. It will make you a talent-plus person beyond the level of those who simply take responsibility for themselves. It is the idea of taking responsibility beyond yourself by serving others. In a speech to the Massachusetts legislature on the eve of his presidency, John F. Kennedy said,

For of those to whom much is given, much is required. And when at some future date the high court of history sits in judgment on each one of us—recording whether in our brief span of service we fulfilled our responsibilities to the state—our success or failure, in whatever office we may hold, will be measured by the answers to four questions. First, were we truly men of courage[?] . . . Secondly, were we truly men of judgement[?] . . . Third, were we truly men of integrity[?] . . . Finally, were we truly men of dedication[?][12]

Self-serving people regard their talent and resources as what they own. Serving people regard their talent and resources as what's on loan.

Holocaust survivor Elie Wiesel, who won the Nobel Peace Prize in 1986, spent the years after his time in the Nazi concentration camps trying to give back to others. He taught as a professor at Boston University. He also traveled extensively giving talks and sharing the wisdom he gained from his life experiences. One of the questions he asked young people was, "How will you cope with the privileges and obligations society will feel entitled to place on you?" As he tried to guide them, he shared his sense of responsibility to others:

What I receive I must pass on to others. The knowledge that I have must not remain imprisoned in my brain. I owe it to many men and women to do something with it. I feel the need to pay back what was given to me. Call it gratitude . . . To learn means to accept the postulate that life did not begin at my birth. Others have been there before me, and I walk in their footsteps.

Practicing responsibility will do great things for you. It will strengthen your talent, advance your skills, and increase your opportunities. It will improve your quality of life during the day and help you to sleep better at night. But it will also improve the lives of the people around you.

If you want your life to be a magnificent story, then realize that you are its author. Every day you have the chance to write a new page in that story. I want to encourage you to fill those pages with responsibility to others and yourself. If you do, in the end you will not be disappointed.

# TALENT + RESPONSIBILITY APPLICATION EXERCISES

1. How good are you about taking care of the small stuff? That really is the prerequisite for being given responsibility for the big stuff. And even if you are being entrusted with huge responsibilities, you must not neglect details in your primary area of responsibility. You also never outgrow the need for responsibilities for small things with the people closest to you, such as your spouse or children. Give yourself a review. Are you taking care of the details in your job? How about at home? How often do you forget small things that are big things for your family members? It can be as big as forgetting an anniversary or birthday, or it can be as small as not picking up dry cleaning or being late for a child's game or recital. If you're neglecting small things, then get back to the basics.

2. Which of the major responsibility lessons are the toughest for you to live out with consistency?

- *Practicing self-discipline*—denying yourself for the sake of something or someone more important. If this is your trouble area, seek assistance from someone who can lend expertise, give you some guidelines, and help you motivate yourself. If you're lacking discipline fiscally, find someone to help you put together a budget. If your health is an issue, see a doctor. If you're overweight, talk to a trainer and a nutritionist.

- *Following through*—taking responsibilities to completion. If you have a tendency to quit, give yourself relatively small goals that require you to stretch. Start in areas where you have passion.

Then with a few wins under your belt, begin tackling other areas of your life.

- *Knowing when others are depending on you*—being there for others. People with this problem area usually lack people skills or are too self-centered. If people skills are your problem, then read a book like Dale Carnegie's How to Win Friends and Influence People or my book Winning with People. If you are too self-focused, then volunteer to help people in serious need.

- *Stepping forward*—not expecting someone else to do what's important to you. You've already done exercises to help you tap into your passion areas, identify your core values, and so on. Review them and determine whether you are taking action in these areas. If you're not, take a bold step. Volunteer, give financially, join an organization, or start your own. Do something by the end of this week.

3. Most people have a tough decision in their jobs or personal lives that is waiting to be made. They put it off and put it off. What's yours? Why aren't you taking action? Write the reasons so that you know without a doubt what they are. Now write down the advantages of making the decision. Are there any clear, concrete, and compelling reasons for putting off the decision? If so, write them down. At this point, you know in your heart what you should do. Do it, and stand by it.

# 13

## TEAMWORK MULTIPLIES YOUR TALENT

In the Academy Award–winning movie *Rocky*, boxer Rocky Balboa describes his relationship with his girlfriend, Adrian: "I've got gaps. She's got gaps. But together we've got no gaps." What a wonderful description of teamwork! It doesn't matter how talented you may be—you have gaps. There are things you don't do well. What's the best way to handle your weaknesses? Partner with others who have strengths in those areas. If you want to do something *really* big, then do it as part of a team.

### EXTRAORDINARY TEAMWORK

In the previous chapter, I mentioned that I recently toured the aircraft carrier USS *Enterprise*. I got that opportunity when my friend, Tom Mullins, invited me to make the trip along with him and a few others. It started when we landed aboard the aircraft, which was already at sea. For twenty-four hours, we received the VIP treatment, touring every part of that magnificent ship. The entire experience was fantastic, but the highlight for me was sitting with Rear Admiral Raymond Spicer, commander of the *Enterprise*'s carrier strike group, and watching F/A-18 Hornet jets taking off and landing at night. What an incredible sight!

There was beauty in the way the jets shot off the deck and others landed, coming to a halt in a mere two seconds. But what struck me even more was the number of people who seemed to be involved in the process and the teamwork that was required. When I asked Admiral Spicer about it, he put me in contact with Lt. Commander Ryan Smith, the V2 Division Officer, who explained the process to me. He said,

> The pilot is seated at the controls of an F/A-18 Hornet as the jet is accelerated from 0 to nearly 160 mph in the span of less than three seconds. As the aircraft climbs away from the carrier, she raises the landing gear and is suddenly alone in the black of night. There are few examples of solitary combat in today's era of modern, networked warfare, but an aviator seated in the cockpit of one of today's Navy fighters still seems like an example in which the accomplishment of a particular objective is entirely dependent on the talent, skill, and effort of one particular, highly trained individual. However, the singular act of catapulting a jet off of the end of one of these carriers is the result of the complex orchestration of scores of individuals, each with a mastery of his or her own specific task. It is the efforts and coordination of these individuals, most of whom are just barely high school graduates, which serve as a truly inspiring example of teamwork.[1]

He then went on to explain the process. Hours before that jet taxis to the catapult for launching, it is being inspected by a team of mechanics and technicians from the Aircraft Squadron. While the pilot is receiving a briefing on the mission, including weather, target information, radio procedures, and navigational information (all of which are produced by teams of sailors), the aircraft is going through an equally rigorous period of preparation. The preflight routine ends only when the pilot has reviewed the aircraft's maintenance records and inspected the aircraft for flight.

Exactly thirty minutes prior to the aircraft's launch time, a specific sequence of steps begins that is always followed with precision. The aircraft carrier's air boss calls for engine starts, a test to make certain that the jets are in proper working order, while the pilot runs through his pre-taxi checks. The aircraft's plane captain is listening to the engines and watching the movement of each control surface as the pilot does his checks. Once it is determined that everything is okay, the aircraft is then topped off with fuel by a crew from the carrier's Fuels Division.

Meanwhile, the aircraft handling officer, seated in flight deck control and using a tabletop model of the carrier's flight deck with scale models of the individual aircraft to keep track of everything, reviews the launch sequence plan with the deck caller. The aircraft handling officer radios the deck caller, telling him which aircraft are reported to be "up" and ready to taxi.

The deck caller leads three separate teams of plane directors and other sailors from the carrier's Flight Deck Division, and each team is responsible for a different area of the flight deck. These teams ensure that each aircraft to be launched is safely unchained, directed around other parked aircraft (often with only inches of clearance), and put in line to be launched—sometimes as the deck of the carrier is pitching and rolling. When the deck caller gets the word from the aircraft handling officer, he leads the plane directors to distribute the aircraft among the four catapults facilitating the fastest possible departure of all the aircraft from the flight deck. As the time of the launch approaches, the directors bring each aircraft to the throat of a catapult, and the jet blast deflector is raised once an aircraft has taxied over it.

On deck, final maintenance checkers walk alongside the aircraft and inspect each panel and component as crew members from the Catapult and Arresting Gear Division hook the aircraft up to the catapult mechanism and ready it for launch. Below deck, other teams are using hydraulics and other equipment to control steam from the nuclear reactor that will be used to power the catapult.

At this time, ordnance personnel arm the aircraft's weapons.

The catapult officer then confirms the weight of the aircraft with the pilot. He also makes note of the wind over the deck and ambient conditions. He performs calculations to determine the precise amount of energy needed to achieve flight.

Even with all of this preparation, no jet would be able to take off if the ship weren't in the proper position. The ship's navigational team, which makes calculations to determine the required speed and heading, has relayed information to the bridge, and by now the ship has completed its turn and has accelerated to proper speed on its directed course.

The aircraft is almost ready for launch. The catapult officer signals to the operators, and the aircraft is hydraulically tensioned into the catapult. At this point, the pilot applies full power to the aircraft's engines and checks to be sure the aircraft is functioning. If the pilot determines that the aircraft is ready for flight, he signals the catapult officer by saluting him. If the catapult officer also receives a thumbs-up from the squadron final checker, he will then give the fire signal to a catapult operator who depresses the fire button and sends the aircraft on its way.

What's amazing is that three more aircraft can be launched right behind it in less than a minute, each having gone through that same procedure. And in just a matter of minutes, that same flight deck can be prepared to receive landing aircraft, one coming on final approach just as the previous one is taxied out of the landing area.

## TEAMWORK TRUTHS

I can think of few things that require such a high degree of precision teamwork with so many different groups of people as the launching of a jet from an aircraft carrier. It's easy to see that teamwork is essential for the task. However, a task doesn't *have* to be complex to need teamwork. In 2001 when I wrote *The 17 Indisputable Laws of Teamwork*, the first law

I included was the Law of Significance, which says, "One is too small a number to achieve greatness." If you want to do anything of value, teamwork is required.

Teamwork not only allows a person to do what he couldn't otherwise do; it also has a compounding effect on all he possesses—including talent. If you believe one person is a work of God (which I do), then a group of talented people committed to working together is a work of art. Whatever your vision or desire, teamwork makes the dream work.

Working together with other people toward a common goal is one of the most rewarding experiences of life. I've led or been part of many different kinds of teams—sports teams, work teams, business teams, ministry teams, communication teams, choirs, bands, committees, boards, you name it. I've observed teams of nearly every type in my

> Teamwork makes the dream work.

travels around the world. And talking to leaders, developing teams, counseling with coaches, and teaching and writing on teamwork have influenced my thinking when it comes to teams. What I've learned I want to share with you:

## 1. Teamwork Divides the Effort and Multiplies the Effect

Would you like to get better results from less work? I think everyone would. That's what teamwork provides. In his book *Jesus on Leadership*, C. Gene Wilkes describes why teamwork is superior to individual effort:

- Teams involve more people, thus affording more resources, ideas, and energy than an individual possesses.

- Teams maximize a leader's potential and minimize her weaknesses. Strengths and weaknesses are more exposed in individuals.

- Teams provide multiple perspectives on how to meet a need or reach a goal, thus devising several alternatives for each situation. Individual insight is seldom as broad and deep as a group's when it takes on a problem.

- Teams share the credit for victories and the blame for losses. This fosters genuine humility and authentic community. Individuals take credit and blame alone. This fosters pride and sometimes a sense of failure.

- Teams keep leaders accountable for the goal. Individuals connected to no one can change the goal without accountability.

- Teams can simply do more than an individual.

It's common sense that people working together can do more than an individual working alone. So why are some people reluctant to engage in teamwork? It can be difficult in the beginning. Teams don't usually come together and develop on their own. They require leadership and cooperation. While that may be more work on the front end, the dividends it pays on the back end are tremendous and well worth the effort.

## 2. Talent Wins Games, but Teamwork Wins Championships

A sign in the New England Patriots' locker room states, "Individuals play the game, but teams win championships." Obviously the Patriot players understand this. Over a four-year period, they won the Super Bowl three times.

> Individuals play the game, but teams win championships.

Teams that repeatedly win championships are models of teamwork. For more than two decades, the Boston Celtics dominated the NBA. Their team has won more championships than any other in NBA history, and at one point during the fifties and sixties, the Celtics won eight championships in a row. During their run, the Celtics never had a player lead the league in scoring. Red Auerbach, who coached the Celtics and then later moved to their front office, always emphasized teamwork. He asserted, "One person seeking glory doesn't accomplish much; everything we've done has been the result of people working together to meet our common goals."

It's easy to see the fruit of teamwork in sports. But it is at least as important in business. Harold S. Geneen, who was director, president, and CEO of ITT for twenty years, observed, "The essence of leadership is the ability to inspire others to work together as a team—to stretch for a common objective." If you want to perform at the highest possible level, you need to be part of a team.

## 3. Teamwork Is Not About You

The Harvard Business School recognizes a team as a small number of people with complementary skills who are committed to a common purpose, performance goals, and approach for which they hold themselves mutually accountable. Getting those people to work together is sometimes a challenge. It requires good leadership. And the more talented the team members, the better the leadership that is needed. The true measure of team leadership is not getting people to work. Neither is it getting people to work hard. The true measure of a leader is getting people to work hard together!

I've studied exceptional team leaders and coaches. Here are what just a few say about getting people to work together:

PAUL "BEAR" BRYANT, legendary Alabama football coach: "In order to have a winner, the team must have a feeling of unity. Every player must put the team first ahead of personal glory."

BUD WILKINSON, author of *The Book of Football Wisdom*: "If a team is to reach its potential, each player must be willing to subordinate his personal goals to the good of the team."

LOU HOLTZ, coach of college football national championship teams: "The freedom to do your own thing ends when you have obligations and responsibilities. If you want to fail yourself— you can—but you cannot do your own thing if you have responsibilities to team members."

MICHAEL JORDAN, most talented basketball player of all time and six-time world champion: "There are plenty of teams in every sport that have great players and never win titles. Most of the time, those players aren't willing to sacrifice for the greater good of the team. The funny thing is, in the end, their unwillingness to sacrifice only makes individual goals more difficult to achieve. One thing I believe to the fullest is that if you think and achieve as a team, the individual accolades will take care of themselves. Talent wins games, but teamwork and intelligence win championships."[2]

All great teams are the result of their players making decisions based on what's best for the rest. That's true in sports, business, the military, and volunteer organizations. And it's true at every level, from the part-time support person to the coach or CEO. The best leaders also put their team first. C. Gene Wilkes observes,

Team leaders genuinely believe that they do not have all the answers— so they do not insist on providing them. They believe they do *not* need to make all key decisions—so they do not do so. They believe they *cannot* succeed without the combined contributions of all the other members of the team to a common end—so they avoid any action that might constrain inputs or intimidate anyone on the team. Ego is *not* their predominant concern.

Highly talented teams possess players with strong egos. One secret of successful teamwork is converting individual ego into team confidence, individual sacrifice, and synergy. Pat Riley, NBA champion coach, says, "Teamwork requires that everyone's efforts flow in a single direction. Feelings of significance happen when a team's energy takes on a life of its own."

## 4. Great Teams Create Community

All effective teams create an environment where relationships grow and teammates become connected to one another. To use a term that is currently popular, they create a *sense of community*. That environment of community is based on trust. Little can be accomplished without it.

On good teams, trust is a nonnegotiable. On winning teams, players extend trust to one another. Initially that is a risk because their trust can be violated and they can be hurt. At the same time that they are giving trust freely, they conduct themselves in such a way to earn trust from others. They hold themselves to a high standard. When everyone gives freely and bonds of trust develop and are tested over time, players begin to have faith in one another. They believe that the person next to them will

> "The mark of community . . . is not the absence of conflict. It's the presence of a reconciling spirit."
>
> —Bill Hybels

act with consistency, keep commitments, maintain confidences, and support others. The stronger the sense of community becomes, the greater their potential to work together.

Developing a sense of community in a team does not mean there is no conflict. All teams experience disagreements. All relationships have tension. But you can work them out. My friend Bill Hybels, who leads a congregation of more than twenty thousand people, acknowledges this:

The popular concept of unity is a fantasy land where disagreements never surface and contrary opinions are never stated with force.

Instead of unity, we use the word *community*. We say, "Let's not pretend we never disagree. We're dealing with the lives of 16,000 people [at the time]. The stakes are high. Let's not have people hiding their concerns to protect a false notion of unity. Let's face the disagreement and deal with it in a good way."

The mark of community . . . is not the absence of conflict. It's the presence of a reconciling spirit. I can have a rough-and-tumble leadership meeting with someone, but because we're committed to the community, we can still leave, slapping each other on the back, saying, "I'm glad we're still on the same team." We know no one's bailing out just because of a conflicting position.

When a team shares a strong sense of community, team members can resolve conflicts without dissolving relationships.

## 5. Adding Value to Others Adds Value to You

"My husband and I have a very happy marriage," a woman bragged. "There's nothing I wouldn't do for him, and there's nothing he wouldn't do for me. And that's the way we go through life—doing nothing for each other!" That kind of attitude is a certain road to disaster for any team—including a married couple.

Too often people join a team for their personal benefit. They want a supporting cast so that they can be the star. But that attitude hurts the team. When even the most talented person has a mind to serve, special things can happen. Former NBA great Magic Johnson paraphrased John F. Kennedy when he stated, "Ask not what your teammates can do for you. Ask what you can do for your teammates." That wasn't just talk for Johnson. Over the course of his career with the Los Angeles Lakers, he started in every position during championship games to help his team.

U.S. president Woodrow Wilson asserted, "You are not here merely to make a living. You are here in order to enable the world to live more amply, with greater vision, with a finer spirit of hope and achievement.

You are here to enrich the world, and to impoverish yourself if you forget the errand." People who take advantage of others inevitably fail in business and relationships. If you desire to succeed, then live by these four simple words: *add value to others*. That philosophy will take you far.

## TALENT + *TEAMWORK* = A TALENT-PLUS PERSON PUTTING THE TALENT-PLUS FORMULA INTO ACTION

All talented people have a choice to make: do their own thing and get all the credit, or do the team thing and share it. My observation is that not only do talented people accomplish more when working with others, but they are also more fulfilled than those who go it alone. My hope is that you choose teamwork over solo efforts. If that is your desire, then do the following:

### 1. Buy into the Law of Significance

Earlier in this chapter I mentioned the Law of Significance from *The 17 Indisputable Laws of Teamwork*: "One is too small a number to achieve greatness." In 2002, when I was teaching on the laws, I challenged members of the audience of ten thousand: "Name one person in the history of mankind who alone, without the help of anyone, made a significant impact on civilization."

A voice from the crowd yelled, "Charles Lindbergh—he crossed the Atlantic Ocean in a plane by himself."

The crowd cheered.

"That's true," I responded, and the crowd cheered louder, thinking I had been stumped. "But did you know," I continued, "that Ryan Aeronautical Engineering designed and built the plane? And did you know that ten millionaires financed the trip?" The crowd exploded. "Are there any more suggestions?" I asked.

I want to give you the same challenge. Think of any significant accomplishment that appears to be a solo act. Then do some research and you will find that others worked with the individuals or supported them so that they could do what they did. No one does anything significant on his own. One is too small a number to achieve greatness. If you buy into that idea, then you will embrace the concept of teamwork. And that will be the foundation upon which you multiply your talent and take it to the highest level. No one can become a talent-plus person without it.

## 2. Include a Team in Your Dream

Journalist and radio host Rex Murphy asserts, "The successful attainment of a dream is a cart and horse affair. Without a team of horses, a cart full of dreams can go nowhere." Teamwork gives you the best opportunity to turn your vision into reality. The greater the vision, the more need there is for a good team.

> Teamwork gives you the best opportunity to turn your vision into reality.

But being willing to engage in teamwork is not the same as actively pursuing a team and becoming part of it. To succeed, you need to get on a team and find your best place in it. That may be as its leader, or it may not. Rudy Giuliani says,

> In reality, a leader *must* understand that success is best achieved through teamwork. From the moment you are put into a leadership position you must demonstrate ultimate humility. A leader must know his weaknesses in order to counterbalance them with the strengths of the team. When I became the Mayor of New York, I had both strengths and weaknesses. For instance, I did not have very much experience in economics. I found members for my team that had experience and great talent in the field of economics. When every member of the team is operating in his or her strengths, your organization will flourish. When crisis comes you will have the people in place to manage every situation with excellence.

If you're not certain about where you ultimately belong on a team, don't let that stop you from engaging in teamwork. Find others who are like-minded in their attitudes and passion, and join them.

## 3. Develop Your Team

If you are a leader on your team, then you must make it your goal to develop your teammates or players. That process begins with having the right people on the team. It's said that people are known by the company they keep. But it can also be said that a company is known by the people it keeps. Jack Welch, former chairman and CEO of General Electric, observed, "If you pick the right people and give them the opportunity to spread their wings—and put compensation as a carrier behind it—you almost don't have to manage them." That's why Patrick Emington said, "It is the greatest folly to talk of motivating anybody. The real key is to help others to unlock and direct their deepest motivators."

The process continues with your doing whatever you can to help people grow and reach their potential. You must do your best to see the abilities of others and help them recognize and develop those abilities. That's what all good leaders do. They don't just become talent-plus people. They help others to become talent-plus people.

## 4. Give the Credit for Success to the Team

The final step to becoming a talent-plus person in the area of teamwork is to give as much of the credit as you can to the people on the team. In his book *Good to Great*, Jim Collins points out that the leaders of the best organizations, what he calls "level-5 leaders," are characterized by humility and a tendency to avoid the spotlight. Does that mean those leaders aren't talented? Of course not. Does it mean they have no egos? No. It means they recognize that everyone on the team is important, and they understand that people do better work and do it with greater effort when they are recognized for their contribution.

If you consider what top leaders and former CEOs say about this, you'll recognize a pattern:

RAY GILMARTIN OF MERCK: "If I were to put someone on the front cover of *Business Week* or *Fortune*, it would be . . . the person who heads up our research organization, not me. Or I would put a team of people on the cover."

LOU GERSTNER OF IBM: "I haven't done this [created the company's turnaround]. It's been 280,000 people who have done it. We took a change in focus, a change in preoccupation, and a great talented group of people . . . and changed the company."

DAN TULLY OF MERRILL LYNCH: "It's amazing what you can do when you don't seek all the credit. I find nothing is really one person's idea."

WALTER SHIPLEY OF CITIBANK: "We have 68,000 employees. With a company this size, I'm not 'running the business' . . . My job is to create the environment that enables people to leverage each other beyond their own individual capabilities."

If you want to help your team go farther and help team members to sharpen their talent and maximize their potential, when things don't go well, take more than your fair share of the blame, and when things go well, give all of the credit away.

One person who has captured my attention lately has been Bono, singer for the rock band U2. I must admit, I'm late in discovering him. His music isn't really my cup of tea. But his passion, leadership, and activism really impress me. In 2005, he was named a Person of the Year by *Time* magazine, along with Bill and Melinda Gates.

There's no doubting Bono's talent. His success in the musical world is obvious. He has penned many hit songs, and U2, which has been together for thirty years, is one of the most successful bands in history. Together the band members have sold more than 170 million albums.[3]

In recent years, Bono has expanded his efforts beyond the world of music. He has become an advocate for African aid and economic development. And he's not just a celebrity lending his name to a cause. Senator Rick Santorum said of him, "Bono understands the issues better than 99% of the members of Congress."[4] And Bono has relentlessly worked at partnering with other people to further the causes he's passionate about. He has met with heads of state, economists, industry leaders, celebrities—anyone who has the potential to add value to the people he desires to help.

Where did Bono learn to rely on others, to be part of a team and enlist the aid of others? Rock stars are supposed to be self-absorbed, iconoclastic, isolated, and indifferent to others. That is what happens to many famous people, and it's the reason many music groups don't stay together. Bono comments,

> There's moments when people are so lost in their own selves, the demands of their own life, that it's very hard to be in a band . . . People want to be lords of their own domain. I mean, everybody, as they get older . . . rids the room of argument. You see it in your family, you see it with your friends, and they get a smaller and smaller circle of people around them, who agree with them. And life ends up with a dull sweetness.[5]

What is Bono's secret, after having been a rock star for more than twenty-five years? He learned teamwork in the band. Bono recognizes his need for others and, in fact, says he can't imagine having been a solo artist. He admits:

> The thing that'll make you less and less able to realize your potential is a room that's empty of argument. And I would be terrified to be on my own as a solo singer, not to have a band to argue with. I mean, I

surround myself with argument, and a band, a family of very spunky kids, and a wife who's smarter than anyone. I've got a lot of very smart friends, a whole extended family of them . . . You're as good as the arguments you get. So maybe the reason why the band hasn't split up is that people might get this: that even though they're only one quarter of U2, they're more than they would be if they were one whole of something else. I certainly feel that way.[6]

I can't think of a better way to say it myself. A talented person who is part of a team—in the right place on the right team—becomes more than he ever could on his own. That's what it means to be a talent-plus person.

# TALENT + TEAMWORK
# APPLICATION EXERCISES

1. How do you think of your talent? Is it something you own or something on loan? Why do you desire success? Do your goals primarily benefit you, or are you simply an instrument being used to benefit others? Do some soul-searching. If you think everything is all about you, you will never be a good team player.

2. What kinds of experiences have you had with teams? Think about how your experience with teams during various phases of your life has impacted your thinking. Write down the kinds of teams you were a part of as a child, as a teenager, and as a young adult. Now try to recall the significant moments, milestones, and experiences with each team. Were they primarily positive or negative? If you had some bad experiences along the way, they may be coloring your thinking and making you reluctant to engage in teamwork. Process through those experiences on the emotional level, and work on seeing the current benefits of being part of a team.

3. How strong is the sense of community on a team of which you are currently a part? Do people trust one another? Do they count on one another when it counts? If not, why not? First, take responsibility for your part in any weakness in the team, and try to make amends for past failures. Work at regaining people's trust. If you have been let down by someone else on the team, go to that person privately and talk about it. Try your best to repair the relationship and start building again.

4. How can you add value to others on your team? Think of three people on your team who you believe have high potential *and* could benefit from talent, skills, or experience you have to offer. Write out a plan for each, outlining how you could help him or her. Then approach each individual with an offer to train or mentor him or her.

5. For the next two weeks, make a commitment to yourself to take no credit for anything that goes right. Praise your employees, coworkers, colleagues, and family members for their contribution. Note the difference it makes in their performance and your relationship with them. I believe that once you've tried it, you will enjoy giving the credit away so much that it will become a regular part of your life.

# THE LAST WORD ON TALENT

Early in 2006, I read a report from *Money* magazine that claimed we were experiencing a worldwide talent shortage:

> ZURICH, SWITZERLAND (REUTERS)—Employers are having difficulty finding the right people to fill jobs despite high unemployment in Europe and the United States, a survey by U.S.-based staffing firm Manpower showed Tuesday.
>
> The survey conducted late in January showed that 40 percent of nearly 33,000 employers in 23 countries across the world were struggling to find qualified job candidates.
>
> "The talent shortage is becoming a reality for a larger number of employers around the world," Manpower's CEO and Chairman Jeffrey Joerres said.[1]

And in what is the number one talent shortage, according to the report? Sales. They wanted more good salespeople.

Every few years, we hear similar statements about certain professions. But the reality is that there never has been nor will there ever be a talent shortage. Talent is God-given. As long as there are people in the world, there will be plenty of talent. What's missing are people who have made the choices necessary to maximize their talent. Employers are really looking for talent-plus people. By now I trust you agree that the key choices we make—apart from the natural talent we already possess—set us apart from others who have talent alone.

William Danforth, who became the owner of the Ralston Purina Company, found a secret of success when he was a young man:

> When I was sixteen, I came to St. Louis to attend the Manual Training School. It was a mile from my boardinghouse to the school. A teacher who lived nearby and I would start for school at the same time every morning. But he always beat me there. Even back then I didn't want to be beaten, and so I tried all the shortcuts. Day after day, however, he arrived ahead of me. Then I discovered how he did it. When he came to each street crossing he would run to the other curb. The thing that put him ahead of me was just "that little extra."

Talent-plus people give a little extra. You see it in the choices they make that multiply and maximize their talent. Because they have given more to *develop their talent*, they are able to give more to others *with their talent*.

I want to encourage you to make the thirteen choices described in this book. And every day remind yourself about how these choices can help you:

1. Belief lifts my talent.
2. Passion energizes my talent.
3. Initiative activates my talent.
4. Focus directs my talent.
5. Preparation positions my talent.
6. Practice sharpens my talent.
7. Perseverance sustains my talent.
8. Courage tests my talent.
9. Teachability expands my talent.
10. Character protects my talent.
11. Relationships influence my talent.
12. Responsibility strengthens my talent.
13. Teamwork multiplies my talent.

Whatever talent you have you can improve. Never forget that the choices you make in the end make you.

Choose to become a talent-plus person. If you do, you will add value to yourself, add value to others, and accomplish much more than you dreamed was possible.

# NOTES

## WHEN IS TALENT ALONE ENOUGH?

1. Malcolm Gladwell, "The Talent Myth," *New Yorker*, 22 July 2002, http://www.gladwell.com/2002/2002_07_22_a_talent.htm.
2. Robert J. Kriegel and Louis Patler, *If It Ain't Broke . . . Break It!* (New York: Warner Books, 1991), 11.

## CHAPTER 1

1. Mark Kriegel, *Namath: A Biography* (New York: Viking), 15.
2. Ibid., 13–14.
3. Ibid., 14.
4. Ibid., 47.
5. Ibid., 234.
6. Used with permission. Copyright 2004–5, Joel Garfinkle. All rights reserved. *Dream Job Coaching*, http://www.dreamjobcoaching.com/articles/court-martial.html.
7. Kriegel and Patler, *If It Ain't Broke . . . Break It!*, 44.
8. Martin Seligman, *Learned Optimism: How to Change Your Mind and Your Life* (New York: Pocket Books, 1998), 99.
9. Kriegel, *Namath*, 57.
10. From Walter D. Wintle, "The Man Who Thinks He Can," *Poems That Live Forever*, comp. Hazel Felleman (New York: Doubleday, 1965), 310.
11. August 26, 1996: Christopher Reeve speaks at the Democratic National Convention," Floor Speeches, PBS, http://www.pbs.org/newshour/convention96/floor_speeches/reeve.html, accessed 2 August 2006.
12. Harvey Mackay, "Be a Believer to be an Achiever," Pioneer Thinking, http://www.pioneerthinking.com/achieve.html, accessed 2 August 2006.
13. Robert H. Schuller, *Tough Times Never Last, But Tough People Do!* (New York: Bantam, 1984), 204, emphasis added.

## CHAPTER 2

1. Ana Figueroa, "Rueben Martinez: Barber and Book Lover," *AARP Segunda Juventud*, April/May 2005, http://www.aarpsegundajuventud.org/english/nosotros/2005-AM/05AM_bookshop.html.
2. "Life and Times" (transcript), KCET News, 11 November 2004, http://www.kcet.org/lifeandtimes/archives/20041109.php.
3. Marco R. della Cava, "Barber Grooms Love of Books," *USA Today*, 10 October 2004, http://www.usatoday.com/life/books/news/2004-10-10-barber-genius-grant_x.htm.
4. Ibid.
5. Interview of Rueben Martinez by Brancaccio, NOW, 28 January 2005, http://www.pbs.org/now/printable/transcriptNOW104_full_print.html.
6. Figueroa, "Rueben Martinez: Barber and Book Lover."

7. Http://www.humanmedia.org/program_martinez.php3.

8. "Life and Times," KCET News.

9. Della Cava, "Barber Grooms Love of Books."

10. Tara Burghart, "MacArthur 'Genius Grants' Awarded," *Seattle Times,* 28 September 2004, http://seattletimes.nwsource.com/html/nationworld/2002048058_genius28.html.

11. Figueroa, "Rueben Martinez: Barber and Book Lover."

12. Kriegel and Patler, *If It Ain't Broke . . . Break It!,* 259.

13. Richard Edler, *If I Knew Then What I Know Now: CEOs and Other Smart Executives Share Wisdom They Wish They'd Been Told 25 Years Ago* (New York: Berkley 1995), 185.

## CHAPTER 3

1. "Northridge Earthquake," Wikipedia, http://en.wikipedia.org/wiki/1994_Northridge_Earthquake.

2. "Lessons for Post-Katrina Reconstruction: A High-Road vs. Low-Road Recovery," 6 October 2005, Economic Policy Institute Briefing Paper #166, 2, http://www.epi.org/content.cfm/bp166.

3. Ibid.

4. "Past Projects: Santa Monica I-10 Freeway," C. C. Myers, Inc., http://www.ccmyers.com/completedprojects.cfm?ID=8.

5. "Lessons for Post-Katrina Reconstruction," 4.

6. "Les Brown," http://www.lesbrown.com/about_les.htm, accessed 2 August 2006.

7. Proverbs 6:6–11 *The Message: The New Testament in Contemporary English,* by Eugene H. Peterson. Copyright © 1993, 1994, 1995, 1996, 2000.

8. http://littlecalamity.tripod.com/Quotes/L.html, accessed 2 August 2006.

9. Edgar A. Guest, "To-morrow," *A Heap O' Livin'* (Chicago: Reilly and Lee, 1916).

## CHAPTER 4

1. Donald E. Demaray, *Laughter, Joy, and Healing* (Grand Rapids: Baker Book House, 1986), 34–35.

## CHAPTER 5

1. Stephen E. Ambrose, *Undaunted Courage: Meriwether Lewis, Thomas Jefferson, and the Opening of the American West* (New York: Simon and Schuster Paperbacks, 1996), 68.

2. Ibid., 27.

3. Ibid., 76 (emphasis added).

4. Ibid., 59.

5. Richard Dillon, *Meriwether Lewis: A Biography* (New York: Coward-McCann, 1965), 30.

6. Ambrose, *Undaunted Courage,* 77.

7. List was created using information from Ambrose, *Undaunted Courage,* pages 87–92.

8. Ibid., 126.

9. Ibid., 114.

10. James P. Ronda, "Lewis and Clark Expedition," Microsoft Encarta Online Encyclopedia 2005, http://encarta.msn.com.

11. Ambrose, *Undaunted Courage,* 14.

12. Don Beveridge Jr. and Jeffrey P. Davidson, *The Achievement Challenge: How to Be a 10 in Business* (Homewood, IL: Irwin Professional, 1987).

13. The New American Standard Bible ®, Copyright © The Lockman Foundation 1960, 1962, 1963, 1968, 1971, 1972, 1973, 1975, 1977. Used by permission. (www.Lockman.org).

14. Kahleen M. Gisenhardt, "Making Fast Strategic Decisions in High-Velocity Environments," *Academy of Management Journal*, Vol. 32, No. 3 (Sept. 1989), 543–76.

## CHAPTER 6

1. Fred Kaplan, *Dickens: A Biography* (Baltimore: Johns Hopkins University Press, 1988), 50.
2. Ibid., 59.
3. Ibid., 58.
4. Ibid., 62.
5. Jane Smiley, *Charles Dickens* (New York: Lipper/Viking, 2002), 26.
6. Kaplan, *Dickens*, 60.
7. Ibid., 64.
8. Smiley, *Charles Dickens*, 3.
9. Ibid., 16.
10. *Reader's Digest*, January 1992, 91.
11. Jon Johnston, *Christian Excellence* (Grand Rapids: Baker Book House, 1985), 30.

## CHAPTER 7

1. Vonetta Flowers with W. Terry Whalin, *Running on Ice: The Overcoming Faith of Vonetta Flowers* (Birmingham, AL: New Hope Publishers, 2005), 25.
2. "Tom Hanks," Box Office Mojo, http://www.boxofficemojo.com/people/chart/?view=Actor &id=tomhanks.htm, accessed 8 May 2006.
3. "Tom Hanks Earns His $25 Million Salary, but Not Jim Carrey," 6 May 2006, http://sg.news.yahoo.com/060506/1/40lm9.html, accessed 8 May 2006.
4. Adapted from Max Isaacson, *How to Conquer the Fear of Public Speaking and Other Coronary Threats* (Rockville Centre, NY: Farnsworth Publishing, 1984), 77.
5. Howard Goodman, "I Don't Regret a Mile," used by permission /Rick Goodman, Goodman and Associates, P.O. Box 158778, Nashville, TN 37215.
6. "One List," *Houston Chronicle*, 1 January 2001, 2D, http://www.chron.com/CDA/archives/archive.mpl?id=2001_3270661, accessed 10 May 2006.
7. George E. Vaillant, *Aging Well: Surprising Guideposts to a Happier Life from the Landmark Harvard Study of Adult Development* (New York: Little, Brown and Company, 2003), 285.
8. Bruce Nash, *The Football Hall of Shame* (New York: Pocket Books, 1991), 21–22.

## CHAPTER 8

1. Winston S. Churchill, "Reflections at Century's End: Man of the Millennium?" The Churchill Centre, http://www.winstonchurchill.org/i4a/pages/index.cfm?pageid=818, accessed 17 May 2006.
2. "10 Facts About Churchill," Churchill Museum and Cabinet War Rooms, http://churchillmuseum.iwm.org.uk/server/show/nav.00i002, accessed 17 May 2006.
3. Douglas S. Russell, "Lt. Churchill, 4th Queen's Own Hussars" (lecture), Boston, 28 October 1995, The Churchill Centre, http://www.winstonchurchill.org/i4a/pages/index.cfm?pageid=638, accessed 17 May 2006.
4. "Malakand Field Force," The Churchill Centre, http://www.winstonchurchill.org/i4a/pages/index.cfm?pageid=176, accessed 2 August 2006.
5. "Churchill, 4th Queen's Own Hussars," The Churchill Centre, http://www.winstonchurchill.org/i4a/pages/index.cfm?pageid=638, accessed 2 August 2006.
6. Churchill, "Reflections."

7. John C. Maxwell, *Winning with People: Discover the People Principles That Work for You Every Time* (Nashville: Thomas Nelson, 2004), 221.
8. Pat Williams, *American Scandal: The Solution for the Crisis of Character* (Shippensburgh, PA: Treasure House, 2003), 290.

## CHAPTER 9

1. Giorgio Vasari, *The Lives of the Artists*, trans. Peter Bondanella (Oxford: Oxford University Press, 1991), 284.
2. "The Moon and the Sky," American Museum of Natural History, http://www.amnh.org/exhibitions/codex/astronom.html, accessed 30 May 2006.
3. "Bill and Melinda Gates Bring Leonardo da Vinci's Codex Leicester to Life," http://www.microsoft.com/BillGates/news/codex.asp, accessed 29 May 2006.
4. Emily Morison Beck, ed., *Bartlett's Familiar Quotations* (Boston: Little, Brown, and Company, 1980), 152.
5. Philip B. Crosby, *Quality Is Free* (New York: Penguin, 1980), 68.
6. J. Konrad Hole, *Diamonds for Daily Living* (World Press, 1996).
7. Proverbs 26:12, New King James Version®. Copyright © 1982 by Thomas Nelson, Inc. Used by permission. All rights reserved.
8. Eric W. Johnson, ed., *A Treasury of Humor* (New York: Ivy Books, 1990), 304.
9. Anonymous.
10. Dan Sullivan and Catherine Nomura, *The Laws of Lifetime Growth: Always Make Your Future Bigger Than Your Past* (San Francisco: Barrett-Koehler Publishers, 2006), 17.
11. Anonymous.

## CHAPTER 10

1. "Dr. Hwang Woo Suk," *Time*, http://www.time.com/time/asia/2004/personoftheyear/people/hwang_woo_suk.html, accessed 3 June 2006.
2. "Hwang Woo-Suk," Wikipedia, http://en.wikipedia.org/wiki/Hwang_Woo-Suk, accessed 3 June 2006.
3. Ibid.
4. "10 Questions for Dr. Hwang Woo Suk," *Time*, 5 December 2005, http://www.time.com/time/asia/magazine/printout/0,13675,501051212-1137709,00.html, accessed 3 June 2006.
5. Nicholas Wade and Choe Sang-Hun, "Researcher Faked Evidence of Human Cloning, Koreans Report," *New York Times*, 10 January 2006, http://www.nytimes.com/2006/01/10/10clone.html, accessed 3 June 2006.
6. Steven Ertelt, "Hwang Woo-Suk Apologizes for Faking Embryonic Stem Cell Research," Lifenews.com, 11 January 2006, http://www.lifenews.com/bio1274.html, accessed 3 June 2006.
7. "Disgraced Korean Cloning Scientist Indicted," *New York Times*, 12 May 2006, http://www.nytimes.com/2006/05/12/world/asia/12korea.html, accessed 3 June 2006.
8. Stan Mooneyham, *Dancing on the Strait and Narrow* (San Francisco: Harper and Row, 1989), 1–2, 68.
9. "Bobby Jones (golfer)," Wikipedia, http://en.wikipedia.org/wiki/Bobby_Jones_%28golfer%29, accessed 6 June 2006.
10. Stephen Covey, *The Seven Habits of Highly Effective People: Restoring the Character Ethic* (New York: Simon and Schuster, 1989), 21.
11. Alexander Solzhenitsyn, *One Day in the Life of Ivan Denisovich* (New York: Signet, 1998), 88.
12. Laura L. Nash, *Good Intentions Aside: A Manager's Guide to Resolving Ethical Problems* (Boston: Harvard Business School Press, 1993), 125.

CHAPTER 11
1. Dan Haseltine, "Foreword," in Dave Urbanski's *The Man Comes Around: The Spiritual Journey of Johnny Cash* (Lake Mary, FL: Relevant Books, 2003), xiv.
2. Urbanski, *The Man*, 50.
3. Ibid., 51.
4. Ibid., 53–54.
5. Johnny Cash with Patrick Carr, *Cash: The Autobiography* (New York: Harper Paperbacks, 1997), 229.
6. Ibid., 232.
7. "Tribute to June by Rosanne Cash," http://www.johnnycash.com/june/may18.html, accessed 13 June 2006.
8. Cash, *Autobiography*, 314.
9. Les Parrott, *High Maintenance Relationships* (Wheaton, IL: Tyndale, 1997).
10. http://home.comcast.net/~b.learn/bob.htm, accessed 13 June 2006.

CHAPTER 12
1. Http://www.climber.org/data/decimal.html.
2. Http://www.supertopo.com/rockclimbing/route.html?r=loeabear.
3. Andrew Todhunter, *Fall of the Phantom Lord: Climbing and the Face of Fear* (New York: Anchor Books, 1998), 44.
4. Craig Vetter, "Terminal Velocity," *Outside*, April 1999, http://outside.away.com/magazine/0499/9904terminal.html, accessed 14 June 2006.
5. Ibid.
6. Todhunter, *Fall*, 43.
7. Ibid., 78.
8. Tony Campolo, *The Covenant Companion*, April 1998.
9. *Business Ethics*, November/December 1996.
10. Williams, *American Scandal*, 174–75.
11. Rudolph W. Giuliani with Ken Kurson, *Leadership* (New York: Hyperion, 2002), 69–70.
12. Speech to Massachusetts legislature (9 January 1961), quoted on www.mass.gov/statehouse/jfk_speech.htm, accessed 4 August 2006.

CHAPTER 13
1. Lt. Commander Smith's description was so complex and detailed that I asked him to e-mail it to me so that I could describe it accurately in this book.
2. Michael Jordan and Mark Vancil, *I Can't Accept Not Trying* (San Francisco: Harper, 1994).
3. "U2," http://en.wikipedia.org/wiki/U2, accessed 21 June 2006.
4. Josh Tyrangiel, "The Constant Charmer," *Time*, 26 December–2 January 2006, 50.
5. Michka Assayas, *Bono in Conversation with Michka Assayas* (New York: Riverhead Books, 2005), 151.
6. Ibid., 152.

THE LAST WORD ON TALENT
1. "Worldwide 'Talent Shortage' Seen by Employers," *Money*, 21 February 2006, http://money.cnn.com/2006/02/21/news/international/jobs_manpower.reut/index.htm.

# ABOUT THE AUTHOR

JOHN C. MAXWELL is an internationally recognized leadership expert, speaker, and author who has sold more than 12 million books. His organizations have trained more than 1 million leaders worldwide. Dr. Maxwell is the founder of Injoy Stewardship Services and EQUIP. Every year he speaks to Fortune 500 companies, international government leaders, and organizations as diverse as the United States Military Academy at West Point and the National Football League. A *New York Times, Wall Street Journal,* and *Business Week* best-selling author, Maxwell was one of 25 authors named to Amazon.com's 10th Anniversary Hall of Fame. Two of his books, *The 21 Irrefutable Laws of Leadership* and *Developing the Leader Within You,* have sold more than a million copies each.

# BECOMING A PERSON OF INFLUENCE

## HOW TO POSITIVELY IMPACT THE LIVES OF OTHERS

### JOHN C. MAXWELL
### JIM DORNAN

*To all those who have been people of influence in*
*our lives,*
*and especially to Eric Dornan,*
*whose life, experiences, and attitude*
*have contributed more significantly*
*than anything else*
*to Jim and Nancy's ability to positively influence*
*people.*

# Contents

# Preface

When the two of us met a few years ago, we sensed instantly that there was great chemistry between us, almost like that of brothers. We had so much in common—despite having very different backgrounds. Jim has spent the last thirty years in the business environment teaching people how to become successful. In the process, he built a worldwide business organization. On the other hand, John has spent the last twenty-eight years working in a nonprofit environment as a pastor, denominational executive, and motivational speaker. He is recognized as one of the top equippers in the United States in leadership and personal growth development.

What we have in common is an understanding of people and of the positive impact that one person's life can have on others. And it all boils down to one idea: influence. We know the power of influence, and we want to share it with you.

So please join us and continue reading. We're going to give you many of our insights, tell some entertaining and informative stories, and share dynamite principles that have the power to change your life—and the lives of all the people you can influence.

# *Acknowledgments*

There are special people in our lives whose encouragement and assistance have made this book possible:

To Margaret Maxwell, whose positive support has made it possible for her husband to become a person of influence.

To Nancy Dornan, an incredible influencer to her husband, her family, and hundreds of thousands of people around the world.

To Mea Brink, for her ideas and assistance on this project.

To Stephanie Wetzel, for her proofing and editing.

To Linda Eggers, the greatest assistant any person could ever have.

To Charlie Wetzel, our writer, for his partnership on this book.

# *Introduction*

When you were a child, what did you want to be when you grew up? Did you dream about being a famous actor or singer? How about president of the United States? Maybe you wanted to become an Olympic athlete or one of the wealthiest people in the world. We all have dreams and ambitions. Undoubtedly, you've accomplished some of yours. But no matter how successful you are now, you still have dreams and goals that are waiting to be fulfilled. And our desire is to help you realize the dreams, to help you realize your potential.

Let's start by doing a little experiment. Take a look at the following list of people. It's quite a diverse group, but they all have one thing in common. See if you can figure out what it is.

JOHN GRISHAM
GEORGE GALLUP
ROBERT E. LEE
DENNIS RODMAN
JAMES DOBSON
DAN RATHER
MADONNA
HIDEO NOMO
JERRY AND PATTY BEAUMONT
RICH DEVOS
MOTHER TERESA
BETH MEYERS
PABLO PICASSO
ADOLF HITLER
TIGER WOODS
ANTHONY BONACOURSI
ALANIS MORRISETTE
GLENN LEATHERWOOD
BILL CLINTON
JOHN WESLEY
ARNOLD SCHWARZENEGGER

*Influence doesn't come
to us instantaneously.
It grows by stages.*

Have you figured it out? What do they have in common? It certainly isn't their professions. The names have been drawn from lists of writers and statesmen, sports figures and artists, evangelists and dictators, actors and business professionals. Both men and women are included. Some are single and others are married. They are of various ages. And many ethnic groups and nationalities are represented. Some of the people are famous, and you probably recognize their names. But you have undoubtedly never heard of others. So what's the key? What do they all have in common? The answer is that *every one of them is a person of influence.*

## EVERYONE HAS INFLUENCE

We created this list almost at random, selecting well-known people as well as ones from our lives. You could just as easily do the same thing. We did it to make a point: Everyone is an influencer of other people. It doesn't matter who you are or what your occupation is. A politician, such as the president of the United States, has tremendous influence on hundreds of millions of people, not only in his own country but around the globe. And entertainers, such as Madonna and Arnold Schwarzenegger, often influence an entire generation of people in one or more cultures. A teacher, such as Glenn Leatherwood, who instructed John and hundreds of others boys in Sunday school, touches the lives of his own students and also indirectly influences all the people those boys grow up to influence.

But you don't have to be in a high-profile occupation to be a person of influence. In fact, if your life in any way connects with other people, you are an influencer. Everything you do at home, at church, in your job, or on the ball field has an impact on the lives of other people. American poet-philosopher Ralph Waldo Emerson said, "Every man is a hero and an oracle to somebody, and to that person, whatever he says has an enhanced value."

If your desire is to be successful or to make a positive impact on your world, you need to become a person of influence. Without influence, there is no success. For example, if you're a salesperson wanting to sell more of your product, you need to be able to influence your customers. If you're a manager, your success depends on your ability to influence your employees. If you're a coach, you can build a winning team only by influencing your players. If you're a pastor, your ability to reach people and grow your church depends on your influence with your congregation. If you want to raise a strong, healthy family, you have to be able to influence your children positively. No matter what your goals are in life or what you want to accomplish, you can achieve them faster, you can be more effective, and the contribution you make can be longer lasting if you learn how to become a person of influence.

> *If your life in any way connects with other people, you are an influencer.*

An amusing story about the impact of influence comes from the administration of President Calvin Coolidge. An overnight guest at the White House was having breakfast with Coolidge one morning, and he wanted to make a good impression on the president. He noticed that Coolidge, having been served his coffee, took the coffee cup, poured some of its contents into a deep saucer, and leisurely added a little bit of sugar and cream. Not wanting to breach any rules of etiquette, the visitor followed the commander in chief's lead, and he poured some of his coffee into his saucer and added sugar and cream. Then he waited for the president's next move. He was horrified to see him place the saucer on the floor for the cat. No one reported what the visitor did next.

# YOUR INFLUENCE IS NOT
# EQUAL WITH ALL PEOPLE

Influence is a curious thing. Even though we have an impact on nearly everyone around us, our level of influence is not the same with everyone. To see this principle in action, try ordering around your best friend's dog the next time you visit him.

You may not have thought much about it, but you probably know instinctively which people you have great influence with and which ones you don't. For example, think of four or five people you work with. When you present an idea to them or make a suggestion, do they all respond in the same way? Of course not. One person may think all your ideas are inspired. Another may view everything you say with skepticism. (No doubt you can identify which one you have the influence with.) Yet that same skeptical person may love every single idea presented by your boss or one of your colleagues. That just shows your influence with her may not be as strong as that of someone else.

Once you start paying closer attention to people's responses to yourself and others, you'll see that people respond to one another according to their level of influence. And you'll quickly recognize how much influence you have with various people in your life. You may even notice that your influence is on many different levels in your household. If you're married and have two or more children, think about how they interact with you. One child may respond especially well to you, while another does better with your spouse. It's a matter of which parent has the greater influence with the child.

# STAGES OF INFLUENCE
# AND THEIR IMPACT

If you've read John's *Developing the Leader Within You,* then you probably remember the description of the five levels of leadership contained in chapter 1. Visually, it looks like this:

**PERSONHOOD**
**PEOPLE DEVELOPMENT**
**PRODUCTION**
**PERMISSION**
**POSITION**

Leadership (which is a specific application of influence) is at its lowest level when it is based on position only. It grows and goes to a higher level as you develop relationships with others. That's when they give you permission to lead beyond the limits of your job description. As you and your followers become more productive together in your work, then your leadership can go to level 3. And when you begin to develop people and help them reach their potential, your leadership moves up to level 4. Only a few people reach level 5 because it requires a person to spend a lifetime developing others to their highest potential.[1]

Influence functions in a similar way. It doesn't come to us instantaneously. Instead, it grows by stages. Visually, it looks something like this:

Let's consider each level:

## Level 1: Modeling

People are first influenced by what they see. If you have children, then you've probably observed this. No matter what you *tell* your children to do, their natural inclination is to follow what they *see you doing*. For most people, if they perceive that you are positive and trustworthy and have admirable qualities, then they will seek you as an influencer in their lives. And the better they get to know you, the greater your credibility will be and the higher your influence can become—if they like what they see.

When you meet people who don't know you, at first you have no influence with them at all. If someone they trust introduces you to them and gives you an endorsement, then you can temporarily "borrow" some of that person's influence. They will assume that you are credible until they get to know you. But as soon as they have some time to observe you, you either build or bust that influence by your actions.

One interesting exception to this modeling process occurs in the case of celebrities. Because of their preoccupation with television, movies, and the media, many people are strongly influenced by others that they have never met. More often than not, they are influenced not by the actual individual, but by the image of that person. And that image may not be an accurate representation of that actress, politician, sports figure, or entertainer. Nonetheless, they admire that person and are influenced by the actions and attitudes they believe that person represents.

> *You can be a model to the masses, but to go to the higher levels of influence, you have to work with individuals.*

## Level 2: Motivating

Modeling can be a powerful influence—either positively or negatively. And it's something that can be done even from a distance. But if you want to make a really significant impact on the lives of other people, you have to do it up close. And that brings you to the second level of influence: motivating.

You become a motivational influencer when you encourage people and communicate with them on an emotional level. The process does two things: (1) It creates a bridge between you and them, and (2) it builds up their confidence and sense of self-worth. When people feel good about you and themselves during the times they're with you, then your level of influence increases significantly.

## Level 3: Mentoring

When you reach the motivational level of influence with others, you can start to see a positive impact in their lives. To increase that impact and make it long-lasting, you have to move up to the next level of influence, which is mentoring.

Mentoring is pouring your life into other people and helping them reach their potential. The power of mentoring is so strong that you can actually see the lives of the persons you are influencing change before your eyes. As you give of yourself, helping them overcome obstacles in their lives and showing them how to grow personally and professionally, you help them achieve a whole new level of living. You can truly make a difference in their lives.

## Level 4: Multiplying

The highest level of influence you can have in others' lives is the multiplication level. As a multiplying influencer, you help people you're influencing to become positive influencers in the lives of others and pass on not only what they have received from you, but also what they have learned and gleaned on their own. Few people ever make it to the fourth level of influence, but everyone has the potential to do so. It takes unselfishness, generosity, and commitment. It also takes time. In order to move up a level in influence with people, you have to give them more individual attention. You can be a model to the masses, but to go to the higher levels of influence, you have to work with individuals.

Bill Westafer, a friend of John's, who formerly worked at Skyline Church in San Diego, observed, "There are people whose feelings and well-being are within my influence. I will never escape that fact." That's a good concept for all of us to remember. If you lead many people or have a high-profile position, you have a greater responsibility because of your increased influence. What you say—and, more important, what you do—is a model for those who follow you. Their actions will reflect your influence.

# YOUR INFLUENCE IS EITHER POSITIVE OR NEGATIVE

Now that you recognize your influence with others, you must think about how you are going to use it. You probably noticed that professional basketball player Dennis Rodman was on the list of influencers at the beginning of this introduction. Many times we've heard Dennis Rodman say that he doesn't want to be a role model. He just wants to be himself. Dennis doesn't understand (or refuses to acknowledge) that he already is a role model. It's not something he can decline. He is an example to everyone in his family, his neighbors, and the people at the neighborhood store where he shops. And because of the profession he has chosen, he is a role model to millions of others—to more people than he would be if he had chosen to be, for example, an auto mechanic. He is influencing others, and he has made a choice concerning the kind of influence he is having.

> ***E**ven if you've had a negative*
> *effect on others in the past,*
> *you can turn that around*
> *and make your impact*
> *a positive one.*

Baseball legend Jackie Robinson noted, "A life isn't significant except for its impact on other lives." Robinson's impact on people in the United States has been incredible. In the mid-1940s, he became the first African-American athlete to play major-league baseball despite prejudice, racial taunts, abuse, and death threats. And he did it with character and dignity. Brad Herzog, author of *The Sports 100,* has identified Robinson as the most influential person in American sports history:

> First, there are those who changed the way the games were played. . . . Then there are the men and women whose presence and performance forever altered the sporting scene in a fundamental manner. . . . And, finally, there are the handful of

sports figures whose influence transcended the playing fields and impacted American culture. . . . Robinson, to a greater extent than anyone else, was all three types in one.[2]

Martin Luther King, Jr., one of the most influential Americans of the twentieth century, acknowledged the positive impact Jackie Robinson made on his life and the cause for which he fought. To African-American baseball pioneer Don Newcombe, King said, "You'll never know what you and Jackie and Roy [Campanella] did to make it possible to do my job."

Most of the time we recognize the influence we have on those who are closest to us in our lives—for good or ill. But sometimes we overlook the impact we can have on other people around us. The anonymous author of this poem probably had that in mind when he wrote,

> *My life shall touch a dozen lives before this day is done,*
> *Leave countless marks for good or ill ere sets the*
>     *evening sun,*
> *This is the wish I always wish, the prayer I always pray;*
> *Lord, may my life help other lives it touches by the way.*

As you interact with your family, your coworkers, and the clerk at the store today, recognize that your life touches many others' lives. Certainly, your influence on your family members is greater than that on the strangers you meet. And if you have a high-profile occupation, you influence people you don't know. But even in your ordinary day-to-day interactions with people, you make an impact. You can make the few moments that you interact with a store clerk and a bank teller a miserable experience, or you can get them to smile and make their day. The choice is yours.

# POSITIVE INFLUENCERS ADD VALUE TO OTHER PEOPLE

As you move up to the higher levels of influence and become an active influencer, you can begin to have a positive influence on people and add value to their lives. That's true for any positive influencer. The baby-sitter who reads to a child encourages him to love books and helps him become a lifelong learner. The teacher who puts his faith, confidence, and love in a little girl helps her to feel valued and good about herself. The boss who delegates to her employees and gives them authority as well as responsibility enlarges their horizons and empowers them to become better workers and people. The parents who know how and when to give their children grace help them to stay open and communicative, even during their teenage years. All of these people add lasting value to the lives of other people.

We don't know what kind of influence you have on others today as you read this book. Your actions may touch the lives of thousands of people. Or you may influence two or three coworkers and family members. The number of people is not what's most important. The crucial thing to remember is that your level of influence is not static. Even if you've had a negative effect on others in the past, you can turn that around and make your impact a positive one. And if your level of influence has been relatively low up to now, you can increase it and become a person of influence who helps others.

In fact, that's what this book is all about. We want to help you become a person of high influence, no matter what stage of life you're in or what you do for a living. You can have an incredibly positive impact on the lives of others. You can add tremendous value to their lives.

## Who Is on the Influence List?

Everyone could sit down and make a list of people who have added value to his or her life. We mentioned that the list at the beginning of this introduction contains the names of some people who have influenced us. Some of the names are big. For example, John considers eighteenth-century evangelist John Wesley to be a significant influence on his life and career. Wesley was a dynamic leader, preacher, and social critic. During his lifetime, he turned the Christian church in England and America upside down, and his thoughts and teachings continue to influence the way churches function and Christians believe even today. John considers Wesley to be the greatest person to have lived since the apostle Paul.

Other people named on that list are not well known, but that in no way lessens their level of influence. For example, Jerry and Patty Beaumont had a profound impact on the lives of Jim and his wife, Nancy. Here's their story:

Nancy and I first met Jerry and Patty almost twenty-five years ago when Nancy and Patty were both pregnant. The Beaumonts were a classy couple—really sharp and confident. We were attracted to them immediately because it seemed that they really had their lives together, and we observed that they were living out their strong spiritual convictions with integrity and consistency.

Nancy met Patty one day while they were in the obstetrician's waiting room. They hit it off instantly and began to build a relationship. We had no idea how much their friendship was going to mean to us just a few months later when our lives got turned upside down.

Nancy and I think back on those days now as a good time in our lives. Our daughter, Heather, was five years old, and we were really enjoying her. We were also just beginning to build our business. It was taking a lot of time and energy to get it going, but it was fun. We were beginning to see that all our work was going to pay off in the future.

When Nancy told me that she was pregnant, I was ecstatic. It meant our little family was about to grow, and we hoped our second child would be a boy.

After nine months of routine pregnancy, Nancy gave birth to our first son, Eric. At first everything appeared to be normal. But a few hours later, the doctors discovered that Eric had been born with some very serious physical problems. His back was open and his spinal cord had not formed properly. They told us he had a condition called spina bifida. To make things worse, his spinal fluid had gotten infected during the delivery, so he was suffering from severe systemic meningitis.

Our whole life seemed to be thrown into chaos. After Nancy's hours of labor, we were exhausted and confused. They told us Eric needed brain surgery, and we had to make a decision right then. Without it, he didn't stand a chance. Even with it, things didn't look good. We cried as they prepared to take our little boy—only a few hours old—and transport him to Children's Hospital for emergency brain surgery. All we could do was pray that he would make it.

We waited for hours, but the doctors finally came out and told us Eric was going to live. We were shaken when we saw him after the surgery. We wondered how someone so small could have so many wires attached to him. The opening in his back was closed, but we could see that they had surgically implanted a shunt tube in his brain to drain off excess spinal fluid and relieve the pressure.

The first year of Eric's life was a blur for us as he repeatedly entered Children's Hospital. In the first nine months, he underwent eleven more surgeries—three of those operations came in one weekend. Things were happening so fast that we were overwhelmed, and we couldn't even comprehend what we might have to face in the future.

While we were trying to survive the midnight trips to the hospital and hold up under the pain and fear we had for Eric, guess who came alongside us and helped us survive each day as it came? Jerry and Patty Beaumont. They had come to the hospital that first day of Eric's life and given us comfort and encouragement while he was in the operating room. They brought food for us and sat with Nancy and me in hospital waiting rooms. And all the while they shared their incredible faith with us.

Most important, they helped us to believe that God had a special plan for Eric and us. "You know," Patty told Nancy one day, "you and Jim can make Eric's problems the center of everything you do, or you can use them as a launching pad for a whole new way of looking at life."

It was then that we turned a corner in our lives. We began looking beyond our circumstances and saw that there was a bigger picture. We realized God had a plan for us as well as Eric, and our faith gave us strength and peace. The Beaumonts had helped us consider and answer some of life's most important questions. From that day on, our entire attitudes changed and we had great hope.

That was more than two decades ago. Jim and Nancy lost touch with the Beaumonts, though they have since tried to find them. Now Eric has grown up and gets around pretty well in his electric wheelchair despite having experienced a stroke during one of his surgeries. He is a constant source of joy, inspiration, and humor for the Dornan family. And though their contact with Jerry and Patty Beaumont lasted only about a year, Jim and Nancy recognize the tremendous value they added to them and still consider them to be two of the greatest influencers in their lives.

Today, Jim and Nancy are people of influence. Their business has expanded into more than twenty-six countries around the world: from Eastern Europe to the Pacific, from Brazil and Argentina to mainland China. Through seminars, tapes, and videos, they impact hundreds of thousands of individuals and families each year. And their business continues to grow. But more important to them, they are sharing their strong values and faith with the people they influence. They are doing all they can to add value to the life of everyone they touch.

Recently, John was talking to Larry Dobbs. He is the president and publisher of the Dobbs Publishing Group, which produces magazines such as *Mustang Monthly, Corvette Fever,* and *Musclecar Review.* They talked about the subject of influence, and Larry shared a little bit of his story: "John, my daddy was a sharecropper, so he never had much. When he died, the only money he left me was a dollar. But he gave me so much more than that. He passed on his values to me." Then Larry said something very insightful: "The only inheritance that a man will leave that has eternal value is his influence."

We don't know exactly what your dream is in life or what kind of legacy you want to leave. But if you want to make an impact, you will have to become a man or woman capable of influencing others. There is no other way of effectively touching people's lives. And if you become a person of influence, then maybe someday when other people write down the names of those who made a difference in their lives, your name just might be on the list.

# *A Person of Influence Has . . .*

# INTEGRITY WITH PEOPLE

A few years ago, while my wife, Nancy, and I were on a business trip to Europe, we celebrated her birthday in London. As her gift, I decided to take her to the Escada boutique to buy her an outfit or two.

She tried on a number of things and liked all of them. And while she was in the dressing room trying to decide which one to pick, I told the salesperson to wrap up the whole lot of it. Nancy tried to protest; she was embarrassed to buy so many things at one time, but I insisted. We both knew she'd get good use out of the clothes. Besides, she looked fabulous in everything.

A couple of days later, we took the long flight out of Heathrow Airport in London to San Francisco International Airport. After we landed, we got in line for the inevitable customs check. When they asked what we had to declare, we told them about the clothes Nancy had bought and the amount we had spent.

"What?" the agent said. "You're declaring clothes?" He read the figure that we'd written and said, "You've got to be kidding!" It's true that we had spent a little bit of money on them, but we didn't think it was *that* big a deal. "What are the clothes made of?" he asked.

That seemed like an odd question. "A bunch of different things," answered Nancy. "Wool, cotton, silk. Everything's different. There are dresses, coats, blouses, shoes, belts, accessories. Why?"

"Each kind of fabric has a different duty," he said. "I'll have to get my supervisor. I don't even know what all the different rates are. Nobody declares clothes." He looked frustrated. "Go ahead and pull everything out and sort it according to what it's made of." As we opened up our bags, he walked away and we could hear him saying to a coworker, "Bobby, you'll never believe this. . . ."

It must have taken us a good forty-five minutes to sort everything out and tally up how much we'd spent on each type of item. The duty turned out to be quite a bit—about two thousand dollars. As we were putting everything back into our suitcase, the agent said, "You know what? I think I know you. Aren't you Jim Dornan?"

"Yes," I answered. "I'm sorry, have we met before?" I didn't recognize him.

"No," he said. "But I've got a friend who's in your organization. Network 21, right?"

"That's right," I said.

"I've seen your picture before. You know," the agent said, "my friend has been telling me that I'd really benefit from hooking up with your organization. But I haven't really listened. Now I'm thinking I should reconsider. He might be right after all. See, most people I see every day try to get all kinds of things through customs without paying duty, even stuff they should know better about. But you guys, you're declaring stuff you could have gotten through with no problem. That's sure a lot of money you could've saved!"

"That may be true," answered Nancy, "but I can spare the money for customs a lot more than I can spare not having a clear conscience."

As we stood in line that day, it didn't even occur to Nancy or me that anyone there might know us. If our intention had been to cheat our way through, we never would have suspected that we'd be recognized. We thought we were anonymous. And I think that is what a lot of people think as they cut corners in life. "Who will ever know?" they say to themselves. But the truth is that other people know. Your spouse, children, friends, and business associates all know. And more important, even if you cover your tracks really well, and they don't know what you are up to, *you do!* And you don't want to give away or sell your integrity for *any* price.

Jim's experience with the customs agent is just one small example of how people today think when it comes to integrity. Sad to say, it no longer appears to be the norm, and when confronted by an example of honest character in action, many people seem shocked. Common decency is no longer common.

## GENUINE INTEGRITY IS NOT FOR SALE

You can see character issues coming up in every aspect of life. A few years ago, for example, financier Ivan Boesky openly described *greed* as "a good thing" while speaking at UCLA's business school. That flawed thinking soon got him into trouble. When his unethical practices on Wall Street came to light, he was fined $100 million and sent to prison for three years. Recently, he was reported to be ruined financially and living on alimony from his former wife.

> *The need for integrity today is perhaps as great as it has ever been. And it is absolutely essential for anyone who desires to become a person of influence.*

Government hasn't been immune to integrity issues either. The Department of Justice is prosecuting public officials as never before, and it recently boasted that it had convicted more than 1,100 in one year—a dubious record.

Just about everywhere you look, you see examples of moral breakdowns. TV preachers fall morally; mothers drown their children; professional athletes are found with drugs and prostitutes in hotel rooms. The list keeps growing. It seems that many people view integrity as an outdated idea, something expendable or no longer applicable to them in our fast-paced world. But the need for integrity today is perhaps as great as it has ever been. And it is absolutely essential for anyone who desires to become a person of influence.

In his best-selling book *The Seven Habits of Highly Effective People,* Stephen Covey wrote about the importance of integrity to a person's success:

> If I try to use human influence strategies and tactics of how to get other people to do what I want, to work better, to be more motivated, to like me and each other—while my character is fundamentally flawed, marked by duplicity or insincerity—then, in the long run, I cannot be successful. My duplicity will breed distrust, and everything I do—even using so-called good human relations techniques—will be perceived as manipulative.
>
> It simply makes no difference how good the rhetoric is or even how good the intentions are; if there is little or no trust, there is no foundation for permanent success. Only basic goodness gives life to technique.[1]

Integrity is crucial for business and personal success. A joint study conducted by the UCLA Graduate School of Management and Korn/Ferry International of New York City surveyed 1,300 senior executives. Seventy-one percent of them said that integrity was the quality most needed to succeed in business. And a study by the Center for Creative Research discovered that though many errors and obstacles can be overcome by a person who wants to rise to the top of an organization, that person is almost never able to move up in the organization if he compromises his integrity by betraying a trust.

# INTEGRITY IS ABOUT THE SMALL THINGS

As important as integrity is to your business success, it's even more critical if you want to become an influencer. It is the foundation upon which many other qualities are built, such as respect, dignity, and trust. If the foundation of integrity is weak or fundamentally flawed, then being a person of influence becomes impossible. As Cheryl Biehl points out, "One of the realities of life is that if you can't trust a person at all points, you can't truly trust him or her at any point." Even people who are able to hide their lack of integrity for a period of time will eventually experience failure, and whatever influence they have temporarily gained will disappear.

Think of integrity as having benefits similar to that of a house's foundation during a huge storm. If the foundation is sound, then it will hold up against the raging waters. But when there are cracks in the foundation, the stress of the storm deepens the cracks until eventually the foundation—and then the whole house—crumbles under the pressure.

*Integrity is the quality most needed to succeed in business.*

That's why it's crucial to maintain integrity by taking care of the little things. Many people misunderstand that. They think they can do whatever they want when it comes to the small things because they believe that as long as they don't have any major lapses, they're doing well. But that's not the way it works. *Webster's New Universal Unabridged Dictionary* describes *integrity* as "adherence to moral and ethical principles; soundness of moral character; honesty." Ethical principles are not flexible. A little white lie is still a lie. Theft is theft—whether it's $1, $1,000, or $1 million. Integrity commits itself to character over personal gain, to people over things, to service over power, to principle over convenience, to the long view over the immediate.

Nineteenth-century clergyman Phillips Brooks maintained, "Character is made in the small moments of our lives." Anytime you break a moral principle, you create a small crack in the foundation of your integrity. And when times get tough, it becomes harder to act with integrity, not easier. Character isn't created in a crisis; it only comes to light. Everything you have done in the past—and the things you have neglected to do—come to a head when you're under pressure.

Developing and maintaining integrity require constant attention. Josh Weston, chairman and CEO of Automatic Data Processing, Inc., says, "I've always tried to live with the following simple rule: 'Don't do what you wouldn't feel comfortable reading about in the newspapers the next day.'" That's a good standard all of us should keep.

# INTEGRITY IS AN INSIDE JOB

One of the reasons many people struggle with integrity issues is that they tend to look outside themselves to explain any deficiencies in character. But the development of integrity is an inside job. Take a look at the following three truths about integrity that go against common thinking:

## 1. *Integrity Is Not Determined by Circumstances*

Some psychologists and sociologists today tell us that many people of poor character would not be the way they are if only they had grown up in a different environment. Now, it's true that our upbringing and circumstances affect who we are, especially when we are young. But the older we are, the greater the number of choices we make—for good or bad. Two people can grow up in the same environment, even in the same household, and one will have integrity and the other won't. Ultimately, you are responsible for your choices. Your circumstances are as responsible for your character as a mirror is for your looks. What you see only reflects what you are.

## 2. *Integrity Is Not Based on Credentials*

In ancient times, brick makers, engravers, and other artisans used a symbol to mark the things they created to show that they were the makers. The symbol that each one used was his "character." The value of the work was in proportion to the skill with which the object was made. And only if the quality of the work was high was the character esteemed. In other words, the quality of the person and his work gave value to his credentials. If the work was good, so was the character. If it was bad, then the character was viewed as poor.

The same is true for us today. Character comes from who we are. But some people would like to be judged not by who they are, but by the titles they have earned or the position they hold, regardless of the nature of their character. Their desire is to influence others by the weight of their credentials rather than the strength of their character. But credentials can never accomplish what character can. Look at some differences between the two:

| Credentials | Character |
|---|---|
| Are transient | Is permanent |
| Turn the focus to rights | Keeps the focus on responsibilities |
| Add value to only one person | Adds value to many people |
| Look to past accomplishments | Builds a legacy for the future |
| Often evoke jealousy in others | Generates respect and integrity |
| Can only get you in the door | Keeps you there |

No number of titles, degrees, offices, designations, awards, licenses, or other credentials can substitute for basic, honest integrity when it comes to the power of influencing others.

## 3. Integrity Is Not to Be Confused with Reputation

Some people mistakenly emphasize image or reputation. Listen to what William Hersey Davis has to say about the difference between character and its shadow, reputation:

> The circumstances amid which you live determine your reputation . . .
> the truth you believe determines your character. . . .
> Reputation is what you are supposed to be;
> character is what you are. . . .
> Reputation is the photograph;
> character is the face. . . .
> Reputation comes over one from without;

character grows up from within. . . .
Reputation is what you have when you come to a new community;
character is what you have when you go away.
Your reputation is made in a moment;
your character is built in a lifetime. . . .
Your reputation is learned in an hour;
your character does not come to light for a year. . . .
Reputation grows like a mushroom;
character lasts like eternity. . . .
Reputation makes you rich or makes you poor;
character makes you happy or makes you miserable. . . .
Reputation is what men say about you on your tombstone;
character is what the angels say about you before the throne of God.

Certainly, a good reputation is valuable. King Solomon of ancient Israel stated, "A good name is more desirable than great riches."[2] But a good reputation exists because it is a reflection of a person's character. If a good reputation is like gold, then having integrity is like owning the mine. Worry less about what others think, and give your attention to your inner character. D. L. Moody wrote, "If I take care of my character, my reputation will take care of itself."

If you struggle with maintaining your integrity, and you're doing all the right things on the *outside*—but you're still getting the wrong results—something is wrong and still needs to be changed on the *inside*. Look at the following questions. They may help you nail down areas that need attention.

## QUESTIONS TO HELP YOU MEASURE YOUR INTEGRITY

1. How well do I treat people from whom I can gain nothing?
2. Am I transparent with others?
3. Do I role-play based on the person(s) I'm with?
4. Am I the same person when I'm in the spotlight as I am when I'm alone?

5. Do I quickly admit wrongdoing without being pressed to do so?
6. Do I put other people ahead of my personal agenda?
7. Do I have an unchanging standard for moral decisions, or do circumstances determine my choices?
8. Do I make difficult decisions, even when they have a personal cost attached to them?
9. When I have something to say about people, do I talk *to* them or *about* them?
10. Am I accountable to at least one other person for what I think, say, and do?

Don't be too quick to respond to the questions. If character development is a serious area of need in your life, your tendency may be to skim through the questions, giving answers that describe how you wish you were rather than who you actually are. Take some time to reflect on each question, honestly considering it before answering. Then work on the areas where you're having the most trouble. And remember this:

> *Many succeed momentarily by what they know;*
> *Some succeed temporarily by what they do; but*
> *Few succeed permanently by what they are.*

The road of integrity may not be the easiest one, but it's the only one that will get you where you ultimately want to go.

## INTEGRITY IS YOUR BEST FRIEND

The esteemed nineteenth-century American writer Nathaniel Hawthorne offered this insight: "No man can for any considerable time wear one face to himself and another to the multitude without finally getting bewildered as to which is the true one." Anytime you compromise your integrity, you do yourself an incredible amount of damage. That's because integrity really is your best friend. It will never betray you or put you in a compromising position. It keeps your priorities right. When you're tempted to take shortcuts, it helps you stay the right course.

When others criticize you unfairly, it helps you keep going and take the high road of not striking back. And when others' criticism is valid, integrity helps you to accept what they say, learn from it, and keep growing.

Abraham Lincoln once stated, "When I lay down the reins of this administration, I want to have one friend left. And that friend is inside myself." You could almost say that Lincoln's integrity was his best friend while he was in office because he was criticized so viciously. Here is a description of what he faced as explained by Donald T. Phillips:

> Abraham Lincoln was slandered, libeled and hated perhaps more intensely than any man ever to run for the nation's highest office. . . . He was publicly called just about every name imaginable by the press of the day, including a grotesque baboon, a third-rate country lawyer who once split rails and now splits the Union, a coarse vulgar joker, a dictator, an ape, a buffoon, and others. The *Illinois State Register* labeled him "the craftiest and most dishonest politician that ever disgraced an office in America. . . ." Severe and unjust criticism did not subside after Lincoln took the oath of office, nor did it come only from Southern sympathizers. It came from within the Union itself, from Congress, from some factions within the Republican party, and, initially, from within his own cabinet. As president, Lincoln learned that, no matter what he did, there were going to be people who would not be pleased.[3]

Through it all, Lincoln was a man of principle. And as Thomas Jefferson wisely said, "God grant that men of principle shall be our principal men."

# INTEGRITY IS YOUR FRIENDS' BEST FRIEND

Integrity is your best friend. And it's also one of the best friends that your friends will ever have. When the people around you know that you're a person of integrity, they know that you want to influence them because of the opportunity to add value to their lives. They don't have to worry about your motives.

Recently, we saw a cartoon in the *New Yorker* that showed how difficult it can be to sort out another person's motives. Some hogs were assembled for a feeding, and a farmer was filling their trough to the brim. One hog turned to the others and asked, "Have you ever wondered *why* he's being so good to us?" A person of integrity influences others because he wants to *bring* something to the table that will benefit them—not *put* them on the table to benefit himself.

If you're a basketball fan, you probably remember Red Auerbach. He was the president and general manager of the Boston Celtics from 1967 to 1987. He truly understood how integrity adds value to others, especially when people are working together on a team. And he had a method of recruiting that was different from that of most NBA team leaders. When he reviewed a prospective player for the Celtics, his primary concern was the young man's character. While others focused almost entirely on statistics and individual performance, Auerbach wanted to know about a player's attitude. He figured that the way to win was to find players who would give their best and work for the benefit of the team. Players who had outstanding ability but whose character was weak or whose desire was to promote only themselves were not really assets.

## THE BENEFIT OF INTEGRITY: TRUST

The bottom line when it comes to integrity is that it allows others to trust you. And without trust, you have nothing. Trust is the single most important factor in personal and professional relationships. It is the glue that holds people together. And it is the key to becoming a person of influence.

Trust is an increasingly rare commodity these days. People have become increasingly suspicious and skeptical. Bill Kynes expressed the feelings of a whole generation when he wrote,

We thought we could trust the *military,*
  but then came *Vietnam;*
We thought we could trust the *politicians,*

but then came *Watergate;*
We thought we could trust the *engineers,*
    but then came the *Challenger disaster;*
We thought we could trust our *broker,*
    but then came *Black Monday;*
We thought we could trust the *preachers,*
    but then came *PTL and Jimmy Swaggart.*
So who can I trust?[4]

At one time you could assume that others would trust you until you gave them a reason not to. But today with most people, you must prove your trustworthiness first. That's what makes integrity so important if you want to become a person of influence. Trust comes from others only when you exemplify solid character.

> *Character is made in the*
> *small moments of our lives.*
> *—Phillips Brooks*

People today are desperate for leaders, but they want to be influenced only by individuals they can trust, persons of good character. If you want to become someone who can positively influence other people, you need to develop the following qualities of integrity and live them out every day:

- **Model consistency of character.** Solid trust can develop only when people can trust you *all the time.* If they never know from moment to moment what you're going to do, the relationship will never deepen to a confident level of trust.
- **Employ honest communication.** To be trustworthy, you have to be like a good musical composition; your words and music must match.
- **Value transparency.** People eventually find out about your flaws, even if you try to hide them. But if you're honest with people and admit your weaknesses, they will appreciate

your honesty and integrity. And they will be able to relate to you better.

- **Exemplify humility.** People won't trust you if they see that you are driven by ego, jealousy, or the belief that you are better than they are.
- **Demonstrate your support of others.** Nothing develops or displays your character better than your desire to put others first. As our friend Zig Ziglar says, help enough other people to succeed, and you will succeed also.
- **Fulfill your promises.** Never promise anything you can't deliver. And when you say you'll do something, follow through on it. A sure way to break trust with others is to fail to fulfill your commitments.
- **Embrace an attitude of service.** We have been put on this earth not to be served, but to serve. Giving of yourself and your time to others shows that you care about them. Missionary-physician Sir Wilfred T. Grenfell held that "the service we render to others is really the rent we pay for our room on this earth." People of integrity are givers, not takers.
- **Encourage two-way participation with the people you influence.** When you live a life of integrity, people listen to you and follow you. Always remember that the goal of influence is not manipulation; it's participation. Only as you include others in your life and success do you permanently succeed.

It has been said that you don't really know people until you have observed them when they interact with a child, when the car has a flat tire, when the boss is away, and when they think no one will ever know. But people with integrity never have to worry about that. No matter where they are, who they are with, or what kind of situation they find themselves in, they are consistent and live by their principles.

## THE BENEFIT OF TRUST: INFLUENCE

When you earn people's trust, you begin to earn their confidence, and that is one of the keys to influence. President Dwight D. Eisenhower expressed his opinion on the subject this way:

In order to be a leader, a man must have followers. And to have followers, a man must have their confidence. Hence, the supreme quality for a leader is unquestionably integrity. Without it, no real success is possible, no matter whether it is on a section gang, a football field, in the army, or in an office. If a man's associates find that he lacks forthright integrity, he will fail. His teachings and actions must square with each other. The first great need, therefore, is integrity and high purpose.

When people begin to trust you, your level of influence increases. And that's when you will be able to start impacting their lives. But it's also the time to be careful because power can be a dangerous thing. In most cases, those who want power probably shouldn't have it, those who enjoy it probably do so for the wrong reasons, and those who want most to hold on to it don't understand that it's only temporary. As Abraham Lincoln said, "Nearly all men can stand adversity, but if you want to test a man's character, give him power."

Few people in the world today have greater power and influence than the president of the United States. George Bush, the nation's forty-first president, had strong beliefs about power and advised, "Use power to help people. For we are given power not to advance our own purposes nor to make a great show in the world, nor a name. There is but one just use of power and it is to serve people." To keep your ambition in check and the focus of your influence on helping and serving others, periodically ask yourself this question: If the whole world followed me, would it be a better world?

## BECOME A PERSON OF INTEGRITY

In the end, you can bend your actions to conform to your principles, or you can bend your principles to conform to your actions. It's a choice you have to make. If you want to become a person of influence, then you better choose the path of integrity because all other roads ultimately lead to ruin.

To become a person of integrity, you need to go back to the fundamentals. You may have to make some tough choices, but they'll be worth it.

## Commit Yourself to Honesty, Reliability, and Confidentiality

Integrity begins with a specific, conscious decision. If you wait until a moment of crisis before settling your integrity issues, you set yourself up to fail. Choose today to live by a strict moral code, and determine to stick with it no matter what happens.

## Decide Ahead of Time That You Don't Have a Price

President George Washington perceived that "few men have the virtue to withstand the highest bidder." Some people can be bought because they haven't settled the money issue before the moment of temptation. The best way to guard yourself against a breach in integrity is to make a decision today that you won't sell your integrity: not for power, revenge, pride, or money—any amount of money.

## Major in the Minor Things

The little things make or break us. If you cross the line of your values—whether it's by an inch or by a mile—you're still out of bounds. Honesty is a habit you ingrain by doing the right thing all the time, day after day, week after week, year after year. If you consistently do what's right in the little things, you're less likely to wander off course morally or ethically.

## Each Day, Do What You Should Do Before What You Want to Do

A big part of integrity is following through consistently on your responsibilities. Our friend Zig Ziglar says, "When you do the things you have to do when you have to do them, the day will come when you can do the things you want to do when you want to do them." Psychologist-philosopher William James stated the idea more strongly: "Everybody ought to do at least two things each day that he hates to do, just for the practice."

Swiss philosopher and writer Henri Frédéric Amiel maintained, "The man who has no inner life is the slave of his surroundings." *Slaves* is the right term to describe people who lack integrity because they often find themselves at the whim of their own and others' changing desires. But with integrity, you can experience freedom. Not only are you less likely to be enslaved by the stress that comes from bad choices, debt, deceptiveness, and other negative character issues, but you are free to influence others and add value to them in an incredible way. And your integrity opens the door for you to experience continued success.

It's almost impossible to overestimate the impact of integrity in the lives of people. You probably remember the Tylenol scare from years ago. Several people were poisoned to death, and investigators traced the cause to contaminated Tylenol capsules. John's friend Don Meyer sent him a commentary on the incident. Here's what it said:

> Some years earlier in their mission statement, they had a line saying they would "operate with honesty and integrity." Several weeks before the Tylenol incident, the president of Johnson and Johnson sent a memo to all presidents of divisions of the company asking if they were abiding by and if they believed in the mission statement. All of the presidents came back with an affirmative answer.

> Reportedly, within an hour of the Tylenol crisis, the president of the company ordered all capsules off the shelf knowing it was a $100 million decision.

> When reporters asked how he could decide so easily and rapidly on such a major decision, his reply was, "I was practicing what we agreed on in our mission statement."

At the bottom of the commentary, Don Meyer wrote this note: "John, it is always easy to do right when you know ahead of time what you stand for."

What's true for Johnson and Johnson is true for you and us. If you know what you stand for and act accordingly, people can trust you. You are a model of the character and consistency that other people admire and want to emulate. And you've laid a good foundation, one that makes it possible for you to become a person of positive influence in their lives.

## *Influence Checklist*
# HAVING INTEGRITY WITH PEOPLE

❏ **Commit yourself to developing strong character.** In the past, have you made it a practice to take full responsibility for your character? It's something that you need to do in order to become a person of influence. Set aside the negative experiences you have had, including difficult circumstances and people who have hurt you. Forget about your credentials or the reputation you've built over the years. Strip all that away, and look at what's left. If you don't see solid integrity in yourself, make the commitment to change today.

Read the following statement, and then sign the line below:

> *I commit myself to being a person of character. Truth, reliability, honesty, and confidentiality will be the pillars of my life. I will treat others as I expect to be treated. I will live according to the highest standards of integrity amid all of life's circumstances.*

Signature: _____ Date: _____

❏ **Do the little things**. Spend the next week carefully monitoring your character habits. Make a note to yourself each time you do any of the following:

- Don't tell the whole truth.
- Neglect to fulfill a commitment, whether it's promised or implied.
- Leave an assignment uncompleted.
- Talk about something that you might have been expected to keep in confidence.

❏ **Do what you *should* do before you do what you *want* to do**. Every day this week, find two items on your to-do list that you should do but that you have been putting off. Complete those tasks before doing anything on the list that you enjoy.

# *A Person of Influence . . .*

# NURTURES
# OTHER PEOPLE

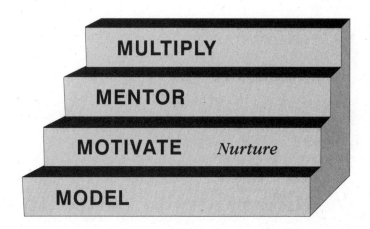

$S$everal years ago Nancy and I decided that we wanted to help our son Eric become a little more independent. In general he does really well. In fact, he participates in many activities that someone who does not use a wheelchair never gets to. But we thought he'd enjoy taking another step in his personal development, so we looked into something we'd heard about called Canine Companions for Independence (CCI), an organization that matches specially trained dogs to people with disabilities.

CCI has been around for about twenty years and has offices all around the country, including in Oceanside, California. That's just a short drive from San Diego, so one Saturday morning we piled into the car and went up the coast to check it out.

Eric was very excited as we got up there and toured the training facility. We met with a few staff members, and we saw a lot of great dogs. We found out that these animals spend the first year of their lives in the homes of volunteers who raise them and teach them basic obedience and socialization skills. Then the dogs are moved to a CCI center where they live and are given specialized training by staff members for the next eight months. They learn how to become working companions to just about every kind of person with disabilities other than blindness. The dogs learn how to open doors, carry objects, and do things like that. Some are trained to help people who are hearing impaired, and they learn to signal their owners when a phone or doorbell rings, a baby cries, a smoke alarm goes off, and so forth. Once a dog is fully trained, it's matched to a new owner, and the two of them go through a kind of "boot camp" to learn how to work together.

Eric loved the idea of getting a dog, and we applied to receive one that would match his needs. For the next several weeks, we waited. And not a day went by that Eric didn't talk about it. Finally, one afternoon we received a call from CCI telling us that they had a dog for Eric, and the next morning, we took off again to Oceanside.

Eric fell in love with Sable immediately. She was an energetic golden retriever who was a little over a year and a half old. The two of them went through boot camp and learned how to work together. Sable could turn lights off and on for Eric, accompany him to the store with money and carry his purchases back for him, and do a bunch of other things.

As boot camp was coming to a close, one of the trainers sat down with Eric and talked with him. He said, "Eric, no matter what else you do or don't do with Sable, be sure of one thing. You have to be the one who feeds her. That's very important. It's the only way to be sure that she will bond with you and look to you as her master."

For Eric, giving the dog love and affection was easy. He enjoyed petting and grooming her, but it was harder for him to learn how to take charge. He has a pretty docile personality. But in time, he learned to feed her, and it eventually became his favorite part of their routine.

Feeding a dog is the best way to create a relationship with her. It not only provides what the dog needs, giving her life and strength, but it also teaches her to trust and follow you. And in most cases, when you do the feeding, the care you give is returned with loyalty, obedience, and affection.

# THE NATURE OF NURTURE

In some regards, people respond similarly to the way some animals do. And like animals, people need to be cared for, not just physically, but emotionally. If you look around, you'll discover that there are people in your life who want to be fed—with encouragement, recognition, security, and hope. That process is called nurturing, and it's a need of every human being.

If you desire to become an influencer in others' lives, start by nurturing them. Many people mistakenly believe that the way to become an influencer is to become an authority figure—correct others' errors, reveal the weak areas they can't easily see in themselves, and give so-called constructive criticism. But what clergyman

John Knox said more than four hundred years ago is still true: "You cannot antagonize and influence at the same time."

At the heart of the nurturing process is genuine concern for others. When you hear the word *nurture,* what do you first think of? If you're like most people, you probably envision a mother cradling a baby. She takes care of her child, protecting him, feeding him, encouraging him, making sure that his needs are met. She doesn't give him attention only when she has spare time or when it's convenient. She loves him and wants him to thrive. Similarly, as you try to help and influence the people around you, you must have positive feelings and concern for them. If you want to make a positive impact on them, you cannot dislike, despise, or disparage them. You must give them love and respect. Or as human relations expert Les Giblin put it, "You can't make the other fellow feel important in your presence if you secretly feel that he is a nobody."

> *If you nurture others but allow them to become dependent on you, you're really hurting them, not helping them.*

You may be wondering why you should take on a nurturing role with the people you want to influence, especially if they are employees, colleagues, or friends—not family members. You may be saying to yourself, Isn't that something they can get somewhere else, for example, at home? The unfortunate truth is that most people are desperate for encouragement. And even if a few people in their lives build them up, you still need to become a nurturer to them because people are influenced most by those who make them feel the best about themselves. If you become a major nurturer in the lives of others, then you have an opportunity to make a major impact on them.

Check and recheck your motives as you help and encourage others. Don't be like a little girl named Emily. Her father, Guy Belleranti, was driving the family home from church one Sunday when the five-year-old girl said, "When I grow up, I want to be like the man who stood in front."

"You want to be a minister?" asked Emily's mother.

"No," said Emily, "I want to tell people what to do."

Your goal is others' growth and independence. If you nurture others but allow them to become dependent on you, you're really hurting them, not helping them. And if you help them because of your desire to meet your needs or to heal the hurts of your past, your relationship with them can become codependent. It's not healthy to try to correct your personal history by reliving it vicariously through others. Besides, codependent people never become positive influencers in the lives of others.

# A Nurturing Influencer Is a Giver

Now that you have a better idea about what it means to nurture others, you're probably ready to learn how to do it with the people in your life: employees, family members, friends, fellow church workers, and colleagues. You do it by focusing on *giving* rather than *getting*. Start by giving to others in these areas:

## Love

Before you can do anything else in the lives of others, you must show them love. Without it, there can be no connection, no future, and no success together. Think back to some key people who have had an impact on your life: an incredible teacher, a fantastic boss, a special aunt or uncle. Undoubtedly, when you spent time with those people, you could sense that they cared about you. And in return, you responded positively to them.

We discovered this example of how love can make a difference in the lives of students. Here is something written by a thoughtful teacher:

I had a great feeling of relief when I began to understand that a youngster needs more than just subject matter. I know mathematics well, and I teach it well. I used to think that was all I needed to do. Now I teach children, not math. I accept the fact that I can only succeed partially with some of them. When I don't have to know all the answers, I seem to have more answers than when I tried to be the expert. The youngster who really made me understand this was Eddie. I asked him one day why he thought he was doing so much better than last year. He gave meaning to my whole new orientation. "It's because I like myself now when I'm with you," he said.[1]

Eddie responded to love in a way that he never would have to knowledge, psychology, technique, or educational theory. When he knew his teacher cared about him, he blossomed.

> ***Without love, there can be no connection, no future, and no success together.***

The length and breadth of our influence on others are directly related to the depth of our concern for them. When it comes to helping people grow and feel good about themselves, there is no substitute for love. Even a tough guy like Vince Lombardi, the legendary coach of the Green Bay Packers, understood the power of love to bring out people's best and make an impact on their lives. He said, "There are a lot of coaches with good ball clubs who know the fundamentals and have plenty of discipline but still don't win the game. Then you come to the third ingredient: If you're going to play together as a team, you've got to care for one another. You've got to *love* each other. Each player has to be thinking about the next guy."

You can positively impact people by nurturing them. It doesn't matter what profession you're in. And it doesn't matter how successful the people around you are or what they have accomplished in the past. Everyone needs to feel valued. Even someone who was once the leader of the free world needs love. In his book *In the Arena,* former president Richard Nixon described his depression following his resignation from the White House and his undergoing surgery. At one point when he was in the hospital, he told his wife, Pat, that he wanted to die.

When he was at the absolute lowest point in his life, a nurse in the hospital came into his room, opened the drapes, and pointed out a small plane that was flying back and forth overhead. It was pulling this sign: GOD LOVES YOU, AND SO DO WE. Ruth Graham, evangelist Billy Graham's wife, had arranged for the plane to fly by the hospital. That's when Nixon experienced a turning point. Seeing that expression of love gave him the courage and desire to keep going and recover.

Take time to express your love and appreciation for the people close to you. Tell them how much they mean to you. Write them notes telling how much you care. Give them a pat on the back and, when appropriate, a hug. Don't ever assume that people know how you feel about them. Tell them. Nobody can be told too often that he or she is loved.

## Respect

We read a story about a woman who moved to a small town. After being there a short time, she complained to her neighbor about the poor service she received at the local drugstore. She was hoping her new acquaintance would repeat her criticism to the store's owner.

The next time the newcomer went to the drugstore, the druggist greeted her with a big smile, told her how happy he was to see her again, and said he hoped she liked their town. He also offered himself as a resource to the woman and her husband as they got settled. Then he took care of her order quickly and efficiently.

Later the woman reported the incredible change to her friend. "I suppose you told him how poor I thought the service was?" she declared.

"Well, no," the neighbor said. "In fact—and I hope you don't mind—I told him you were amazed at the way he had built up this small town drugstore, and that you thought it was one of the best-run drugstores you'd ever seen."[2]

That woman's neighbor understood that people respond to respect. In fact, most people will do nearly anything for you if you treat them respectfully. And that means making it clear to them that their feelings are important, their preferences are respected, and their opinions are valuable. It means giving them the benefit of the doubt. Or as poet-philosopher Ralph Waldo Emerson put it, "Every man is entitled to be valued by his best moments."

Where love focuses on giving to others, respect shows a willingness to receive from them. Respect acknowledges another person's ability or potential to contribute. Listening to other people and putting their agenda ahead of your own reflect your respect for them and have the potential to make you and them more successful. According to a recent study by Teleometrics International reported in the *Wall Street Journal,* executives understand the power of respect. Among the sixteen thousand executives surveyed, the researchers concentrated on a group of high achievers. Within that group, all had positive attitudes about their subordinates, frequently sought their advice, regularly listened to their concerns, and treated them with respect.

If you have had the opportunity to work in many environments, and you have worked for both types of people—those who *have* and those who *have not* shown you respect—you understand how motivational respect can be. And you also know that you are more easily influenced by people who treat you well.

## Sense of Security

Another important part of nurturing is giving people a sense of security. People are reluctant to trust you and reach their potential when they are worried about whether they're safe with you. But when they feel secure, they are in a position to respond positively and do their best. Virginia Arcastle remarked, "When people are made to feel secure and important and appreciated, it will no longer be necessary for them to whittle down others in order to seem bigger in comparison."

Part of making people feel secure comes from integrity, which we talked about in the previous chapter. People feel secure with you when your actions and words are consistent and conform to a high moral code that includes respect. Former Notre Dame head football coach Lou Holtz addressed that issue when he said, "Do what's right! Do the best you can and treat others the way you want to be treated because they will ask three questions: (1) Can I trust you? (2) Are you committed? . . . (3) Do you care about me as a person?"

People desire security not only from you but also from their environment. Good leaders recognize this and create an environment where people can flourish. Mike Krzyzewski, successful head basketball coach of Duke University, understands the impact a leader can make when he provides security to the people who follow him: "If you set up an atmosphere of communication and trust, it becomes a tradition. Older team members will establish your credibility with newer ones. Even if they don't like everything about you, they'll still say, 'He's trustworthy, committed to us as a team.'"

Not until people can completely trust you will you be able to positively influence them and have an impact on their lives.

## Recognition

A too common mistake, especially among leaders in the marketplace, is failure to share recognition and show appreciation to others. For example, J. C. Staehle did an analysis of workers in America and found that the number one cause of dissatisfaction among employees was their superiors' failure to give them credit. It's difficult for people to follow someone who doesn't appreciate them for who they are and what they do. As former secretary of defense and World Bank president Robert McNamara said, "Brains are like hearts—they go where they are appreciated."

Recognition is greatly appreciated by everyone, not just people in business and industry. Even a little bit of recognition can go an incredibly long way in a person's life. For example, we recently read a story written by Helen P. Mrosla, a teaching nun. She told about her experience with Mark Eklund, a student she had taught in third grade and then again in junior high math. Here's her story:

> One Friday [in the classroom] things just didn't feel right. We had worked hard on a new concept all week, and I sensed that the students were growing frustrated with themselves—and

edgy with one another. I had to stop this crankiness before it got out of hand. So I asked them to list the names of the other students in the room on two sheets of paper, leaving a space between each name. Then I told them to think of the nicest thing they could say about each of their classmates and write it down.

It took the remainder of the class period to finish the assignment, but as the students left the room, each one handed me their paper. . . .

That Saturday, I wrote down the name of each student on a separate sheet of paper, and I listed what everyone else had said about that individual. On Monday I gave each student his or her list. Some of them ran two pages. Before long, the entire class was smiling. "Really?" I heard whispered. "I never knew that meant anything to anyone!" "I didn't know others liked me so much!"

No one ever mentioned those papers in class again. I never knew if they discussed them after class or with their parents, but it didn't matter. The exercise had accomplished its purpose. The students were happy with themselves and one another again.

That group of students moved on. Several years later, after I had returned from a vacation, my parents met me at the airport. As we were driving home, Mother asked the usual questions about the trip: How the weather was, my experiences in general. There was a slight lull in the conversation. Mother gave Dad a sideways glance and simply said, "Dad?" My father cleared his throat. "The Eklunds called last night," he began.

"Really?" I said. "I haven't heard from them for several years. I wonder how Mark is."

Dad responded quietly. "Mark was killed in Vietnam," he said. "The funeral is tomorrow, and his parents would like it if you could attend." To this day I can still point to the exact spot on I-494 where Dad told me about Mark.

I had never seen a serviceman in a military coffin before. . . . The church was packed with Mark's friends. [His old classmate] Chuck's sister sang "The Battle Hymn of the Republic." Why did it have to rain on the day of the funeral? It was difficult enough at the grave side. The pastor said the usual prayers and the bugler played taps. One by one those who loved Mark took a last walk by the coffin and sprinkled it with holy water.

I was the last one to bless the coffin. As I stood there, one of the soldiers who had acted as a pallbearer came up to me. "Were you Mark's math teacher?" he asked. I nodded as I continued to stare at the coffin. "Mark talked about you a lot," he said.

After the funeral most of Mark's former classmates headed to Chuck's farmhouse for lunch. Mark's mother and father were there, obviously waiting for me. "We want to show you something," his father said, taking a wallet out of his pocket. "They found this on Mark when he was killed. We thought you might recognize it."

Opening the billfold, he carefully removed two worn pieces of notebook paper that had obviously been taped, folded and refolded many times. I knew without looking that the papers were the ones on which I had listed all the good things each of Mark's classmates had said about him. "Thank you so much for doing that," Mark's mother said. "As you can see, Mark treasured it."

Mark's classmates started to gather around us. Chuck smiled rather sheepishly and said, "I still have my list. It's in the top drawer of my desk at home." John's wife said, "John asked me to put his in our wedding album." "I have mine too," Marilyn said. "It's in my diary." Then Vicki, another classmate, reached into her pocketbook, took out her wallet and showed her worn and frazzled list to the group. "I carry this with me at all times," Vicky said without batting an eyelash. "I think we all saved our lists."

That's when I finally sat down and cried.[3]

What would make so many adults hold on to pieces of paper they had received years before as kids, some of them carrying those pages with them everywhere they went—even into battle in a rice paddy halfway around the world? The answer is appreciation. Everyone is incredibly hungry for appreciation and recognition. As you interact with people, walk slowly through the crowd. Remember people's names and take time to show them you care. Make other people a priority in your life over every other thing, including your agenda and schedule. And give others recognition at every opportunity. It will build them up and motivate them. And it will make you a person of significant influence in their lives.

## Encouragement

An experiment was conducted years ago to measure people's capacity to endure pain. Psychologists measured how long a barefooted person could stand in a bucket of ice water. They found that one factor made it possible for some people to stand in the ice water twice as long as others. Can you guess what that factor was? It was encouragement. When another person was present, giving support and encouragement, the sufferers were able to endure the pain much longer than their unencouraged counterparts.

> *When a person feels encouraged, he can face the impossible and overcome incredible adversity.*

Few things help a person the way encouragement does. George M. Adams called it "oxygen to the soul." German philosopher-poet Johann Wolfgang von Goethe wrote, "Correction does much, but encouragement after censure is as the sun after a shower." And William A. Ward revealed his feelings when he said: "Flatter me, and I may not believe you. Criticize me, and I may not like you. Ignore me, and I may not forgive you. Encourage me, and I will not forget you."

The ability to influence is a natural by-product of encouragement. Benjamin Franklin wrote in a letter to naval commander John Paul Jones, "Hereafter, if you should observe an occasion to give your officers and friends a little more praise than is their due, and confess more fault than you can justly be charged with, you will only become the sooner for it, a great captain." Jones evidently learned the lesson. He eventually became a hero of the American Revolution and later achieved the rank of rear admiral in the Russian navy.

Just as encouragement makes others want to follow you, withholding praise and encouragement has the opposite effect. We read an account by Dr. Maxwell Maltz that shows the incredible negative impact a person can have when he doesn't encourage persons close to him. Maltz described a woman who came to his office seeking his help. Evidently, her son had moved from her home in the Midwest to New York where Maltz had his practice. When their son was only a boy, the woman's husband died, and she ran his business, hoping to do so only until the son became old enough to take it over. But when the son became old enough, he didn't want to be involved with it. Instead, he wanted to go to New York and study. She came to Maltz because she wanted him to find out why her son had behaved that way.

A few days later the son came to Maltz's office, explaining that his mother had insisted on the visit. "I love my mother," he explained, "but I've never told her why I had to leave home. I've just never had the courage. And I don't want her to be unhappy. But you see, Doctor, I don't want to take over what my father started. I want to make it on my own."

"That's very admirable," Maltz said to him, "but what do you have against your father?"

"My father was a good man and worked hard, but I suppose I resented him," he said. "My father came up the hard way. And he thought he should be tough on me. I guess he wanted to build self-reliance in me or something. When I was a boy, he never encouraged me. I can remember playing catch with him out in the yard. He'd pitch and I'd catch. We had a game to see if I could catch ten balls in a row. And, Doctor, he'd never let me catch the tenth ball! He'd throw eight or nine to me, but he always threw the tenth ball into the air, or into the ground, or where I couldn't catch it." The young man paused for a moment and then said, "He would never let me catch the tenth ball—never! And I guess I had to leave home and the business he started because I wanted somehow to catch that tenth ball!"

Lack of encouragement can hinder a person from living a healthy, productive life. But when a person feels encouraged, he can face the impossible and overcome incredible adversity. And the person who gives the gift of encouragement becomes an influencer in his life.

# WHAT THEY RECEIVE

To become a nurturer, learn to be other-minded. Instead of thinking of yourself, put others first. Instead of putting others in their place, try to put *yourself* in their place. That's not always easy. Only when you have a sense of peace about yourself and who you are will you be able to be other-minded and give yourself away to others. But the rewards of nurturing are many. When you nurture people, they receive several things:

## *Positive Self-Worth*

Nathaniel Branden, a psychiatrist and expert on the subject of self-esteem, states that no factor is more decisive in people's psychological development and motivation than the value judgments they make about themselves. He says that the nature of self-evaluation has a profound effect on a person's values, beliefs, thinking processes, feelings, needs, and goals. In his view, self-esteem is the most significant key to a person's behavior.

A poor self-concept can have all kinds of negative effects on a person's life. Poet T. S. Eliot asserted, "Half of the harm that is done in this world is due to people who want to feel important. . . . They do not mean to do harm. . . . They are absorbed in the endless struggle to think well of themselves." Poor self-worth creates an invisible ceiling that can stop a person from attempting to rise above self-imposed limitations.

If you are confident and have a healthy self-image, then you may be saying, "Hey, I can see trying to boost a child's self-worth, but when it comes to my employees or colleagues, let them take care of themselves. They're adults. They need to get over it." The reality is that most people, whether they're seven or fifty-seven, could use help with their feelings about themselves. They would love to have their sense of identity boosted. If you question that, try this experiment. Ask a couple of people you know to write down on a piece of paper all their personality strengths. Each person usually comes up with about half a dozen. Then ask them to write down all their weaknesses. Most of the time, the lists of weaknesses are at least twice as long!

Eighteenth-century writer-critic Samuel Johnson expressed this thought: "Self-confidence is the first great requisite to great under-takings." Self-esteem impacts every aspect of a person's life: employment, education, relationships, and more. For example, the National Institute for Student Motivation conducted a study showing that the impact of self-confidence on academic achieve-ment is greater than that of IQ. And Martin Seligman, a professor of psychology at the University of Pennsylvania, discovered that people with high self-esteem get better-paying jobs and are more successful in their careers than people with low self-esteem. When he surveyed representatives of a major life insurance com-pany, he found that those who expected to succeed sold 37 per-cent more insurance than those who did not.

If you want to help people improve their quality of life, become more productive at work, and develop more positive relationships, then build their self-worth. Make them feel good about themselves, and the positive benefits will spill over into every aspect of their lives. And when they begin to experience those benefits, they will be grateful to you.

## *Sense of Belonging*

Belonging is one of the most basic human needs. When people feel isolated and excluded from a sense of communion with oth-ers, they suffer. Albert LaLonde pointed out the dangers of this iso-lation: "Many young people today have never experienced a deep emotional attachment to anyone. They do not know how to love and be loved. The need to be loved translates itself into the need to belong to someone or something. Driven by their need . . . they will do anything to belong."

Positive influencers understand this need for a sense of belong-ing and do things that make people feel included. Parents make sure their children feel like important members of the family. Spouses make the person to whom they are married feel like a cherished equal partner. And bosses let their employees know that they are valued members of the team.

Great leaders are particularly talented at making their followers feel they belong. Napoleon Bonaparte, for example, was a master at making people feel important and included. He was known for wandering through his camp and greeting every officer by name. As he talked to each man, he asked about his hometown, wife, and family. And the general talked about a battle or maneuver in which he knew the man had taken part. The interest and time he took with his followers made them feel a sense of camaraderie and belonging. It's no wonder that his men were devoted to him.

If you desire to become a better nurturer of people, develop an other-person mind-set. Look for ways to include others. Become like the farmer who used to hitch up his old mule to a two-horse plow every day and say, "Get up, Beauregard. Get up, Satchel. Get up, Robert. Get up, Betty Lou."

One day his neighbor, hearing the farmer, asked, "How many names does that mule have?"

"Oh, he has only one," answered the farmer. "His name is Pete. But I put blinders on him and call out all the other names so he will think other mules are working with him. He has a better attitude when he's a part of a team."

## Perspective

Another thing that people gain when they are nurtured is a better perspective on themselves. Most people receive more than their share of negative comments and criticism from others—so much that they sometimes begin to lose sight of their value. There is a telling example of this in *A Touch of Wonder* by Arthur Gordon. He relates the story of a friend who belonged to a club at the University of Wisconsin. It was comprised of several bright young men who had genuine talent for writing. Each time they met, one of the men would read a story or essay he had written, and the rest of the group would dissect and criticize it. The viciousness of their comments prompted them to call themselves the Stranglers.

On the same campus, some women formed a group, and they called themselves the Wranglers. They also read their manuscripts to one another, but instead of showering criticism on one another, they tried to find positive things to say. Every member was given encouragement, no matter how weak or undeveloped her writing was.

> ## *For most people, it's not what they are that holds them back. It's what they think they're not.*

The results of the two groups' activities came to light twenty years later when the careers of the classmates were examined. Of the talented young men in the Stranglers, not one of them had made a name for himself as a writer. But half a dozen successful writers emerged from the Wranglers, even though they had not necessarily shown greater promise. And some of the women had gained national prominence, such as Pulitzer prize–winner Marjorie Kinnan Rawlings.[4]

For most people, it's not what they are that holds them back. It's what they think they're not. The Stranglers undoubtedly made one another suspect that they were unqualified to write, and in time they became convinced of it. Who knows what kind of talent was squashed by their negativism? But if someone in the group had taken the initiative to be nurturing instead of negative, maybe another Hemingway, Faulkner, or Fitzgerald would have emerged and given the world another library of masterpieces.

Everyone appreciates being nurtured, even great men and women. A small exhibit at the Smithsonian Institution bears this out. It contains the personal effects found on Abraham Lincoln the night he was shot: a small handkerchief embroidered "A. Lincoln," a country boy's penknife, a spectacle case repaired with cotton string, a Confederate five-dollar bill, and a worn-out newspaper clipping extolling his accomplishments as president. It begins, "Abe Lincoln is one of the greatest statesmen of all time. . . ."[5]

As we mentioned in the previous chapter, Lincoln faced fierce criticism while in office, and it would have been easy for him to become totally discouraged. That article, worn with repeated reading, undoubtedly helped him during some very difficult times. It nurtured him and helped him retain his perspective.

## Feeling of Significance

Woody Allen once quipped, "My only regret in life is that I'm not someone else." And while he probably said that to get a laugh, with the relationship problems he has had over the years, we can't help wondering how much truth there is to his comment. In life, the price tag that the world puts on us is almost identical to the one we put on ourselves. People who have a great deal of self-respect and who believe that they have significance are usually respected and made to feel valued by others.

When you nurture people and add value to them without expecting anything in return, they feel significant. They realize that they are valued, that they matter to others. And once they consistently feel positive about themselves, they're free to live more positively for themselves and others.

## Hope

Writer Mark Twain warned, "Keep away from people who try to belittle your ambitions. Small people always do that, but the really great make you feel that you, too, can become great." How do most people feel when they're around you? Do they feel small and insignificant, or do they believe in themselves and have hope about what they can become?

The key to how you *treat* people lies in how you *think* about them. It's a matter of attitude. How you act reveals what you believe. Johann Wolfgang von Goethe emphasized, "Treat a man as he appears to be and you make him worse, But treat a man as if he already were what he potentially could be, and you make him what he should be."

Hope is perhaps the greatest gift you can give others as the result of nurturing because even if their sense of self is weak and they fail to see their own significance, they still have a reason to keep trying and striving to reach their potential in the future.

In *Building Your Mate's Self-Esteem*, Dennis Rainey tells a wonderful story about nurturing hope that can lead to the development of tremendous potential. He says that there was a boy named Tommy who had a particularly hard time in school. He continually asked questions, and he never could quite keep up. It seemed that he failed every time he tried something. His teacher finally gave up on him and told his mother that he could not learn and would never amount to much. But Tommy's mother was a nurturer. She believed in him. She taught him at home, and each time he failed, she gave him hope and encouraged him to keep trying.

What ever happened to Tommy? He became an inventor, eventually holding more than one thousand patents, including those of the phonograph and the first commercially practical incandescent electric lightbulb. His name was Thomas Edison.[6] When people have hope, there is no telling how far they can go.

# How to Become a Natural Nurturer

Maybe you weren't born a nurturing person. Many people find it hard to be loving and positive to others, especially if the environment they grew up in wasn't particularly uplifting. But anyone can become a nurturer and add value to others. If you cultivate a positive attitude of other-mindedness, you, too, can become a natural at nurturing and enjoy the added privilege of influence in the lives of others. Here's how to do it:

- **Commit to them.** Make a commitment to become a nurturer. Making a commitment to help people changes your priorities and your actions. Love for others always finds a way to help; indifference to others finds nothing but excuses.
- **Believe in them.** People rise or fall to meet the expectations of those closest to them. Give people your trust and hope, and they will do everything they can to keep from letting you down.

- **Be accessible to them.** You can't nurture anyone from a distance. You can only do it up close. When you first start the process with people, you may need to spend a lot of time with them. But as they gain confidence in themselves and the relationship, they will require less personal contact. Until they reach that point, make sure they have access to you.
- **Give with no strings attached.** If you need people, you cannot lead them. And nurturing is an aspect of leadership. Instead of trying to make a transaction out of it, give freely without expecting anything in return. Nineteenth-century economist Henry Drummond wisely observed, "You will find as you look back upon your life that the moments when you have really lived are the moments when you have done things in a spirit of love."
- **Give them opportunities.** As the people you nurture gain strength, give them additional opportunities to succeed and grow. You will continue to nurture them, but as time goes by, their actions and accomplishments will help them remain secure, respected, and encouraged.
- **Lift them to a higher level.** Your ultimate goal should always be to help people go to a higher level, to reach their potential. Nurturing is the foundation upon which they can begin the building process.

Walt Disney is reported to have said that there are three kinds of people in the world. There are well-poisoners who discourage others, stomp on their creativity, and tell them what they can't do. There are lawn-mowers, people who have good intentions but are self-absorbed, who mow their own lawns but never help others. And there are life-enhancers. This last category contains people who reach out to enrich the lives of others, who lift them up and inspire them. Each of us needs to do everything in our power to become a life-enhancer, to nurture people so that they are motivated to grow and reach their potential. It is a process that takes time. (And in coming chapters, we'll share insights that will show you how to help people take additional steps in that process.)

One of the most inspiring stories of encouragement and nurturing we've ever heard concerns John Wesley—an influencer we mentioned in this book's introduction. In 1791, Wesley wrote a letter to William Wilberforce, a member of England's Parliament who was in the midst of fighting for the abolition of the British slave trade. The letter, which has since become famous, said this:

London, February 26, 1791
Dear Sir:

Unless the divine power has raised you up . . . I see not how you can go through your glorious enterprise, in opposing that execrable villainy, which is the scandal of religion, of England, and of human nature. Unless God has raised you up for this very thing, you will be worn out by the opposition of men and devils. But "if God be for you, who can be against you?" Are all of them stronger than God? O "be not weary in well doing!" Go on, in the name of God and in the power of His might, till even American slavery (the vilest that ever saw the sun) shall vanish away before it. . . .

That He who has guided you from your youth up, may continue to strengthen you in this and all things, is the prayer of,

Your affectionate servant,
J. Wesley

Four days later, Wesley was dead at age eighty-eight, yet his influence in Wilberforce's life continued for years. Wilberforce did not succeed in convincing Parliament to abolish slavery at that time, but he didn't give up the fight. He kept at it for decades despite slander, vilification, and threats. And when he thought he couldn't go on, he looked to Wesley's letter for encouragement. Finally, in 1807, the slave trade was abolished. And in 1833, several months after Wilberforce's death, slavery was outlawed in all of the British Empire.

Though condemned by many during his career, Wilberforce was buried with honor in Westminster Abbey, one of the most esteemed men of his day. Part of his epitaph reads:

*Eminent as he was in every department of public labour,*
   *And a leader in every work of charity,*
*Whether to relieve the temporal or the spiritual wants*
   *of his fellow men*
*His name will ever be specially identified*
   *With those exertions*
*Which, by the blessing of God, removed from England*
   *The guilt of the African slave trade,*
*And prepared the way for the abolition of slavery*
   *in every colony of the Empire.*

Maybe there is a William Wilberforce in your life, just waiting to be nurtured to greatness. The only way you'll ever know is to become a nurturer who is other-minded and adds value to the people you meet.

## *Influence Checklist*
# NURTURING OTHER PEOPLE

❑ **Develop a nurturing environment in your home, place of business, or church**. Make it your goal to make the people around you feel loved, respected, and secure. To do that, commit to eliminating all negative criticism from your speech for one month and searching for only positive things to say to others.

❑ **Give special encouragement.** Pick two or three people to encourage this month. Send each person a short handwritten note every week. Make yourself accessible to these people. And give of your time without expecting something in return. At the end of the month, examine your relationships with them for positive change.

❑ **Rebuild bridges.** Think of one person with whom you have tended to be negative in the past. (It can be anyone: a colleague, a family member, or an employee, for instance.) Go to that person and apologize for your past actions or remarks. Then find the quality you most admire about the person and tell him or her about it. During the following weeks, look for ways to build and strengthen the relationship.

# *A Person of Influence Has . . .*

# FAITH IN PEOPLE

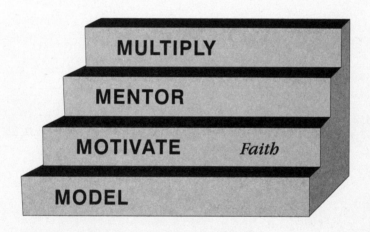

J im grew up in Niagara Falls, New York. Today the population is about 60,000, but when Jim lived there, it had closer to 100,000 people. It was a thriving industrial center, with companies such as DuPont Chemical. It also had cultural offerings, a strong one-hundred-year-old university, and other attractions, but the main focus of the town then was the incredible natural wonder of the falls, as it still is today.

The Iroquois called it *Niagara,* meaning "thunder of waters." It's an awesome sight. Every minute more than 12 million cubic feet of water drop a distance of about 180 feet over the edge of the falls. And its total width, including both the Canadian and the American portions, measures more than 3,100 feet. It is rightly called one of the natural wonders of the world. Jim says,

> Back when we were growing up, we heard a lot of stories about the falls and the daredevil stunts people used to pull—like Annie Edson Taylor's going over the falls in a barrel and things like that. One of the great legends of the town was a French acrobat named Charles Blondin who lived from 1824 to 1897. He crossed over the entire width of the falls on a tightrope back in 1859. That must have taken nerves of steel since a fall certainly would have killed him. In fact, he crossed the falls several times. He did it once with a wheelbarrow, another time blindfolded, and yet another time on stilts. They say he was quite remarkable. He continued performing even into his seventies.
>
> One of the most incredible feats he performed was crossing the falls on a tightrope while carrying a man on his back. Can you imagine that? I guess just crossing over by himself wasn't tough enough for him! But as difficult as that feat must have been on Blondin, I can't help wondering how he got someone to go with him. That's what you call trust: to climb onto the back of a man who is going to walk more than half a mile on *a rope* suspended over one of the most powerful waterfalls in the world.
>
> I used to think about that as a kid. What would it be like to see the falls from up on a rope above them? And more important, what person would trust me to carry him across the falls the way that man trusted Blondin?

# FACTS ABOUT FAITH IN PEOPLE

We can't tell you the identity of the man Blondin carried across the falls, but there is no question that he had great faith in the French acrobat. After all, he put his life in the man's hands. You don't see that kind of trust in others every day. But the times you do, it is a very special thing.

Faith in people is an essential quality of an influencer when working with others, yet it's a scarce commodity today. Take a look at the following four facts about faith:

## 1. Most People Don't Have Faith in Themselves

Not long ago we saw a *Shoe* comic strip by Jeff MacNelly that showed Shoe, the crusty newspaper editor, standing on the mound in a baseball game. His catcher said to him, "You've got to have faith in your curve ball." In the next frame Shoe remarked, "It's easy for him to say. When it comes to believing in myself, I'm an agnostic."

> *When you believe in people, they do the impossible.*
> *—Nancy Dornan*

That's the way too many people feel today. They have trouble believing in themselves. They believe they will fail. Even when they see a light at the end of the tunnel, they're convinced it's a train. They see a difficulty in every possibility. But the reality is that difficulties seldom defeat people; lack of faith in themselves usually does it. With a little faith in themselves, people can do miraculous things. But without it, they have a really tough time.

## 2. Most People Don't Have Someone Who Has Faith in Them

In *Just for Today,* James Keller tells this story: "A sidewalk flower vendor was not doing any business. Suddenly a happy thought struck him and he put up this sign: 'This gardenia will make you feel important all day long for 10 cents.' All at once his sales began to increase."

In our society today, most people feel isolated. The strong sense of community that was once enjoyed by most Americans has become rare. And many people don't have the family support that was more common thirty or forty years ago. For example, evangelist Bill Glass noted, "Over 90 percent of prison inmates were told by parents while growing up, 'They're going to put you in jail.'" Instead of teaching their children to believe in themselves, some parents are tearing them down. For many people, even those who are closest to them don't believe in them. They have no one on their side. No wonder even a little thing like a flower can make a difference in how a person approaches the day.

## 3. Most People Can Tell When Someone Has Faith in Them

People's instincts are pretty good at knowing when others have faith in them. They can sense if your belief is genuine or phony. And truly having faith in someone can change her life. Jim's wife, Nancy, often says, "When you believe in people, they do the impossible."

In his book *Move Ahead with Possibility Thinking,* John's friend Robert Schuller, pastor of the Crystal Cathedral in Garden Grove, California, tells a wonderful story about an incident that changed his life as a boy. It occurred when his uncle had faith in him and showed it in his words and actions:

His car drove past the unpainted barn and stopped in a cloud of summer dust at our front gate. I ran barefooted across the splintery porch and saw my uncle Henry bound out of the car. He was tall, very handsome, and terribly alive with energy. After many years overseas as a missionary in China, he was visiting our Iowa farm. He ran up to the old gate and put both of his big hands on my four-year-old shoulders. He smiled widely, ruffled my uncombed hair, and said, "Well! I guess you're Robert! I think you are going to be a preacher someday." That night I prayed secretly, "And dear God, make me a preacher when I grow up!" I believe that God made me a POS-SIBILITY THINKER then and there.

As you work to become a person of influence, always remember that your goal is not to get people to think more highly of you. It's to get them to think more highly of themselves. Have faith in them, and they will begin to do exactly that.

> ## *Difficulties seldom defeat people; lack of faith in themselves usually does it.*

## 4. *Most People Will Do Anything to Live Up to Your Faith in Them*

People rise or fall to meet your level of expectations for them. If you express skepticism and doubt in others, they will return your lack of confidence with mediocrity. But if you believe in them and expect them to do well, they will go the extra mile trying to do their best. And in the process, they and you benefit. John H. Spalding expressed the thought this way: "Those who believe in our ability do more than stimulate us. They create for us an atmosphere in which it becomes easier to succeed."

If you've never been one to trust people and put your faith in them, change your way of thinking and begin believing in others. Your life will quickly improve. When you have faith in others, you give them an incredible gift. Give others money, and it's soon spent. Give resources, and they may not be used to their best advantage. Give help, and people will often find themselves back where they started in a short period of time. But give them your faith, and they become confident, energized, and self-reliant. They become motivated to acquire what they need to succeed on their own. And then later if you share money, resources, and help, they're better able to use them to build a better future.

## FAITH IS BELIEF IN ACTION

In the late 1800s, a salesman from back east arrived at a frontier town somewhere on the Great Plains. As he was talking to the owner of a general store, a rancher came in, and the owner excused himself to take care of his customer. As they talked, the salesman couldn't help overhearing their conversation. It seemed the rancher wanted credit for some things he needed.

"Are you doing any fencing this spring, Jake?" asked the storekeeper.

"Sure am, Bill," said the rancher.

"Fencing in or fencing out?"

"Fencing in. Taking in another 360 acres across the creek."

"Good to hear it, Jake. You got the credit. Just tell Steve out back what you need."

The salesman was dumbfounded. "I've seen all kinds of credit systems," he said, "but never one like that. How does it work?"

"Well," said the storekeeper, "let me tell you. If a man's fencing out, that means he's scared, trying to just hold on to what he's got. But if he's fencing in, he's growing and trying to improve. I always give credit to a man who's fencing in because that means he believes in himself."

Having faith in people requires more than just words or positive feelings about them. We have to back it up with what we do. As W. T. Purkiser, professor emeritus of religion at Point Loma College, clearly saw: "Faith is more than thinking something is true. Faith is thinking something is true to the extent that we act on it."

If you want to help other people and make a positive impact on their lives, you have to treat them with that kind of confidence. Ralph Waldo Emerson said, "Trust men and they will be true to

you; treat them greatly and they will show themselves great."
Become a believer in people, and even the most tentative and
inexperienced people can bloom right before your eyes.

# HOW TO BECOME A
# BELIEVER IN PEOPLE

We're fortunate because we grew up in positive, affirming
environments. As a result, we have an easy time believing in people and expressing that belief. But we realize that not everyone
had the benefit of a positive upbringing. Most people need to
*learn* how to have faith in others. To build your belief in others,
try using these suggestions, created using the initial letters of the
word *BELIEVE*.

## Believe in Them Before They Succeed

Have you ever noticed how many people support a sports
team as soon as it starts winning? That happened here in San
Diego a couple of years ago when the Chargers won their division, then won all their play-off games leading into the Super
Bowl. The whole town went crazy. You could see the team's
lightning bolt symbol everywhere: on people's houses, on the
back windows of cars, on lapel pins, and so forth.

During the height of the Chargers' success, a couple of local
radio personalities named Jeff and Jer rallied the people of San
Diego by sponsoring a big event at the stadium one morning.
Their plan was to give the people who showed up T-shirts in the
team colors and have them line up in the parking lot in the shape
of a giant lightning bolt. Then they would take a picture of it from
a helicopter and put it in the newspaper the next morning. A couple of thousand people were required to pull it off, but they
hoped enough would show to make it happen. Imagine their surprise when so many people showed up that they ran out of T-
shirts, and ended up surrounding the "human bolt" with a border
of extras. It was such a big deal that some of the news services
picked it up and televised it on the national news.

Everyone loves a winner. It's easy to have faith in people who have already proved themselves. It's much tougher to believe in people *before* they have proved themselves. But that is the key to motivating people to reach their potential. You have to believe in them first, before they become successful, and sometimes before they even believe in themselves. French writer and moralist Joseph Joubert said, "No one can give faith unless he has faith. It is the persuaded who persuade." You need faith in others before you can persuade them to believe in themselves.

Some people in your life desperately want to believe in themselves but have little hope. As you interact with them, remember the motto of French World War I hero Marshal Ferdinand Foch: "There are no hopeless situations; there are only men and women who have grown hopeless about them." Every person has seeds of greatness within, even though they may currently be dormant. But when you believe in people, you water the seeds and give them the chance to grow. Every time you put your faith in them, you're giving life-sustaining water, warmth, food, and light. And if you continue to give encouragement through your belief in them, these people will bloom in time.

## Emphasize Their Strengths

We mentioned previously that many people mistakenly think that to be influential in other people's lives, they have to be an "authority" and point out others' deficiencies. People who try that approach become like Lucy from the comic strip *Peanuts* by Charles Schulz. In one strip Lucy told poor Charlie Brown, "You, Charlie Brown, are a foul ball in the line drive of life! You're in the shadow of your own goal posts! You are a miscue! You are three putts on the eighteenth green! You are a seven-ten split in the tenth frame. . . . You are a missed free throw, a shanked nine iron and a called third strike! Do you understand? Have I made myself clear?" That's hardly a way to positively impact the life of another person!

The road to becoming a positive influence on others lies in exactly the opposite direction. The best way to show people your faith in them and motivate them is to focus your attention on their strengths. According to author and advertising executive Bruce Barton, "Nothing splendid has ever been achieved except by those who dared believe that something inside them was superior to circumstances." By emphasizing people's strengths, you're helping them believe that they possess what they need to succeed.

> ***B**elieving in people* **before**
> *they have proved themselves*
> *is the key to motivating people*
> *to reach their potential.*

Praise them for what they do well, both privately and publicly. Tell them how much you appreciate their positive qualities and their skills. And anytime you have the opportunity to compliment and praise them in the presence of their family and close friends, do it.

## List Their Past Successes

Even when you emphasize people's strengths, they may need further encouragement to show them you believe in them and to get them motivated. Entrepreneur Mary Kay Ash advised, "Everyone has an invisible sign hanging from his neck saying, 'Make me feel important!' Never forget this message when working with people." One of the best ways to do that is to help people remember their past successes.

The account of David and Goliath presents a classic example of how past successes can help a person have faith in himself. You may remember the story from the Bible. A nine-foot-tall Philistine champion named Goliath stood before the army of Israel and taunted them every day for forty days, daring them to send out a warrior to face him. On the fortieth day a young shepherd named David came to the front lines to deliver food to his brothers, who were in Israel's army. While he was there,

he witnessed the giant's contemptuous display of taunts and challenges. David was so infuriated that he told King Saul of Israel
that he wanted to face the giant in battle. Here's what happened:

> David said to Saul, "Let no one lose heart on account of this
> Philistine; your servant will go and fight him." Saul replied,
> "You are not able to go out against this Philistine and fight
> him; you are only a boy, and he has been a fighting man
> from his youth." But David said to Saul, "Your servant has
> been keeping his father's sheep. When a lion or a bear
> came and carried off a sheep from the flock, I went after it,
> struck it and rescued the sheep from its mouth. When it
> turned on me, I seized it by its hair, struck it and killed it.
> Your servant has killed both the lion and the bear. . . . The
> LORD who delivered me from the paw of the lion and the
> paw of the bear will deliver me from the hand of this Philis-
> tine."[1]

David looked back on his past successes, and he had confidence in his future actions. And of course, when he faced the
giant, he felled him like a tree, using nothing but a rock and sling.
And when he cut off Goliath's head, his success inspired his fellow countrymen; they routed the Philistine army.

Not everyone has the natural ability to recognize past successes and draw confidence from them. Some people need help.
If you can show others that they have done well in the past and
help them see that their past victories have paved the way for
future success, they'll be better able to move into action. Listing
past successes helps others believe in themselves.

# Instill Confidence When They Fail

When you have encouraged people and put your faith in them,
and they begin to believe they can succeed in life, they soon
reach a critical crossroads. The first time or two that they fail—
and they will fail because it's a part of life—they have two
choices. They can give in or go on.

Some people are resilient and willing to keep trying in order
to succeed, even when they don't see immediate progress. But
others aren't that determined. Some will collapse at the first sign

of trouble. To give them a push and inspire them, you need to keep showing your confidence in them, even when they're making mistakes or doing poorly.

One of the ways to do that is to tell them about your past troubles and traumas. Sometimes people think that if you're currently successful, you have always been that way. They don't realize that you have had your share of flops, failures, and fumbles. Show them that success is a journey, a process, not a destination. When they realize that you have failed and yet still managed to succeed, they'll realize that it's okay to fail. And their confidence will remain intact. They will learn to think the way baseball legend Babe Ruth did when he said, "Never let the fear of striking out get in the way."

# Experience Some Wins Together

It's not enough just knowing that failure is a part of moving forward in life. To really become motivated to succeed, people need to believe they can win. John, like many of us, got a taste for winning when he was just a kid. He says,

> Growing up, I idolized my brother Larry, who is two and a half years older than I am. After my parents, he was probably the greatest influencer in my life when I was a kid. Larry has always been a great leader and an excellent athlete. And whenever we played basketball, football, or baseball with the kids in the neighborhood, Larry was a captain.
>
> A lot of times when they picked teams, I would be one of the last picked, because I was younger and smaller than most of the kids. But as I got older, Larry began picking me more, and that always made me feel good, not only because it meant my brother cared about me, but because I knew that when Larry picked me, I was going to be on the winning team. You see, Larry was a fierce competitor, and he didn't like losing. He always played to win, and he usually did. Together we put quite a few wins under our belts, and I came to expect victory when I played with my brother.

Winning is motivating. Novelist David Ambrose acknowledged this truth: "If you have the will to win, you have achieved half your success; if you don't, you have achieved half your failure." Coming alongside others to help them experience some wins with you gives them reasons to believe they will succeed. And in the process, they sense victory. That's when incredible things begin to happen in their lives. Take a look at this comparison between what happens when people sense victory versus when they expect defeat:

| When People Sense Victory | When People Sense Defeat |
|---|---|
| They sacrifice to succeed. | They give as little as possible. |
| They look for ways to win. | They look for excuses. |
| They become energized. | They become tired. |
| They follow the game plan. | They forsake the game plan. |
| They help other team members. | They hurt others. |

To help people believe they can achieve victory, put them in a position to experience small successes. Encourage them to perform tasks or take on responsibilities you know they can handle and do well. And give them the assistance they need to succeed. As Greek orator Demosthenes said, "Small opportunities are often the beginning of great enterprises." In time as their confidence grows, they will take on more difficult challenges, but they will be able to face them with confidence and competence because of the positive track record they're developing.

## Visualize Their Future Success

We heard about an experiment performed with laboratory rats to measure their motivation to live under different circumstances. Scientists dropped a rat into a jar of water that had been placed in total darkness, and they timed how long the animal would continue swimming before it gave up and allowed itself to drown. They found that the rat usually lasted little more than three minutes.

Then they dropped another rat into the same kind of jar, but instead of placing it in total darkness, they allowed a ray of light to shine into it. Under those circumstances, the rat kept swimming for thirty-six hours. That's more than seven hundred times longer than the one in the dark! Because the rat could see, it continued to have hope.

If that is true of laboratory animals, think of how strong the effect of visualization can be on people, who are capable of higher reasoning. It's been said that a person can live forty days without food, four days without water, four minutes without air, but only four seconds without hope. Each time you cast a vision for others and paint a picture of their future success, you build them up, motivate them, and give them reasons to keep going.

## Expect a New Level of Living

German statesman Konrad Adenauer observed: "We all live under the same sky, but we don't all have the same horizon." As an influencer, you have the goal of helping others see beyond today and their current circumstances and dream big dreams. When you put your faith in people, you help them to expand their horizons and motivate them to move to a whole new level of living.

> *To help people believe they can achieve victory, put them in a position to experience small successes.*

Integral to that new way of living is a change in attitude. According to Denis Waitley, "The winner's edge is not in a gifted birth, a high IQ, or in talent. The winner's edge is all in the attitude, not aptitude. Attitude is the criterion for success." As people's attitudes change from doubt to confidence—in themselves and their ability to succeed and reach their potential—everything in their lives changes for the better.

Jim and Nancy gained incredible insights about the power of putting their faith into others several years ago when they decided to take a chance with their son Eric on a mountain in Utah. Here's Jim's account of it:

> When you have a disabled child, you constantly fight a battle of emotions between providing him new experiences and protecting him from injury or failure. Our life with Eric has been no exception. Despite his limitations, which include having to use a wheelchair and having very little use in his right hand, Eric has a great positive spirit. And often if there is hesitation to try new things, it comes from Nancy and me rather than him.
>
> About five years ago Nancy got the idea that we should take Eric skiing. She had heard from a friend about a place in Park City, Utah, called the National Ability Center. There they offer people with disabilities instruction and assistance in snow skiing, swimming, tennis, waterskiing, horseback riding, rafting, and other activities. She thought the experience would be great for his self-esteem.
>
> I have to admit, I was skeptical about it from the very beginning. Knowing how difficult the sport is for me, I had trouble imagining Eric racing down a 10,000-foot mountain. And that wasn't helped by the knowledge that a blow to Eric's head could cause him to have a seizure that would put him in the hospital for more brain surgery. But Nancy had faith that Eric could do it, and when she believes, so does he. And off we went to give it a try.
>
> When we got up to Deer Valley and met some of the people who work at the National Ability Center, I started to feel a little bit better about it. They were professional and extremely positive, and they showed us the equipment that Eric would be using, a type of bi-ski with a molded seat. Eric would be put in the chair and steer using a bar attached to outrigger skis.
>
> When we started to fill out paperwork, we were momentarily paralyzed when we read the waiver that said that Eric would be "engaging in activities that involve risk of serious injury, including permanent disability and death." It made the risk seem very real, but by this time Eric was very excited and we didn't want him to see any hesitation from us.

After Velcro-fastening Eric into his bi-ski and giving him some pointers, Stephanie, his young instructor, took him up the bunny slope. About ten minutes later, we got excited as we saw Eric coming down the hill with the biggest smile on his face. We were so proud of him that we were giving him high fives and patting him on the back. I thought to myself, *That wasn't so bad.*

Then off they went again. What we didn't know was that this time they were going to the top of the mountain. At the bottom of the hill we waited. And waited. We weren't sure whether we'd see Eric come down the mountain on his skis or on a stretcher with the ski patrol. Finally after about thirty minutes, we saw him and Stephanie come around a bend and ski to the bottom of the slope. His cheeks were flushed, and he was grinning like the Cheshire cat. He loved it.

"Move over, Dad," he said as he blew past us. "I'm going up again."

Eric skied every day on that trip. In fact, when he finished skiing one day, he told us, "Stephanie didn't take me up the mountain today."

"Oh," said Nancy, "then who skied with you?"

"Some one-legged guy," answered Eric.

"What!" screeched Nancy. "What do you mean some one-legged guy?"

"Yep," said Eric, "a one-legged guy." And then Eric smiled mischievously and said, "Want to know how he lost his leg? Avalanche!"

Eric has been skiing every year since then, and his life hasn't been the same. He now has confidence that he never had before, and he is willing to try just about anything. He swims three days a week, works out with weights, plays power soccer, and does other sorts of things. I guess you could say that he has adopted the motto of the National Ability Center as his own: "If I Can Do This, I Can Do Anything!"

If they had done things Jim's way, Eric never would have gotten the chance to experience what he did on that mountain in Utah five years ago. Jim loves Eric with all his heart, but he tends to want to play it safe. Putting your faith in others involves taking a chance. But the rewards outweigh the risks. Robert Louis

Stevenson said, "To be what we are, and to become what we are capable of becoming, is the only end of life." When you put your faith in others, you help them reach their potential. And you become an important influencer in their lives.

## *Influence Checklist*
# HAVING FAITH IN PEOPLE

❏ **Find a strength.** Think about someone you'd like to encourage. Find a strength that the person has, and point it out to him or her. Use your interaction as an opportunity to express confidence in the person.

❏ **Build on past successes.** If you have to give someone a difficult assignment in the near future, take some time to recall his or her past successes. Then when you meet with the person, review those past successes. (If you go through this process and can't recall any past successes, that's a sign you've spent too little time getting to know the person. Plan to spend some time together to get better acquainted.)

❏ **Help others overcome defeat.** If you have colleagues, friends, employees, or family members who have recently experienced a defeat of some kind, take time to chat with them about it. Let them tell you the whole story, and when they're done, make it clear that you value them and still believe strongly in them.

❏ **Start off right.** The next time you recruit new people for your organization, start the relationships right. Instead of waiting until after they prove themselves to praise them, make it a point to repeatedly express your faith in them and their ability *before* they give you results. You'll be pleased by their desire to live up to your positive expectations.

# *A Person of Influence . . .*

# LISTENS TO PEOPLE

If you were going on a job interview today, what would you say is the most important skill you would need? Is it writing, to create a knockout résumé? Or maybe salesmanship? After all, isn't that what you do on an interview, sell yourself? Or how about charisma? If you're charismatic, you're sure to get the job you want, right?

Or let's say that instead of going on an interview, you were going to spend your day recruiting, whether for business prospects, ministry workers, or people to play on your softball team. What skill would you need as a recruiter? Discernment? An eye for talent? The ability to cast vision and get people excited? Or maybe it would be hard-nosed negotiation skills?

Better yet, let's say your job today was to supply new ideas for your organization. What qualities would you need? Creativity? Intelligence? Would you need a good education? What is the number one ability you would need?

No matter which one of these three tasks you were to take on today, you would need one skill over all others, more than talent, discernment, or charm. It is the one skill that all great leaders recognize as indispensable to their ability to influence others and succeed. Have you guessed what it is? It's the ability to listen.

Not everyone is quick to learn the lesson of the importance of listening. Take, for example, Jim's experience:

> Fresh from Purdue University's engineering school, I started out in the corporate environment at McDonnell-Douglas where they had about 40,000 employees. I was working in the advanced design group for the DC-10 doing wind-tunnel analyses and computer simulations of the airplane's performance.
>
> But it didn't take me long to realize that I wasn't going to be there for my whole career. Some of the guys I worked with had been there two decades, and nothing had changed in them for those twenty years. They were in a holding pattern, waiting for the gold watch. But I wanted to make a greater impact on my world.
>
> That's when I started to pursue other business opportunities, and when I found the right one, I began trying to

recruit others to join me. Back then my strategy was to meet people in the huge employee cafeteria. After waiting in line to get my lunch, I'd look for a seat next to a sharp-looking guy who was sitting by himself, and I'd strike up a conversation with him. The first chance I got, I'd bombard him with information and try to persuade him with impressive facts and irrefutable logic. I managed to intimidate a few people with the force of my convictions, but I was unsuccessful in building a productive relationship with anyone.

I'd been doing this for several months, with very little success, when one day I was just talking with a guy from another department. He was telling me about the frustrations he was having with his boss, and about some problems he was having at home. He just found out his oldest child needed braces, their old clunker of a car was on its last legs, and he wasn't sure how he was going to make it. I really felt for the guy, and I wanted to get to know him better. Then suddenly, I realized that I could help him out. He was feeling powerless on the job, and he had money problems—two things that could be helped by being in business for himself. So I started to tell him about my business and explain how it might solve some of his problems. And to my shock he was actually very interested.

That day it hit me: *What an idiot I've been! I can't succeed with others by dumping information on them. If I want to help them or have a positive impact on people, I need to learn how to listen to them!*

## THE VALUE OF LISTENING

Edgar Watson Howe once joked, "No man would listen to you talk if he didn't know it was his turn next." Unfortunately, that accurately describes the way too many people approach communication—they're too busy waiting for their turn to really listen to others. But people of influence understand the incredible value of becoming a good listener. For example, when Lyndon B. Johnson was a junior senator from Texas, he kept a sign on his office wall that read, "You ain't learnin' nothin' when you're doin' all the talkin'." And Woodrow Wilson, the twenty-eighth American president, once said, "The ear of the leader must ring with the voices of the people."

The ability to skillfully listen is one key to gaining influence with others. Consider these benefits to listening that we've found:

## Listening Shows Respect

Psychologist Dr. Joyce Brothers said, "Listening, not imitation, may be the sincerest form of flattery." Whenever you don't pay attention to what others have to say, you send them the message that you don't value them. But when you listen to others, you communicate that you respect them. Even more, you show them that you care. German-born philosopher-theologian Paul Tillich commented, "The first duty of love is to listen."

A mistake that people often make in communicating is trying very hard to impress the other person. They try to make themselves appear smart, witty, or entertaining. But if you want to relate well to others, you have to be willing to focus on what they have to offer. Be *impressed and interested,* not *impressive and interesting.* Poet-philosopher Ralph Waldo Emerson acknowledged, "Every man I meet is in some way my superior, and I can learn of him." Remember that and listen, and the lines of communication will really open up.

## Listening Builds Relationships

Dale Carnegie, author of *How to Win Friends and Influence People,* advised, "You can make more friends in two weeks by becoming a good listener than you can in two years trying to get other people interested in you." Carnegie was incredibly gifted at understanding relationships. He recognized that people who are self-focused and who talk about themselves and their concerns all the time rarely develop strong relationships with others. David Schwartz noted in *The Magic of Thinking Big,* "Big people monopolize the listening. Small people monopolize the talking."

By becoming a good listener, you are able to connect with others on more levels and develop stronger, deeper relationships because you are meeting a need. Author C. Neil Strait pointed out that "everyone needs someone who he feels really listens to him." When you become that important listener, you help that person. And you take a significant step toward becoming a person of influence in his or her life.

## Listening Increases Knowledge

Wilson Mizner said, "A good listener is not only popular everywhere, but after a while he knows something." It's amazing how much you can learn about your friends and family, your job, the organization you work in, and yourself when you decide to really listen to others. But not everyone clues in to this benefit. For example, we heard a story about a tennis pro who was giving a lesson to a new student. After watching the novice take several swings at the tennis ball, the pro stopped him and suggested ways he could improve his stroke. But each time he did, the student interrupted him and gave his opinion of the problem and how it should be solved. After several interruptions, the pro began to nod his head in agreement.

When the lesson ended, a woman who had been watching said to the pro, "Why did you go along with that arrogant man's stupid suggestions?"

> *You'll never know how close you are to a million-dollar idea unless you're willing to listen.*

The pro smiled and replied, "I learned a long time ago that it is a waste of time to try to sell real *answers* to anyone who just wants to buy *echoes.*"

Beware of putting yourself into a position where you think you know all the answers. Anytime you do, you'll be putting yourself in danger. It's almost impossible to think of yourself as "the expert" and continue growing and learning at the same time. All great learners are great listeners.

One common problem as people gain more authority is that they often listen to others less and less, especially the people who report to them. While it's true that the higher you go, the less you are required to listen to others, it's also true that your need for good listening skills increases. The farther you get from the front lines, the more you have to depend on others to get reliable information. Only if you develop good listening skills early, and then continue to use them, will you be able to gather the information you need to succeed.

As you proceed through life and become more successful, don't lose sight of your need to keep growing and improving yourself. And remember, a deaf ear is evidence of a closed mind.

## Listening Generates Ideas

Fresh, innovative ideas help us to find new ways to solve old problems, to generate new products and processes to keep our organizations growing, and to continue growing and improving personally. Plutarch of ancient Greece asserted, "Know how to listen, and you will profit even from those who talk badly."

When we think about innovative companies that never seem to run out of ideas, 3M immediately comes to mind. That company seems to develop new products faster than just about any other manufacturer. The organization has a reputation for being open to employees' ideas and for listening to customers. In fact, a representative of 3M said the number one resource for product ideas was customer complaints.

Good companies have a reputation for listening to their people. Chili's restaurants, one of the nation's best-run food service chains according to *Restaurants and Institutions* magazine, is known for that quality too. Almost 80 percent of its menu has come from suggestions made by unit managers.

What's good for effective companies is good for individuals. When you consistently listen to others, you never suffer for ideas. People love to contribute, especially when their leader shares the credit with them. If you give people opportunities to share their thoughts, and you listen with an open mind, there will always be a flow of new ideas. And even if you hear ideas that won't work, just listening to them can often spark other creative thoughts in you and others. You'll never know how close you are to a million-dollar idea unless you're willing to listen.

## Listening Builds Loyalty

A funny thing happens when you don't make a practice of listening to people. They find others who will. Anytime employees, spouses, colleagues, children, or friends no longer believe they are being listened to, they seek out people who will give them what they want. Sometimes the consequences can be disastrous: the end of a friendship, lack of authority at work, lessened parental influence, or the breakdown of a marriage.

> *Nobody ever* **listened** *himself or herself out of a sale.*

On the other hand, practicing good listening skills draws people to you. Karl Menninger, psychiatrist, author, and one of the founders of the Menninger Foundation, said, "The friends who listen to us are the ones we move toward, and we want to sit in their radius." Everyone loves a good listener and is attracted to him or her. And if you consistently listen to others, valuing them and what they have to offer, they are likely to develop a strong loyalty to you, even when your authority with them is unofficial or informal.

## Listening Is a Great Way to Help Others and Yourself

Roger G. Imhoff urged, "Let others confide in you. It may not help you, but it surely will help them." At first glance, listening to others may appear to benefit only them. But when you become a good listener, you put yourself in a position to help yourself too. You have the ability to develop strong relationships, gather valuable information, and increase your understanding of yourself and others.

# COMMON BARRIERS TO LISTENING

Few people have reached their potential when it comes to listening. If you aren't as skilled at listening as you would like to be, then the first thing to do to improve your ability is to be aware of common barriers to listening:

## *Overvaluing Talking*

A comic once described listening as being "composed of the rude interruptions between my exclamations." Many people's attitudes about listening agree with that statement more than they would like to admit. For example, if you asked six people how they could improve their communication skills, most of them would describe the need to become more persuasive or sharpen their public speaking skills. Few would cite a desire to listen better.

Most people overvalue talking and undervalue listening, even those in people-related jobs, such as sales. But the truth is that effective communication is not persuasion. It's listening. Think about it: Nobody ever *listened* himself or herself out of a sale.

Good communicators know to monitor their talking-to-listening ratio. President Abraham Lincoln, considered one of the most effective leaders and communicators in our nation's history, said, "When I'm getting ready to reason with a man, I spend one third of my time thinking about myself and what I am going to say—and two thirds thinking about him and what he is going to say." That's a good ratio to maintain. Listen twice as much as you speak.

## *Lacking Focus*

For some people, especially those with high energy, slowing down enough to really listen can be challenging. Most people tend to speak about 180 words a minute, but they can listen at 300 to 500 words a minute. That disparity can create tension and cause a listener to lose focus. Most people try to fill up that communication gap by finding other things to do, such as daydream, think about their daily schedule or mentally review their to-do list, or watch other people. It's similar to what we do when we drive a car. We rarely just watch the road and do nothing else. Usually we look at the scenery, eat and drink, talk, or listen to the radio.

If you want to become a better listener, however, you need to learn to direct that energy and attention positively by concentrating on the person you're with. Observe body language. Watch for changes in facial expression. Look into the person's eyes. Management expert Peter Drucker remarked, "The most important thing in communication is to hear what isn't being said." If you expend your extra energy by observing the other person closely and interpreting what he or she says, your listening skills will improve dramatically.

## Experiencing Mental Fatigue

Former president Ronald Reagan told an amusing story about two psychiatrists, one older and one younger. Each day they showed up at work immaculately dressed and alert. But at the end of the day, the younger doctor was frazzled and disheveled while the older man was as fresh as ever.

"How do you do it?" the younger psychiatrist finally asked his colleague. "You always stay so fresh after hearing patients all day."

The older doctor replied, "It's easy. I never listen."[1]

Whenever you listen to others for extended periods of time, the effect can be exhausting. But any kind of mental fatigue can negatively affect your ability to listen.

We heard a story about an eighty-nine-year-old woman with hearing problems. She visited her doctor, and after examining her, he said, "We now have a procedure that can correct your hearing problem. When would you like to schedule the operation?"

"There won't be any operation because I don't want my hearing corrected," said the woman. "I'm eighty-nine years old, and I've heard enough!"

If you're tired or facing difficult circumstances, remember that to remain an effective listener, you have to dig up more energy, concentrate, and stay focused.

## Stereotyping

Stereotyping others can be a huge barrier to listening. It tends to make us hear what we expect rather than what another person actually says. Most of us may think that we don't fall into this trap, but we all do to some degree. Read the following humorous list of stereotype breakers from a piece called "Things I'd Like to Hear—But Won't" created by David Grimes. If you never expect to hear any of these things from the people listed, then you may be guilty of stereotyping:

*From my auto mechanic:*
"That part is much less expensive than I thought."
"You could get that done more cheaply at the garage down the street."
"It was just a loose wire. No charge."

*From a store clerk:*
"The computerized cash register is down. I'll just add up your purchases with a pencil and paper."
"I'll take a break *after* I finish waiting on these customers."
"We're sorry we sold you defective merchandise. We'll pick it up at your home and bring you a new one or give you a complete refund, whichever you prefer."

*From a contractor:*
"Whoever worked on this before sure knew what he was doing."
"I think I came in a little high on that estimate."

*From the dentist:*
"I think you're flossing too much."
"I won't ask you any questions until I take the pick out of your mouth."

*From a restaurant server:*

"I think it's presumptuous for a waiter to volunteer his name, but since you ask, it's Tim."

"I was slow and inattentive. I cannot accept any tip."[2]

These statements are clever. And they are also a reminder that it's a bad idea to stereotype others. Whenever you treat people strictly as members of a group rather than as individuals, you can get into trouble. So watch out. If you talk to people and find yourself thinking of them as computer geeks, typical teenagers, ditsy blondes, stiff engineer types, or some other representative of a group instead of as individual people, beware. You may not really be listening to what they have to say.

## Carrying Personal Emotional Baggage

Nearly everyone has emotional filters that prevent him or her from hearing certain things that other people say. Your past experiences, both positive and negative, color the way you look at life and shape your expectations. And particularly strong experiences, such as traumas or incidents from childhood, can make you tend to react strongly whenever you perceive you are in a similar situation. As Mark Twain once said, "A cat who sits on a hot stove will never sit on a hot stove again. He'll never sit on a cold stove either. From then on, that cat just won't like stoves."

If you've never worked through strong past emotional experiences, you may be filtering what others say through those experiences. If you're preoccupied with certain topics, if a particular subject makes you defensive, or if you frequently project your point of view onto others, you may need to work through your issues before you can become an effective listener.

Sigmund Freud stated, "A man with a toothache cannot be in love," meaning that the toothache doesn't allow him to notice anything other than his pain. Similarly, anytime a person has an ax to grind, the words of others are drowned out by the sound of the grindstone.

## Being Preoccupied with Self

Probably the most formidable barrier to listening is preoccupation with self. Many years ago we saw a TV sketch that illustrates this point really well. A husband was watching television, and his wife was trying to engage him in conversation:

WIFE:     Dear, the plumber didn't make it in time to fix the leak by the hot water heater today.

HUSBAND: Uh-huh.

WIFE:     So the pipe burst and flooded the basement.

HUSBAND: Quiet. It's third down and goal to go.

WIFE:     Some of the wiring got wet and almost electrocuted Fluffy.

HUSBAND: Oh, no, they've got a man open. Shoot! Touchdown.

WIFE:     The vet says he'll be better in a week.

HUSBAND: Can you get me something to eat?

WIFE:     The plumber finally came and said that he was happy our pipe broke because now he can afford to go on vacation.

HUSBAND: Aren't you *listening?* I said I'm hungry!

WIFE:     And, Stanley, I'm leaving you. The plumber and I are flying to Acapulco in the morning.

HUSBAND: Can't you please stop all that yakking and get me something to eat? The trouble around here is that nobody ever listens to me.

If you don't care about anyone but yourself, you're not going to listen to others. But the ironic thing is that when you don't listen, the damage you do to yourself is ultimately even greater than what you do to other people.

# HOW TO DEVELOP LISTENING SKILLS

According to Brian Adams, author of *Sales Cybernetics,* during the average waking day, we spend most of it listening. He offers the following statistics:

9 percent of the day is spent writing
16 percent of the day is spent reading
30 percent of the day is spent speaking
45 percent of the day is spent *listening*[3]

So you probably agree that listening is important. But what does it mean to listen? We heard a story about a high school music appreciation class that provides a meaningful answer to that question. The teacher of the class asked for a volunteer to explain the difference between listening and hearing. At first no one wanted to answer, but finally, a student raised his hand. When the teacher called on him, he said, "Listening is *wanting* to hear."

That answer is a great start. To become a good listener, you have to want to hear. But you also need some skills to help you. Here are nine suggestions to help you become a better listener:

## 1. Look at the Speaker

The whole listening process begins with giving the other person your undivided attention. As you interact with someone, don't catch up on other work, shuffle papers, do the dishes, or watch television. Set aside the time to focus only on the other person. And if you don't have the time at that moment, then schedule it as soon as you can.

## 2. Don't Interrupt

Most people react badly to being interrupted. It makes them feel disrespected. And according to Robert L. Montgomery, author of *Listening Made Easy,* "It's just as rude to step on people's ideas as it is to step on their toes."

People who tend to interrupt others generally do so for one of these reasons:

- They don't place enough value on what the other person has to say.
- They want to impress others by showing how smart or intuitive they are.

- They're too excited by the conversation to let the other person finish talking.

If you are in the habit of interrupting other people, examine your motives and determine to make a change. Give people the time they need to express themselves. And don't feel that one of you has to be speaking all the time. Periods of silence give you a chance to reflect on what's been said so that you can respond appropriately.

## 3. Focus on Understanding

Have you ever noticed how quickly most people forget the things they hear? Studies at institutions such as Michigan State, Ohio State, Florida State, and the University of Minnesota indicate that most people can recall only 50 percent of what they hear immediately after hearing it. And as time passes, their ability to remember continues to drop. By the next day, their retention is usually down to about 25 percent.

One way to combat that tendency is to make your goal understanding rather than just remembering facts. Lawyer, lecturer, and author Herb Cohen emphasized, "Effective listening requires more than hearing the words transmitted. It demands that you find meaning and understanding in what is being said. After all, meanings are not in words, but in people."

To increase your understanding of others as you listen, follow these guidelines offered by Eric Allenbaugh:

1. Listen with a head-heart connection.
2. Listen with the intent of understanding.
3. Listen for the message and the message behind the message.
4. Listen for both content and feelings.
5. Listen with your eyes—your hearing will be improved.
6. Listen for others' interest, not just their position.
7. Listen for what they are saying and not saying.
8. Listen with empathy and acceptance.
9. Listen for the areas where they are afraid and hurt.
10. Listen as you would like to be listened to.[4]

As you learn to put yourself in the other person's place, your ability to understand will increase. And the greater your ability to understand, the better listener you will become.

## 4. Determine the Need at the Moment

The ability to discern the other person's need at the moment is part of becoming an effective listener. People talk for so many different reasons: to receive comfort, to vent, to persuade, to inform, to be understood, or to relieve nervousness. Often people talk to you for reasons that don't match your expectations.

A lot of men and women find themselves in conflict because they occasionally communicate at cross-purposes. They neglect to determine the need of the other person at the moment of interaction. Men usually want to fix any problems they discuss; their need is resolution. Women, on the other hand, are more likely to tell about a problem simply to share it; they often neither request nor desire solutions. Anytime you can determine the current need of the people you're communicating with, you can put whatever they say into the appropriate context. And you will be better able to understand them.

## 5. Check Your Emotions

As we've already mentioned, most people carry around emotional baggage that causes them to react to certain people or situations. Anytime that you become highly emotional when listening to another person, check your emotions—especially if your reaction seems to be stronger than the situation warrants. You don't want to make an unsuspecting person the recipient of your venting. Besides, even if your reactions are not due to an event from your past, you should always allow others to finish explaining their points of view, ideas, or convictions before offering your own.

## 6. Suspend Your Judgment

Have you ever begun listening to another person tell a story and started to respond to it before he or she was finished? Just about everyone has. But the truth is that you can't jump to con-clusions and be a good listener at the same time. As you talk to others, wait to hear the whole story before you respond. If you don't, you may miss the most important thing they intend to say.

## 7. Sum Up at Major Intervals

Experts agree that listening is most effective when it's active. John H. Melchinger suggests, "Comment on what you hear, and individualize your comments. For example, you can say, 'Cheryl, that's obviously very important to you.' It will help keep you on track as a listener. Get beyond, 'That's interesting.' If you train yourself to comment meaningfully, the speaker will know you are listening and may offer further information."

A technique for active listening is to sum up what the other person says at major intervals. As the speaker finishes one sub-ject, paraphrase his or her main points or ideas before going on to the next one, and verify that you have gotten the right mes-sage. Doing that reassures the person and helps you stay focused on what he or she is trying to communicate.

## 8. Ask Questions for Clarity

Have you ever noticed that top reporters are excellent listen-ers? Take someone like Barbara Walters, for example. She looks at the speaker, focuses on understanding, suspends judgment, and sums up what the person has to say. People trust her and seem to be willing to tell her just about anything. But she prac-tices another skill that helps her to gather more information and increase her understanding of the person she is interviewing. She asks good questions.

If you want to become an effective listener, become a good re-porter—not a stick-the-microphone-in-your-face-and-bark-ques-tions-at-you reporter, but someone who gently asks follow-up questions and seeks clarification. If you show people how much you care and ask in a nonthreatening way, you'll be amazed by how much they'll tell you.

## 9. *Always Make Listening Your Priority*

The last thing to remember when developing your listening skills is to make listening a priority, no matter how busy you become or how far you rise in your organization. A remarkable example of a busy executive who made time for listening was the late Sam Walton, founder of Wal-Mart and one of the richest men in America. He believed in listening to what people had to say, especially his employees. He once flew his plane to Mt. Pleasant, Texas, landed, and gave instructions to his copilot to meet him about one hundred miles down the road. He then rode in a Wal-Mart truck the rest of the way just so that he could chat with the driver. We should all give listening that kind of priority.

---

*If you show people how much you care and ask questions in a nonthreatening way, you'll be amazed by how much they'll tell you.*

---

Many people take for granted the ability to listen. Most people consider listening to be easy, and they view themselves as pretty good listeners. But while it's true that most people are able to hear, fewer are capable of really listening.

In our careers, we have done a lot of speaking. Between the two of us, we speak to several hundred thousand people every year. Jim's wife, Nancy, does a lot of speaking—and believe us, she is a great talker! But she is also a wonderful listener, and sometimes when she speaks, she talks about communication and the importance of listening. Not long ago she gave a talk about listening that emphasized giving other people the benefit of the doubt and trying to see things from their point of view.

In the audience that day was a man named Rodney. Though he was happily married and had a young son, he had been previously married and had two daughters with his first wife. And he was having problems with her. She was constantly calling him and asking for more money for herself and the two girls. They argued continually, and she was driving him so nuts that he had already hired an attorney and was preparing to sue her.

But when Rodney heard Nancy speak about listening that day, he realized how insensitive he had been to his ex-wife, Charlotte. A couple of days later he called her and asked if they could meet. She was suspicious of Rodney and even asked her attorney to call him to find out what he was up to. But eventually, Rodney convinced them that he just wanted to talk, and finally, Charlotte agreed to see him.

They met at a coffee shop, and Rodney said, "Charlotte, I want to listen to you. Tell me what your life is like. I do care about you and the kids."

"I didn't think you cared about the girls at all," she said as she began to cry.

"I do," he said. "I'm sorry. I've only been thinking of myself, and I haven't been thinking of you. Please forgive me."

"Why are you doing this?" she asked.

"Because I want to make things right," he answered. "I've been angry for so long that I couldn't see straight. Now, tell me how things are going for you and the girls."

For a while, Charlotte could only sob. But then she started telling him about her struggles as a single parent and how she was doing her best to bring up the girls, but that it didn't seem like enough. They talked for hours, and as they did, the beginning of a new foundation of mutual respect formed. In time, they believe they will be able to become friends again.

Rodney is probably not alone. Can you think of people you haven't been listening to lately? And what are you going to do about it? It's never too late to become a good listener. It can change your life—and the lives of the people in your life.

## *Influence Checklist*
# LISTENING TO PEOPLE

❏ **Measure your listening skills.** Have someone who knows you well use the following questions to evaluate your listening skills according to the nine qualities of good listening discussed in this chapter. Ask him or her to explain any no answers. And don't interrupt or defend yourself as you receive the explanation.

1. Do I usually look at the speaker while he or she is talking?
2. Do I wait for the speaker to finish talking before I respond?
3. Do I make understanding my goal?
4. Am I usually sensitive to the speaker's immediate need?
5. Do I make it a practice to check my emotions?
6. Do I regularly suspend my judgment until I get the whole story?
7. Am I in the practice of summing up what the speaker says at major intervals?
8. Do I ask questions for clarity when needed?
9. Do I communicate to others that listening is a priority?

❏ **Strategy for improvement.** Based on the answers received, list three ways you could improve your listening skills:

1._____

2._____

3._____

Commit yourself to making those improvements during the coming weeks.

❏ **Schedule a listening occasion.** Make an appointment with the most important person in your life this week, and plan to spend an hour together just communicating. Give that person your undivided attention, and spend at least two-thirds of the time just listening to him or her.

# *A Person of Influence . . .*

# UNDERSTANDS PEOPLE

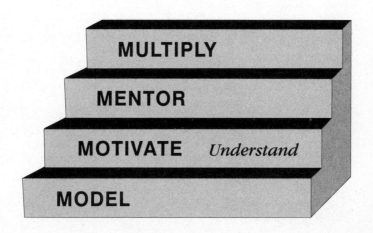

The other night over dinner, the two of us were talking, and we started to explore some questions. How does a person build an organization? What does it take? What is the key to being successful? For example, what did it take for a person like Jim to build a business organization that's active in twenty-six countries and impacts the lives of hundreds of thousands of people? Or in the case of John, what did it take to triple the size of his church—making it the largest in its denomination—and in the process increase its budget from around $800,000 to more than $5 million, and raise active involvement by volunteers from just 112 to more than 1,800 people?

It doesn't matter whether your business is creating computer software, selling books, serving food in a restaurant, building houses, or designing airplanes. The key to success is understanding people. Jim says,

> I'm not like John. I didn't grow up with an orientation toward people. He took Dale Carnegie courses while he was still in high school and went off to college knowing he would be in a people job. I went to Purdue University and studied aeronautical engineering. By the time I finished with my bachelor's degree, I thought there were two keys to success in any job: hard work and technical skills. It never even occurred to me that people skills had any value.
>
> I entered my first job ready to work and loaded with technical knowledge. Purdue had given me a first-rate education, and I had always believed in working hard. But it didn't take me long to realize that success in business means being able to work with people. In fact, all of life is dealing with people. I found that to be true not only professionally as an engineer, a consultant, and an entrepreneur, but in every aspect of living, whether I was interacting with my family, working with one of my kids' teachers, or socializing with friends.
>
> If you can't understand people and work with them, you can't accomplish anything. And you certainly can't become a person of influence.

# UNDERSTANDING PEOPLE
# PAYS GREAT DIVIDENDS

In *Climbing the Executive Ladder,* authors Kienzle and Dare said, "Few things will pay you bigger dividends than the time and trouble you take to understand people. Almost nothing will add more to your stature as an executive and a person. Nothing will give you greater satisfaction or bring you more happiness."

> ***When we understand the other fellow's viewpoint— understand what he is trying to do—nine times out of ten he is trying to do right.***
> ***—Harry Truman***

The ability to understand people is one of the greatest assets anyone can ever have. It has the potential to positively impact every area of your life, not just the business arena. For example, look at how understanding people helped this mother of a preschooler. She said,

> Leaving my four-year-old son in the house, I ran out to throw something in the trash. When I tried to open the door to get back inside, it was locked. I knew that insisting that my son open the door would have resulted in an hour-long battle of the wills. So in a sad voice, I said, "Oh, too bad. You just locked yourself in the house." The door opened at once.

Understanding people certainly impacts your ability to communicate with others. David Burns, a medical doctor and professor of psychiatry at the University of Pennsylvania, observed, "The biggest mistake you can make in trying to talk convincingly is to put your highest priority on expressing your ideas and feelings. What most people really want is to be listened to, respected, and understood. The moment people see that they are being understood, they become more motivated to understand your point of view." If you can learn to understand people—how they think, what they feel, what inspires them, how they're likely to act and react in a given situation—then you can motivate and influence them in a positive way.

# WHY PEOPLE FAIL TO UNDERSTAND OTHERS

Lack of understanding concerning others is a recurrent source of tension in our society. We once heard an attorney say, "Half of all the controversies and conflicts that arise among people are caused not by differences of opinion or an inability to agree, but by their lack of understanding for one another." If we could reduce the number of misunderstandings, the courts wouldn't be as crowded, there would be fewer violent crimes, the divorce rate would go down, and the amount of everyday stress most people experience would drop dramatically.

If understanding is such an asset, why don't more people practice it? There are many reasons:

## Fear

Seventeenth-century American colonist William Penn advised, "Neither despise or oppose what thou dost not understand," yet many people seem to do exactly the opposite. When they don't understand others, they often react by becoming fearful. And once they start fearing others, they rarely try to overcome their fear in order to learn more about them. It becomes a vicious cycle.

Unfortunately, fear is evident in the workplace when it comes to employees' reactions toward their leaders. Laborers fear their managers. Middle managers are intimidated by senior managers. Both groups are sometimes afraid of executives. The whole situation causes undue suspicion, lack of communication, and reduced productivity. For example, according to Dr. M. Michael Markowich, vice president of human resources at United Hospitals, Inc., employees are reluctant to suggest ideas. Here are some reasons why:

- They think their ideas will be rejected.
- They feel co-workers won't like the ideas.
- They think they won't get credit if the ideas work.
- They're afraid the boss will be threatened by the ideas.
- They're concerned that they'll be labeled as troublemakers.
- They're afraid of losing their jobs if they suggest ideas that don't work.[1]

The common thread in all of these reasons is fear. Yet in a healthy work environment, if you give others the benefit of the doubt and replace fear with understanding, everyone can work together positively. All people have to do is follow the advice of President Harry Truman, who said, "When we understand the other fellow's viewpoint—understand what he is trying to do—nine times out of ten he is trying to do right."

## Self-Centeredness

When fear isn't a stumbling block to understanding, self-centeredness often is. Someone remarked, "There are two sides to every question—as long as it doesn't concern us personally." That's the way too many people think. Everyone is not self-centered on purpose; it's just in the nature of people to think of their own interests first. If you want to see an example of that, play with a two-year-old child. He naturally chooses the best toys for himself and insists on his own way.

One way to overcome our natural self-centeredness is to try to see things from other people's perspectives. Talking to a group of salespeople, Art Mortell shared this experience: "Whenever I'm losing at chess, I consistently get up and stand behind my opponent and see the board from his side. Then I start to discover the stupid moves I've made because I can see it from his viewpoint. The salesperson's challenge is to see the world from the prospect's viewpoint."[2]

That's the challenge for every one of us, no matter what our profession. There is a quote that John filed away years ago called "A Short Course in Human Relations." You may have already heard it because it's been around for a while. But it reminds us of what our priorities should be when dealing with other people:

The least important word: I
The most important word: We
The two most important words: Thank you.
The three most important words: All is forgiven.
The four most important words: What is your opinion?
The five most important words: You did a good job.
The six most important words: I want to understand you
    better.

Changing your attitude from self-centeredness to understanding requires desire and commitment to always try to see things from the other person's point of view.

## Failure to Appreciate Differences

The next logical step after leaving behind self-centeredness is learning to recognize and respect everyone else's unique qualities. Instead of trying to cast others in your image, learn to appreciate their differences. If someone has a talent that you don't have, great. The two of you can strengthen each other's weaknesses. If others come from a different culture, broaden your horizons and learn what you can from them. Your new knowledge will help you relate not only to them, but also to others. And celebrate people's differences in temperament. Variety makes for interesting dynamics between people. For instance, John has a choleric-sanguine temperament, which means he loves to have fun and enjoys making decisions in the blink of an eye. On the other hand, Jim is a melancholy-phlegmatic. He is a great thinker and processor of information, and when he needs to make decisions, he gathers as much data as he can to make wise choices. Separate, we do well. But we're even more effective when the two of us are together.

Once you learn to appreciate other people's differences, you come to realize that there are many responses to leadership and motivation. Joseph Beck, the president of the Kenley Corporation, recognized that truth when he said that an influencer "must realize that different people are motivated in different ways. A good basketball coach, for example, knows when a player needs encouragement to excel and when a player needs a 'kick in the pants.' The main difference is that all players need encouragement and only some need a 'kick in the pants.'"

## Failure to Acknowledge Similarities

As you learn more about people and get to know others well, you soon begin to realize that people have a lot in common. We all have hopes and fears, joys and sorrows, victories and problems. Probably the time when people are least likely to recognize their common ground with others is during adolescence. We came across a story that illustrates this:

> A teenage girl was talking to her father about all of her problems. She told him of the terrible peer pressure she faced, about conflicts with friends, and difficulties with schoolwork and teachers. In an attempt to help her put everything in perspective, he told her that life was not as dark as it might seem and, in fact, much of her worry was perhaps unnecessary.
>
> "That's easy for you to say, Dad," she replied. "You already have all your problems over with."

All people have an emotional reaction to what's happening around them. To foster understanding, think of what *your* emotions would be if you were in the same position as the person you're interacting with. You know what you would want to happen in a given situation. Chances are that the person you're working with has many of the same feelings.

We found a wonderful example of a person who understands this approach. A candy store sold its exotic chocolates only by the pound. In the store was one particular salesclerk who always had customers lined up waiting while other salesclerks stood around with nothing to do. The owner of the store noticed how the customers flocked to her and finally asked for her secret.

"It's easy," she said. "The other girls scoop up more than a pound of candy and then start taking away. I always scoop up less than a pound and then add to it. The customers feel that I'm looking out for them and getting them their money's worth."

# THINGS EVERYBODY NEEDS TO UNDERSTAND ABOUT PEOPLE

Knowing what people need and want is the key to understanding them. And if you can understand them, you can influence them and impact their lives in a positive way. If we were to boil down all the things we know about understanding people and narrow them down to a short list, we would identify these five things:

## 1. Everybody Wants to Be Somebody

There isn't a person in the world who doesn't have the desire to be someone, to have significance. Even the least ambitious and unassuming person wants to be regarded highly by others.

John remembers the first time these feelings were stirred strongly within him. It was back when he was in the fourth grade:

> I went to my first basketball game when I was nine years old. I can still see it in my head. I stood with my buddies in the balcony of the gym. The thing that I remember most wasn't the game; it was the announcement of the starting lineups. They turned all the lights out, and then some spotlights came on. The announcer called out the names of the starters, and they ran out to the middle of the floor one by one with everybody in the place cheering.
>
> I hung over the balcony that day as a fourth-grade kid and said, "Wow, I'd like that to happen to me." In fact, by the time the introductions were over, I looked at my friend Bobby Wilson, and I said, "Bobby, when I get to high

school, they're going to announce my name, and I'm going to run out in the spotlight to the middle of that basketball floor. And the people are going to cheer for me because I'm going to become somebody."

I went home that night and told my dad, "I want to be a basketball player." Soon afterward, he got me a Spalding basketball, and we put a goal on the garage. I used to shovel snow off that driveway to practice my foul shots and play basketball, because I had a dream of becoming somebody.

It's funny how that kind of dream can impact your life. I remember in sixth grade we played intramural basketball, and our team won a couple of games, so we got to go to the Old Mill Street Gym in Circleville, Ohio, where I'd seen that basketball game in the fourth grade. When we got there, instead of going out onto the floor with the rest of the players as they were warming up, I went over to the bench where those high school players had been two years before. I sat right where they had, and I closed my eyes (the equivalent of turning the lights out in the gym). Then in my head I heard my name announced, and I ran out in the middle of the floor.

It felt so good to hear that imaginary applause that I thought, *I'll do it again!* So I did. In fact, I did it three times, and all of a sudden I realized that my buddies weren't playing basketball; they were just watching me in disbelief. But I didn't even care because I was one step closer to being the person I'd dreamed about becoming.

Everybody wants to be regarded and valued by others. In other words, everybody wants to be somebody. Once that piece of information becomes a part of your everyday thinking, you'll gain incredible insight into why people do the things they do. And if you treat every person you meet as if he or she were the most important person in the world, you'll communicate that he or she *is* somebody—to you.

## 2. *Nobody Cares How Much You Know Until He Knows How Much You Care*

To be an influencer, you have to love people before you try to lead them. The moment that people know that you care for and about them, the way they feel about you changes.

Showing others that you care isn't always easy. Your greatest times and fondest memories will come because of people, but so will your most difficult, hurting, and tragic times. People are your greatest assets and your greatest liabilities. The challenge is to keep caring about them no matter what.

We came across something called "Paradoxical Commandments of Leadership." Here's what it says:

People are illogical, unreasonable, and self-centered—love them anyway.

If you do good, people will accuse you of selfish ulterior motives—do good anyway.

If you're successful, you'll win false friends and true enemies—succeed anyway.

The good you do today will perhaps be forgotten tomorrow—do good anyway.

Honesty and frankness make you vulnerable—be honest and frank anyway.

The biggest man with the biggest ideas can be shot down by the smallest man with the smallest mind—think big anyway.

People favor underdogs but follow only hot dogs—fight for the few underdogs anyway.

What you spend years building may be destroyed overnight—build anyway.

People really need help but may attack you if you help them—help them anyway.

Give the world the best that you have and you will get kicked in the teeth—give the world the best that you have anyway.[3]

If better is possible, then good is not enough.

If you want to help others and become a person of influence, keep smiling, sharing, giving, and turning the other cheek. That's the right way to treat people. Besides, you never know which people in your sphere of influence are going to rise up and make a difference in your life and the lives of others.

## 3. *Everybody Needs Somebody*

Contrary to popular belief, there are no such things as self-made men and women. Everybody needs friendship, encouragement, and help. What people can accomplish by themselves is almost nothing compared to their potential when working with others. And doing things with other people tends to bring contentment. Besides, Lone Rangers are rarely happy people. King Solomon of ancient Israel stated the value of working together this way:

> Two are better than one,
>   because they have a good return for their work:
> If one falls down,
>   his friend can help him up.
> But pity the man who falls
>   and has no one to help him up!
> Also, if two lie down together, they will keep warm.
>   But how can one keep warm alone?
> Though one may be overpowered,
>   two can defend themselves.
> A cord of three strands is not quickly broken.[4]

People who try to do everything alone often get themselves into trouble. One of the wildest stories we've ever seen on this subject came from the insurance claim form of a bricklayer who got hurt at a building site. He was trying to get a load of bricks down from the top floor of a building without asking for help from anyone else. He wrote:

> It would have taken too long to carry all the bricks down by hand, so I decided to put them in a barrel and lower them by a pulley which I had fastened to the top of the building. After tying the rope securely at ground level, I then went up to the top of the building, I fastened the rope around the barrel,

loaded it with bricks, and swung it over the sidewalk for the descent. Then I went down to the sidewalk and untied the rope, holding it securely to guide the barrel down slowly. But since I weigh only 140 pounds, the 500 pound load jerked me from the ground so fast that I didn't have time to think of letting go of the rope. As I passed between the second and third floors I met the barrel coming down. This accounts for the bruises and the lacerations on my upper body.

I held tightly to the rope until I reached the top where my hand became jammed in the pulley. This accounts for my broken thumb.

At the same time, however, the barrel hit the sidewalk with a bang and the bottom fell out. With the weight of the bricks gone, the barrel weighed only about 40 pounds. Thus my 140 pound body began a swift descent, and I met the empty barrel coming up. This accounts for my broken ankle.

Slowed only slightly, I continued the descent and landed on the pile of bricks. This accounts for my sprained back and broken collar bone.

At this point I lost my presence of mind completely, and I let go of the rope and the empty barrel came crashing down on me. This accounts for my head injuries.

And as for the last question on your insurance form, "What would I do if the same situation rose again?" Please be advised I am finished trying to do the job all by myself.

Everybody needs somebody to come alongside and help. If you understand that, are willing to give to others and help them, and maintain the right motives, their lives and yours can change.

## 4. Everybody Can Be Somebody When Somebody Understands and Believes in Her

Once you understand people and believe in them, they really can become somebody. And it doesn't take much effort to help other people feel important. Little things, done deliberately at the right time, can make a big difference, as this story from John shows:

> For fourteen years I was privileged to pastor a very large congregation in the San Diego area where we did a wonderful Christmas program every year. We used to do twenty-eight performances, and altogether about thirty thousand people saw it each year.
>
> The show always included a bunch of kids, and one of my favorite parts of the show several years ago was a song in which three hundred kids dressed like angels sang while holding candles. Toward the end of the song, they walked off the stage, came up the aisles, and exited out of the lobby in the front of the church.
>
> During the first performance, I decided to wait for them back in the lobby. They didn't know I was going to be there, but as they went by I clapped, praised them, and said, "Kids, you did a great job!" They were surprised to see me, and they were glad for the encouragement.
>
> For the second performance, I did the same thing again. And I could see as they started to walk up the aisles, they were looking back expectantly to see if I was standing there to cheer them on. By the third performance of the night, as they turned the corner to come up the aisle, they had smiles on their faces. And when they got to the lobby, they were giving me high fives and having a great time. They knew I believed in them, and it made all of them feel that they were somebody.

When was the last time you went out of your way to make people feel special, as if they were somebody? The investment required on your part is totally overshadowed by the impact it makes on them. Everyone you know and all the people you meet have the potential to be someone important in the lives of others. All they need is encouragement and motivation from you to help them reach their potential.

## 5. Anybody Who Helps Somebody Influences a Lot of Bodies

The final thing you need to understand about people is that when you help one person, you're really impacting a lot of other people. What you give to one person overflows into the lives of all the people that person impacts. The nature of influence is to multiply. It even impacts you because when you help others and your motives are good, you always receive more than you can ever give. Most people are so genuinely grateful when another person makes them feel that they're somebody special that they never tire of showing their gratitude.

# CHOOSE TO UNDERSTAND OTHERS

In the end, the ability to understand people is a choice. It's true that some people are born with great instincts that enable them to understand how others think and feel. But even if you aren't an instinctive people person, you can improve your ability to work with others. Every person is capable of having the ability to understand, motivate, and ultimately influence others.

If you truly want to make a difference in the lives of others, then make up your mind to possess . . .

## The Other Person's Perspective

Mark McCormack, author of *What They Don't Teach You at Harvard Business School,* wrote about an amusing story for *Entrepreneur* magazine. It illustrates the value of recognizing other people's perspectives. He said, "A few years ago I was standing in an airport ticket line. In front of me were two children fighting over an ice cream cone. In front of them was a woman in a mink coat. I could see this was an accident waiting to happen. Should I interfere? I was still pondering this when I heard the girl tell the boy, 'If you don't stop, Charlie, you'll get hairs from that lady's coat on your cone.'"

Most people don't look beyond their own experience when dealing with others. They tend to see other people and events in the context of their own position, background, or circumstances. For example, Pat McInally of the NFL's Cincinnati Bengals said, "At Harvard they labeled me a jock. In the pros they consider me an intellectual." Though he had not changed, other people's perceptions of him had.

Whenever you look at things from the other person's perspective, you'll receive a whole new way of looking at life. And you'll find new ways of helping others. A story from the book *Zadig* by Voltaire shows the value of looking at people and situations in a new way.

A country's ruler was upset because his favorite horse was missing. The king sent couriers throughout the land to look for it, but to no avail. In desperation, the king offered a great reward. Many came hoping to win it and searched for the horse, but they all failed. The horse had disappeared.

A simpleton at the king's court sought an audience with the monarch, and told him that he could find the horse.

"You!" exclaimed the king. "You can find my horse when all others have failed?"

"Yes, sire," answered the simpleton.

"Then do it," said the king, who had nothing to lose.

Within hours the horse was back at the palace, and the king was astounded. He immediately had his treasurer issue a handsome reward to the man, and asked him to explain how he had found it when many men considered wise had not.

"It was easy, sire," said the simpleton. "I merely asked myself, 'If I was a horse, where would I go?' And putting myself in his place, I soon found him."

## Personal Empathy

Another quality that you need if you want to understand and help others is personal empathy. Not everyone is naturally empathetic, as is evident in this story about a Kansas preacher. It seems that the preacher was returning home after a visit to New England, and one of his parishioners met him at the train station.

"Well," asked the preacher, "how are things at home?"

"Sad, real sad, Pastor," answered the man. "A cyclone came and wiped out my house."

"Well, I'm not surprised," said the unsympathetic parson with a frown. "You remember I've been warning you about the way you've been living. Punishment for sin is inevitable."

"It also destroyed your house, Pastor," added the layman.

"It did?" the pastor said, momentarily surprised. "Ah, me, the ways of the Lord are past human understanding."

Don't wait for your house to be blown down to have feelings about people's troubles and shortcomings. Reach out to others with a strong hand but a soft heart, and they'll respond to you positively.

## A Positive Attitude About People

Author Harper Lee wrote, "People generally see what they look for and hear what they listen for." If you have a positive attitude about people, believe the best of them, and act on your beliefs, then you can have an impact on their lives. But it all starts with the way you think of others. You can't be a positive influencer if your thinking is like this:

When the other fellow takes a long time, he's slow.
  When I take a long time, I'm thorough.
When the other fellow doesn't do it, he's lazy.
  When I don't do it, I'm busy.
When the other fellow does something without being told, he's
    overstepping his bounds.
  When I do it, that's initiative.
When the other fellow overlooks a rule of etiquette, he's rude.
  When I skip a few rules, I'm original.
When the other fellow pleases the boss, he's an apple polisher.
  When I please the boss, it's cooperation.
When the other fellow gets ahead, he's getting the breaks.
  When I manage to get ahead, that's just the reward for hard
    work.

Your attitude toward people is one of the most important choices you'll ever make. If your thinking is positive, you can really make an impact on them. Pastor Robert Schuller, a strong proponent of positive thinking, tells the following story in *Life Changers:*

"I'm the greatest baseball player in the world," the little boy boasted as he strutted around his backyard. Shouldering his bat, he tossed a baseball up, swung, and missed. "I am the greatest ball player ever," he reiterated. He picked up the ball again, swung, and missed again. Stopping a moment to examine his bat, he stooped and picked up his ball. "I am the greatest baseball player who ever lived!" The momentum of his swing nearly knocked him down. But the ball plopped, unscathed, at his feet. "Wow!" he exclaimed. "What a pitcher!"[5]

If you want to become a person of influence, have an attitude toward others similar to the attitude that little boy had about himself.

> *If you treat every person you meet as if he or she were the most important person in the world, you'll communicate that he or she is somebody— to you.*

Jim was reminded of the importance of understanding people and seeing things from their perspective when visiting his aging parents in New York recently:

My parents are in their upper eighties, and they worked hard all their lives. My dad was the city editor of the Niagara Falls *Gazette,* and my mother was the night supervising nurse at Niagara Falls Memorial Hospital. She worked many years from 11 P.M. to 7 A.M. when I was young so that she could be home to get me up for school, make breakfast, and pack my lunch. And then she was there when I got home from school each afternoon. I hardly realized she worked. Growing up we always lived in a very small house. After they retired, they sold it and moved to a small apartment to live on their modest pensions.

Like most people who have been blessed financially, Nancy and I are always looking for ways to help our parents and repay them in some small way for the positive things they have done for us over the years. Recently, we thought we could help them by leasing them a penthouse unit in the most prestigious apartment building in the city. It was incredible and even had a view of Niagara Falls.

But after about six months, my parents asked if they could move out. My mother's eyesight was now so poor that she couldn't see the Falls. Dad, on the other hand, could see the Falls fine but was made extremely uncomfortable by being up so high. We were disappointed that they didn't like it, but we readily agreed to move them back into their small apartment.

My desire to help them was still strong, so one day after we got them squared away in their place, I took Mom to the store. Though she claimed she didn't need anything, I did manage to talk her into letting me get her a few items: a new trash can, some flatware, a small radio, and a new toaster—the old one had *shot* the toast out like a cannon when it was done. And it made me feel good when I overheard her showing the toaster to a neighbor and saying, "My *son* bought this for us!"

Nancy and I had wanted to get them big things, but that's not what was important to them. They were happy with a toaster. Oh, yes, there was one other item they finally admitted that they could use: a small tree for the front of their apartment. They thought it would be nice to have some shade in the summer when they sat outside. "But they're so expensive," my mother said. "Just get us a sapling."

We wanted them to have shade *today,* not fifteen years from now. So we went out and got them the biggest tree we could find. It didn't take a lot of money to make them happy, just a little understanding.

Not everyone learns that lesson. Lots of people try to push their own agenda—and then they wonder why they have no pull with others. To make an impact on others, find out what people want and then help them get it. That's what motivates them. And that's what makes it possible for you to become a person of influence in their lives.

## *Influence Checklist*
# UNDERSTANDING PEOPLE

❏ **Rate your understanding.** Use the following scale to rate your ability to understand people (circle the rating that applies to you):

Superior     I can nearly always anticipate how people will feel and react in any given situation. Understanding is one of my strongest abilities.

Good     Most of the time what people do and want makes sense to me. I consider my ability to understand people an asset.

Fair     I'm surprised by people just as often as I'm able to anticipate their thinking. I consider my ability to understand others to be average.

Poor     Most of the time people's feelings and motivations are mysteries to me. I definitely need to do better in this area.

❏ **Understanding action plan.** If you rated yourself superior, then you should be sharing your skill by teaching others how to better understand people. If you rated yourself good, fair, or poor, keep striving to learn and improve. You can improve your ability immediately by asking yourself these four questions each time you meet new people:

1. Where did they come from?
2. Where do they want to go?
3. What is their need now?
4. How can I help?

❏ **Activate your positive attitude.** If your ability to understand people isn't as good as you'd like it to be, the root cause may be that you don't value others as highly as you could. As you interact with people remember the words of Ken Keyes, Jr.: "A loving person lives in a loving world. A hostile person lives in a hostile world: Everyone you meet is your mirror."

# 6

## *A Person of Influence . . .*

# ENLARGES
# PEOPLE

$O$nce you have been a model of integrity with others and successfully motivated them, you're ready to take the next step in the process of becoming a person of influence in their lives. Jim has a story that will give you an idea of what that next step looks like:

Over the years, Eric has been through more than thirty individual brain operations, but that has never stopped him from being mentally sharp and full of optimism. And his great sense of humor keeps all of us entertained.

During one of his many surgeries, Eric experienced an interoperative stroke. The resulting loss of muscle balance has limited the use of his right hand and given him severe curvature of the spine. After a couple of years, that required another surgery in which the doctors performed spinal fusion and implanted steel rods from the base of his neck to his pelvis. He spent three months in a full body cast during his long recovery, and as a result, many of his previous abilities were reduced dramatically. But Eric came through it all with characteristically positive spirits.

After Eric's spinal surgery, Nancy could no longer handle him alone, so we decided it was time to employ a full-time home attendant to lift him, help with his daily life, and assist him with his ongoing rehabilitation. We knew the type of person we wanted to hire, but we had no idea where or how to locate him.

One day while Nancy was talking to one of our medical contacts, she heard about a person named Fernando. He sounded great. "He's the perfect person," our friend had said, "but you'll never get him."

Nancy's response was, "Just give us his number, and let us worry about whether or not we can get him."

A few weeks later we hired him, and he has been wonderful. Fernando had been a life skills trainer for Sharp Hospital, and though he was only five years older than Eric, he had already been a manager of a group home for abused kids and had worked in the field of rehab for seven years. He and Eric bonded immediately. Fernando provided a perfect combination of professional skills and companionship.

It's difficult to describe what a wonderful gift God has provided to Eric and our family in the person of Fernando. He sees his mission as that of enlarging Eric, to keep him growing toward his full potential. Fernando constantly learns new information and techniques in his field, and he seeks ways to expose Eric to new experiences and to challenge him to grow. As a result, Eric's life hasn't been the same. In the time that the two of them have been doing things together, Eric has done a lot more than go skiing every year. He has learned to jet ski—I never could have visualized Eric going forty miles per hour on the water, but Fernando believed Eric could do it, and so he did it. Eric also volunteers as a tutor with second graders, studies German, works in our office two days a week, swims a couple of days a week, and has begun to work out with weights. It's hard for us to remember that Eric is severely limited physically, because his life is full, challenging, and expanding every day.

One of Eric's greatest experiences since teaming with Fernando has been his involvement in power soccer. It's a new sport played by people using power wheelchairs. They meet in gymnasiums where they compete as teams and score goals using a large ball. Eric loves it and usually prefers to play goalie.

Not long ago Fernando took Eric to Vancouver, Canada, to compete in a power soccer tournament. It was quite an experience for Eric. They flew together, rented a car, got their hotel room, and got around town—just the two of them. Eric loved it, especially competing in the five-day tournament where he scored two goals. And best of all, his team won the gold medal!

We had never seen Eric so excited as he was when he returned from the tournament. He wore his gold medal home on the plane, and I don't think he touched the ground for days. Since then, his confidence has been so strong that he's willing to tackle just about any kind of challenge. And for that, Fernando deserves a lot of the credit.

> Without his belief in Eric and his desire to expand his
> world, none of this would ever have happened.

To become a person of influence and to make a positive
impact on people, you have to come alongside them and really
get involved in their lives. That's what Fernando did and continues to do with Jim's son Eric. And that's what you need to do with
the people for whom you want to make a difference. Modeling a
life of integrity is an important first step in becoming an influencer because it creates a strong foundation with others. And the
next natural step is motivating people. As you nurture people,
show your faith in them, listen to their hopes and fears, and
demonstrate your understanding of them, you build a strong relational connection and give them incentive to succeed—and to be
influenced by you. But if you want people to be able to *really*
grow, improve, and succeed, you have to take the next step with
them. You have to become a mentor to them.

## THE MEANING OF MENTORING

Giving people the *motivation* to grow without also providing
them the *means* of doing it is a tragedy. But the mentoring process offers people the opportunity to turn their potential into reality, their dreams into destiny. Mentors impact eternity because
there is no telling where their influence will stop.

Nineteenth-century British statesman William Gladstone
asserted, "He is a wise man who wastes no energy on pursuits for
which he is not fitted; and he is wiser still who from among the
things he can do well, chooses and resolutely follows the best."
Most people don't have a natural knack for spotting their greatest areas of potential. They need help doing it, especially as they
begin growing and striving to reach their potential. And that's
why it's important for you to become a mentor in the lives of the
people you desire to help. You need to lead them in their areas
of personal and professional growth until they are able to work
in these areas more independently.

The authors of *The Leadership Challenge,* James M. Kouzes and
Barry Z. Posner, offer insights on leadership that pertain to the

subject of mentoring: "Leaders are pioneers. They are people who venture into unexplored territory. They guide us to new and often unfamiliar destinations. . . . The unique reason for having leaders—their differentiating function—is to move us forward. Leaders get us going someplace."

> *Mentors impact eternity because there is no telling where their influence will stop.*

Leading mentors move the people they are developing into growth and areas of strength. In this chapter and in the next three, we'll focus on four ways of accomplishing the task of mentoring others: enlarging people, helping them navigate through life's problems, connecting with them on a deeper level, and empowering them to reach their potential.

## ENLARGING OTHERS IS AN INVESTMENT

Author Alan Loy McGinnis observed, "There is no more noble occupation in the world than to assist another human being—to help someone succeed." Helping others enlarge themselves is one of the most incredible things you can ever do for them. As John says in his book *The Success Journey,* growing to reach your potential is one of the three components to being successful (along with knowing your purpose and sowing seeds that benefit others).

Robert Gross, former president of Lockheed Aircraft Corporation, once explained to his supervisors, "It's one thing to build a product; it's another thing to build a company, because companies are nothing but men, and the things that come out of them are no better than the people themselves. We do not build automobiles, airplanes, refrigerators, radios, or shoestrings. We build men. *The men build the product.*"

When you enlarge others, you do several things:

## Raise Their Level of Living

Denis Waitley said, "The greatest achievements are those that benefit others." Anytime you help people to enlarge themselves in any area of their lives, you benefit them because you make it possible for them to step up to a new level of living. As people develop their gifts and talents, learn new skills, and broaden their problem-solving abilities, their quality of living and level of contentment improve dramatically. No one can grow and remain unaffected in the way he lives his life.

> *When you enlarge others, you seize an opportunity to help them reach their potential.*

## Increase Their Potential for Success

Businessman George Crane claimed that "there is no future in any job. The future lies in the man who holds the job." When you enlarge other people, you brighten their future. When they expand their horizons, improve their attitudes, increase their skills, or learn new ways to think, they perform and live better. And that increases their potential.

## Increase Their Capacity for Growth

When you help people enlarge themselves, you aren't giving them only a temporary, short-term shot in the arm or tools that will help them only today. Enlarging has long-term benefits. It helps them become better equipped, and it increases their capacity to learn and grow. After being enlarged, whenever they receive a resource or opportunity, they are better able to use it to its greatest benefit. And their growth begins to multiply.

## Increase the Potential of Your Organization

If the people you are working to enlarge are a part of a group—no matter whether it is a business, church, sports team, or club—then the whole group benefits from their growth. For example, if many people in your organization improve themselves even slightly, the quality of your whole organization increases. If a few people improve themselves a lot, the potential for growth and success increases due to the increased leadership of these people. And if both kinds of growth occur as the result of your enlarging, hang on because your organization is about to take off!

Fred Smith, a friend of John, is an excellent leader, entrepreneur, and business consultant. Fred had been advising a group of twenty young CEOs and meeting with them monthly for about three years when he decided that they needed to spend some time on their own. So he told them he would not be coming back to see them for a while. They continued to get together without him, but eventually, they asked him to come back for a visit. When he did, they presented him with a piece of Baccarat crystal. On it were etched the words *He stretched us.*

Fred has been stretching and enlarging others for decades because he realizes the incredible value added not only to the people being stretched, but also to all the people they influence. Most people are funny; they want to get ahead and succeed, but they are reluctant to change. They are often willing to grow only enough to accommodate their *problems;* instead, they need to grow enough to achieve their *potential.* That's why they need help from you. Authors Helen Schucman and William Thetford aptly said, "Every situation, properly perceived, becomes an opportunity." When you enlarge others, you seize an opportunity to help them reach their potential.

French essayist Michel Eyquem de Montaigne wrote, "The value of life lies not in the length of days, but in the use we make of them; a man may live long yet live very little." When you enlarge others, you help them make the most of the time they have and raise their quality of life.

## MAKE YOURSELF AN ENLARGER

For many people, just because they want to enlarge others doesn't necessarily mean they are ready for the task. They usually need to do some work on themselves first. As in most instances, if you want to do more for others, you have to become more yourself. That's never more valid than in the area of mentoring. You can teach what you know, but you can reproduce only what you are.

Leadership experts Warren Bennis and Bert Nanus spoke to this issue: "It is the capacity to develop and improve their skills that distinguishes leaders from their followers." In your preparations to take on the task of helping others enlarge themselves, the first thing you need to do is improve and enlarge yourself because only when you are growing and enlarging yourself are you able to help others do the same. Just as people will not follow a person whose leadership skills are weaker than their own, they will not learn to grow from someone who isn't growing. Not only must you be on a higher level in your personal growth, but you must continue to grow on an ongoing basis. (You can probably remember how little you respected one of your high school teachers or college professors who had obviously stopped learning and growing decades earlier—possibly the day he received his degree!)

Albert Schweitzer maintained that "the great secret of success is to go through life as a man who never gets used up." When you make it a goal to continually learn and enlarge yourself, you become the kind of person who can never be "used up." You're always recharging your batteries and finding better ways to get things done. To determine whether you are still growing, ask yourself what you're still looking forward to. If you can't think of anything or you're looking back instead of ahead, your growth may be at a standstill.

It has been said, "The greatest obstacle to discovery is not ignorance. It is the illusion of knowledge." Many people lose sight of the importance of personal growth once they finish their formal education. But don't let that happen to you. Make your growth one of your top priorities starting today. There is no time to waste. As Scottish writer and thinker Thomas Carlyle put it, "One life; a little gleam of time between two eternities; no second chance for us forever more." Any day that passes without personal growth is an opportunity lost to improve yourself and to enlarge others.

# CAREFULLY CHOOSE
# PERSONS TO ENLARGE

Once you've done some growing and you're ready to help others enlarge themselves, you need to start thinking about the people you will choose to work with. You have to be selective. You should try to be a model of integrity to all people, whether they're close to you or total strangers. And you should make it your goal to motivate all of the people you have a relationship with—family members, employees, fellow church volunteers, colleagues, and friends. But you can't take the time to enlarge everybody in your life; it's too involved a process. That's why you need to work first with the most promising people around you, the ones most likely to be receptive to growth.

In *Killers of the Dream,* Lillian Smith wrote, "We in America— and men across the earth—have trapped ourselves with that word equality, which is inapplicable to the *genus* man. I wish we would forget it. Stop its use in our country: Let the communists have it. It isn't fit for men who fling their dreams across the skies. It is fit only for a leveling down of mankind." We certainly desire for all people to have equal access to opportunities and justice, but we know that everyone doesn't respond equally to his environment or advantages. And that's true for the people you will have the opportunity to develop. Some people are eager to be enlarged. Others don't care about personal growth or won't grow under your care. It's your job to figure out which is which.

As you think about the people you want to enlarge, keep the following guidelines in mind:

- **Select people whose philosophy of life is similar to yours.** The underlying values and priorities of the people you desire to enlarge need to be similar to yours. If you and they don't have the basics in common, you may end up working at cross-purposes, and you won't experience the effectiveness you would like. Roy Disney, Walt's brother and partner, said, "It's not hard to make decisions when you know what your values are." And if you and the people you mentor have similar values, you will be able to make harmonious decisions as you work together.

- **Choose people with potential you genuinely believe in.** You can't help people you don't believe in. Give your best mentoring effort to people who have the greatest potential— the ones for whom you can see a promising future—not the ones for whom you feel sorry. Nurture, love, and motivate hurting people. But pour yourself into the people who will grow and make a difference.

- **Select people whose lives you can positively impact.** Not everyone you are capable of developing would benefit from what you have to offer. Look for a fit between their potential and your strengths and experience.

- **Match the men and women to the mountains.** We would like all the people we mentor to reach their full potential and develop into stars. After all, the greatest mentors develop people to a level beyond their ability. But the truth is that while all people can move to a higher level than they currently occupy, not everyone is capable of climbing to the highest levels. A successful enlarger evaluates the potential of others and places them in a position to succeed.

- **Start when the time is right.** Start the process at the right time in the lives of others. You've probably heard the expression "strike while the iron is hot." It means to act on a situation at the right time. We've heard that the saying goes back to the fourteenth century. It comes from the practice of

Becoming a Person of Influence

blacksmiths who needed to strike metal when it was exactly the right temperature in order to mold it into the precise shape desired. You have to do the same thing with the people you want to enlarge. Start too soon, and they don't yet see the need to grow. Start too late, and you've missed your best opportunity to help them.

Once you've found the right people, keep in mind that you need to get their permission before you start enlarging them. People love to be encouraged and motivated, so you don't need their consent to do either one. But the mentoring process really works only when both parties know the agenda, agree to it, and give it 100 percent effort.

# MAKE IT A PRIORITY TO TAKE THEM THROUGH THE ENLARGING PROCESS

Enlarging others can be rewarding and fun, but it also takes time, money, and work. That's why you have to commit yourself to the process and make it a top priority. John's friend Ed Cole says, "There is a price to pay to grow. Commitment is the price." Once you've made the commitment, you're ready to go. The following suggestions will help you maximize the enlarging process:

## *See Their Potential*

Composer Gian Carlo Menotti forcefully stated, "Hell begins on that day when God grants us a clear vision of all that we might have achieved, of all the gifts we wasted, of all that we might have done that we did not do."[1] Unrealized potential is a tragic waste. And as an enlarger, you have the privilege of helping others discover and then develop their potential. But you can't do that until you *see* their potential.

Olympic gold medal swimmer Geoffrey Gaberino sums it up this way: "The real contest is always between what you've done and what you're capable of doing." Whenever you look at people you desire to enlarge, try to discern what they are capable of doing. Look for the spark of greatness. Watch and listen with your heart as well as your eyes. Find their enthusiasm. Try to visualize what they would be doing if they overcame personal obstacles, gained confidence, grew in areas of promise, and gave everything they had. That will help you to see their potential.

## Cast a Vision for Their Future

Former presidential speechwriter Robert Orben urged, "Always remember there are only two kinds of people in this world—the realists and the dreamers. The realists know where they're going. The dreamers have already been there." To add value to the people you enlarge, travel ahead of them in your mind's eye and see their future before they do. You become able to cast a vision for their future that helps to motivate and enlarge them.

Someone once said, "Don't let yourself be pressured into thinking that your dreams or your talents aren't prudent. They were never meant to be prudent. They were meant to bring joy and fulfillment into your life." That's great advice. People will never succeed beyond their wildest dreams unless they have some pretty wild dreams. When you cast a vision for others, you help them see their potential and their possibilities. And when you add to that vision your faith in them, you spark them to action. The great British statesman Benjamin Disraeli declared, "Nurture great thoughts for you will never go higher than your thoughts." Help people have great thoughts about themselves, and they will begin to live like the people they can become.

## Tap into Their Passion

As an enlarger of people, you are to help people want to grow, and one way to do that is to tap into their passion. Everybody— even the quietest, least demonstrative person—has a passion for something. You just have to find it. As scientist Willis R. Whitney pointed out, "Some men have thousands of reasons why they cannot do what they want to, when all they need is one reason why they can."

As you look for others' passions, go beyond the surface of their daily wants. Look deep within them. Harold Kushner perceptively wrote, "Our souls are not hungry for fame, comfort, wealth, or power. Those rewards create almost as many problems as they solve. Our souls are hungry for meaning, for the sense that we have figured out how to live so that our lives matter, so that the world will at least be a little bit different for our having passed through it."

Once you discover their passion, tap into it. Show them how it can activate their potential to the point that they will be able to realize their vision for their lives. Passion can help them make their dreams come true. And as U.S. President Woodrow Wilson said, "We grow by dreams. All big [individuals] are dreamers. They see things in the soft haze of a spring day, or in the red fire on a long winter's evening. Some of us let those great dreams die, but others nourish and protect them; nourish them through bad days until they bring them to the sunshine and light which comes always to those who sincerely hope that their dreams will come true." Passion is the fuel that helps people nourish and protect their dreams.

## Address Character Flaws

As you explore how you can help others enlarge themselves, you need to address any character issues they may have. As we mentioned in Chapter 1, integrity is the foundation upon which everything else must stand in people's lives. No matter how much enlarging you do, if the foundation isn't solid, there's going to be trouble.

When examining the character of others, remember to look beyond their reputation. Abraham Lincoln made this distinction: "Character is like a tree and reputation like its shadow. The shadow is what we think of it; the tree is the real thing." Take time to really get to know the people you're enlarging. Observe them in various situations. If you get to know people well enough to know how they react in most situations, you'll have an idea of where any character shortcomings might be.

Martin Luther King, Jr., said, "The ultimate measure of a man is not where he stands in moments of comfort and convenience, but where he stands at times of challenge and controversy." Your goal should be to help the people you're developing to stand strong in the midst of challenges. But you have to start with the little things. Author and corporate leader Joseph Sugarman observed, "Every time you are honest and conduct yourself with honesty, a success force will drive you toward greater success. Each time you lie, even with a little white lie, there are strong forces pushing you toward failure." Help others learn to conduct themselves with integrity in every situation, and they will be ready to grow and reach their potential.

## Focus on Their Strengths

When some people begin to work with others on their development, they often gravitate to weaknesses rather than strengths. Maybe that's because it's so easy to see others' problems and shortcomings. But if you start by putting your energies into correcting people's weaknesses, you will demoralize them and unintentionally sabotage the enlarging process.

We recently heard a baseball story that addresses the subject of people's weaknesses. One afternoon in St. Louis, Stan Musial was having a great game against Chicago pitcher Bobo Newsom. Stan first hit a single, then a triple, and then a home run. When Stan came up to bat for the fourth time, Chicago manager Charlie Grimm decided to yank Bobo and take a chance on a rookie relief pitcher. As the young rookie went to the mound from the bull pen and received the ball from Newsom, he asked, "Say, has this guy Musial got any weaknesses?"

"Yeah," replied Newsom, "he can't hit doubles."

Instead of focusing on weaknesses, pay attention to people's strengths. Sharpen skills that already exist. Compliment positive qualities. Bring out the gifts inherent in them. Weaknesses can wait—unless they are character flaws. Only after you have developed a strong rapport with them and they have begun to grow and gain confidence should you address areas of weakness. And then handle them gently one at a time.

## Enlarge Them One Step at a Time

Ronald Osborn noted, "Unless you try to do something beyond what you have already mastered, you will never grow." To enlarge others, help them take growth steps that stretch them regularly without overwhelming or discouraging them.

For each person, that process will look different. But no matter where people are from or where they are going, they need to grow in certain areas. We suggest that you include the following four areas in the development process:

**1. *Attitude.*** More than anything else, attitude determines whether people are successful and able to enjoy life. And attitude impacts not only every area of their own lives, but it also influences others.

**2. *Relationships.*** The world is made up of people, so everybody has to learn to interact effectively with others. The ability to relate to others and communicate with them can affect marriage, parenting, occupation, friendships, and more. If people can get along, they can get ahead in just about any area of life.

**3. *Leadership.*** Everything rises and falls on leadership. If the people you're developing plan to work with others, they have to learn to lead them. If they don't, they'll be carrying the whole load themselves in everything they do.

**4. *Personal and professional skills.*** You may be surprised to see that we're listing this last. But the truth is that if thinking isn't positive and skills at working with people are missing, all the professional skills in the world are of little benefit. As you help people grow, work from the inside out. It's not what happens *to* people that makes a difference; it's what happens *in* them.

## Put Resources in Their Hands

To help people grow, no matter what area you're addressing, put resources in their hands. Whenever either one of us meets with someone we're developing, we always try to take something with us to give to them—books, tapes, magazine articles, anything uplifting or instructive that we can get our hands on. Nothing gives us greater joy than to know that we've helped someone take another step in growth. That's one reason both of us are constantly creating resources for people's growth. If you can't find exactly what you're looking for to help people, you may want to give from your experience.

The next time you're ready to meet with people whom you want to enlarge, take an active hand in the process. Clip articles written on one of their areas of interest. Give them copies of a book that impacted your life. Or put into their hands tapes that will teach and inspire them. If you keep doing that, not only will the people you develop love the time they spend with you, but each time you meet you'll see that they've grown just a little more toward their potential.

## Expose Them to Enlarging Experiences

Implementing a plan for growth enlarges people. But sometimes they need something more to give them a fresh burst of energy and inspiration. Author and champion for the blind Helen Keller said, "One can never consent to creep when one feels an impulse to soar." When you expose people to enlarging experiences, you plant within them that desire to soar.

Conferences and seminars, meetings with outstanding men and women, and special events have made a tremendous impact on us. They always take us out of our comfort zone, move us to think beyond ourselves, or challenge us to go to new levels of living. But remember that events and meetings don't make people grow. They *inspire* people to make important decisions that can change the direction of their lives. The growth itself comes from what people do daily after they have made a decision.

## Teach Them to Be Self-Enlargers

According to Philip B. Crosby, "There is a theory of human behavior that says people subconsciously retard their own intellectual growth. They come to rely on clichés and habits. Once they reach the age of their own personal comfort with the world, they stop learning and their mind runs on idle for the rest of their days. They may progress organizationally, they may be ambitious and eager, and they may even work night and day. But they learn no more."

Once you've gotten people to value growth enough to start enlarging themselves, you've broken through a strong barrier. But the next step is to get them to keep growing on their own. It has been said that the goal of all teachers should be to equip students to get along without them. The same can be said of people who seek to enlarge others. As you work with others and help them to enlarge themselves, give them what they need so that they learn to take care of themselves. Teach them to find resources. Encourage them to get out of their comfort zone on their own. And point them toward additional people who can help them learn and grow. If you can help them to become lifelong learners, you will have given them an incredible gift.

> *A successful enlarger evaluates the potential of others and places them in a position to succeed.*

We've heard it said, "No one becomes rich unless he enriches another." When you enrich others by helping them grow and enlarge themselves, you not only bring joy to them and yourself, but you also increase your influence and their ability to touch others' lives.

At the beginning of this chapter we told you about how Fernando has enriched the life of Jim and Nancy's son Eric. But there is more to the story:

> Since Eric played in that power soccer tournament, he has really changed. He has become more assertive, and he is pursuing his goals with more enthusiasm. For example, Eric has now decided that he wants to try to play tennis, so Fernando has started working with him to get him ready. As I mentioned earlier, Eric has begun weight training. But he has also taken another step to help make tennis possible, a step that at first scared Nancy and me.
>
> Since his stroke, Eric's right hand is extremely limited in what it can do, so he really has full use of only his left hand.

But to play tennis, he would have to use his good left hand to hold the racket. What was Fernando's solution? He waited until Nancy and I were out of town and switched Eric's wheelchair controls over to his bad hand. We didn't think it was possible, but it was. Eric now drives right-handed, and as soon as he is ready, he is going to take up tennis.

Eric also does other things that simply astound us. For example, he works in the office, and he puts himself into bed at night. But that's nothing compared to some of his goals: someday Eric wants to be able to drive a car.

Fernando's mentoring and coaching of Eric have been fantastic. We always wanted the best for Eric, but we discovered that we were overly protective. The whole process has enlarged us and broadened our horizons. And of course, it's incredible to see Eric grow and change as he has. But he, Nancy, and I are not alone in that. Even the enlarger has become enlarged. Fernando is changing and growing too. He has always been the consummate professional, but we're now seeing a softer, more loving side that was previously hidden. And recently he told Nancy, "I'm learning that I have to really give to have joy in my life."

What nineteenth-century American philosopher-poet Ralph Waldo Emerson said is true: "It is one of the most beautiful compensations of this life that no man can sincerely try to help another without helping himself." If you give yourself to enlarging others and assisting them in reaching their potential, the rewards you reap will be almost as great as the ones of the people you help.

## *Influence Checklist*
# ENLARGING PEOPLE

❏ **Whom will you enlarge?** Write down the names of the top
three candidates for you to enlarge. Remember to pick people
whose philosophy of life is similar to yours, whose potential
you believe in, whose lives you can positively impact, and
who are ready for the process.

1. _____
2. _____
3. _____

❏ **Enlargement agenda.** Use the following grid to develop your
strategy for enlarging the three persons you selected:

|  | **Person 1** | **Person 2** | **Person 3** |
|---|---|---|---|
| **Name** | _____ | _____ | _____ |
| **Potential** | _____ | _____ | _____ |
| **Passion** | _____ | _____ | _____ |
| **Character Issue(s)** | _____ | _____ | _____ |
| **Greatest Strength** | _____ | _____ | _____ |
| **Next Step in Development** | _____ | _____ | _____ |
| **Resource for Current Need** | _____ | _____ | _____ |
| **Next Enlarging Experience** | _____ | _____ | _____ |

# *A Person of Influence . . .*

# NAVIGATES FOR OTHER PEOPLE

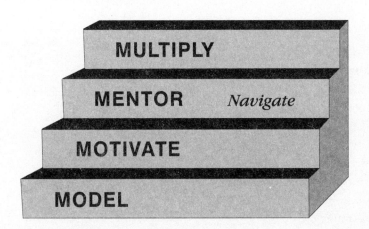

Helping people enlarge themselves and develop their potential makes it possible for them to go to a whole new level of living. But no matter how much they grow and learn, they will still face obstacles. They will make mistakes. They will run into problems in their personal and professional lives. And they will encounter circumstances that they won't be able to get through well without some help.

John tells a story about a time when he decided to help a whole planeload of people get through a tough day together:

I travel a lot because of the speaking I do around the country, and sometimes that leads to unusual situations. I remember one particular evening when I was in the airport in Charlotte, North Carolina, getting ready to fly to Indianapolis, Indiana. I was on the phone up to the last minute, and then I dashed up to my gate and met Dick Peterson, the president of INJOY, expecting to run onto the plane just before the doors closed. But to my surprise, the waiting area had about fifty or sixty people moping around in it.

I looked at Dick and said, "What's going on?"

"Well," said Dick, "it looks like we won't get to fly out for a while yet."

"What's the problem?" I asked.

"I don't know," he said.

So I went up and talked to the agent at the gate, and he told me, "The flight attendants aren't here yet, and we can't allow anyone to board until they come." Then he announced the same thing over the PA system, and I could see everyone in the waiting area kind of deflate. They looked miserable.

I looked at Dick, and I said, "You know, let's see if we can help these people out." So we went to a snack counter close by, and I told the woman there, named Denise, "I'd like sixty Coca-Colas, please."

She stared at me a moment and finally said, "You want sixty?"

Then I explained to her, "There are a whole bunch of passengers down at that next gate who are disappointed, and they need something to boost their morale."

"You're not kidding? You're going to buy one for everybody?" she asked.

"You bet."

She paused for a moment, then said, "Can I help?"

She, Dick, and I took those drinks down to the people at the gate, and I could see that they weren't sure what to think. So I said, "May I have your attention, please? My name is John Maxwell. Since we're not going to leave for thirty to forty-five minutes, I thought I would at least get you something to drink. It's on the house."

We started passing out the Cokes, and I could tell they thought I was weird. So did the airline personnel. But after a while I began to develop rapport with them, and when they found out the flight attendants were on the ground and would be at the gate soon, I was finally able to talk them into letting us get on the plane.

As soon as we all got on the plane, I saw a large basket of peanuts, granola bars, and goodies in the galley, and I thought to myself, *Hey, they ought to have something to eat with that Coca-Cola.* So I went down the aisle giving out the goodies. In only five minutes I had served them all something to eat, and they were drinking their Cokes. About this time the flight crew rushed aboard. They were very apologetic. They got on the plane's PA system right away and said, "Ladies and gentlemen, we're going to get started right away. As soon as we can, we'll begin the beverage service."

Well, they could hear a lot of laughter and chattering in the cabin, and one of the flight attendants said to the other, "What's going on here?"

"Hi, my name's John," I said. "They're not too worried about your service right now. I've already given everybody something to drink and some snacks to eat. In fact, would it be all right if I talked to everybody a moment?" They laughed and said, "Sure. Why not?"

As we taxied out to the runway, they let me talk. "Hi, folks," I said, "this is your friend, John Maxwell. Please buckle up. We'll be airborne in a few moments, and as soon as we're in the air, I'll be back again to serve you."

We had a great time on that flight. I talked to everybody and helped serve drinks. When we landed, I asked if I could talk to everybody one last time. "Gang," I said, "this is John. I'm so glad you were on this flight today. Didn't we have a wonderful time?" Everyone clapped and cheered. "Now when we get off, I'm going to go down to the baggage claim area. If any of you have any problems, please see me, and we'll immediately take care of the situation."

While I was down in the baggage area helping people find their luggage, a man came up to me and said, "This has been great. I'm from Florida, and I've got some grapefruit with me. Here, have a grapefruit."

"Thank you very much," I said. "You know, I've got a brother who lives in Florida—in Winterhaven."

"That's where I live!" he said. "What's your name again? John Maxwell? Wait! Is your brother's name Larry and his wife, Anita?"

"That's correct."

"I know them!" he said. "Anita serves on a board with me. I'm going to call them right now. They won't believe it." He hurried off toward a bank of phones. "I've traveled for years," he said, "and nothing like this has ever happened before!"

What could have been a miserable plane ride of tired, grumpy people turned out to be an experience that nobody on that flight will ever forget. Why? Because one person decided to take others under his wing and help them through a potentially unpleasant situation. It's a process that we call *navigating*.

Most people need help working through some of life's difficulties. That plane flight probably wasn't more than an inconvenience for most of those passengers, but they still enjoyed being coached through the experience by someone with a good attitude. That kind of assistance is needed and appreciated by most people, especially when life's complicated problems hit closer to home, and people have a tougher time with them.

A person well known for trying to help people work through their problems is Ann Landers. Talking about what she has learned from people through the letters she has received for her column, Ann Landers said,

> I've learned plenty—including, most meaningfully, what Leo Rosten had in mind when he said, "Each of us is a little lonely, deep inside, and cries to be understood." I have learned how it is with the stumbling, tortured people in this world who have nobody to talk to. The fact that the column has been a success underscores, for me at least, the central tragedy of our society, the disconnectedness, the insecurity, the fear that bedevils, cripples, and paralyzes so many of us. I have learned that financial success, academic achievement, and social or political status open no doors to peace of mind or inner security. We are all wanderers, like sheep, on this planet.[1]

The people in your life with whom you have influence need your help, especially the ones who are trying to go to a new level, start a new venture, or enter a new phase of life. They need someone to lead and guide them. Mel Ziegler, founder of Banana Republic, outlined a leader's ability to navigate when he wrote: "A leader discovers the hidden chasm between where things are and where things would better be, and strings up a makeshift bridge to attempt the crossing. From the other side he guides those who dare to cross his rickety traverse until the engineers can build a sturdier span for all."[2]

*A **leader is one who sees more than others see, who sees farther than others see, and who sees before others do.**
—Leroy Eims*

Ziegler painted a vivid picture. But for most people, the leadership they need isn't just a one-time event, a single chasm to cross. Most people need guidance on a fairly continual basis until they can get their lives together, and then they can be encouraged to make the trip under their own power. It's more like an ocean voyage that you have to navigate them through than a chasm you have to coax them to cross. You've got to help them find their way, spot icebergs, and weather stormy seas, and you've got to take the trip with them—at least until they are on the right course and can learn to navigate on their own.

## A Navigator Identifies the Destination

A good navigator helps people identify their destination. In *Be the Leader You Were Meant to Be,* Leroy Eims wrote, "A leader is one who sees more than others see, who sees farther than others see, and who sees before others do." In the previous chapter, we talked about the importance of casting a vision of people's future so that they are encouraged to grow. The next step is to show them their destination in a more concrete way. Most people who are dissatisfied and discouraged feel that way because they haven't grabbed hold of a vision for themselves. It has been said, "To bury our dreams is to bury ourselves, for we are really 'such stuff as dreams are made on.' God's dream for us is to reach our potential." You have to help others discover their dream and then get them moving toward it. If there is no movement, then there can be no navigation. And any movement will be progress only if it's in the direction of the destination.

You may already recognize much of the potential of the people you're trying to mentor, but you need to know more about them. To help them recognize the destination they will be striving for, you need to know what really matters to them, what makes them tick. To do that, find out these things:

- **What do they cry about?** To know where people truly want to go, you need to know what touches their hearts. Passion and compassion are compelling motivators. It has been said that the great men and women of history were great not for what they owned or earned, but for what they

gave their lives to accomplish. Listen with your heart and
you are likely to discover the things for which others are
willing to give themselves.

- **What do they sing about?** Frank Irving Fletcher observed,
  "No man can deliver the goods if his heart is heavier than his
  load." There is a big difference between the things that touch
  people's hearts and the things that weigh them down. In the
  long run, people need to focus a lot of energy on what gives
  them joy. Looking for enthusiasms in the people you mentor will give you another clue concerning their intended destination.

- **What do they dream about?** Napoleon Hill said, "Cherish
  your visions and your dreams as they are the children of
  your soul; the blueprints of your ultimate achievements." If
  you can help people discover their dreams and truly believe
  in them, you can help them become the persons they were
  designed to be.

# A NAVIGATOR PLOTS THE COURSE

When you consider people's passions, potential, and vision,
you are better able to see where they really want to go because
you view them with more depth and discernment. Often, people
say that their goal is happiness or success, but if they identify
such a surface thing as their destination, they're sure to be disappointed. As John Condry emphasized, "Happiness, wealth, and
success are by-products of goal-setting; they cannot be the goal
themselves."

Once you as the navigator assist others in identifying a vision
for their lives, you need to help them find a way to make it a reality. And that means plotting a course and setting goals. J. Meyers
said, "A #2 pencil and a dream can take you anywhere." No
doubt he understood the value of planning and putting goals in
writing. That doesn't mean that things always go as you expect,
but you have to start with a game plan. A good rule of thumb is
to set your goals in concrete and write your plans in sand.

To help people plot their course, give attention to these areas:

## Where They Need to Go

You would be amazed by how far off track some people can get when trying to reach their goals. As E. W. Howe wrote in *Success Is Easier Than Failure,* "Some people storm imaginary Alps all their lives, and die in the foothills cursing difficulties that do not exist." People who have not yet experienced success often have no idea what it takes to get from where they are to where they want to go. They throw themselves into a labyrinth of activity because they don't recognize that they can take an easier path. As the navigator, you are to show them the best course.

## What They Need to Know

We heard an amusing story about a husband who wanted to help his wife because he suspected she had a hearing problem. One night he positioned himself across the room from her with her back to him, and softly he said, "Can you hear me?" He didn't get an answer from her, so he moved closer and repeated, "Can you hear me now?" Still nothing. He moved closer and asked, "Can you hear me?" He heard no response, so finally he repeated the question from directly behind her. She turned to face him and said, "For the fourth time, *Yes!*"

Too many people out there are similar to that husband. They want to succeed and help others, but their misunderstanding or lack of knowledge hinders them. A good navigator recognizes the blind spots in others, gently identifies them, and helps people overcome them.

## How They Need to Grow

When you are navigating for others, remember that they can't make the whole trip in a day. They have to grow into their goals and take things one step at a time. An experiment performed by Alfred J. Marrow, a company president with a Ph.D. in psychology, illustrated this fact. He was interested in finding a way to help new unskilled employees reach optimum performance and match the standards of his skilled, experienced employees as quickly as possible.

Marrow decided to divide some new employees into two groups. With the first, he asked the unskilled workers to match the production of the skilled ones by the end of twelve weeks. With the second group, he established escalating weekly goals. Each week's goal was slightly more ambitious than the one from the week before.

> ***A** #2 pencil and a dream*
> *can take you anywhere.*
> *—J. Meyers*

In the first group with the single goal, only 66 percent of the workers were able to meet his expectations. But the second group with the intermediate goals performed significantly better and was able to match the production averages of the company's experienced laborers more quickly.[3]

As you work with people, help them to figure out not only their long-term destination, but also the smaller steps along the way. Help them identify attainable goals that will give them confidence, and they'll make progress.

## A NAVIGATOR THINKS AHEAD

Few things are more discouraging than being blindsided, especially when someone who could have helped you stands by and watches it happen. That's why thinking ahead for others is part of your task as a navigator. As people's leader and mentor, you have been places they have not yet gone, had experiences they have not been through, and gained insights they have not yet developed. You have the ability to prepare them for what they are going to face. If you don't, you're not helping them the way you should, and you are no longer performing one of your most important functions as a leader. American humorist Arnold H. Glasow saw the significance of this: "One of the tests of leadership is to recognize a problem before it becomes an emergency." That's something the less-experienced persons you're helping cannot at first do on their own.

Here are four things you should help them understand as they get under way:

## 1. Everybody Faces Problems

Someone quipped, "If you keep your head when all about you are losing theirs, you just don't understand the problem." As you mentor people and help them grow, you may find that they expect to someday reach a point in their lives when their problems disappear. But they need to realize that everybody has problems. No matter how far they go or how successful they become, they will continue to face difficulties. Or as writer and artists' advocate Elbert Hubbard said, "The man who has no more problems to solve is out of the game."

The Barna Research Group surveyed more than twelve hundred people to gather information on the problems they faced. They were asked to identify their single most serious need or problem. Here are their answers along with the percentage of people who ranked the problems most pressing:

| | |
|---|---|
| 39% | Financial |
| 16% | Job-Related |
| 12% | Personal Health |
| 8% | Time and Stress |
| 7% | Parenting |
| 6% | Educational Attainment |
| 3% | Fear of Crime |
| 3% | Personal Relationships[4] |

As you can see, people face a variety of problems, with money being the greatest. Be prepared to give them assistance. And remember to settle your own issues before trying to help others with theirs.

## 2. Successful People Face More Problems Than Unsuccessful People

Another common misconception is that successful people have achieved because they didn't have problems. But that isn't true. In his book *Holy Sweat,* Tim Hansel tells this story:

> In 1962, Victor and Mildred Goertzel published a revealing study of 413 famous and exceptionally gifted people. The study was called *Cradles of Eminence.* These two researchers spent years trying to understand the source of these people's greatness, the common thread which ran through all of these outstanding people's lives. The most outstanding fact was that almost all of them, 392, had to overcome very difficult obstacles in order to become who they were. Their problems became opportunities instead of obstacles.[5]

Not only do people overcome obstacles to become successful, but even after they have achieved a level of success, they continue to face problems. The bad news is that the higher people go—personally and professionally—the more complicated life gets. Schedules get tighter, money issues increase, and greater demands are put on successful people. But the good news is that if they continue to grow and develop themselves, their ability to deal with problems will also increase.

## 3. Money Doesn't Solve Problems

Another faulty belief is that money solves all problems. The opposite is actually true—people with money tend to be less content and have additional problems. For example, Ernie J. Zelinski cites a recent survey showing that a higher percentage of people making more than $75,000 a year are dissatisfied with their incomes than of those making less than $75,000 a year. He also noted:

> A larger percentage of the rich have alcohol and drug problems than the general population. I have a theory about how well off we will be with a lot of money. If we are happy and handle problems well when we are making $25,000 a year, we will

be happy and handle problems well when we have a lot more money. If we are unhappy and don't handle problems well on $25,000 a year, we can expect the same of ourselves with a lot of money. We will be just as unhappy and handle problems as ineffectively, but with more comfort and style.[6]

The bottom line is that you should try to help people understand that money is no substitute for the basic problem-solving skills they need to develop. Financial problems are usually a symptom of other personal problems.

## 4. Problems Provide an Opportunity for Growth

As you look ahead and help people, realize that while problems can cause pain, they also provide an excellent opportunity for growth. Or as author Nena O'Neill put it, "Out of every crisis comes the chance to be reborn."

The people of Enterprise, Alabama, understand that idea. In their town stands a monument to the Mexican boll weevil, erected in 1919. The story behind it is that in 1895, the insect destroyed the county's major crop, cotton. After that disaster, local farmers began to diversify, and the peanut crop of 1919 far exceeded the value of even the best ones comprised of cotton. On the monument are the following words: "In profound appreciation of the boll weevil and what it has done as the herald of prosperity. . . . Out of a time of struggle and crisis has come new growth and success. Out of adversity has come blessing."

As you have certainly observed, not everyone approaches life's problems in the same way. Historian Arnold Toynbee believed that all people react in one of four ways under difficult circumstances:

1. Retreat into the past
2. Daydream about the future
3. Retreat within and wait for someone to rescue them
4. Face the crisis and transform it into something useful

As you help others, let them know there may be rough waters ahead. Show them that it's wise to plan ahead as best they can.

And when trouble comes, encourage them to face it and try to become better as a result.

# A Navigator Makes
# Course Corrections

We've heard that back before the time of sophisticated electronic navigational equipment, the ship's navigator used to take a reading of the stars at a particular time in the middle of the night, determine how far off course the vessel was, and make adjustments to its course. No matter how accurately the original course had been laid out or how carefully the helmsman had followed his orders, the ship always got off course and needed adjustments.

People are the same way. No matter how focused they are or how well they plan, people will still get off course. The problem comes when they have difficulty making course corrections—either because they don't know they're off course, or because they don't know what they should do to fix things. Not everyone is a natural problem solver. For most people, it's a skill they must learn. John Foster Dulles, secretary of state during the Eisenhower administration, proposed that "the measure of success is not whether you have a tough problem to deal with, but whether it's the same problem you had last year." As the navigator, you can help people avoid that situation.

## Teach Them Not to Listen to
## Doubting Critics

In the book *Principle-Centered Leadership,* Stephen Covey tells how Columbus was once invited to a banquet where he was given the most honored place at the table. A shallow courtier who was jealous of him asked abruptly, "Had you not discovered the Indies, are there not other men in Spain who would have been capable of the enterprise?"

Columbus made no reply but took an egg and invited the company to make it stand on end. They all attempted to do it, but none succeeded, whereupon the explorer tapped it on the table, denting one end, and left it standing.

"We all could have done it that way!" the courtier cried.

"Yes, if you had only known how," answered Columbus. "And once I showed you the way to the New World, nothing was easier than to follow it."

> ***When you are navigating for others, remember that they can't make the whole trip in a day.***

The truth is that it's a hundred times easier to criticize others than to find solutions to problems. But criticism gets you nowhere. Alfred Armand Montapert summed it up this way: "The majority see the obstacles; the few see the objectives; history records the successes of the latter, while oblivion is the reward of the former." Help the people within your influence to ignore the critics and keep their eyes on the big picture. Show them that the best way to silence critics is to solve the problem and move on.

## Coach Them Not to Be Overwhelmed by Challenges

A rookie major-league baseball player faced pitcher Walter Johnson for the first time when Johnson was in his prime. The batter took two quick strikes and headed for the dugout. He told the umpire to keep the third strike—he had seen enough.

When faced with tough problems, just about anybody is likely to get discouraged. That's why it's a good idea to coach people through their problems, especially early on in the mentoring process while you're first helping them to navigate. Encourage them to maintain a positive attitude, and give them strategies for problem solving.

Management expert Ken Blanchard recommends a four-step problem-solving process that includes (1) thinking about the problem in order to make it specific, (2) forming theories for solving it, (3) forecasting the consequences of carrying out the theories, and (4) then choosing which method to use based on the big picture. Blanchard says, "Whether you choose a vacation or a spouse, a party or a candidate, a cause to contribute to or a creed to live by—think!" There are no impossible problems. Time, thought, and a positive attitude can solve just about anything.

## Encourage Them to Seek Simple Solutions

There are a couple of keys to the most effective method of problem solving. The first is recognizing that the simple way to solve a problem is better than the most clever one. An example from the life of Thomas Edison illustrates this point well. It's said that Edison had a unique way of hiring engineers. He would give the applicant a lightbulb and ask, "How much water will it hold?" There were two ways the engineers usually went about solving the problem. The first way was to use gauges to measure all the angles of the bulb, and then use those figures to calculate the surface area. That approach sometimes took as long as twenty minutes. The second way was to fill the bulb with water and then pour the contents into a measuring cup, which usually took about one minute.[7] Edison never hired the engineers who used the first method. He didn't want the engineers to impress him—he wanted them to provide simple results.

The second element in effective problem solving is the ability to make decisions. Thomas J. Watson, Jr., former head of IBM, believed that solving problems quickly was essential to making progress. "Solve it," he declared. "Solve it quickly, solve it right or wrong. If you solve it wrong, it will come back and slap you in the face, and then you can solve it right. Lying dead in the water and doing nothing is a comfortable alternative because it is without risk, but it is an absolutely fatal way to manage a business." And it's also a terrible way for people to manage their lives. Help others to realize when they need to make course adjustments, find simple solutions that they think will work, and then

execute them without delay. Don't let them continue traveling off
course for any length of time.

## Instill Confidence in Them

One pitfall of helping others with their problems and mistakes
is that they can doubt themselves. Continually encourage the
people you help. George Matthew Adams said, "What you think
means more than anything else in your life. More than what you
earn, more than where you live, more than your social position,
and more than what anyone else may think about you." The size
of the persons and the quality of their attitude are more important than the size of any problem they may face. If your people
remain confident, they will be able to overcome any obstacle.

## A NAVIGATOR STAYS WITH THE PEOPLE

Finally, a good navigator takes the trip with the people he is
guiding. He doesn't give directions and then walk away. He travels alongside his people as a friend. Author and conference
speaker Richard Exley explained his idea of friendship this way:
"A true friend is one who hears and understands when you share
your deepest feelings. He supports you when you are struggling;
he corrects you, gently and with love, when you err; and he for-
gives you when you fail. A true friend prods you to personal
growth, stretches you to your full potential. And most amazing of
all, he celebrates your successes as if they were his own."

As you come alongside some of the people within your influence and mentor them, you and they may experience difficult
times together. You won't be perfect and neither will they, but
just keep in mind Henry Ford's words: "Your best friend is he
who brings out the best that is within you." Do your best to follow that objective, and you will help a lot of people.

Once people learn to become effective problem solvers and
can navigate for themselves, their lives begin to change dramatically. No longer do they feel powerless in the face of life's difficult circumstances. They learn to roll with the punches—and

even to duck a few. And once problem solving becomes a habit, no challenge seems too large.

Jim is an excellent thinker and problem solver. He has navigated through some pretty interesting situations over the years. Recently, he recounted a story that you will undoubtedly enjoy:

A couple of years ago while Nancy and I were hosting a business seminar aboard a large cruise ship in the Caribbean, we were called away to an important business meeting in Michigan. We had no problem getting to the meeting because arrangements had been made for us to be picked up by a private jet at the airport in San Juan, Puerto Rico. But leaving Michigan and getting back turned out to be quite another story.

Our plan was to return on the same jet the next day and meet the ship at its next port. From there the ship would return to Miami, and we could continue teaching our seminar. But in Michigan when we began to depart, our aircraft developed a problem and had to return to the hangar. That caused a serious problem for us. There were no commercial flights to our destination, nor were there any private planes with enough range to get us down to St. Martin, which is some fifteen hundred miles off the coast of Florida.

Missing the seminar simply was not an option for us, so we looked at other possibilities. The best we could do was take an available private jet to Atlanta and work on finding another plane to take us the rest of the way.

By the time we touched down in Atlanta, we had managed to arrange for another plane, and it was ready and waiting for us. As soon as our plane came to a stop, we gathered up our things and scrambled over to the other jet. You can imagine how relieved we were to get on board and get in the air.

We weren't on our way for very long before we found out that our current flight was going to get us on the island exactly fifteen minutes after the ship was scheduled to depart. "We've got to get them to delay the ship," I said.

The pilot started working on the problem via radio and managed to contact the ship's captain from the cockpit. He agreed to a twenty-minute delay. Then the pilot worked on getting us a quick clearance through customs. And when word came back that we would be able to do it, we started getting optimistic.

We dashed to the first taxi we could find and headed out, but almost immediately, we hit a huge traffic jam.

"How far is it to the ship?" Nancy asked.

"On the other side of the island," the driver answered.

"How long will that take?'

"Fifteen, maybe twenty minutes."

"We need to make it in less than ten," I said, offering him a really good tip.

He looked at me, looked at the money, and said, "Yes, sir." He pulled the cab over onto the sidewalk and made a quick turn up an alley. We went over curbs, through lights, and weaved down alleys and side streets in a blur. We felt as if we were on Mr. Toad's Wild Ride at Disneyland. It seemed like we saw the back of every building on the island. But then we shot through a narrow opening between two buildings and careened out into the sunlight onto a pier—and the ship was in sight, its horn sounding its imminent departure.

As we screeched to a halt at the end of the pier, we piled out of the cab. That's when we began to hear the cheering. Evidently, word had gotten to our people on the ship that we were fighting to make our way back to them. And when we finally had a second to look up, we could see more than five hundred people on deck whooping and clapping and cheering to celebrate our arrival.

"Who are you anyway?" our driver asked. I just handed him the money and said, "Thanks for your help." Then Nancy and I ran for the gangway. It hadn't been easy, but we had made it.

The ability to navigate problems and overcome obstacles is a skill that anyone can learn, but it takes practice. If Jim and Nancy had faced that same situation twenty years before, they probably would not have made it to that ship. But over the years, they've developed an incredible ability to make things happen, not only in their own lives, but also in the lives of others.

You can have that same ability. Become a navigator in the lives of others. You will be able to use your influence to help them move up to the next level in their lives, and if you assist them during their darkest hours, you will make friends of them for life.

## *Influence Checklist*
# NAVIGATING FOR OTHER PEOPLE

❏ **Identify their destination.** Think about the three people you've decided to enlarge. What are their destinations? Observe what makes them cry, sing, and dream. Write those things down here:

Person 1: _____

Cry: _____

Sing: _____

Dream: _____


Person 2: _____

Cry: _____

Sing: _____

Dream: _____


Person 3: _____

Cry: _____

Sing: _____

Dream: _____

❏ **Look ahead.** Based on your experience and knowledge of these people, list the difficulties you think they are likely to face in the near future:

1. _____

2. _____

3. _____

❏ **Plan ahead.** How can you help them navigate through these potential problems? Write down what you can do and when you should do it.

1. _____

2. _____

3. _____

# *A Person of Influence . . .*

# CONNECTS
# WITH PEOPLE

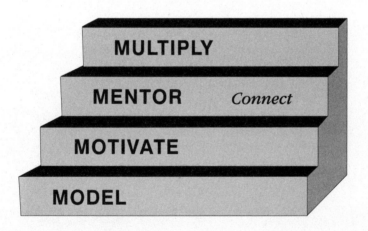

Have you ever been to a family or school reunion? It can be fun because it gives you a chance to connect with people you haven't seen in a long time. John recently went to a reunion of sorts, and he had an incredible time. Let him tell you about it:

My first job out of college in 1969 was at a little church in Hillham, Indiana. I was the senior pastor there for three years. The church really grew during the short time Margaret and I were there, so much so that we had to construct a new church building in 1971 to hold all the people. We look back on those three years as a crucial growing time in our lives that we really enjoyed and benefited from.

Recently, I got a phone call from that little country church. The person on the phone excitedly explained they were getting ready to celebrate the twenty-five-year anniversary of the building we constructed. They were preparing to have a big service and invite everybody for miles around to come celebrate with them. And then the person on the other end of the phone paused and cleared his throat. And he finally asked, "Dr. Maxwell, would you be willing to come back and preach that Sunday service for us?"

"I would love to come back and preach at your service," I told him. "It would be an honor. You just tell me the day, and I'll be there."

During the next few months, I spent some time thinking about how I could make their anniversary a great day for them. The last thing I wanted to do was come back as some kind of conquering hero. I knew I needed to find ways to connect with them.

The first thing I did was get them to send me a copy of their church directory with the pictures and names of all the people in their congregation. There in the book were many faces I recognized. Some people had less hair than I remembered, and much of that hair was now gray, but I knew the faces behind those twenty-five years of wrinkles. And there were many others who were new to me. Sons and daughters of the people I loved, and some new names

I didn't recognize. I spent many hours poring over those pictures and memorizing those names.

Then I prepared the best message I could, one filled with stories of our common experiences. I shared some of my mistakes and recounted all of their victories. I wanted them to know that they shared in my success. They were king makers, and I felt very privileged to have served them for three years and benefited from their loving support and care for me.

But I knew that more important than the message I preached or anything else I could do would be the time I was able to spend with the people. So when the time came, Margaret and I flew in early, and we spent Saturday afternoon with some of the old-timers who had been such a vital part of our ministry twenty-five years before. We shared a lot of wonderful recollections. I talked to them about some of my fondest memories, and they surprised me with a few stories of their own. For instance, there was one man in a wheelchair who had been a teenager when I was the pastor there. He had been in an accident that left him in a coma. I had visited him and his family several times in the hospital, and one night I shared my faith with him as he lay unconscious in his bed. I left Hillham soon after that to go to my next church, and until my current visit, I hadn't known he had ever awakened from the coma.

"Do you remember coming into the hospital and talking to me twenty-five years ago?" he asked.

"I sure do," I answered.

"So do I," he told me. "I remember that day as clear as can be. I wasn't able to answer you, but I heard every word you said. That's the day I became a believer." And he told me about how his faith had impacted other people in the community. It was a very special time.

The next day, I got to the church early to shake the hands of the people as they came into the sanctuary. It was wonderful to get to meet so many of the people and be able to greet them by name. And I preached a message of affirmation to them. Even though they had done some wonderful things since I had last seen them, I told them that I could see that in the next twenty-five years lay their greatest potential. Their best days were still ahead of them. And when I left, I felt as though I had not only renewed some old acquaintances, but also had made a lot of new friends.

The time John spent with the people in Hillham was brief, but in that short time, he was able to do something that was important to them and him. He was able to connect with them.

# CONNECTING ENABLES OTHERS TO TRAVEL TO A HIGHER LEVEL

Connection is a very important part of the process of mentoring others. And it's absolutely critical if you want to influence people in a positive way. When you navigate for others, you come alongside them and travel their road for a while, helping them handle some of the obstacles and difficulties in their lives. But when you connect with them, you are asking them to come alongside you and travel your road for your and their mutual benefit.

When we think of connecting with people, we compare it to trains and what happens to them in a train yard. The cars sitting on the tracks in a train yard have a lot of things going for them. They have value because they're loaded with cargo; they have a destination; and they even have a route by which to get to that destination. But they don't have a way of getting anywhere on their own. To do anything of value, they have to hook up with a locomotive.

Have you ever been to a train yard and watched how unrelated and disconnected pieces of equipment come together to form a working train? It's quite a process. It all begins with the locomotive. First, it switches itself onto the same track as the car it's going to pick up. Then it moves to where the car is, backs up to it, makes contact with it, and connects. Once it's all hooked up, together they move toward their destination.

A similar thing must happen before you can get people to go with you on a journey. You have to find out where they are, move toward them to make contact, and connect with them. If you can do that successfully, you can take them to new heights in your relationship and in their development. Remember, the road to the next level is always uphill, and people need help to make it to that higher level.

# Nine Steps for Connecting
# with People

Fortunately, you don't have to be an engineer to connect with people, but it does take effort to make connection happen. You'll need communication skills, a desire to help people grow and change, and a sense of personal mission or purpose—after all, you have to know where you're going to take others along.

Take a look at the following steps, and use them to help you connect with the people you influence:

## 1. Don't Take People for Granted

You can connect with people and lead them only if you value them. Weak leaders sometimes get so caught up in the vision of where they're going that they forget the people they're trying to lead. But you can't take people for granted for any length of time before your leadership begins to fall apart. And you won't be able to connect with them.

A wonderful story from former Speaker of the House Tip O'Neill reveals what can happen when you take people for granted. He said that on one election day, an elderly neighbor came up to him after leaving the polls and said, "Tip, I voted for you today even though you didn't ask me."

O'Neill was surprised. "Mrs. O'Brien," he said, "I've known you all my life. I took your garbage out for you, mowed your lawn, shoveled snow for you. I didn't think I had to ask."

"Tip," she said in a motherly tone, "it's always *nice* to be asked." O'Neill said he never forgot that piece of advice.

Valuing people is the first step in the connection process, but it has additional benefits. When you let people know that you don't take them for granted, they turn around and do the same for you. John was reminded of this by his friend and colleague Dan Reiland. John will tell you the story:

> Margaret and I spent a long weekend with Dan and his wife, Patti, not too long ago. Dan has worked with me for fifteen years, first as my executive pastor at Skyline Church where I was the senior pastor, and now as a vice president at INJOY. We spent the weekend at a resort hotel in Laguna Beach. It was great. We enjoyed the pool and spa, ate some great meals, and had a wonderful time together.
>
> As Margaret and I were checking out, I went to the front desk to pay the bill and discovered that Dan had beaten me there and already taken care of everything. Later I talked to him and said, "Dan, you didn't have to do that. I wanted to treat you and Patti."
>
> "No, John," said Dan, "it was our pleasure. You do so much for us; I never want to take you for granted."

John's friend Coach Bill McCartney, former head football coach of the Colorado State Buffaloes, said, "Anytime you devalue people, you question God's creation of them." You can never tell people too often, too loudly, or too publicly how much you love them.

## *You can connect with people and lead them only if you value them.*

## 2. Possess a Make-a-Difference Mind-Set

If you desire to accomplish something great and really want to see it happen, you need to possess a make-a-difference attitude. Anytime you don't believe you can make a difference, you won't. How do you cultivate a solid make-a-difference mind-set?

***Believe you can make a difference.*** Every person on this earth—including you—has the potential to make a difference. But you can do it only if you believe in yourself and are willing to give yourself away to others. As Helen Keller said, "Life is an exciting business and most exciting when lived for others." You may not be able to help *everybody,* but you can certainly help *somebody.*

***Believe what you share can make a difference.*** The two of us spend a large part of our lives connecting and communicating with people. Between the two of us, we impact more than one million people every year. If we believed that what we share with others couldn't make a difference, we would quit tomorrow. But we know that we can help others change their lives. We believe that everything rises and falls on leadership. We're certain that people's attitudes make or break them. And we know that there is no joy, peace, or meaning in life without faith.

You have to believe that what you have to offer others can make a difference in their lives. No one wants to follow a person without conviction. If you don't believe, neither will other people.

***Believe the person you share with can make a difference.*** We've read about something called a reciprocity rule in human behavior. It states that over time, people come to share similar attitudes toward one another. In other words, if we hold a high opinion of you and continue to hold that opinion, eventually, you will come to feel the same way about us. That process builds a connection between us, and it opens the way for a powerful partnership.

***Believe that together you can make a big difference.*** Mother Teresa is a living example of a truth she once expressed: "I can do what you can't do, and you can do what I can't do. *Together* we can do great things." No one ever achieves alone what he can do when partnering with others. And anybody who doesn't recognize that falls incredibly short of her potential.

There is a story about a famous organist in the 1800s that illustrates the importance of recognizing valuable partnerships. The musician traveled from town to town giving concerts. In each town, he hired a boy to pump the organ during the concert. After one particular performance, he couldn't shake the boy. He even followed the organist back to his hotel.

"We sure had us a great concert tonight, didn't we?" said the boy.

"What do you mean *we?*" said the musician. "*I* had a great concert. Now why don't you go home?"

The next night when the organist was halfway through a magnificent fugue, the organ suddenly quit. The organist was stupefied. Then suddenly, the little boy stuck his head around the corner of the organ, grinned, and said, "We ain't having a very good concert tonight, are *we?*"

If you want to connect with people and take them with you to a higher level, recognize the difference you can make as a team, and acknowledge it at every opportunity.

## 3. Initiate Movement Toward Them

According to Tom Peters and Nancy Austin, "The number one managerial productivity problem in America is, quite simply, managers who are out of touch with their people and out of touch with their customers."[1] Lack of contact and communication is a problem that affects many people, not just managers in organizations. Maybe that's why sales expert Charles B. Ruth says, "There are many cases of salesmen who have nothing to offer a prospect except friendship out-selling salesmen with everything to offer—except friendship."[2]

We believe there are many reasons why people don't connect with one another more than they do. A primary reason, especially within organizations, is that many leaders believe that it is the follower's responsibility to initiate contact with them. But the opposite is true. To be effective, leaders must be initiators. If they don't go to their people, meet them where they are, and initiate the connection, then 80 percent of the time no connection will be made.

## 4. Look for Common Ground

Anytime you want to connect with another person, start where both of you agree. And that means finding common ground. If you have developed good listening skills, as we talked about in Chapter 4, you'll probably be able to detect areas where you have common experience or views. Talk about hobbies, where you've lived, your work, sports, or children. What you discuss isn't as important as your attitude. Be positive, and try to see things from the other person's point of view. Being open and likable is half the battle. As it's sometimes said, "All things being equal, people will do business with people they like. All things not being equal, they still will."

Sometimes even when you find common ground, you can face obstacles in the communication process. If you detect that people you're trying to connect with are tentative about your approaching them, then try to meet them on emotional common ground. An excellent way to do that is to use something called *feel, felt, found* to help them relate to you. First, try to sense what they *feel,* and acknowledge and validate the feelings. If you've had similar feelings in the past, then share with them about how you've also *felt* the same way before. Finally, share with them what you've *found* that has helped you work through the feelings.

Once you make it a regular practice to look for common ground with others, you'll find that you can talk to just about anybody and meet her where she is. And when you can do that, you can make a connection.

## 5. Recognize and Respect Differences in Personality

We are capable of finding common ground with others, but at the same time we need to acknowledge that we're all different. And that's one of the great joys of life, though we didn't always see it that way. An excellent tool for understanding other people is a book by John's friend Florence Littauer called *Personality Plus.* In it, she describes four basic personality types:

- *Sanguine:* desires fun; is outgoing, relationship oriented, witty, easygoing, popular, artistic, emotional, outspoken, and optimistic.

- *Melancholy:* desires perfection; is introverted, task oriented, artistic, emotional, goal oriented, organized, and pessimistic.
- *Phlegmatic:* desires peace; is introverted, unemotional, strong-willed, relationship oriented, pessimistic, and purpose driven.
- *Choleric:* desires power or control; is strong-willed, decisive, goal oriented, organized, unemotional, outgoing, outspoken, and optimistic.[3]

Just about everyone you try to connect with falls into one of these categories (or has characteristics from two complementary categories). For example, John is a classic choleric-sanguine. He loves to have fun, he is decisive, and he naturally takes charge in just about any situation. Jim, on the other hand, is melancholy-phlegmatic. He is an analytical thinker who's not driven by emotion, and he generally keeps his own counsel.

As you connect with others, recognize and respect their differences in motivation. With cholerics, connect with strength. With melancholics, connect by being focused. With phlegmatics, connect by giving assurance. And with sanguines, connect with excitement.

Playwright John Luther understood this point: "Natural talent, intelligence, a wonderful education—none of these guarantees success. Something else is needed: the sensitivity to understand what other people want and the willingness to give it to them." Pay attention to people's personalities, and do your best to meet them where they are. They'll appreciate your sensitivity and understanding.

## 6. Find the Key to Others' Lives

Industrialist Andrew Carnegie had an uncanny ability for understanding people and what was important to them. It's said that when he was a boy in Scotland, he had a rabbit that had a litter of bunnies. To feed them, Carnegie asked the neighborhood boys to collect clover and dandelions. In return, each boy got to name a bunny after himself.

Carnegie did something similar as an adult that showed his understanding of people. Because he wanted to sell his steel to the

Pennsylvania Railroad, when he built a new steel mill in Pittsburgh, he named it the J. Edgar Thompson Steel Works after the president of the Pennsylvania Railroad. Thompson was so flattered by the honor that he thereafter purchased all his steel from Carnegie.

You don't have to be a Carnegie to connect with people. You just need to know what's important to them. Everybody has a key to his or her life. All you need to do is find it. Here are two clues to help you do it: To understand a person's mind, examine what he has already achieved. To understand his heart, look at what he aspires to do. That will help you find the key, and once you do find it, use it with integrity. Turn the key only when you have the person's permission, and even then use that key only for his benefit, not your own—to help, not to hurt.

## 7. *Communicate from the Heart*

Once you've initiated a connection with others, found common ground, and discovered what really matters to them, communicate to them what really matters to you. And that requires you to speak to them from your heart.

A young man with a brand-new degree in psychology was asked to deliver a speech to a group of senior citizens. For forty-five minutes he talked to them on how to live your twilight years gracefully. When the speech was over, an eighty-year-old woman came up to the young speaker and said, "Your vocabulary and pronunciation were excellent, but I must tell you one thing that you'll come to understand as you get older, you don't know what you're talking about!"

Being genuine is the single most important factor when communicating with others, whether one-on-one or before large audiences. No amount of knowledge, technique, or quick-wittedness can substitute for honesty and the genuine desire to help others.

Abraham Lincoln was well known for communicating well with others, and at the heart of that skill was his ability to speak from the heart. In 1842, Lincoln addressed members of the Washington Temperance Society. During his speech titled "Charity in Temperance Reform," he made the following observation: "If you would win a man to your cause, first convince him that you are his sincere friend. . . . Assume to dictate to his judgment, or to command his action, or to mark him as one to be shunned and despised, and he will retreat within himself. . . . You shall no more be able to pierce him than to penetrate the hard shell of a tortoise with a rye straw."[4]

As you communicate with others to build connections with them, share from your heart and be yourself.

## 8. Share Common Experiences

To really connect with others, you have to do more than find common ground and communicate well. You need to find a way to cement the relationship. Joseph F. Newton said, "People are lonely because they build walls instead of bridges." To build bridges that connect you to people in a lasting way, share common experiences with them.

> *No one ever achieves alone what he can do when partnering with others.*

The two of us have enjoyed sharing experiences with others for years. For example, whenever John hires a new member of his executive staff, he always takes that person on the road with him to several of his conferences. He does that not only because he wants the new staff member to become familiar with the services the company offers to its customers, but also because they can travel together and get to know each other in a wide variety of settings. Nothing bonds people together like racing through impossible traffic in an unfamiliar city to get to the airport and then running with your bags down the concourse to scramble onto a plane at the last minute!

The common experiences you share with others don't have to be that dramatic (although adversity definitely brings people together). Share meals with people. Go to a ball game together. Take people out on a call or visitation with you. Anything you experience together that creates a common history helps to connect you to others.

A wonderful story of connection comes from the career of Jackie Robinson, the first African-American to play major-league baseball. Robinson faced jeering crowds, death threats, and loads of abuse in just about every stadium he visited while breaking baseball's color barrier. One day in his home stadium in Brooklyn, he committed an error, and immediately, his own fans began to ridicule him. He stood at second base, humiliated, while the fans jeered. Then shortstop Pee Wee Reese came over and stood next to him. He put his arm around Robinson and faced the crowd. The fans grew quiet. It's said that Robinson later claimed that Reese's arm around his shoulder saved his career.

Look for ways to build bridges with people within your influence, especially during times when they experience adversity. The connections you make will strengthen your relationships incredibly and prepare you for the journey you can take together.

## 9. Once Connected, Move Forward

If you want to influence others, and you desire to get them moving in the right direction, you must connect with them before you try to take them anywhere. Attempting to do it before connecting is a common mistake of inexperienced leaders. Trying to move others before going through the connection process with them can lead to mistrust, resistance, and strained relationships. Always remember that you have to share yourself before you try to share the journey. As someone once observed, "Leadership is cultivating in people today, a future willingness on their part to follow you into something new for the sake of something great." Connection creates that willingness.

A challenge for any influencer is connecting with people from another culture. Jim has had a lot of experience in this area since he works with people in twenty-six countries. He found it particularly interesting working with people in the Eastern bloc countries formerly controlled by the Soviet Union:

> When we first started working with people in Eastern Europe, it was really a unique experience. We had experienced very little exposure to their culture and values, and

we found that things we accept in everyday business were foreign to people who had endured fifty years of Communist rule.

Most people in America have been raised on Judeo-Christian ethical and moral values. We often take that for granted, along with the benefits of free enterprise and capitalism. Our new friends in countries like Poland, Hungary, and the Czech Republic, however, were used to surviving in a corrupt world of oppressive government, propaganda, and little-to-no-ethical teaching as we know it. Their environment led them to believe that success comes only to those who work *around* the rules and beat the cheaters at their own game. We found that many people embraced a success-at-any-cost mind-set and almost a pride in how cleverly they could break the rules.

We believed it was important to show these wonderful people that real success was possible only when a person behaved ethically and stood on the principles of integrity and trust. It seemed like a big job, but the people were smart, and we were working with some great young professionals who were hungry to learn the secrets of true success.

We began the process by doing everything we could to connect with people in those countries. In some ways, that has been one of our greatest challenges as influencers. But we were able to find a few key people, and we came alongside them as friends and mentors. We began navigating them through this new paradigm of ethical living and principle-centered business. And we invested a lot of time in getting to know them better and connecting with them on this worthwhile journey. Our goal was to give them tools to positively impact the people in their country.

This is still an ongoing journey for us. But whether we are working with people in Eastern Europe, mainland China, or another part of the world, we recognize that people are basically the same. Everyone wants to be successful and happy and is eager to learn from others who have gone ahead of them. But you can't make a significant impact in people's lives until you personally connect with them. Only then can you take them on a journey and really make a difference.

Jim and Nancy are making an impact that is being felt around the world. They understand that influence means relating to people, raising them up, and then turning them loose to reproduce themselves in others' lives. Connecting is a fundamental step in that process. But before people can go to the highest level and reproduce their influence in others, there is one more step they need to take: They need to be empowered. And that is the subject of the next chapter.

## *Influence Checklist*
# CONNECTING WITH PEOPLE

❑ **Measure your current connection.** How strong is your connection with the top people whose lives you are influencing? Do you know the key to each person's life? Have you established common ground? Are there common experiences that bond you together? If your connection is not as strong as it could be, remember that it's your role to be the initiator. Schedule time in the coming week to have coffee, share a meal, or just chat with each person.

❑ **Connect at a deeper level.** If you've never spent any kind of meaningful time with your top people in a nonprofessional setting, schedule a time to do so in the coming month. Plan a retreat or a getaway weekend, and include your spouses. Or take them to a seminar or conference. The main thing is to give yourselves opportunities to connect on a deeper level and share common experiences.

❑ **Communicate your vision.** Once you've made a strong connection with your people, share your hopes and dreams. Cast vision for your common future, and invite them to join you on the journey.

# *A Person of Influence . . .*

# EMPOWERS
# PEOPLE

$A$ big part of Jim's business includes meeting fairly often with some of his key leaders, and because they come from around the country and all over the world, he makes it a goal to schedule meetings in various locations. One place that has become a favorite of his and Nancy's over the years is Deer Valley near Salt Lake City, Utah. Recently, when they were there with some of their leaders, something interesting happened. Jim will tell you about it:

> Deer Valley is really a beautiful setting. In the winter it's great for skiing, and in the summer it's got gorgeous forested mountains and meadows full of wildflowers. We really enjoy vacationing there and using it as a place to meet with some of our people.
>
> This past year we spent time with a group of about ten couples at some condos in Deer Valley right on the ski slopes. We all had a wonderful time.
>
> When we were ready to leave, we packed up our belongings and swung by the rental office to check out on the way to the airport. But as we worked to get our bill squared away, we discovered that one couple in our party had inadvertently left their room key in their condo.
>
> "I'm going to have to charge you $25 for the lost key," the desk clerk said.
>
> I have to admit I was a little surprised. We had been their customers for eight years. And we had spent thousands of dollars with them in the past week. "Look," I said, "I appreciate that you have a policy about missing keys, but the key is in their room. And if we were to go back and get it, we'd miss our flight. Can't you just forget the charge?"
>
> "No," he said, "the rule is that I have to add the charge to your bill." Even when I reminded him of our history with their company and told him that I didn't feel good about the extra charge, he wouldn't budge. In fact, he got more rigid, and I got really irritated. As I stood there waiting, I calculated in my mind how much money we had spent there over the years, and I figured out that he was jeopardizing our $100,000 history with their company for a $25 key!

We finally left and paid the fee. On the way to the airport, Nancy and I talked about the incident, and I thought about how it really wasn't the desk clerk's fault. The problem was with the owner who had failed to train him properly.

"That kind of thing drives me crazy," she said. "Some people just don't get it. You know who's just the opposite of that?" she asked. "Nordstrom. They're unbelievable. I didn't tell you about what happened the other night before we left for Deer Valley. I went down to Nordstrom to get Eric a pair of pajamas. I picked out some that I knew he'd like, but I told the salesgirl that I needed the pants hemmed and that we were leaving on a trip early the next morning. She didn't blink and offered to have them done that night and drive them out to us at home.

"And that was the only thing I bought!" added Nancy. "It's not like I had spent a lot of money. She did that just for a pair of pajamas."

Stories of the excellent service at Nordstrom department stores have become legendary. Anyone who shops there can attest to it. Their employees are exceptional because the company is built on the principle of *empowerment*. That philosophy of empowering employees is capsulized in the following brief statement that every employee receives when he or she begins working for the company:

### Welcome to Nordstrom
We're glad to have you with
our Company.
Our number one goal is to provide
outstanding customer service.
Set both your personal and
professional goals high.
We have great confidence in your ability to achieve them.
Nordstrom Rules:
Rule #1: Use your good
judgment in all situations.
There will be no additional rules.
Please feel free to ask
your department manager,

store manager, or division general
manager any question
at any time.[1]

Nordstrom stores emphasize people, not policies. They believe in their people, they encourage them to achieve excellence, and they release them to do it. As Tom Peters said, "Techniques don't produce quality products or pick up the garbage on time; people do, people who care, people who are treated as creatively contributing adults." The managers and staff at that rental office in Deer Valley would benefit greatly from learning that lesson.

## WHAT IT MEANS TO EMPOWER OTHERS

An English artist named William Wolcott went to New York in 1924 to record his impressions of that fascinating city. One morning he was visiting in the office of a former colleague when the urge to sketch came over him. Seeing some paper on his friend's desk, he asked, "May I have that?"

*The act of empowering others changes lives, and it's a win-win situation for you and the people you empower.*

His friend answered, "That's not sketching paper. That's ordinary wrapping paper."

Not wanting to lose that spark of inspiration, Wolcott took the wrapping paper and said, "Nothing is ordinary if you know how to use it." On that ordinary paper Wolcott made two sketches.

Later that same year, one of those sketches sold for $500 and the other for $1,000, quite a sum for 1924.

People under the influence of an empowering person are like paper in the hands of a talented artist. No matter what they're made of, they can become treasures.

The ability to empower others is one of the keys to personal and professional success. John Craig remarked, "No matter how much work you can do, no matter how engaging your personality may be, you will not advance far in business if you cannot work through others." And business executive J. Paul Getty asserted, "It doesn't make much difference how much other knowledge or experience an executive possesses; if he is unable to achieve results through people, he is worthless as an executive."

*When you empower people, you're not influencing just them; you're influencing all the people they influence.*

When you become an empowerer, you work with and through people, but you do much more. You enable others to reach the highest levels in their personal and professional development. Simply defined, empowering is giving your influence to others for the purpose of personal and organizational growth. It's sharing yourself—your influence, position, power, and opportunities— with others with the purpose of investing in their lives so that they can function at their best. It's seeing people's potential, sharing your resources with them, and showing them that you believe in them completely.

You may already be empowering some people in your life without knowing it. When you entrust your spouse with an important decision and then cheerfully back him up, that's empowering. When you decide that your child is ready to cross the street by herself and give her your permission to do so, you have empowered her. When you delegate a challenging job to an employee and give her the authority she needs to get it done, you have empowered her.

The act of empowering others changes lives, and it's a win-win situation for you and the people you empower. Giving others your authority isn't like giving away an object, such as your car, for example. If you give away your car, you're stuck. You no longer have transportation. But empowering others by giving them your authority has the same effect as sharing information: You haven't lost anything. You have increased the ability of others without decreasing yourself.

# QUALIFICATIONS OF AN EMPOWERER

Just about everyone has the potential to become an empowerer, but you cannot empower everyone. The process works only when certain conditions are met. You must have:

## Position

You cannot empower people whom you don't lead. Leadership expert Fred Smith explained, "Who can give permission for another person to succeed? A person in authority. Others can encourage, but permission comes only from an authority figure: a parent, boss, or pastor."

You can encourage and motivate everybody you meet. You can enlarge or help navigate for anyone with whom you have built a mentoring relationship. But to *empower* people, you have to be in a position of *power* over them. Sometimes that position doesn't have to be formal or official, but other times it does. For example, if we went to a restaurant to have lunch with you one day, and we weren't happy about how long it was taking to get our food, we could never empower you to go into the kitchen to fix our meal for us. We don't have that authority, so we certainly can't give it away to you. The first requisite of empowerment is having a position of authority over the people you want to empower.

## Relationship

The second requirement for empowering people is having a
relationship with them. Nineteenth-century writer Thomas Carlyle
said, "A great man shares his greatness by the way he treats little
men." Although the people you empower are not "little," they can
be made to feel that way if you don't value your relationship with
them.

It has been said that relationships are forged, not formed. They
require time and common experience. If you have made the
effort to connect with people, as we talked about in the previous
chapter, by the time you're ready to empower them, your relationship should be solid enough for you to be able to lead them.
And as you do, remember what Ralph Waldo Emerson wrote,
"Every man [or woman] is entitled to be valued by his [or her] best
moments." When you value people and your relationships with
them, you lay the foundation for empowering others.

## Respect

Relationships cause people to want to be with you, but respect
causes them to want to be empowered by you. Mutual respect is
essential to the empowerment process. Psychiatrist Ari Kiev
summed it up this way: "If you wish others to respect you, you
must show respect for them. . . . Everyone wants to feel that he
counts for something and is important to someone. Invariably,
people will give their love, respect, and attention to the person
who fills that need. Consideration for others generally reflects
faith in self and faith in others." When you believe in people, care
about them, and trust them, they know it. And that respect
inspires them to want to follow where you lead.

## Commitment

The last quality a leader needs to become an empowerer is
commitment. USAir executive Ed McElroy stressed that "commitment gives us new power. No matter what comes to us—sick-
ness, poverty, or disaster, we never turn our eye from the goal."
The process of empowering others isn't always easy, especially
when you start doing it for the first time. It's a road that has many

bumps and sidetracks. But it is one that's worth traveling because the rewards are so great. As Edward Deci of the University of Rochester stated, "People must believe that a task is inherently worthwhile if they are to be committed to it." If you need a reminder of the value of empowering others, remember this: When you empower people, you're not influencing just them; you're influencing all the people they influence. That's impact!

If you have authority in people's lives, have built relationships with them, respect them, and have committed yourself to the process of empowerment, you're in a *position* to empower them. But one more crucial element of empowering needs to be in place. You need to have the right attitude.

Many people neglect to empower others because they are insecure. They are afraid of losing their jobs to the people they mentor. They don't want to be replaced or displaced, even if it means that they would be able to move up to a higher position and leave their current one to be filled by the person they mentor. They're afraid of change. But change is part of empowerment—for the people you empower and for yourself. If you want to go up, there are things you have to be willing to give up.

If you're not sure about where you stand in terms of your attitude toward the changes involved with empowering others, answer these questions:

## QUESTIONS TO ASK
## BEFORE YOU GET STARTED

1. Do I believe in people and feel that they are my organization's most appreciable asset?
2. Do I believe that empowering others can accomplish more than individual achievement?
3. Do I actively search for potential leaders to empower?
4. Would I be willing to raise others to a level higher than my own level of leadership?
5. Would I be willing to invest time developing people who have leadership potential?
6. Would I be willing to let others get credit for what I taught them?

7. Do I allow others freedom of personality and process, or do I have to be in control?
8. Would I be willing to publicly give my authority and influence to potential leaders?
9. Would I be willing to let others work me out of a job?
10. Would I be willing to hand the leadership baton to the people I empower and truly root for them?

If you answer no to more than a couple of these questions, you may need an attitude adjustment. You need to believe in others enough to give them all you can and in yourself enough to know that it won't hurt you. Just remember that as long as you continue to grow and develop yourself, you'll always have something to give, and you won't need to worry about being displaced.

# HOW TO EMPOWER OTHERS TO THEIR POTENTIAL

Once you have confidence in yourself and in the persons you wish to empower, you're ready to start the process. Your goal should be to hand over relatively small, simple tasks in the beginning and progressively increase their responsibilities and authority. The greener the people you're working with, the more time the process will take. But no matter whether they are raw recruits or seasoned veterans, it's still important to take them through the whole process. Use the following steps to guide you as you empower others:

## 1. Evaluate Them

The place to start when empowering people is to evaluate them. If you give inexperienced people too much authority too soon, you can set them up to fail. If you move too slowly with people who have lots of experience, you can frustrate and demoralize them.

Sometimes when leaders misjudge the capabilities of others, the results can be comical. For example, we read about an incident from the life of Albert Einstein that illustrates this point. In 1898, Einstein applied for admittance to the Munich Technical Institute and was rejected because he would "never amount to much." As a result, instead of going to school, he worked as an inspector at the Swiss Patent Office in Bern. And with the extra time he had on his hands, he worked at refining and writing his theory of relativity.

Remember that all people have the potential to succeed. Your job is to see the potential, find out what they lack to develop it, and equip them with what they need. As you evaluate the people you intend to empower, look at these areas:

- **Knowledge.** Think about what people need to know in order to do any task you intend to give them. Don't take for granted that they know all that you know. Ask them questions. Give them history or background information. Cast a vision by giving them the big picture of how their actions fit into the organization's mission and goals. Knowledge is not only power; it's empowering.

- **Skill.** Examine the skill level of the people you desire to empower. Nothing is more frustrating than being asked to do things for which you have no ability. Look at what people have done before as well as what they're doing now. Some skills are inherent. Others need to be learned through training or experience. Your job as the empowerer is to find out what the job requires and make sure your people have what they need to succeed.

- **Desire.** Greek philosopher Plutarch remarked, "The richest soil, if uncultivated, produces the rankest weeds." No amount of skill, knowledge, or potential can help people succeed if they don't have the desire to be successful. But when desire is present, empowerment is easy. As seventeenth-century French essayist Jean La Fontaine wrote, "Man is made so that whenever anything fires his soul, impossibilities vanish."

## 2. Model for Them

Even people with knowledge, skill, and desire need to know what's expected of them, and the best way to inform them is to show them. People do what people see. A little parable about a

farm boy who lived in a mountainous region of Colorado illustrates this point. One day the boy climbed to a high place and
found an eagle's nest with eggs in it. He snatched one of the eggs
while the eagle was away, took it back to the farm, and put it
under a sitting hen who had a brood of eggs.

The eggs hatched one by one, and when the eaglet came out
of his shell, he had no reason to believe he was anything other
than a chicken. So he did everything that the other chickens did
on the farm. He scratched around the yard looking for grain, he
tried his best to cluck, and he kept his feet firmly planted on the
ground, even though the fence around the pen wasn't more than
several feet high.

That went on until he towered over his would-be siblings and
his adopted mother hen. Then one day an eagle flew over the
chicken yard. The young eagle heard its cry and saw it swoop
down on a rabbit in the field. And at that moment, the young
eagle knew in his heart that he wasn't like the chickens in the
yard. He spread his wings, and before he knew it, he was flying after the other eagle. Not until he had seen one of his kind
flying did he know who he was or what he was capable of
doing.

The people you desire to empower need to see what it looks
like to fly. As their mentor, you have the best opportunity to show
them. Model the attitude and work ethic you would like them to
embrace. And anytime you can include them in your work, take
them along with you. There is no better way to help them learn
and understand what you want them to do.

## *3. Give Them Permission to Succeed*

As a leader and influencer, you may believe that everyone
wants to be successful and automatically strives for success, probably as you have. But not everyone you influence will think the
same way you do. You have to help others believe that they can
succeed and show them that you want them to succeed. How do
you do that?

- **Expect it.** Author and professional speaker Danny Cox
  advised, "The important thing to remember is that if you
  don't have that inspired enthusiasm that is contagious—

whatever you do have is also contagious." People can sense your underlying attitude no matter what you say or do. If you have an expectation for your people to be successful, they will know it.

- **Verbalize it.** People need to hear you tell them that you believe in them and want them to succeed. Tell them often that you know they are going to make it. Send them encouraging notes. Become a positive prophet of their success.

- **Reinforce it.** You can never do too much when it comes to believing in people. Leadership expert Fred Smith has made it a habit to give people plenty of positive reinforcement. He says, "As I recognize success, I try to stretch people's horizons. I might say, 'That was terrific!' but I don't stop there. Tomorrow I might return, repeat the compliment, and say, 'Last year, would you have believed you could do that? You may be surprised at what you can accomplish next year.'"

Once people recognize and understand that you genuinely want to see them succeed and are committed to helping them, they will begin to believe they can accomplish what you give them to do.

## 4. Transfer Authority to Them

The real heart of empowerment is the transfer of your authority—and influence—to the people you are mentoring and developing. Many people are willing to give others responsibility. They gladly delegate tasks to them. But empowering others is more than sharing your workload. It's sharing your power and ability to get things done.

Management expert Peter Drucker asserted, "No executive has ever suffered because his subordinates were strong and effective." People become strong and effective only when they are given the opportunity to make decisions, initiate action, solve problems, and meet challenges. When you empower others, you're helping them develop the ability to work independently under your authority. W. Alton Jones offered this opinion: "The man who gets the most satisfactory results is not always the man with the most brilliant single mind, but rather the man who can best co-ordinate the brains and talents of his associates."

As you begin to empower your people, give them challenges you know they can rise to meet and conquer. It will make them confident and give them a chance to try out their new authority and learn to use it wisely. And once they've begun to be effective, give them more difficult assignments. A good rule of thumb is that if someone else can do a job 80 percent as well as you do, delegate it. In the end, your goal is to empower others so well that they become capable of meeting nearly any challenge that comes their way. And in time, they will develop their own influence with others so that they no longer require yours to be effective.

## 5. *Publicly Show Your Confidence in Them*

When you first transfer authority to the people you empower, you need to tell them that you believe in them, and you need to do it publicly. Public recognition lets them know that you believe they will succeed. But it also lets the other people they're working with know that they have your support and that your authority backs them up. It's a tangible way of sharing (and spreading) your influence.

John is especially talented at empowering people and publicly showing them his confidence, and he has an interesting story about one of his greatest successes in empowerment:

> I mentioned in the last chapter that Dan Reiland has worked with me for fifteen years. When Dan first started with me, he was an intern, fresh out of graduate school. He had a lot of talent, but he still had some rough edges. I worked with him quite a bit—modeling, motivating, and mentoring him—and in a short time he grew to be a first-rate pastor.
>
> In just a few years, he became one of my key players. When we had a new program that needed to be created and implemented, I frequently looked to Dan, empowered him to take on the task, and gave him my full confidence and authority. And he took care of it. Time after time, I'd give him a major project, he would work through the whole process, implement it, raise up leaders to run it,

then come to me for another task. He continually worked himself out of a job.

In 1989, about six or seven years after Dan began working for me, I came to a point where I realized I needed to hire an executive pastor, a kind of chief administrative officer. And I knew right away that I wanted Dan to fill the position.

Now I knew that when you raise up a leader from within the ranks, there are often resentment and resistance from some of that person's colleagues. But I had a strategy. As I began to transfer my authority to Dan, I tried my best not to miss an opportunity to publicly praise him, show my confidence in him, and remind everyone that Dan spoke with my authority. As a result, the rest of the staff quickly rallied around him, and he was empowered as their new leader.

As you raise up leaders, show them and and their followers that they have your confidence and authority. And you will find that they quickly become empowered to succeed.

## 6. Supply Them with Feedback

Although you need to publicly praise your people, you can't let them go very long without giving them honest, positive feedback. Meet with them privately to coach them through their mistakes, miscues, and misjudgments. At first, some people may have a difficult time. During that early period, be a grace giver. Try to give them what they need, not what they deserve. And applaud any progress that they make. People do what gets praised.

## 7. Release Them to Continue on Their Own

No matter who you are working to empower—your employees, children, colleagues, or spouse—your ultimate aim should be to release them to make good decisions and succeed on their own. And that means giving them as much freedom as possible as soon as they are ready for it.

President Abraham Lincoln was a master at empowering his leaders. For example, when he appointed General Ulysses S. Grant as commander of the Union armies in 1864, he sent him this message: "I neither ask nor desire to know anything of your plans. Take the responsibility and act, and call on me for assistance."

That's the attitude you need as an empowerer. Give authority and responsibility, and offer assistance as needed. John and I have been fortunate to have been empowered by key people in our lives since we were kids. Probably the person who has been the most empowering in John's life is his father, Melvin Maxwell. He always encouraged John to be the best person he could be, and he gave him his permission and his power whenever he could. Years later as they talked about it, Melvin told John his philosophy: "I never consciously limited you as long as I knew what you were doing was morally right." Now that's an empowering attitude!

## THE RESULTS OF EMPOWERMENT

If you head up any kind of organization—a business, club, church, or family—learning to empower others is one of the most important things you'll ever do as its leader. Empowerment has an incredibly high return. It not only helps the individuals you raise up by making them more confident, energetic, and productive, but it also has the ability to improve your life, give you additional freedom, and promote the growth and health of your organization.

Farzin Madjidi, program liaison for the city of Los Angeles, has expressed his beliefs concerning empowerment: "We need leaders who empower people and create other leaders. It's no longer good enough for a manager to make sure that everybody has something to do and is producing. Today, all employees must 'buy in' and take ownership of everything they're doing. To foster this, it's important that employees should make decisions that most directly affect them. That's how the best decisions are made. That's the essence of empowerment." When it comes down to it, empowering leadership is sometimes the only real advantage one organization has over another in our competitive society.

As you empower others, you will find that most aspects of your life will change for the better. Empowering others can free you personally to have more time for the important things in your life, increase the effectiveness of your organization, increase your influence with others and, best of all, make an incredibly positive impact on the lives of the people you empower.

Jim recently received a letter from someone he has spent several years motivating, mentoring, and empowering. His name is Mitch Sala, and here's his letter:

> Dear Jim,
>
> I know you are in the process of writing a book on influence, and I feel the need to put pen to paper to express my deep respect and love for you and Nancy and tell you about the profound impact you've had on my life.
>
> Your influence on me started before we even met when I listened to one of your tapes for the first time. Your vision, positive attitude, and committed faith were inspiring, and Nancy's ability to put life and its obstacles in proper perspective helped me to see my world in a new way.
>
> As I observed you, I sensed an incredible depth of character in you. I admired that and wanted it myself. And it made me want to get to know you better, to develop our relationship. I had never really developed close friendships before, so that was new for me. You see, I grew up in Africa where my father ran a large sawmill in the forest. My older brother and sister were away at school, so I pretty much grew up without other kids around. I was kind of a loner. When I was eight, they sent me to traditional [boarding] school. It was good for my education, but bad for my self-image. It left me feeling like a loser.
>
> As an adult, those feelings drove me to work hard and try to prove myself, but I still felt empty no matter what I did. And I was failing at the things that mattered to me most: being a good husband and father.
>
> But you became an influence in my life at just the right time. You understood me and made me feel accepted despite my mistakes and failings. You've helped me to grow in my family life, financially, and spiritually. Everything has changed in my life.

Jim's positive influence has helped Mitch Sala change his life. Jim has taken him through the entire process. He has modeled a life of integrity to him. He has motivated and mentored him. He has empowered him. And over the years, Mitch has become a world-class influencer. Through his business enterprises and public speaking, Mitch touches the lives of hundreds of thousands of people every year in more than twenty countries around the world. And best of all, he is using his influence to raise up more leaders who are learning how to positively impact the lives of many more people. He has reproduced his influence in others, which is the subject of the final chapter of this book.

## *Influence Checklist*
# EMPOWERING PEOPLE

❏ **Give others more than just something to do.** If you lead a
business, a department, a family, a church, or any other kind
of organization, you are probably preparing to hand off some
responsibilities to others. Before you officially start the process, carefully plan your strategy for passing the baton by
using the following checklist:

Describe the task: _____

Name the person to whom you will give it: _____

What knowledge does the task require? _____

_____

Does the person have the required knowledge?  ❏ Yes ❏ No

What skills does the task require? _____

_____

Does the person have the skills required?        ❏ Yes ❏ No

Have you modeled how you want the job done? ❏ Yes ❏ No

Have you given the person the authority and permission to
succeed?                                         ❏ Yes ❏ No

Have you publicly given the person your confidence?
                                                 ❏ Yes ❏ No

Have you privately supplied the person with feedback? ¨
                                                 ❏ Yes ❏ No

Have you set a date to release the person to continue on his
or her own?                                      ❏ Yes ❏ No

Repeat this process with every task you intend to delegate
until it becomes second nature. Even when someone you
empower is successful and established in performance, continue praising, encouraging, and showing your confidence
publicly.

# *A Person of Influence . . .*

# REPRODUCES OTHER INFLUENCERS

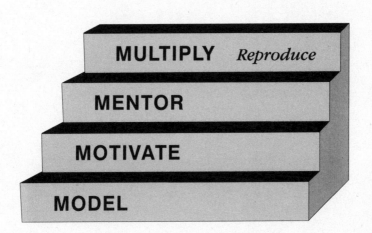

At the beginning of this book, we told you about influencers and specifically about some of the people who have made an impact on our lives, people like Glenn Leatherwood, who was John's Sunday school teacher in seventh grade—and Jerry and Patty Beaumont, who took Jim and Nancy under their wing around the time Eric was born. Our lives have been filled with wonderful people of influence. But the greatest value has been added to our lives by people who not only influenced us, but also made influencers of us. In John's case, his father, Melvin Maxwell, has shaped and molded him the most, helping him to become an outstanding leader. And in the case of Jim, that place is probably held by Rich DeVos:

> I grew up in a great family. We had lots of love, even though there wasn't much money. My father's views on politics and economics were pretty liberal, and his advice to me was to go to college and get a good job. But when I was in my twenties, I heard Rich DeVos speak for the first time, and I was mesmerized. He introduced me to a whole new paradigm. He talked about free enterprise, the worth of the individual, dreams, freedom, and "compassionate capitalism." He also talked about his faith in God and encouraged people to live with integrity and passion. I had never before heard any philosophy that made so much sense as his simple message of personal achievement. I was forever changed.

Today, of course, Rich DeVos is one of the most influential businessmen in the world. He is a founder and past president of Amway; he owns the NBA's Orlando Magic; he is the president of Gospel Films and the DeVos Foundation; and he is frequently asked to give advice on business matters to presidents and other influential leaders. Jim has looked up to him as a leader and mentor, and over the years, he has come to call Rich his friend.

Rich DeVos understands the value of raising up leaders, people who are able to become influencers in their own right. In some ways, teaching others to become leaders is like handing off the baton in a relay race. If you run well but are unable to pass the baton to another runner, you lose the race. But if you run well, recruit and train other good runners, and learn to hand off the baton smoothly, you can win. And when it comes to influence, if you can do that process repeatedly, you can multiply your influence incredibly.

# THE POWER OF MULTIPLICATION

In the work with people that the two of us have done, we've had to learn to hand off the baton. We never could have been successful if we hadn't. And now we want to hand it off to you. If you've moved successfully through the influence process, you've learned how to run the race. You understand how important it is for you to model integrity. You've learned to motivate people by nurturing them, having faith in them, listening to them, and giving them understanding. You understand that people really grow only when you mentor them. They have to be enlarged, navigated through life's difficulties, connected with, and empowered. Right now, you're running a good race. And if you've mentored others, you've got them running now too. But it's time to pass the baton, and if you don't get it into their hands, the race is over. They will have no reason to keep running, and the momentum will die with them.

That's why the reproduction phase of becoming a person of influence is so significant. Take a look at some benefits of creating leaders in your organization who are able to not only follow you but also influence others and raise them up:

- **Reproducing leaders raises your influence to a new level.** Anytime you influence people who either do not or cannot exercise influence with others, you limit your influence. But when you influence leaders, you indirectly influence all the people they influence. The effect is multiplication. (This idea is treated in greater depth in John's book *Developing the Leaders Around You.*) The greater your influence, the greater the number of people you can help.

- **Reproducing leaders raises the new leaders' personal potential.** Whenever you help others become better leaders, you raise the bar on their potential. Leadership is the lid on a person's ability to perform and influence. A person acting independently who doesn't practice leadership can accomplish only so much, personally or professionally. But as soon as people understand leadership and start practicing leadership principles, they blow the lid off personal potential. And if they lead people who lead others, the potential for what they can achieve is almost limitless.

- **Reproducing leaders multiplies resources.** As you develop leaders, you'll find that your resources increase in value. You have more time because you can share the load and increasingly delegate authority. As the people on your staff learn leadership, they become wiser and more valuable as advisers. And as an added bonus, you receive personal loyalty from just about everyone you raise up.

- **Reproducing leaders ensures a positive future for your organization.** G. Alan Bernard, president of Mid Park, Inc., put the issue of raising up leaders into perspective: "A good leader will always have those around him who are better at particular tasks than he is. This is the hallmark of leadership. Never be afraid to hire or manage people who are better at certain jobs than you are. They can only make your organization stronger." Not only does it make an organization stronger when you develop leaders, but it gives that organization a strong future. If only a couple of people in the organization are capable of doing the leading, the organization can't flourish when they retire or anything happens to them. It may not even be able to survive.

John had the opportunity in 1995 to see exactly how an organization reacts when its leader leaves after equipping and empowering many strong leaders within it. Following fourteen years of leading and reproducing leaders at Skyline Wesleyan Church, John resigned from his position as senior pastor. He left so that he could devote himself full-time to INJOY, his organization that offers seminars and materials for leadership growth and personal development. And the result of his move? Skyline is doing very well. In fact, about a year after John left, he received a note from Jayne Hansen, an INJOY employee whose husband, Brad, was on staff at Skyline.

Dear John,

I was just thinking about Skyline and how it is really thriving since you've left. . . . It's such an absolute TRIBUTE to the kind of leadership and lay ministry that you developed. We have a living example of the saying "practice what you preach" unfolding as we see the fruit of your labor. I can tell anyone without question that the principles you teach work. I can think of no greater honor than that a man pour his life into something, leave, and have it flourish! What a shame it would be to have a ministry die on the vine when one man leaves.

Thank you for pouring your life into us.

Your friend,
Jayne

Mentoring people and developing their leadership potential really can make a huge difference—for your organization, for your people, and for you.

## AWAKEN THE REPRODUCER IN YOU

Everyone has the potential to multiply influence by developing and reproducing leaders. To awaken the reproducer in you, make the following principles a part of your life:

### *Lead Yourself Well*

Being able to lead others begins with leading yourself well. You can't reproduce what you don't have. As entrepreneur and Chick-Fil-A restaurant chain founder Truett Cathy said, "The number one reason leaders are unsuccessful is their inability to lead themselves."

When we think about self-leadership, many qualities come to mind: integrity, right priorities, vision, self-discipline, problem-solving skills, a positive attitude, and so forth. Desire and a game plan for personal development can help you cultivate these qualities, but the greatest obstacle to becoming a leader may be yourself. Psychologist Sheldon Kopp remarked about this problem: "All the significant battles are waged within the self."

If you haven't already put yourself on a program for growth and leadership development, start today. Listen to tapes. Go to conferences. Read enlightening books. (John's *Developing the*

*Leader Within You* is an excellent primer for leadership development.) If you make personal growth your weekly goal and daily discipline, you can become a reproducer of leaders. Nineteenth-century theologian H. P. Liddon clearly saw this connection when he stated, "What we do on some great occasion will probably depend on what we already are; and what we are will be the result of previous years of self-discipline." Personal development pays dividends.

## Look Continually for Potential Leaders

Former Notre Dame head football coach Lou Holtz said of a subject he knew well: "You've got to have good athletes to win, I don't care who the coach is." The same thing is true in your personal and professional lives. You need good people with leadership potential if you're going to reproduce leaders. Industrialist Andrew Carnegie emphasized that "no man will make a great leader who wants to do it all himself or get all the credit for doing it." Effective developers of people are always on the lookout for potential leaders.

It's said that "when the student is ready, the teacher appears." But it's also true that when the teacher is ready, the student appears. If you keep developing yourself as a leader, you will soon be ready to develop others. And if you want to be a great reproducer of leaders, you need to seek out and recruit the best people possible.

## Put the Team First

Great developers of leaders think of the welfare of the team before thinking of themselves. J. Carla Northcutt, who receives John's monthly INJOY Life Club tapes, stated, "The goal of many leaders is to get people to think more highly of the leader. The goal of a great leader is to help people to think more highly of themselves."

Bill Russell was a gifted basketball player. Many consider him to be one of the best team players in the history of professional basketball. Russell observed, "The most important measure of how good a game I played was how much better I'd made my teammates play." That's the attitude necessary to become a great reproducer of leaders. The team has to come first.

Do you consider yourself to be a team player? Answer each of the following questions to see where you stand when it comes to promoting the good of the team:

## SEVEN QUESTIONS FOR A
## SUCCESSFUL TEAM ORIENTATION

1. Do I add value to others?
2. Do I add value to the organization?
3. Am I quick to give away the credit when things go right?
4. Is our team consistently adding new members?
5. Do I use my "bench" players as much as I could?
6. Do many people on the team consistently make important decisions?
7. Is our team's emphasis on creating victories more than producing stars?

If you answered no to a few of these questions, you may want to reevaluate your attitude toward the team. It has been said, "The ultimate leader is one who is willing to develop people to the point that they eventually surpass him or her in knowledge and ability." That should be your goal as you multiply your influence by developing leaders.

## Commit Yourself to Developing Leaders, Not Followers

We believe that our country is experiencing a leadership crisis today. Not long ago, we saw an article in the *New Republic* that addressed the issue. In part it read, "Two hundred years ago, a little republic on the edge of the wilderness suddenly produced people like Jefferson, Hamilton, Madison, Adams, and others. Yet the total population was only 3,000,000 people. Today, we have over 200 million. Where are the great people? We should have 60 Franklins in a cover story on leadership. The search was in vain."

Ralph Nader, consumer advocate and founder of the Center for Responsive Law, declared, "The function of a leader is to produce more leaders, not more followers." Maybe two hundred years ago, people understood that better. But today, producing leaders isn't a priority for many people. Besides, developing other leaders isn't always easy or simple, especially for people who are natural leaders. As management expert Peter Drucker observed, "People who excel at something can rarely tell you how to do it."

That's why it's important for a person who wants to raise up other leaders to be committed to the task. We've said it before and we'll repeat it here: Everything rises and falls on leadership. When you raise up and empower leaders, you positively impact yourself, your organization, the people you develop, and all the people their lives touch. Reproducing leaders is the most important task of any person of influence. If you want to make an impact, you have got to be committed to developing leaders.

# MOVING FROM MAINTENANCE TO MULTIPLICATION

Many people live in maintenance mode. Their main goal is to keep from losing ground rather than trying to make progress. But that's the lowest level of living when it comes to the development of people. If you want to make an impact, you must strive to become a multiplier. Take a look at the five stages that exist between maintenance and multiplication, starting with the lowest:

## *1. Scramble*

About 20 percent of all leaders live on the lowest level in the development process. They are not doing anything to develop people in their organization, and as a result, their attrition rate is off the charts. They can't seem to keep anyone they recruit. That's why we say they're in the scramble stage—they spend most of their time scrambling to find people to replace the ones they lose. You may know some small business owners who seem to stay in scramble mode. The morale in their organization stays low, and it doesn't take long for them to burn out from exhaustion.

## 2. Survival

The next stage in the development ladder is survival mode. In it, leaders do nothing to develop their people, but they do manage to keep the people they have. About 50 percent of all organizational leaders function this way. Their organizations are average, their employees are dissatisfied, and no one is developing personal potential. No one really benefits from this approach to leadership. Everyone merely survives from day to day without much promise or hope for the future.

## 3. Siphon

About 10 percent of all leaders work at developing their people into better leaders, but they neglect to build their relationships with their people. As a result, their potential leaders leave the organization to pursue other opportunities. In other words, they are siphoned off from the organization. That often leads to frustration on the part of the leader because other people benefit from their effort, and they must devote a lot of time to looking for replacements.

## 4. Synergy

When leaders build strong relationships, develop people to become good leaders, empower them to reach their potential—and are able to keep them in the organization—something wonderful happens. It's often called synergy, meaning that the whole is greater than the sum of its parts because the parts interact well together and create energy, progress, and momentum. An organization on the synergy level has great morale and high job satisfaction. Everyone benefits. Only about 19 percent of all leaders reach this level, but those who do are often considered the very best there are.

## 5. Significance

Many people who reach the synergy level never try to go any farther because they don't realize they can take one more step in the development process, and that's to the significance level. Leaders on that level develop and reproduce leaders who stay in the organization, work to reach their potential, and in turn develop leaders. And that's where influence really multiplies. Only about 1 percent of all leaders make it to this level, but the ones who do are able to tap into almost limitless growth and influence potential. A handful of leaders continually functioning on the significance level can make an impact on the world.

# HOW TO RAISE UP LEADERS
# WHO REPRODUCE LEADERS

In an article published by the *Harvard Business Review,* author Joseph Bailey examined what it took to be a successful executive. In conducting his research, he interviewed more than thirty top executives and found that every one of them learned firsthand from a mentor.[1] If you want to raise up leaders who reproduce other leaders, you need to mentor them.

We've been told that in hospital emergency rooms, nurses have a saying: "Watch one, do one, teach one." It refers to the need to learn a technique quickly, jump right in and do it with a patient, and then turn around and pass it on to another nurse. The mentoring process for developing leaders works in a similar way. It happens when you take potential leaders under your wing, develop them, empower them, share with them how to become persons of influence, and then release them to go out and raise up other leaders. Every time you do that, you plant seeds for greater success. And as novelist Robert Louis Stevenson advised, "Don't judge each day by the harvest you reap but by the seeds you plant."

Now you know what it takes to become a person of influence, to positively impact the lives of others. Being an influencer means . . .

- modeling *integrity* with everyone you come into contact with.
- *nurturing* the people in your life to make them feel valued.
- showing *faith* in others so that they believe in themselves.
- *listening* to them so that you can build your relationship with them.
- *understanding* them so that you can help them achieve their dreams.
- *enlarging* them in order to increase their potential.
- *navigating* them though life's difficulties until they can do it themselves.
- *connecting* with them so that you can move them to a higher level.
- *empowering* them to become the person they were created to be.
- *reproducing* other leaders so that your influence continues to grow through others.

Over the years, Jim and I have worked hard to make this process more than a mere set of principles or method of working. We have sought to make investing in others a way of living. And as time goes by, we keep working to become better developers of people. Our reward is seeing the impact we make on the lives of other people. Listen to this story from Jim:

One of the greatest things about becoming a person of influence is that you actually get to see the lives of others change before your eyes. I told you in the previous chapter about Mitch Sala, whom I got to see blossom into a person of impact. But what I didn't tell you is that Mitch has became more than just an influencer. He has gone through the entire development process himself and now is a great *reproducer* of influencers too.

One of his greatest success stories is a man named Robert Angkasa. Robert is from Indonesia, holds an MBA from Sydney University, and used to work for Citibank, where he had risen to become a vice president in Jakarta by the time he was thirty years old.

Robert has always worked hard. He put himself through school driving a taxi, working in restaurant kitchens, and cleaning stadiums after concerts. But a few years ago, he met Mitch Sala. Mitch took Robert under his wing, motivated him, mentored him, and empowered him to become a person of influence.

Robert says, "The turning point in my life came when I met Mitch. At first, all I noticed was that he was a kind person. But the more time I spent with him, the more I realized that I wanted to be like him while still being myself. Mitch taught me that the way to success was through integrity and hard work. Today I am tasting the sweetness of a new life. I enjoy the financial security that's come from hard work, but more than that, I am becoming a better person. The pleasure that I get from helping others is enormous and gives me great satisfaction. I am a better person, husband, and family man. I owe a lot of who I am today to Mitch. He is a mentor, a friend, and a parent. I thank God every day for all his blessings that I've received through Mitch. And what I am trying to do now is be to others what he's been to me. I want to help others have a better life. The words *Thank you* don't seem sufficient, but they're the best words I can find."

Today Robert impacts the lives of thousands of people throughout Indonesia, Malaysia, China, and the Philippines. He is one of several key business leaders whom Mitch is now mentoring. And Robert's influence is continuing to increase daily.

My friend, you have the same potential as Robert Angkasa, Mitch Sala, or Jim Dornan. You can become a person of influence and impact the lives of many people. But the decision is yours. You can either develop your influence potential or let it remain unrealized. Jim gave the baton to Mitch. Mitch found Robert and taught him to run. He has successfully given the baton to Robert, and now he is running. There is one more leg—and the baton is ready. Now is your chance. Reach out your hand, take the baton, and finish the race that only you can run. Become a person of influence, and change your world.

## *Influence Checklist*
# REPRODUCING OTHER INFLUENCERS

❑ **Develop your own leadership potential.** The way to be prepared to teach others leadership is to continue developing your own leadership potential. If you haven't already put yourself on a personal plan for growth, start today. Select tapes, books, and magazines that you will review weekly for the next three months. Growth comes only if you make it a habit.

❑ **Find people with leadership potential.** As you continually enlarge and empower the people around you, some will emerge as potential leaders. Choose the person with the greatest potential for special mentoring, and talk to him or her about developing greater leadership skills. Proceed only if the person wants to be developed and agrees to mentor others in leadership in the future.

❑ **Teach the person to be a leader, not just perform tasks.** Give the person complete access to you, and spend lots of time modeling leadership. Devote time each week to increasing the person's leadership potential by teaching, sharing resources, sending him or her to seminars, and so forth. Do everything in your power to help that person reach his or her leadership potential.

❑ **Multiply.** When the person becomes a good leader, help him or her select someone to mentor in the area of leadership. Release them to work together, and find yourself a new potential leader so that you can keep repeating the process.

# *Notes*

## Introduction
1. John C. Maxwell, *Developing the Leader Within You* (Nashville: Thomas Nelson, 1993), 5–12.
2. Brad Herzog, *The Sports 100: The One Hundred Most Important People in American Sports History* (New York: MacMillan, 1995), 7.

## Chapter 1
1. Stephen R. Covey, *The Seven Habits of Highly Effective People: Restoring the Character Ethic* (New York: Simon and Schuster, 1989).
2. Proverbs 22:1 NIV.
3. Donald T. Phillips, *Lincoln on Leadership: Executive Strategies for Tough Times* (New York: Warner Books, 1992), 66–67.
4. Bill Kynes, "A Hope That Will Not Disappoint," quoted in *Best Sermons 2* (New York: Harper and Row, 1989), 301.

## Chapter 2
1. Everett Shostrom, *Man the Manipulator.*
2. *Bits and Pieces.*
3. Jack Canfield and Mark Victor Hansen, "All the Good Things," in *Chicken Soup for the Soul* (Deerfield Beach, Fla.: Health Communications, 1993), 126–28.
4. Arthur Gordon, "The Gift of Caring," in *A Touch of Wonder.*
5. Greg Asimakoupoulos, "Icons Every Pastor Needs," *Leadership,* fall 1993, 109.
6. Dennis Rainey and Barbara Rainey, *Building Your Mate's Self-Esteem* (Nashville: Thomas Nelson, 1993).

## Chapter 3
1. 1 Samuel 17:32–37 NIV.

## Chapter 4
1. Quoted by Fred Barnes in the *New Republic.*
2. David Grimes, (Sarasota, Florida) *Herald-Tribune.*
3. Brian Adams, *Sales Cybernetics* (Wilshire Book Co., 1985), 110.
4. Eric Allenbaugh, *Wake-Up Calls* (Austin: Discovery Publications, 1992), 200.

## Chapter 5

1. M. Michael Markowich, *Management Review,* cited in *Behavioral Sciences Newsletter.*
2. Art Mortell, "How to Master the Inner Game of Selling," vol. 10, no. 7.
3. Kent M. Keith, *The Silent Revolution: Dynamic Leadership in the Student Council,* (Cambridge, Mass: Harvard Student Agencies) 1968.
4. Ecclesiastes 4:9–12 NIV.
5. Robert Schuller, ed., *Life Changers* (Old Tappan, N.J.: Revell).

## Chapter 6

1. Quoted in Og Mandino, *The Return of the Ragpicker.*

## Chapter 7

1. *Saturday Review.*
2. Quoted in advertisement, *Esquire.*
3. Mortimer R. Feinberg, *Effective Psychology for Managers.*
4. "The Top Problems and Needs of Americans," *Ministry Currents,* January–March 1994.
5. Tim Hansel, *Holy Sweat* (Waco: Word, 1987), 134.
6. Ernie J. Zelinski, *The Joy of Not Knowing It All* (Edmonton, Alberta, Canada: Visions International Publishing, 1995), 114.
7. David Armstrong, *Managing by Storying Around,* quoted in *The Competitive Advantage.*

## Chapter 8

1. Tom Peters and Nancy Austin, *A Passion for Excellence.*
2. Charles B. Ruth, *The Handbook of Selling* (Prentice-Hall).
3. Florence Littauer, *Personality Plus* (Grand Rapids: Revell, 1983), 24–81.
4. Carl Sandberg, *Lincoln: The Prairie Years.*

## Chapter 9

1. *The Nordstrom Way,* 15–16.

## Chapter 10

1. Joseph Bailey, "Clues for Success in the President's Job," *Harvard Business Review* (special edition), 1983.

# Books by Dr. John C. Maxwell
## Can Teach You How to Be A REAL Success

### RELATIONSHIPS

Everyone Communicates, Few Connect

Encouragement Changes Everything

25 Ways to Win With People

Winning With People

Relationships 101

The Treasure of a Friend

The Power of Partnership in the Church

Becoming a Person of Influence

Be A People Person

The Power of Influence

Ethics 101

### ATTITUDE

Self-Improvement 101

Success 101

The Difference Maker

How Successful People Think

The Journey From Success to Significance

Attitude 101

Failing Forward

Your Bridge to a Better Future

Living at the Next Level

The Winning Attitude

Be All You Can Be

The Power of Thinking Big

Think on These Things

The Power of Attitude

Thinking for a Change

### EQUIPPING

Teamwork 101

My Dream Map

Put Your Dream to the Test

Make Today Count

The Choice Is Yours

Mentoring 101

Talent is Never Enough

Equipping 101

Developing the Leaders Around You

The 17 Essential Qualities of a Team Player

Success One Day at a Time

The 17 Indisputable Laws of Teamwork

Your Road Map for Success

Today Matters

Partners in Prayer

### LEADERSHIP

Leadership Promises For Your Work Week

Leadership Gold

Go for Gold

The 21 Most Powerful Minutes
in a Leader's Day

Revised & Updated 10th Anniversary
Edition of The 21 Irrefutable
Laws of Leadership

The 360 Degree Leader

Leadership Promises for Every Day

Leadership 101

The Right to Lead

The 21 Indispensable Qualities of a Leader

Developing the Leader Within You

The Power of Leadership

# GiANT is a growth company.

We help grow organizations by growing their leaders. GiANT Impact has created many corporate training tools based on the writings of John C. Maxwell. We partner with John Maxwell to inspire transformation of self, team, and community.

## LEARNING AND GROWTH EXPERIENCES

Behavior and Values Assessments

Public and Private Workshops
*Leadership, Attitude, Influence, Relationships, Teamwork, Communication*

Custom Corporate Training Programs
*Tailored to the needs of the organization*

Events
*Leader retreats and exclusive conferences*

Resources
*Periodicals, CDs, DVDs, and more*

Mentoring
*John Maxwell's monthly Maximum Impact Club*

Intentional Leader Pathing Plans
*Customized leadership programs to help individuals, teams and/or entire organizations be intentional about growth.*

Performance Coaching
*Industry captains guide leaders and fast-trackers through a confidant model*

Self Leadership Programs
*Daily self-study activities to develop life-changing behaviors*

Lunch & Learns
*Guided curriculum for lunch-time book discussions and team building.*

Visit **www.giantimpact.com** or call **(877) 225-3311 TODAY** to learn more about bringing John Maxwell content to your organization and your personal leadership journey.